Fundamentals of

SPEECH COMMUNICATION

Fundamentals of

SPEECH COMMUNICATION

T H E   C R E D I B I L I T Y   O F   I D E A S

Bert E. Bradley

Auburn University

ωcb

Wm. C. Brown Publishers

Dubuque, Iowa

Book Team

Editor *Stan Stoga*
Developmental Editor *Kathy Law Laube*
Designer *K. Wayne Harms*
Production Editor *Harry Halloran*
Photo Research Editor *Michelle Oberhoffer*
Visual Processor *Reneé Pins*
Product Manager *Marcia H. Stout*

wcb group

Chairman of the Board *Wm. C. Brown*
President and Chief Executive Officer *Mark C. Falb*

wcb

Wm. C. Brown Publishers, College Division

Executive Vice-President, General Manager *G. Franklin Lewis*
Editor in Chief *George Wm. Bergquist*
Director of Production *Beverly Kolz*
National Sales Manager *Bob McLaughlin*
Manager of Design *Marilyn A. Phelps*
Production Editorial Manager *Colleen A. Yonda*
Photo Research Manager *Faye M. Schilling*

Cover illustration by Peter Eastwood

Library of Congress Catalog Card Number: 87-70091

ISBN 0-697-04281-2

Published in the United States by Wm. C. Brown Publishers
2460 Kerper Boulevard, Dubuque, IA 52001

Printed in the United States of America
10 9 8 7 6 5 4 3 2

CONTENTS

PART 1
BASIC CONSIDERATIONS

1
THE COMMUNICATION PROCESS 4

2
THE FIRST SPEECH 20

3
UNDERSTANDING PERFORMANCE APPREHENSION 30

4
RESPONSIBILITIES OF SPEAKERS: ETHICAL DIMENSIONS   46

5
RESPONSIBILITIES OF RECEIVERS: EFFECTIVE LISTENING   56

PART 2
PREPARATION

6
CREATING CREDIBILITY   70

PART 3
THE SPEECH

10
STRUCTURING THE SPEECH
146

11
BEGINNING AND ENDING THE
SPEECH   174

12
NONVERBAL PRESENTATION
194

13
USING REASONING   220

14
DEVELOPING CONTENT   240

PART 4
FORMS OF COMMUNICATION

16
SPEAKING TO INFORM   298

17

SPEAKING TO PERSUADE
316

18

SPEECHES FOR SPECIAL OCCASIONS 346

APPENDIX A THE CRITICISM OF SPEECHES 357

APPENDIX B MODEL SPEECHES 371

GLOSSARY 392

PHOTO CREDITS 400

NAME INDEX 401

SUBJECT INDEX 406

PREFACE

Fundamentals of Speech Communication: The Credibility of Ideas is written for college students enrolled in an introductory public speaking course. This book, first published in 1974, has been written with a solid grounding in theoretical principles, yet balanced with suggestions for practical application. Many years of teaching public speaking have reinforced my belief that it is just as important, if not more so, to explain *why* something is done as it is to simply state that it should be done.

The field of speech communication is the heir of time-proven principles discovered through scholarly study by many people separated by time, geography, and culture. As in the first four editions, this classic heritage lives on in the fifth edition. Yet, where possible and appropriate, a great deal of contemporary experimental research from the fields of speech, psychology, and sociology has been used in developing and supporting the theories presented throughout the book. Why are numerous empirical studies cited and discussed? Because it is critical to help students understand that research is important in achieving credibility in their own public speaking roles.

This research-based orientation has proven successful over the years. The book's success is evidenced not only by its continuing popularity, but also by the numerous books that have appeared on the market that take the same approach.

Organization of the Book

Fundamentals of Speech Communication has been structured to accommodate myriad course outlines. Most professors enjoy using the book as it is currently arranged, but others find they like to shuffle the chapters around. Each chapter is designed to stand alone so an instructor can change the chapter sequencing without loss of continuity or clarity. The book is organized into four parts containing eighteen chapters.

Part I, "Basic Considerations," discusses the fundamental principles in the speech-making process. Chapter 2 is devoted to explaining what students can expect from their first public speaking experience. Critical to building students' confidence as speech-makers is the chapter on "Understanding Performance Apprehension." Also in this first part, students are asked to consider the ethical dimensions to speech-making and to learn how to become effective listeners.

Part II, "Preparation" discusses how to approach speech-making. Students are shown how to create ethos, how to understand audience attitude, how to select the subject and the purpose of a speech, and the appropriate method of speech presentation.

Part III, "The Speech" gets into the nuts and bolts of speech-making. In this part, students will learn how to structure the speech, and how to begin and end the speech. Nonverbal and reasoning skills are also presented. Students will learn how to develop content and how to create meaning in their speeches.

Part IV, "Forms of Communication" presents, in an in-depth fashion, various types of speeches, including those to inform and those to persuade, as well as those for special occasions.

Learning Aids

Each chapter begins with an **outline** to acquaint students with the material and to help them structure their study of the chapter. At the end of each chapter, a **summary** briefly reiterates the main concepts presented in the chapter, and numerous **exercises** ask students to apply what they have learned. This active participation is intended to help students better retain the material they've just read. Finally, the **notes** provide students with a plethora of research sources.

At the end of the book, students will find two invaluable **appendices.** First, there are seven sample speeches, four of which are written by experienced students. The other three are speeches written by professional people. All seven should serve as models for students as they write and present their own speeches throughout the term.

Finally, this edition contains a **glossary,** which contains the most important terms from the book that students should know.

New to this Edition

Throughout the thirteen years that this book has been on the market, readers have made numerous suggestions about what information they would like to see in the book. Ongoing efforts to accommodate them have resulted in material that is clear, current, and as credible as possible. The fifth edition includes:

1. A new chapter on performance apprehension. Because of the overwhelmingly positive response to inclusion of this topic in the last edition, it was taken of the appendix and placed it near the front of the book (Chapter 3).

2. A new chapter (2) on the first speech. Again, this has been added to the front of the book to prepare students early in the process of speech-making. Students will be better prepared when they give their first speech after reading and practicing the material presented in this chapter.

3. A new chapter on occasional speaking to provide information and advice about various kinds of special speeches, such as those to entertain, commemorate, introduce, present, and nominate.

4. Expansion of the section on visual and audio aids in chapter 14. The use of clear, accurate, and engaging audio-visual aids is receiving increased attention in public speaking education. This section shows students how to use the most appropriate and effective visuals in their presentation.

5. A new Introduction about the value of studying speech communication to provide students background information about the discipline and its relevancy to their lives.

6. Seven new sample speeches at the end of the book, an increase from two in the last edition.

7. The transfer of the speech criticism chapter to the appendix where it serves as a resource for effectively analyzing speeches. This change was made in response to reviewer comments.

8. Removal of some material from the previous edition in order to accommodate the numerous additions to the book and keep it within a manageable length. An overwhelming number of people responding to that edition indicated that they didn't cover small group discussion in their basic public speaking course.

9. A glossary so students have ready access to definitions of the most important terms and concepts presented in the book.

10. Updated content with current examples and recent research findings.

Ancillaries

The **instructor's manual** continues to function as an invaluable resource for both the novice and experienced professor.

The first section of the manual discusses instructional objectives, course procedures, and administrative concepts. The second section's focus on individual chapters includes overviews, summaries, objectives, key terms, additional resources, and a variety of communication assignments. The third section examines the criticism of speeches, presents model speeches, and discusses evaluation and grading procedures. Speech evaluation forms have been added to this edition of the **instructor's manual.** Test items for each chapter are in the fourth section.

A new ancillary we are providing this year is **wcb**'s TestPak, a free, computerized testing service available to adopters of *Fundamentals of Speech Communication.* **wcb** will send you the test item file, program diskette, and user's guide. With these you'll be able to create your own tests, answer sheets, and answer keys. You can also modify or delete test questions or add your own questions to the diskettes we provide.

Acknowledgements

I am indebted to the following individuals who reviewed this project and contributed to the development of this edition:

Marvin De Boer
University of Central Arkansas, Conway
Charlene Handford
Louisiana State University, Shreveport
Thomas E. Harris
University of Evansville
Robert D. Leffingwell
Slippery Rock University
David Snowball
Augustana College, Rock Island
James Tolhuizen
Indiana University Northwest, Gary
Dorothy Williamson-Ige
Indiana University Northwest, Gary

INTRODUCTION

THE VALUE OF STUDYING SPEECH COMMUNICATION

Rhetorical theory has its roots deep in antiquity. Almost three thousand years before the birth of Christ, a book written in Egypt, *The Precepts of Kagemni and Ptah-Hotep,* offered rules for speaking in certain situations. Homer's *Iliad* and *Odyssey* both record speeches made by major characters and give testimony of the esteem in which speechmaking was held. The development of a substantial theory of rhetoric did not come, however, until there was a widespread need for the ability of self-expression. This need arose in the fifth century B.C.

On the island of Sicily, which had been ruled for a number of years by tyrants, the people revolted and deposed the tyrants. As a result of the confusion over rival property claims and questionable citizenship rights, many Sicilians were required to go to court to plead their own cases, in the custom of the day. From the necessity of this situation, Corax and his pupil, Tisias, are commonly credited with preparing what is considered to be the first manual on public speaking. They defined rhetoric as the art of persuasion, designated five parts for a persuasive speech—proem, narration, argument, subsidiary remarks, and peroration—and explained the use of probability for rhetorical arguments.

As the people of Athens, Greece, developed democratic government in the fourth century B.C., the need arose for theorists and teachers of the art of rhetoric. Teachers of public speaking, known as Sophists, became numerous. Some entered the profession for the money they could make, others because they had a sincere interest in helping people to develop the ability to speak effectively. Plato was upset by the practices of some of the Sophists, and he attempted to belittle the accomplishments and the significance of rhetoric. Ultimately, however, he was forced to acknowledge its importance, and in the *Phaedrus* he set forth a theoretical skeleton of rhetoric that still can be defended. One of his students, Aristotle, then wrote *The Rhetoric,* which is as applicable today as it was then.

With these early rhetorical principles, the Greek people were able to participate more effectively in their newly created democratic society. In the approximately twenty-five hundred years between that time and today, thousands of critics and theorists have expanded, clarified, and improved rhetorical principles.

Those of us who understand rhetorical principles today can meet our responsibilities as citizens. We can analyze public issues, identify valid and invalid arguments, evaluate evidence, and organize positions on current problems.

Understanding the following principles will increase your appreciation of this course:

1. Speakers are made, not born. Public speaking is a learned skill. This is not to deny that some people are able to use the principles more skillfully than others, but whether that is due to inborn traits or to growing up in an environment that fostered and developed those skills is not clear. What we do know is that taking a public speaking course improves the speaking abilities of everyone. So you can be assured that at the end of this course, if you have applied yourself to learning and practicing the principles presented, you will be a better and more effective speaker.

Wendell Phillips, the renowned antislavery agitator, began his speech training at Boston Latin School where he "distinguished himself" in public speaking. Following graduation, Phillips entered Harvard College, "where . . . rhetoric and oratory were a highly important part of the curriculum, being, in fact, the only field in which students were required to take work through the entire four years."[1] After graduation Phillips entered Harvard Law School where he continued "his training in speechmaking in the Moot Court."[2] Thus, "he had a thorough training in rhetoric, oratory, and declamation in Harvard College." In fact, one of his biographers says that this training "was the foundation of his later success as a public speaker."[3]

Woodrow Wilson's earliest ambition was to be a leader. In his view, oratory was "the first tool of leadership: 'Its object is persuasion and conviction—the control of other minds. . . .'"[4] To prepare himself as a speaker, he became a member of a debating society at Davidson College, delivering orations and participating in debates. Later at Princeton University he actively participated in a debating society, and while a law student at the University of Virginia was an active member of the Jefferson debating society. Thus did he develop and hone the skills that were to make him a highly effective public speaker.

John C. Calhoun obtained his earliest formal education at the age of thirteen from a school run by his brother-in-law. A Friday afternoon debating club offered the opportunity for "his first formal training in public speaking." Two years later he entered Yale University as a junior. There he participated in disputations that occurred "twice each week during the junior and senior years."[5] As a member of one of the debating societies, he had ample opportunity to improve his speaking ability.

Following graduation from Yale University, he enrolled in Judge Reeve's law school at Litchfield, Conn. His participation in the law school debating society, according to Calhoun, "added to his powers of extemporaneous debating."[6]

These examples are not unusual. If space permitted, many more could be added. If you want to become an effective public speaker, you must work at carefully learning the principles and diligently practicing their use.

2. Understanding speech communication principles makes you a more effective citizen in a democratic society. Edwin J. Delattre, then director of the National Humanities Faculty in Concord, Mass., said in 1977 that "Practice in reading, writing, speaking, listening . . . enables us to think more rigorously and to imagine more abundantly. These activities free us to possibilities that are new, at least to us, and they unbind us from portions of our ignorance about living well."[7]

With the knowledge of and ability to use the principles of public speaking, you can speak out on the issues you deem important. That gives you influence on the vital decisions that are made by citizens in a democracy. In addition, your knowledge of those principles enables you to recognize and publicize the fallacious and devious tactics of demagogues. Thus, you are not only able to weaken or nullify the influence of those who employ illegitimate methods, you are also able to present your arguments in ethical, responsible, and valid ways. The ultimate result is government policies based on legitimate evidence, sound reasoning, and effective argumentation.

3. Improving your speaking ability will make you a more effective and more confident participant in your occupation as well as in society. John M. Harbert III, a civil engineer who has business interests around the world, hires numerous engineers but says, "Only a select few will reach senior management." He observes that those "few aren't necessarily more knowledgeable than the others. . . . The difference is that they have developed the skill to communicate. All the knowledge in the world is useless unless you can share it."[8] In the late 1970s, an American Council on Education task force made essentially the same point. After studying higher education, they concluded that associate and bachelor degrees "should attest to at least . . . three types of accomplishment." One of those types of accomplishment, the Council said, is "competence in analytical, *communication* (italics added), quantitative, and synthesizing skills."[9]

In a recent study by two business administration professors, the authors noted that 90 percent of their respondents testified "that the ability to communicate orally was very important . . . and only one percent indicated that the ability to communicate orally was not important." One hundred percent of their respondents reported that the ability to communicate orally was "very important to success" in the following "job categories: clerical/secretarial, marketing, personnel, production/plant management, public relations, and teaching." The respondents also indicated that they spent approximately 37 percent "of their work time speaking, 19 percent listening, 16 percent writing, and 13 percent reading." These respondents strongly confirm the value of oral communication in their daily lives.[10]

One professional personnel consultant advises clients to "be sure you do not ignore communications and 'people' skills—written and oral. These are important at almost everything you do." She points out that young workers frequently find that their technical skills help them most at the beginning of their careers. Later, however, "people" skills are the most important. "Ultimately," she says, "someone with moderately good technical skills and very good people skills will outshine the techno-whizzes who have let their ability to communicate droop." She advises those who have ignored communication skills, therefore, to "develop public speaking skills."[11]

As you improve your skills, you will gain the confidence needed to participate more actively in discussions of public policy. As you participate more, you will begin to notice that others are paying attention to your contributions and supporting positions that you advocate. You will begin to notice that your personal influence on decisions is increasing. People will not only want to hear what you have to say, they will actively seek your counsel if you have not voluntarily offered it.

4. Developing individual citizens' speech skills is essential to democratic society. There will always be those individuals who prefer a form of government that grants them maximum power and authority. Some of them will have sufficient speaking skills to confuse and mislead many others into helping set up a form of government that provides minimum influence for the many and maximum authority for the few. The presence of a large number of citizens who have the speaking ability to oppose these self-interested authoritarians will help to persuade other less informed citizens to reject these potential self-interested leaders.

5. Speech is basic to social intercourse. The ability to communicate ideas orally becomes more crucial daily because most of our daily contacts with others involve speech communication. Our associates make judgments about our intellect, our abilities, our motivations, our knowledge, and our sociability on the basis of our spoken communication. Many surveys have shown that speaking and listening constitute more than one-half of our communication experiences each day.

Think for a minute of how you carry on relationships with other people. It is predominantly with speech. In your discussions you discover that you have mutual interests and concerns with others. Immediately, there begins to develop a bond between you and them. Without speech, neither you nor they might have been able to discover those mutual concerns. Speech, therefore, enables you to develop relationships with other people.

But, you say, I am talking about conversation, and that is not public speaking. True, but the principles used in developing an effective speech are the same principles that are used in conversational speech. In good conversation you have to be concerned about the topics you are going to introduce; you have to think about how you are going to organize the information you present, what supporting materials you will use for the ideas you introduce into the conversation, what language will be appropriate for the person you are talking to, and how you are going to use your voice to emphasize ideas and communicate meaning to your conversational partner.

Someone has said that a public speech should be an extended conversation. That position is not totally valid, but a good public speech has many of the qualities of a good conversation—and a good conversation has many of the qualities of a good speech.

6. Developing effective oral communication is a necessary ingredient of a liberal education. No person who lacks the ability to communicate orally can be considered to have completed a liberal education. In his inaugural address as president of Susquehanna University, Jonathan C. Messerli noted that any definition of a liberal education "will include the need to help students learn how to think, how to communicate, and how to have something to communicate."[12]

Notes

1. Willard Hayes Yaeger, "Wendell Phillips," in *History and Criticism of American Public Address,* ed. W. Norwood Brigance (New York: McGraw-Hill Book Co., Inc., 1943), I, 330. Used by permission.
2. *Ibid.,* I, 332.
3. *Ibid.,* I, 333.
4. Dayton David McKean, "Woodrow Wilson," in *History and Criticism of American Public Address,* ed. W. Norwood Brigance (New York: McGraw-Hill Book Co., Inc., 1943), II, 968–71. Used by permission.
5. Herbert L. Curry, "John C. Calhoun," in *History and Criticism of American Public Address,* ed. W. Norwood Brigance (New York: McGraw-Hill Book Co., Inc., 1943), II, 640–41. Used by permission.
6. *Ibid.,* II, 641–42.
7. Edwin J. Delattre, "The Humanities Can Irrigate Deserts," *The Chronicle of Higher Education,* October 11, 1977, p. 32. Excerpted from *The Chronicle of Higher Education.* Reprinted with permission.
8. *The Birmingham News,* May 7, 1979, p. 22. Used by permission.
9. *The Chronicle of Higher Education,* February 6, 1978, p. 9. Excerpted from *The Chronicle of Higher Education.* Reprinted with permission.
10. Martha H. Rader and Alan P. Wunsch, *Journal of Business Communication,* 17 (1980):35. Used by permission.
11. Ruth Walker, "Earnings: Raw Material for your Financial Plans," *The Birmingham News,* February 24, 1985, p. 5–B.
12. Jonathan C. Messerli, "Church and State: the Limited Partners of Church-Related Colleges," *The Chronicle of Higher Education,* May 1, 1978, p. 40. Used by permission.

Fundamentals of
SPEECH COMMUNICATION

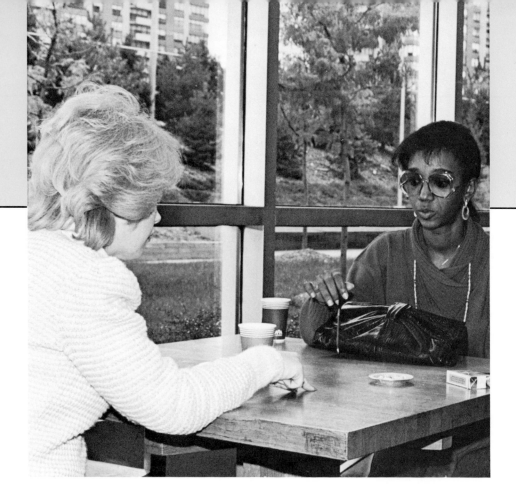

PART 1

BASIC CONSIDERATIONS

1

THE COMMUNICATION PROCESS

W hy is human communication a subject of study in so many disciplines? A moment's reflection tells us: it touches human beings daily. Through intrapersonal communication we consider a personal problem and devise a solution to it. Through interpersonal communication we tell friends about memorable experiences, a stranger obtains directions to the home of a friend, a parent lets a child know he is loved, an air traffic controller talks an airliner safely onto the runway through rain and fog. Through public communication we present to a local service club the details of a new company policy to establish better relations with the community.

What happens if communication is faulty? Sometimes very little. If you order an egg over-light and the one you get is scrambled, little harm is done. But if an air traffic controller's report that the altitude of an airplane is one hundred feet is received as two hundred feet, a tragic crash may occur. If a parent's message of love is not received clearly by a child, a serious personality problem may develop.

Not only is communication important in simply conveying information, it is also an especially important problem-solving device. By means of arbitration meetings, labor and management explore each other's positions and ultimately may resolve their differences. By means of small group communication, a city council analyzes the city's need for a new water plant, examines alternative proposals, and finally adopts what it judges the best solution. By means of public speeches, proponents of different views can take their cases to the people concerned.

Some, recognizing its importance, have suggested communication as a cure-all for solving problems in our society. Thus we hear almost daily that if only two groups could "communicate," they could resolve their problems. Without denying the importance of communication, we know it will not automatically solve every problem in our world. In some instances, it may even increase the difficulty by revealing that differences are greater than assumed.

Human communication takes many forms, such as interviews, conversations, small group communication, public communication, and mass communication. In this book, we will concentrate on one of these forms: public communication.

Credibility and the Communicator

The main theme of this book is that successful acts of communication—whether from one to one, to a few, or to many—depend on the credibility of ideas.

When democratic government came to ancient Athens, and all citizens were given the right to address the Assembly, many found themselves unable to take advantage of the privilege because they had not been taught to speak effectively.

Soon, teachers of rhetoric, or speech communication, were numerous in Athens. Known as Sophists, some of those teachers considered the principles they taught as a means of giving effectiveness to the speaker. Aristotle—one of the most important of all writers on rhetoric—believed, on the other hand, that *speech communication principles are a means of giving effectiveness to the speaker's ideas*. That concept will be pervasive in this book.

The student of speech communication who learns the principles of creating the credibility of ideas is apt to communicate with others more effectively and to analyze the communication attempts of others more intelligently. The credibility of ideas may stem from several sources: the message content, the organization of the message, the language of the communication effort, the communication situation, the communicator's delivery, or the communicator's attributes. Credibility is seldom created by a single factor alone. Usually several factors must work together.

The remainder of this book will discuss the principles by which you can establish the effectiveness and credibility of your ideas.

Definition of Communication

Communication is the process by which we develop and share meaning. This definition precludes no form of human communication—from two people's developing and sharing meaning for the sheer joy of communicating, to the public communicator's developing and sharing meaning in order to influence the attitudes and behaviors of others.

Figure 1.1 shows the elements that are involved in the communication process. Before discussing those elements, however, we need to clarify their roles and relationships by considering six characteristics of the process itself.

1. Communication is *dynamic* rather than static. The elements act individually and also interact with each other. Communication is not a discrete act, but a number of actions that produce certain effects that in turn produce results, and so on. In any communicative effort, therefore, you must constantly be aware of the other elements involved and continually adapt to their changes.
2. It is *continuous*. There is a continuity of each of the parts. Your understanding of the world begins the day you are born and continues until the day you die. Throughout this time you communicate with others, and they communicate with you. Even as you express ideas to a listener, your mutual understanding of those ideas is developing, as a result of both the listener's response to them and your own reaction to that listener's response. Furthermore, communication goes on after you and the listener go your separate ways, as each of you continues to think about and respond to what the other said and did. There is no beginning and no end to communication. Though your death may end your role as receiver, it does not stop your role as source.

Figure 1.1
A model of the speech communication process.

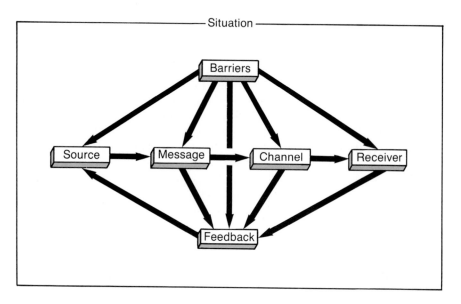

3. It is *complex*. Many naively perceive the act of speech communication as a simple one: somebody speaks and somebody listens. Therefore, they reason, communication has taken place. Initiating efforts to communicate may be easy, but achieving communication is difficult. Some even speak of the transfer of ideas from one person to another. Nothing could be further from the truth. Don't expect to transfer your ideas to another; the best that can be done is to stimulate a hearer to think about the meaning expressed. Even if you cause the listener to think, you cannot always make that listener think about the meaning you have in mind, because communication occurs at many levels and reflects many influences. The listener may not be stimulated to think about the meaning in the way you wanted.

4. It is *irreversible*. Just as the process of turning iron into steel cannot be reversed, the process of communication cannot be turned back. If you call a friend an offensive name and later apologize, the effect cannot be totally erased. Once a message has been sent and received, the effect it produces becomes a factor in all later messages.

5. It is *nonsequential*. The elements in the communication process are not necessarily in any particular order. They may occur in any sequence— linear, circular, or any other—or they may occur in a random order. The positions of the parts in the following communication model in figure 1.1 are constantly interchanging. For example, the model shows the source before the message, yet the message may have been developing in the source's mind long before it is presented to another person. The placement of barriers in the figure does not clearly

demonstrate that the barriers can start to block the message even before the source begins. Also, the figure does not indicate that the message and channel are interrelated and generally are inseparable. Moreover, feedback can begin before the source starts a message, although the figure does not show this.

6. It is *unrepeatable*. We cannot re-create an act of communication. Since participants are changed because of it, they cannot repeat the process because they bring altered meanings to any later acts of communication. If you miss a class lecture, for example, there is no way you can get the same information; no classmates' notes will have all the information, nor will the professor be able to repeat the lecture for you because the verbal and nonverbal interactions that came from your classmates will be missing. As Heraclitus said long ago, a person cannot step into the same river twice because both are different the second time. Because other factors in an act of communication do not remain static, their changes also prevent the repetition of communication.[1]

In short, communication is a process consisting of a number of independent and interdependent steps leading to the attainment of an end. In speech communication that end is the developing and sharing of some specific meaning. Never let the simplicity of the end obscure the complexity of the process.

Elements of the Speech Communication Process

The complex process of speech communication must be understood if effective, meaningful communication is to occur. We can grasp the process better if we break it into its constituent parts and diagram them in a model as in figure 1.1. Are we to interpret this model literally? No, it is *analogous* with the communication process, not a replica of it. We must also keep in mind that the speech communication process is different from certain biological processes in which the parts cannot be interchanged and must occur in a fixed sequence. Understand that, in some important ways, we distort the communication process when we discuss the elements in isolation. Basically there are seven elements in the process: (1) the source, (2) the message, (3) the channel, (4) the receiver, (5) barriers, (6) feedback, and (7) the situation.

The Source

The source in speech communication is the person who makes the decision to communicate. As a communicator you may decide to communicate with yourself (intrapersonal speech communication), with another person (interpersonal speech communication), or with a number of other persons (public communication). You may have one or more of three intents: (1) *to inform*, as when you tell a stranger how to get to a particular place in town; (2) *to entertain*, as when you tell someone a joke; (3) *to persuade*, as when you explain to a friend reasons for staying in college. In some instances you may

have more than one purpose because you are talking to more than one audience. A labor leader explaining to the union members how an impending strike will be carried out if negotiations break down is attempting to inform them. If television cameras are present to carry these remarks to the nation, however, the labor leader may be trying to persuade management and the public that the union is serious and unyielding in its contract demands.

You determine the purpose of a speech. Even if you give a speech to inform or entertain and the listeners end up being persuaded, the purpose of the speech is still to inform or to entertain. Or you may give a speech to persuade, but the listeners may only be informed. In some instances your purpose may be to persuade, but the speech is given as an informative one. Although many informative and persuasive speeches use communicative principles similarly, there are some speeches in which the principles are applied in different ways, as explained in chapters 12 and 13.

You are limited to the information you have accumulated on the topic through experience and investigation. Your ability to generate a message is further circumscribed by your perceptions, your thoughts, and your feelings.

Significantly influencing the impact of the message will be characteristics that make you appealing or unappealing to the particular audience being addressed. If you have a poor image with a specific group of listeners, attempt to remove or compensate for that image. On the other hand, if you have a good image, take advantage of it.

The Message	Determine the meaning you want to convey to the particular receivers. Your message should consist of your ideas, attitudes, and values. It can be communicated in a number of different forms. It may be presented in written form—an essay, letter, poem, novel, drama, political pamphlet. It may be delivered orally—a conversation, interview, group discussion, debate, informal speech, formal speech. It may be developed nonverbally, through music, painting, sculpture, and action. From one point of view, these forms are channels for a message. In fact, however, the form and the ideas are intertwined, and together become the message.

Speech is the most proficient form of communication. Horowitz and Newman had forty subjects speak and write for two minutes after thinking about a given topic for thirty seconds. The results showed that spoken communication produced significantly more ideas and subordinate ideas than written communication, even when the time limit for writing was extended to twelve minutes.[2] When speaking was compared with handwriting, typing, and stenotyping, it again proved more proficient.[3]

You can also use nonverbal communication, which is meaning communicated by bodily action, facial expression, vocal inflection, and other non-language sounds. Whether you want to or not, you usually communicate nonverbally, and it may be more important than the verbal communication.

We frequently force a receiver to resolve conflicting verbal and nonverbal cues. The response to these different cues will vary according to such factors as the age group of the receiver and the sex of the source. One group of experimenters found that children believe verbal cues more than nonverbal ones. Children interpreted the comments more negatively than adults when adult women made critical comments while smiling. The children tended to ignore the nonverbal cue, the smile, whereas it caused adults to interpret the message as neutral. All subjects, children and adult, responded more to the conflicting nonverbal cues of a woman than to similar cues from a man. Bugental and her colleagues pointed out "that if a woman frowned and said something complimentary in a pleasant tone of voice, her sincerity was doubted—her communication was rated as neutral at best and was described as sarcastic." When the same cues were given by a man, the message "was rated positively" and he was described "as sincere or complimentary."[4]

This book will help you communicate, mainly by conveying ideas in the form of an informal or formal oral message, although many of the principles are applicable in other forms of communication. Put your message together in such a way that the listeners believe your ideas. It should hold their attention and cause them to respond in the desired manner. Be concerned about the selection of specific ideas; use the most effective means of organizing them; choose language that will transmit the denotative and connotative meanings desired; and present the finished message in such a way that nothing will prevent the listener from focusing on the meaning communicated by the relevant verbal and nonverbal stimuli.

Basic Considerations

You may consider the channel for speech communication from two points of view. First, the channel is the means by which you transmit an oral message to a listener. Two senses are involved—hearing and sight. Air waves carry vibrations created by your voice to the outer ear of the listener. These vibrations induce nerve impulses that travel to the listener's brain for interpretation into your orginal sounds and words. Meanwhile, light waves carry your image and actions to the receiver's eye. Nerve impulses then travel to the visual center of the brain where the sensation becomes perception. Thus these aural and visual cues transmit the communicative stimuli from you, the source, to the receiver. **The Channel**

Second, the channel is the type of speech communication you use. You may speak in a face-to-face situation with no artificial aids, in a face-to-face situation with the aid of an amplifying system, from a radio studio to an unseen audience who cannot see you, from a TV studio to an unseen audience who can see you, or to a live audience with the message being transmitted by radio or TV to an unseen audience.

Whatever channel you use to transmit the message, adapt your speaking in order to make the most effective use of the particular channel. If you are using the telephone, you may have no concern for eye contact and bodily action. In a face-to-face situation, however, direct eye contact and effective use of bodily action are necessary.

A receiver is any person who perceives the message. It may not be the person for whom the message was intended. Attempt to determine who the receivers will be. What is their age, their sex, their educational background, their economic status? What characteristics do they have in common with one another: membership in the same organization? Similar occupational backgrounds? Similar concerns about one or more contemporary problems? How much information do the receivers have on the topic of the message? Do they have as much as, more than, or less than you? What attitudes do the listeners hold? Will the majority of them be opposed, neutral, or favorably disposed toward your topic and purpose? If they are opposed, will they be strongly opposed or mildly opposed? If they are favorable to your position, will they be strongly favorable or mildly favorable? If the listeners are neutral, what kind of neutrality is it? Neutrality for some persons means that they are undecided, that they have not made up their minds. These listeners may be easily moved to a new position. For others, neutrality may constitute a committed position arrived at after careful deliberation. McGinnies found, for example, that many Japanese students were committed to a position of neutrality on the issue of the cold war between the United States and the USSR. This was not an attitude held because they didn't know or didn't care, but a firmly committed attitude arrived at and held deliberately.[5] **The Receiver**

With the above information in hand, decide how much and what kind of information to include and how to convey it to the listeners in order to achieve your purpose.

Unless the people for whom the message is intended are listening, communication will be either nonexistent or distorted. Those who can and do listen will attempt to decode the message. Words will be interpreted to have a particular meaning, which may or may not be the same as you intended. Or the listener may see certain actions and attach a specific meaning to them. The meaning attached can vary from person to person and group to group.

After the receiver has decoded the message and decided what he thinks the intended meaning is, he makes some kind of response to it: he may ignore it, reject it, applaud it, boo it, behave in opposition to it, or behave in accord with it.

Basic Considerations

Barriers sometimes interfere with the communicative process. What are barriers? They are any factors that cause an incorrect meaning, or no meaning, to be communicated to a receiver.

In most cases you want to communicate a meaning that accurately reflects both the reality of the topic under discussion and your attitude toward that reality. Sometimes, however, you are prevented from perceiving the reality of a situation because of your personal biases or attitudes, ignorance or lack of some information, or inability to perceive the events. For example, you may believe that all Southerners are racists, so when you meet someone with a Southern dialect, you may avoid that person even though he is the farthest thing from a bigot. On other occasions, you may have arrived at a meaning that is consistent with reality, but be unable to communicate that meaning to a listener because of an inadequate vocabulary. Or you may possess certain characteristics that cause the listener to focus on you rather than on the message. All these things, and others like them, constitute barriers in the source because they interfere with effective communication.

How do you create barriers? You may organize the message so poorly that the listener simply cannot comprehend its meaning. You may develop the ideas so poorly that the listener finds them unbelievable. You may choose a word, such as "ain't," that stirs in the listener reactions that are actually detrimental to your purpose, or you may select an ambiguous word that leaves the listener confused or with a different understanding from the one intended. You may deliver the message in such a way that the listener cannot focus on its substance but is distracted by irrelevant and meaningless actions.

Interference may occur in the channel of the communication—a baby crying in the audience, a loud sound outside the room, a room that is too hot. Anything that interferes with the receiver's perception of the source, such as a lectern that is too high for the speaker, or an improperly used microphone, can become an interference in the channel. For example, some speakers turn alternately away from and toward the microphone, causing the loudness level to change drastically. Some become so enamored of the mike that they talk to it rather than to the listeners. Some set up distracting noises by handling the mike, smacking their lips, pounding on the lectern, or rattling notes close by—all sounds that are magnified by the public address system.

Barriers may exist within the listeners. A person who had little sleep the night before may be unable to concentrate on your statements. One who had an unpleasant argument at home before coming to the speech may relive that controversy in her mind instead of attending to you. An individual may be in pain and unable to focus on your thoughts. Obviously, these problems are beyond your control, but they are barriers that the listener can often eliminate or overcome. Other barriers may exist in the listener, however, which you can affect. Some listeners may have had unpleasant experiences that certain words cause them to recall; you can avoid those words if you have previously analyzed the audience and are aware of this situation. Some may react unfavorably to incorrect grammar, nonfluencies, or a monotonous voice.

Figure 1.2

A helical spiral as a representation of human communication. Dance's helical spiral graphically demonstrates that communication is an on-going process, as feedback from the listener returns to a speaker who has moved on from the point at which the feedback was instigated. From Human Communication Theory: Original Essays, *edited by Frank E. X. Dance. Copyright © 1967 by Holt, Rinehart & Winston, Inc. Reprinted by permission of Holt, Rinehart & Winston, Inc.*

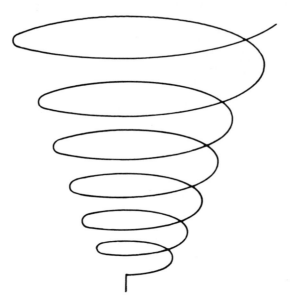

Feedback

Feedback consists of the reactions and responses of the listeners that you perceive. They enable you to adapt what you are saying to communicate more precisely. Feedback begins the moment you go in front of an audience, even before you say anything, and continues constantly until you and the audience part. In many instances feedback continues even after you and the listeners have gone to other activities. Such feedback comes in the form of printed comment, letters, and public opinion polls, which provide information about your efforts.

Some have described the communicative process as circular—the speaker verbalizes certain thoughts and ideas, the listener responds, the speaker perceives the response, the speaker verbalizes new thoughts adapted to the listener's response, and the cycle continues. Frank Dance, however, has suggested that the communicative process is not circular, but helical. By this he means that the response of the listener never finds you, the speaker, where you were when you stated the idea to which the listener responded. You have moved on; and since the feedback never returns to exactly the same point as that from which the original statement began, the process cannot be circular. Dance conceives of the process as ever moving to a higher plateau; consequently, he describes it as a helical or spiral process,[6] as shown in figure 1.2.

If we keep in mind that it is merely an analogy to clarify the communicative process, then viewing the process as helical can be helpful, because this model does stress that feedback always finds the speaker at a different point from that to which the feedback pertains. However, it is misleading to let the helical model make us believe that communication is always moving to a higher plateau, for feedback can force you, the speaker, backward, instead of letting you spiral upward.

What can cause you to regress? You may misinterpret the feedback. The listener's action may not be a response to you or your message. For example, you may see a key member of the audience lean over and put his head in his hands. Although the action may simply reflect fatigue on the part of the receiver, you may interpret the action to mean you have just said something with which the listener disagrees. A frown may indicate disapproval of what you are saying, or it may mean that the listener just experienced the pangs of indigestion. Even if the response is to your message, you may not recognize it as such or may misinterpret its meaning. A listener's whispered comment, which causes the neighbor to smile and nod her head, may be interpreted as a favorable reaction. The listener, however, may have said, "I think he's crazy," to which the second listener nodded agreement.

Whether feedback causes communication to advance or regress, it is an important part of the process. It helps you perceive whether your ideas are being understood, accepted, or attended to. You cannot afford to be ignorant of, or to ignore, feedback from listeners.

Probably the single most influential element in the speech communication process is the situation. It is the element that not only binds all the others together, but also largely fixes their characteristics. It is the situation that often determines who the speaker will be. On the floor of the Senate, no one except a senator or the chaplain can be a speaker. In a local church on Sunday morning, certain areas in the church may be limited to the clergy. Other situations are less structured in determining the speaker; but the situation, to a large extent, is a limiting factor on who will be permitted or motivated to speak. The kind of people who will be present also is influenced by the situation. Few nonchurch members, and still fewer atheists, will be present at the Sunday morning church service. Democratic political rallies attract few Republicans; Republican political rallies attract few Democrats.

Even the message is affected by the situation. It may affect what should or should not be said, how the message should be organized, what language is appropriate. The use of a message inappropriate to the situation may have a negative effect instead of the positive effect it would have in an appropriate situation.

The mood of the people is affected by the situation. The mood of students at an orientation lecture is different from the mood of those students in a classroom listening to a lecture. And both of these moods will be quite different from the one at a football rally. If you fail to adapt your message to the situation, you stand little chance of being a credible speaker.

The Situation

The situation affects the polarization of an audience. Polarization occurs when listeners focus their attention intensely upon the speaker. An auditorium affects polarization by causing listeners to sit facing the speaker, whereas listeners standing at an outdoors speech may face in several directions easily. Music, especially martial music, preceding the speech facilitates focusing attention on the speaker. Decoration of the meeting place with colored bunting, organizational symbols, or nationalistic symbols helps in polarizing an audience. A podium that puts the speaker above the level of the listeners, or lighting that directs the focal point to the speaker makes it easier for the listeners to attend to the speaker. On the other hand, a barren-looking room or one that has a wide, open space between the listeners and the speaker makes it more difficult for polarization to occur.

The channel chosen for the transmission of the message depends on the situation. Without an amplifying system, a face-to-face speech cannot be given to an audience of fifty thousand in a football stadium. Yet the use of an amplifying system to aid in talking to an audience of twenty-five in a small room appears ludicrous.

Feedback is influenced by the situation. If there are fifty thousand people present, it is impossible for the speaker to perceive most of the responses of the hearers. If the speech is given from a practically empty studio to a television audience, there is no feedback for the speaker to perceive. If the speech is given to a class of graduate students who have some expertise on the topic, the speaker will probably receive much highly sophisticated feedback from listeners.

Summary

Although communication is not a panacea for the world's ills, it is extremely important because it permits people to transmit instructions, convey feelings and attitudes, and cope in a rational way with problems that confront us.

The most effective communicator develops credibility to aid in communication, the process by which we develop meaning and share it with others.

To better control our communication, we must understand the communication process itself, which is dynamic, continuous, complex, irreversible, nonsequential, and unrepeatable. There are seven elements in the communicative process: (1) the source, (2) the message, (3) the channel, (4) the receiver, (5) barriers, (6) feedback, and (7) the situation. But we must remember that no part can be entirely isolated from the others. With an appreciation and understanding of these elements, you can proceed rationally to improve your communicative efforts.

Basic Considerations

Exercises

1. Analyze the classroom in which you are to speak. Describe how you would arrange it for maximal and minimal support to aid in establishing your credibility.

2. Go to a fund-raising dinner or a similar speaking situation. Explain in detail how you would alter the communicative situation to better support development of the speaker's credibility. For example: Would you place the speaker in a different location? Would you rearrange the seating of the audience? Would you change the decoration of the room? Would you have the speaker dress differently?

3. Describe barriers to effective communication that exist in your classroom situation. Explain how you as a speaker plan to cope with them to prevent their affecting your credibility.

4. Analyze the receivers in your classroom: What attributes of theirs must you consider for your next speaking assignment? In what ways will you adapt to these characteristics to improve your credibility?

5. Attend a public lecture on campus. Describe the feedback available to the speaker. Explain in what ways this speaker used it to enhance his or her credibility and in what ways he or she failed to use it.

6. Using the same speech as in exercise 5, describe the plan of organization used by the speaker. Did the speaker state a purpose? Were the main points identified? If so, how? Were the speaker's ideas easy or difficult to follow? Why?

7. Again using the same speech, describe the content of the speech. What kinds of supporting materials did the speaker use? statistics? examples? personal experiences? testimony? opinion polls? Were sources of the content provided? Did you feel that the content was credible? Why or why not?

8. Using the same speech, describe the language used. Was it clear? Was it appropriate? Was it wordy? Did it seem original? Did it have vitality?

9. Analyze a communicative effort of one of your classmates. Which elements of the communicative process did this classmate consider in establishing credibility? Which did he or she not consider?

10. Pair off with a classmate and take turns interviewing each other according to the following guidelines:
    a. Decide who will be the first to be interviewed.
    b. Conduct a ten-minute interview, focusing on the questions below. The interviewer should take notes and feed back to the interviewee a paraphrase after each question. The goals are openness and accurate listening.
    c. After ten minutes repeat the process by switching roles.
    d. Take about three minutes to talk about the interviewing experience.
    e. Give a brief report to the entire class on the person whom you interviewed.

Notes

1. Although there are differences, this discussion of the communicative process relies heavily upon that of Dean C. Barnlund. He believes communication is circular; I believe it is nonsequential. See D. C. Barnlund, "A Transactional Model of Communication," in K. K. Sereno and C. D. Mortensen, eds., *Foundations of Communication Theory* (New York: Harper & Row, 1970), pp. 83–102.
2. M. W. Horowitz and J. B. Newman, "Spoken and Written Expression: An Experimental Analysis," *Journal of Abnormal and Social Psychology* 68 (1964):640–47.
3. M. W. Horowitz and A. Berkowitz, "Structural Advantage of the Mechanism of Spoken Expression as a Factor in Differences in Spoken and Written Expression," *Perceptual and Motor Skills* 19 (1964):619–25.
4. D. E. Bugental, J. W. Kaswan, and L. R. Love, "Perception of Contradictory Meanings Conveyed by Verbal and Nonverbal Channels," *Journal of Personality and Social Psychology* 16 (1970):647–55.
5. E. McGinnies, "Studies in Persuasion: III. Reactions of Japanese Students to One-Sided and Two-Sided Communications," *Journal of Social Psychology* 70 (1966):87–93.
6. F. E. X. Dance, *Human Communication Theory* (New York: Holt, Rinehart and Winston, 1967), pp. 295–96.

2

THE FIRST SPEECH

*I*n a short time, before you have had a chance to read much of this book, you will be asked to prepare and deliver your first speech. You may be unduly concerned about this first speech. For many, it will be your first effort and you may not feel ready to prepare and give a speech because you have never given one before. Undoubtedly you have given parts of a speech before. For example, you have told someone of an exciting, boring, or unusual experience you have had. In relating that experience you used some of the same principles that you will use in making a speech. Once you realize that you have often used many of the principles before, you will understand that giving a speech is not such a difficult task. The important thing is to learn the principles that make a speech different from relating a single experience. This chapter will explain how to prepare and present that first speech.

Approach the First Speech with a Positive Attitude

First, recognize the benefits that this speech will have for you. It will permit the other students in class to get to know you better. They can see how you think, how you react to unexpected happenings in the situation, whether you have a sense of humor, or what experiences you have had. It will give you an opportunity to affect their thought processes. You can introduce them to new information that will affect how they think about the topic on which you speak. Never overlook the influence that an effective speaker has on listeners' beliefs and attitudes.

Second, this first speech will begin to develop and hone the public speaking skills that will be so valuable to you for the rest of your life. The principles that you learn will help you to cogently argue a political position; how to clearly explain a procedure; how to enthusiastically present a new idea to a colleague or supervisor.

Select a Subject for Your Speech

First, select the subject area from which you will draw your specific topic for the speech. Make a list of subjects that you are interested in; then check the ones on which you have had experience. Your best choice will generally be an area in which you have had experience—scouting, cheerleading, student government, or perhaps in political campaigns. Next, you will want to consider your potential audience. Since your classmates will be your audience, it will not be difficult to ascertain the information you need about their interests, experiences, and knowledge. This will be one of the most homogeneous audiences you will ever address. Learn everything you can about your classmates, and select a subject they will be interested in. The final factor to consider in selecting a subject is the occasion. In this case, the occasion is a classroom assignment. Be sure you have met the requirements stated by your professor, such as type of speech, time limits, and so on.

Now that you have considered your interests, knowledge, and experience, your listeners' interests, knowledge, and experience, and the occasion of the speech, you are ready to select your subject.

Suppose you had experience as a cheerleader in high school, so you decide that would be a good topic to speak on. Think about the experiences (funny, exciting, happy, sad) you have had as a cheerleader. Think about your attitudes and convictions toward cheerleading. As a result of these thoughts, you may decide that you don't want to tell them how to be a cheerleader, however, because probably none of them will ever be one. College cheerleaders have usually been high school cheerleaders. Give your classmates some information that will be meaningful. Focus on an aspect of cheerleading that will help them to understand what cheerleaders do or what they accomplish. Or focus on facets of cheerleading that are relevant to people in other occupations, such as teachers, salespersons, ministers, or nurses.

One of the functions and values of this first speech is to let your classmates begin to understand and know something about you. For example, you might decide to tell them something about what you learned from cheerleading.

Develop Your Purpose and Supporting Materials

First, phrase a sentence that tells specifically what you are going to say about your subject. This is called a central idea sentence, thesis sentence, or topic sentence. It tells the audience specifically what you are going to talk about. It is phrased in the following way: "This morning I want to talk to you about three things I learned from cheerleading."

Second, consider the main ideas that can be used to develop the thesis sentence. In this case, you might decide that there were six things you learned from cheerleading: leadership, sportsmanship, cooperation, imagination, friendliness, ethusiasm. You realize that you cannot develop six main ideas in the time you have alloted for your first speech, so you decide to develop only three. After you have selected the ideas you are going to use to develop your thesis sentence, you should then phrase each of them in a complete sentence. These will be the main points in the body of your speech.

Third, develop the supporting materials for each of your three main points. Three types of evidence that can be used are facts, statistics, and testimony. Methods of developing supporting materials are by definition, comparison, description, classification, narration, restatement, and explanation. These methods of developing evidence are the means of giving life and vitality to your ideas. Narration, for example, is the telling of a story, and stories are what people like to hear, because they give flesh and blood to your points. Stories also help to hold the attention of listeners because people are usually curious to know how a story will end.

You may define each of your three points, then give an example of each. You may find a statement that someone has made about one or more of your points. Go to the library and look up your topic in relevant sources. Check

your subject in the card catalog to see if there are any books that deal with it. Next, check the *Readers' Guide to Periodical Literature* and the *Social Science Index* for periodical articles on your subject. For your first speech, these indexes will probably provide you with all the information you will need. You will also want to focus on personal experiences as the primary method of clearly developing each of your points for your listeners. If selected carefully, this information should increase your credibility with your listeners because you will have established that you have had personal experience with the topic, and have also done research to verify and authenticate your experience.

Organize the Speech

You should now prepare an outline of your speech. When you have completed the above three phases, you will have the thesis sentence and the body of your speech. To these two parts should be added an introduction and conclusion. The outline of these four parts will look like this:

I. Introduction
II. Thesis Sentence: This morning I want to explain to you three qualities that cheerleading taught me.

III. Body of the speech
    A. Cheerleading taught me leadership.
        1. Definition of leadership.
        2. Testimony concerning leadership.
        3. Personal experience with leadership.
    B. Cheerleading taught me sportsmanship.
        1. Definition of sportsmanship.
        2. Example of sportsmanship.
        3. Personal experience with sportsmanship.
    C. Cheerleading taught me imagination.
        1. Definition of imagination.
        2. Example of imagination.
        3. Personal experience with imagination.
IV. Conclusion

After you have completed the body of your speech, you are ready to prepare an introduction and conclusion. You can't prepare them earlier because you cannot know what to introduce and conclude until you have completed the body of the speech.

In the introduction, your primary purpose is to get the attention of the listeners. You can do one or more of several things. You can explain the relevance of this topic to your audience—you can relate a memorable experience, you can describe the importance of the topic for you or your listeners, or you can relate a humorous event. The important thing is to keep it brief, to the point, and have it well prepared. This is where you make your first and most important impression on the listeners.

In the conclusion, you can summarize what you have said, you can focus on a humorous aspect, you can challenge the listeners to use the information in some way. The conclusion should be brief, relevant, and well prepared. This final impression will probably be the one most listeners will remember, and that memory will greatly affect their reaction to your speech.

Develop Language

Do not be misled by the heading of this unit. You are not to develop language in the sense of fixing permanently or even semi-permanently the language you will use to present the speech. What you want to do is to develop several ways of phrasing the ideas you are going to present. In some cases, you may create a strikingly original way of expressing an idea, and you want to use that sequence of words each time you present the speech. That is acceptable, providing you don't let it begin to sound memorized. For the most part, however, you want to avoid an habitual use of language in presenting the same speech.

At this point in the course, you should be primarily concerned about two aspects of language: familiarity and clarity. Primarily use words that you are accustomed to using. Do not, however, use incorrect or inappropriate words, no matter how much you might use them in other situations. Don't try to

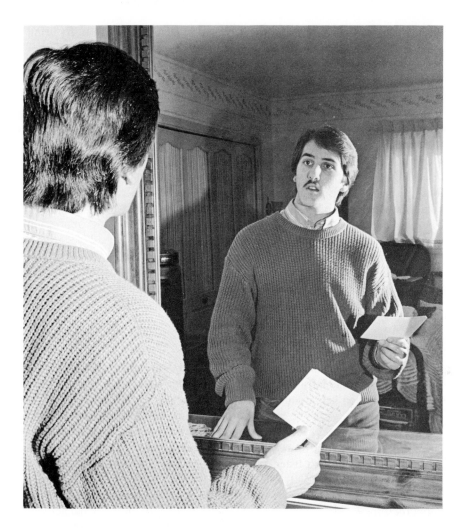

impress your listeners by using "big" words or unfamiliar words. Use your own vocabulary that is appropriate. The words that you are accustomed to using will flow more easily and give a sense of naturalness to your speech.

Choose words that clearly and unambiguously express your ideas. Think of synonyms that will convey the same idea, so that you will have a choice of language when you give the speech.

If you stress familiarity and clarity of language, you will have no problems in communicating in this first speech.

Practicing the Speech

Prepare for delivering your speech by practicing it. Do not write out the speech. Using your prepared outline, practice talking about each of the points that you have decided to include in the speech. A speech that sounds memorized has little chance of being effective. Moreover, it is difficult to make adjustments and adaptations with a memorized speech. Each time you practice the speech, be sure you use different wording so you don't memorize it. By using different wording each time you practice the speech, you will not be upset if you forget a particular word when you actually give it. Since you will have used different words each time you practiced the speech, you will have several words to choose from. When you deliver your speech to the audience, you won't have to worry about forgetting what you want to say, because you will have a reservoir of words for each of your main ideas. As a result, your speech will possess a spontaneity of language; it will not sound memorized. You will sound as though you are conversing with the audience.

To practice your speech, prepare a key word outline of your speech on four-by-six note cards. Three-by-five note cards are less desirable because they hold so much less information that you must have a greater number of them. The consequent greater shuffling of the cards gives the listeners the impression that you are heavily dependent on your notes.

By practicing from a key word outline, you will naturally vary your language each time you practice. That will help you develop a conversational mode of delivery, reduce your dependence on your notes, and provide a larger number of words to choose from to express your ideas.

Delivering the Speech

Your first appearance in front of the audience is extremely important. Walk purposely and confidently to the lectern, lay your notes on it, look at your listeners, and then begin your speech in a confident tone of voice. If you do not have a lectern, go to the center of the podium, look at your listeners, and then begin your speech. Remember, your personality and character are important. Don't be afraid to reveal them to your listeners. They can have as strong an impact on your listeners as any words and ideas you can utter.

Speaking Behavior

Maintain good eye contact with your listeners. Look them straight in the eyes, not at their foreheads or chins or chests, but directly in the eyes. Avoid nervous mannerisms: shifting weight from side to side, playing with note cards, saying "uh," frequently putting your hands in your pockets and taking them out, rattling coins or keys in pockets. Do not influence the listeners negatively by apologizing for your speech effort. If your apology is for something you should have done and didn't, then the apology is insufficient. If it is for something over which you had no control, then it is irrelevant. In either case, forget the apology.

Use plenty of signposts in the speech. These serve as transitions and guides for your listeners to tell them where you have been and where you are going. These are important in oral communication because the listener cannot go back over the material that has been presented the way a reader can turn back and reread a page. Examples of signposts are: "My first point is. . ." "Let me move on to my second point," "however," "nevertheless," "furthermore," "moreover," "therefore," "consequently." Examples of summaries are: "I have presented three reasons. . ." "The point I have tried to make is. . ." "Let me summarize. . . ."

Speak in a firm, clear voice. If the listeners can't hear what you are saying, **Voice**
you are not communicating with them. Vary the pitch, rate, and loudness in
keeping with the meaning of your statements. Avoid sounding memorized. The
best way to shun this fault is to prevent memorization of the speech, as previously described.

Use a conversational tone. This will suggest spontaneity and intimacy
which will contribute to improved communication. Using a conversational mode
does not mean that you should speak as you do in conversation but that you
should use the qualities characteristic of effective conversation.

In the first place, even good conversationalists must adjust to the public
speaking situation. Volume must be increased; gestures must be enlarged so
they are easily seen; the speaking rate must be adapted to the acoustics of the
room.

Second, some people are poor conversationalists—they speak too low,
they speak in a monotone, they muffle their articulation, they use too many
vocalized pauses, they speak too slowly or they speak too fast. If these ineffective methods are used in speaking to an audience, the speaker will be just
as ineffective as he is in conversation.

What, then, are those qualities that are present in effective conversation? James Winans says,

You will have carried over into your public delivery the most desirable qualities of
conversational speaking when you maintain upon the platform—

  1. Full realization of the content of your words as you utter them, and
  2. A lively sense of communication.[1]

Directness, enthusiasm, absence of self-consciousness, a communicative
attitude—these are the qualities you are striving for when you try to achieve
the "conversational mode." If you move mechanically through words you have
memorized or written on note cards, you often lose the vitality of tone that is
present when you turn your thoughts into words as you proceed through the
speech. Language becomes more informal when you use a "conversational
mode." More personal pronouns—*I, you, me, we, our, your*—are used, contributing to the impression that you are talking directly to each listener.

The conclusion is the final impression you will leave with your listeners. Make **Conclusion**
it a good one! Prepare it carefully. Avoid notes, so that you can look directly
at the members of your audience during the final moments of your speech. Do
not rush. When you have completed your conclusion, pause briefly before
leaving the podium. Then walk confidently and positively to your seat. Do not,
by facial expressions or bodily actions, indicate displeasure with your effort.
The listeners may think you have done an outstanding job. Don't influence
them negatively—after the speech is over. Unless you requested to speak to
the group, do not say "thank you" at the end of your speech. In most cases,
any statement of appreciation should come from those whom you addressed.
Sometimes a "Thank you" maintains audience rapport and appreciation for
the speaker.

Criticism of the Speech

Following completion of your speech or a group of speeches, there will probably be a period of oral criticism by your professor and your classmates. Depending upon your attitude and that of your classmates, this can be a constructive or traumatic experience. Listen positively to the comments. Realize that most of the people in the class will be sympathetic to your efforts; they will be trying to help you. Recognize that the critics are able to perceive things that you cannot. If they identify problems that you don't know how to correct, ask them for suggestions. Consider this criticism period as a time to begin preparation for the next speech. Write down the important comments so that you can begin working on them immediately.

Finally, consider this first speech an opportunity—to get to present yourself to your classmates, to begin to develop speech skills that will serve you for the rest of your life, to read and react to the reactions of your listeners.

Summary

In developing your first speech, maintain a positive attitude. Keep in mind that you have information that will be new to your classmates. Select a subject on which you have had experience and which you know something about. Develop a specific purpose, identify main ideas, and support those ideas with as much personal experience as possible. Organize the speech into four main parts: introduction, thesis sentence, body, and conclusion. Consider the language that you are going to use. Be sure you have chosen words that communicate accurately and clearly your main ideas. Practice the speech until you are comfortably familiar with it. Deliver the speech confidently in a conversational tone with good eye contact and effective body actions. Accept criticism after the speech positively and consider this criticism period as a beginning of preparation for the next speech. Good luck and have fun!

Basic Considerations

Exercises

1. Read at least one of the student speeches in Appendix B. Identify the elements that made the speech appropriate to that student. Do you feel that the student knew what he or she was talking about? What made you feel that way? Do you consider the speech an effective one? Why or why not?
2. Read one of the non-student speeches. Does the speaker use any of the methods that the student speaker did? Does the speaker use any methods not used by the student speaker? Do you consider the speech a good one? Why or why not?

Notes

1. J. A. Winans, *Speech-Making* (New York: D. Appleton-Century Co., 1938), p. 25.

3

UNDERSTANDING PERFORMANCE APPREHENSION

Seventy-five per cent of the respondents in a recent poll identified giving a speech as a cause of social anxiety, the second highest ranking out of ten events.[1] In fact, a look at the ten events reveals that all ten involve and depend upon communication. For most beginning speakers, performance apprehension, or stage fright as it is popularly called, is a well-known but little understood phenomenon. The purpose of this chapter is to dispel the mystery of performance apprehension and assist in your mental preparation for a communicative effort. An understanding of the nature and causes of performance apprehension will aid you in coping with it, intelligently using and benefitting from this psychological and physiological reaction.

The Term *Stage Fright* is a Misnomer

An understanding of stage fright begins with the knowledge that the term *stage fright* is unclear. As a matter of fact, speech teachers have been unable to devise a clear, consistent, meaningful definition of stage fright. Much experimental research has been conducted on this problem, but even here researchers have failed to define the term. Clevenger called attention to this fact and observed that "the measuring instrument in a stage fright experiment is not only the measurement of the stage fright, it is the definition as well."[2] Three different measuring instruments have been used to measure "the amount of fright a speaker says he has, the amount his audience says he has, and the amount a meter says he has." The important fact for consideration is that these three measurements have very little relationship to one another, or as Clevenger says, they "operate with only moderate interdependence during the course of a public speech."[3]

Stage fright is a misnomer because the inclusion of the term *fright* gives the impression that fear is present. Some have even defined the reaction as fear. This book contends, however, that a person with so-called stage fright is not experiencing fear, but anxiety or apprehension about the performance. The speaker is not afraid of the audience or the situation. The speaker's personal feelings about the quality of the speaking effort and its outcome causes anxiety or tension. Psychologists Shaffer and Shoben clearly differentiate between fear and anxiety:

The feeling-tone of anxiety is much like that of fear, but the two emotions can be distinguished in a number of ways. Typically, fear is evoked by a present and external stimulus, such as a ferocious dog or a narrowly escaped accident. Anxiety usually relates to the anticipation of a future situation, an apprehension of a probable pain, loss, or threat. Also anxiety is most often stimulated by qualities of a person himself rather than by external events. A boy *fears* a larger bully but has *anxiety* about his own strength, competence, or acceptance in the group. Anxiety is therefore a relatively late-emerging emotional pattern, since it depends upon some ability to foresee the future and upon some degree of socially acquired evaluation of one's self.[4]

In this book, then, stage fright will be defined as *a normal form of anxiety, or emotional tension, occurring in anyone confronted with a situation in which the performance is important and the outcome uncertain.* It should be noted that this definition does not restrict the reaction to speakers or to certain speakers. What we are really talking about is *performance apprehension.*

Performance Apprehension is Not Peculiar to Certain People

Unfortunately, the terms *stage fright* or *communication apprehension* give the impression that this reaction is an abnormal one and is peculiar to certain people on the stage—public speakers and actors—or persons involved in some act of communication. The truth is that the reaction is not abnormal and is not peculiar to any group; it is found in many people—athletes before an athletic event, actors and musicians before a performance, teachers before a class, job applicants before an interview. A teammate of Bill Russell, the great center and former coach of the Boston Celtics basketball team, reports that Russell "has left his lunch in men's rooms all over the country."[5] When Jerry West, the outstanding player of the Los Angeles Lakers basketball team, was an equally outstanding player for West Virginia University, *Time* reported:

The night before a game, the high-strung forward from West Virginia is often so taut that he takes a sedative. In the dressing room his hands are wet with sweat, and waiting on the bench, he has even retched into a towel. Then the game begins, and Jerry West, 21, sets his long face in a stony mask and begins to release his tremendous store of nervous energy.[6]

The late Paul Lynde, star of stage, screen, and television, confessed: "I have never gotten over being terrified in front of an audience. Oh, I know most performers get the jitters before they go on. My reaction is more like nervous collapse."[7]

Singer Linda Ronstadt was asked if she still experienced stage fright when she sang. She responded, "Always. I think everybody does, whether they admit it or not. My face twitches. I've seen myself on television, my cheek kind of doing a dance."[8]

The chief pilot of Air Force One, the plane that flies President Reagan wherever he wants to go, responded to questions about his job: "You bet I was nervous the first time I took it up," he said, "and I still am. Every time. But if I wasn't, it would be time to get out. I have butterflies and if I didn't, that means I'm not concentrating. That person in the back is the most important man in the world."[9]

A feature story on great teachers in U.S. colleges included historian Carl Schorske, a highly stimulating lecturer at the University of California, Berkeley. According to the report, Schorske . . . still gets butterflies. "But if I have no tension," he says, "there's no spring. You must go in there with tension, and you should end up feeling worn out." Once on stage, Schorske gestures, grins, whispers, employs the full range of a booming baritone voice.

He covers three centuries of European intellectual history in his most popular course, shifts spontaneously to suit the mood of his audience ("It's almost a cabaret thing") as he explores Locke, Rousseau, Kant, Mill, Marx, and Freud. "He inspires an awful lot of hero worship from extremely bright people," says sandaled coed Regina James.[10]

It seems clear that performance apprehension is not peculiar to speakers.

This reaction is not an unusual one for speakers, inexperienced or experienced. Some beginning speakers have the idea they alone have this response. Rest assured, you are in large and good company. In a study of two groups of college students, 210 in one group and 277 in the second group, Knower found that "fifty-six percent of the first group and 61 percent of the second group listed some form of nervousness as one of their speech problems." In another study of 512 high school speech students, Knower discovered that "seventy-four percent of them judged themselves to be at least somewhat nervous when

Performance Apprehension and Students

speaking."[11] Although different students experience performance apprehension in varying degrees, Low and Sheets, on the basis of their research, concluded, "No significant differences were found between students with the most stage fright and students with the least stage fright in: 1. General intelligence. 2. Quantitative reasoning ability. 3. The more important phases of personality. 4. Their interest in the fields of science, mechanics, nature, and business."[12]

You do not have to worry about being abnormal, therefore, because you experience more emotional tension than some of your classmates.

Experienced speakers also have emotional tension prior to a speaking engagement. After studying thirty experienced public speakers, including lawyers, ministers, businessmen, educators, and state supreme court judges, Wrenchley concluded that "seventy-six percent of the interviewees stated that they did have stage fright or, as many termed it, a nervousness or tension before speaking."[13] Coincidentally, Kniseley also reported after studying sixty prominent speakers that 76 percent experienced some form of performance apprehension.[14] An examination of Wrenchley's data reveals that 76 percent is a conservative conclusion on her part, for only one speaker gave a categorically negative answer. The difference in interpretation apparently stems from Wrenchley's failure to define what she meant by stage fright.

It is interesting to read some of the replies from experienced speakers when Wrenchley asked: "Do you manifest any signs of stage fright before speaking?"

Speaker #3: Yes, a little nervous until I get started. Never had stage fright so badly that I have been blocked. I generally know what I want to say and as soon as I get into it, the tension leaves. I don't particularly like to speak, but am like Fanny Hurst about writing, "Never happy when I'm writing, much unhappier when I'm not."

Speaker #4: Oh, yes, definitely. People who do not talk do not realize. One who is perfectly relaxed isn't so apt to do so well. Most artists are very nervous. Every speaker who is experienced goes through different stages of stage fright. Much of it is dispelled after the speech is under way.

Speaker #10: Always a little nervous, and it was my joy to know that W. J. Bryan was always nervous. One never retires from the mental strain or apprehension with a large or small audience. I have always had it but have learned to do away with it. Am as free as a bird when I'm really in my speech.

Speaker #26: Yes, and everyone has it. That is excellent speakers do.[15]

Before his State of the Union address to Congress and the nation in 1983, President Reagan "admitted to feeling stage jitters akin to those he experienced during his acting days."[16]

Beginning speakers can take comfort, then, from the knowledge that the phenomenon we call stage fright is not peculiar to certain people, nor even to certain groups of people. The reactions occur in athletes, actors, musicians, teachers, speakers—in short, they occur in anyone who is confronted with a situation in which the performance is important and the outcome uncertain.

Figure 3.1

When the body perceives an emergency situation, certain organs in the body begin to prepare it for a better physical and mental effort.

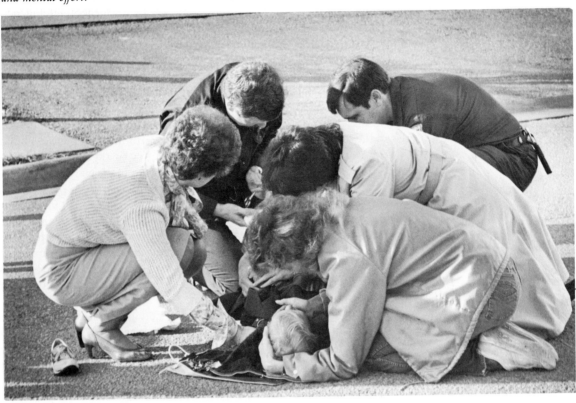

Performance Apprehension Causes Helpful Physiological Reactions

This emotional tension, or anxiety, results in a physiological reaction that prepares the body for a better physical and mental effort. Located within the human body are organs designed to function only when triggered by what is perceived to be an emergency situation. Just as it would be wasteful and inefficient for an automobile engine to use all its 350 horsepower when the car was going twenty-five miles an hour, so it would be wasteful and inefficient for the human body to operate at peak efficiency under normal circumstances.

When an emergency is perceived, however, these organs are ready to go into operation. The adrenal gland pumps adrenalin into the system. The arrival of adrenalin at the muscles increases their vitality and reaction time. Larger quantities of sugar are released from the pancreas to convert the sugar into energy, giving the body greater strength to cope with physical problems. Numerous red corpuscles are discharged into the bloodstream from the spleen. Breathing is quickened, thus bringing in more oxygen and expelling the carbon dioxide more rapidly. The pulse rate speeds up so that more fresh blood arrives at the muscles, the heart, the brain, and the central nervous system with larger quantities of oxygen. Blood is diverted away from its normal process of picking up digested food from the stomach and intestines and is now directed to the muscles, heart, brain, and central nervous system to provide these organs with more oxygen and energy. The brain is thus capable of thinking with greater clarity, perceptiveness, and quickness; the muscles are capable of exerting a more intense physical effort; the central nervous system is capable of reacting more quickly. Because of these physiological changes, the human body can perform at a much higher level than under normal conditions.

A few years ago newspapers carried an account of a mother who lifted a small foreign car off her son on whom it had fallen. While his mother held the car, the son scrambled to safety. The mother performed this amazing physical feat even though she stood less than five feet in height and weighed less than 100 pounds. Undoubtedly the emergency organs of the body enabled that mother to aid her son so well.

Not long afterwards newspapers carried another story of a father who saved his son in a similar manner. The father was on a ladder painting his house while his son was working under their car which was jacked up off the ground with the rear wheels removed. Hearing a noise the father turned to see the car—a normal-sized American car—with the rear axle resting on his son's chest. Jumping off the ladder, the father ran, grabbed the rear of the car, and lifted it so his son could slide out.

A number of years ago a woman lifted—not once, but twice—a slab of marble weighing approximately 300 pounds that was lying on a child. Normally this woman could not lift a hundred pounds, but under these extreme circumstances the emergency organs of her body enabled her to lift a weight several times what she normally could.

These are examples of what physiological changes can do to enable an individual to cope with situations better if he will just learn to utilize them. They can also help the speaker. The novelist I. A. R. Wylie tells how she discovered the efficacy of these reactions,

When I first came to the United States and found out that my publishers expected me to make a speech at a public dinner, I was almost sick with fear. I had never made a speech in my life; in a group of people I was tongue-tied with shyness. To my amazement I found myself speaking fluently, telling stories, sounding—as I was told afterward—like a practiced speaker. I had, in fact, been scared right out of myself to the discovery of someone I hadn't dreamed existed. Now after many years of practice I am, I suppose, really a practiced speaker. But I rarely rise to my feet without a throat constricted with terror and a furiously thumping heart. When, for some reason, I *am* cool and self-assured the speech is always a failure. I need fear to spur me on.[17]

Greg Norman, the Australian golfer, now understands the value of this emotional tension. In the summer of 1986, he led the U.S. Open tournament by one stroke at the beginning of the final round. He played poorly and did not win the tournament. Later in the summer, he led the British Open by one stroke at the beginning of the final round. This time, however, he increased

his lead to five strokes and won the tournament. In talking to reporters after the tournament, Norman said, "I wanted to be nervous today . . . I wasn't nervous on the final day of the U.S. Open, and I was flat . . . (Today) I didn't tell my wife I was nervous. But I was. . . ."[18]

It is important to note, however, that *these reactions do not take place if there is no uncertainty within the individual over the outcome of the performance or if the outcome is considered unimportant.* Many upsets in athletic contests can be traced to this cause. Members of an athletic team expected to win easily—but who lose—report almost without exception that they had no occurrence of the familiar "butterflies in the stomach" prior to the contest. William Jennings Bryan, outstanding speaker of the first part of this century who gave literally thousands of speeches, reports in his autobiography that he failed to experience "butterflies in his stomach" on only one occasion. And, he said, that was the worst speech he ever gave.

Performance Apprehension Can Be Harmful

To say that the phenomenon of performance apprehension is helpful is not to say that it cannot be harmful, for it can. An individual can have so much anxiety, or emotional tension, that it will result in extreme physiological reactions. A college football player recounted his experience in his first varsity football game in high school. Shortly before the game was to begin, the coach informed him that he was to be responsible for the opening kickoff. On taking the field, the referee, apparently sensing his nervous tension, came over to him and said: "Son, just keep your eyes on that ball, and when you hear my whistle, run up there and kick it as far as you can." With that, the young player fixed his concentration on the ball ready on the tee. Hearing a whistle, he ran forward, kicked the ball, and watched it sail off on the longest kick he had ever made. He was running after it as hard as he could when he suddenly realized he was the only person moving. From the darkness around him he heard the voice of his coach yelling, "Stop! Stop!" The whistle he had heard was the whistle of the band director beginning the national anthem.

Obviously, this youthful football player had received too much help from his emergency organs. Most of us have witnessed the inexperienced speaker who goes blank or whose voice becomes tremulous or whose hands shake so badly he cannot hold his notes or gesture properly. It seems safe to conclude, then, that performance apprehension can be harmful. It can be harmful because the speaker gets too much help. This can occur for two reasons.

First, it can occur because the individual's experience is too limited for the significance of the duties he is asked to perform. The football player above, for example, simply was asked to do too much for his limited experience when the coach asked him to make the kickoff—the most important chore at the beginning of the game—in his first varsity game. If you were asked to give your first speech over nationwide television, this would be too great a responsibility for your limited experience. A background of success in less important situations must be built up before coping with important situations.

Observe how professional football coaches carefully protect and develop promising rookies; they are generally kept on the bench for the first two or three games of the season so they merely get the feel of being a professional player. Then they are often put into a game when there will be little pressure on them. In some instances a professional coach has refused to use an outstanding rookie in a championship game for fear the pressure would be too much for him and destroy his confidence for future seasons.

Avoid speaking situations of great significance until a background of successful minor experiences has been established. This is one of the values you receive from the speech course you are taking. You have an opportunity to gain much experience before your peers in a relatively unimportant situation; after all, only your grade in the course and your standing among your peers are influenced by these speeches—a job promotion or some equally important result does not hinge upon your effort.

A second factor that contributes to making performance apprehension harmful has to do with not understanding the origin of the rapid breathing, the moist palms, the butterflies in the stomach, the other physiological reactions, and the consequent lack of knowledge as to how to cope with these physiological changes. That brings us, then, to the means by which you may learn to control performance apprehension.

Performance Apprehension Can Be Controlled

Many beginning speakers, and even some experienced ones, ask "How can I get rid of speech apprehension?" The answer is you do not want to get rid of it—what you want to do is learn to control it. The emotional tension, or anxiety, is a beneficial reaction that the public speaker must not be without. This fact was well understood by the football coach who chose his starting lineup in the dressing room prior to a game by asking his players to hold out their hands. If a player's hands were dry, he got no consideration for the starting team because the coach took this as an indication the player was not physically and mentally "keyed up." The coach chose his players from among those whose hands were moist, which indicated they were experiencing anxiety, or emotional tension. Harry Emerson Fosdick, outstanding radio minister, also was fully aware of the importance of these reactions for a speaker.

Impatient to meet his audience face to face, he often had to take sedatives on Saturday night in order to get his rest for Sunday's adventure. "Not anxiety, but tension that was a stimulus" caused him to be "aroused." In his judgment, "Any man who isn't tense before he speaks can't speak. Fear is not something to be feared, but something to be sublimated."[19]

After a penetrating study, Robinson concluded: *"The complete absence of feelings of apprehension is neither normal nor a desirable state."*[20] With this fact in mind, let us examine seven ways in which the speaker can learn to control performance apprehension.

The first method for controlling performance apprehension is to develop the proper attitude toward it. Realize that the physiological changes that take place are normal and beneficial and prepare you for a better effort, both physically and mentally. The knowledge that the anxiety, or emotional tension, before a speech is normal and beneficial arms you with a healthy, wholesome attitude which serves to short-circuit the process that causes too much performance apprehension.

Develop Proper Attitude toward Performance Apprehension

When you first perceive the situation as an important one, a message goes out from the central nervous system activating the emergency organs. Unfortunately, many speakers, unaware of the origin and possessing the wrong attitude, misinterpret the accompanying physiological changes as indications that the situation is getting worse. Consequently, another message goes out from the central nervous system to the emergency organs. The resulting increase in the physiological changes causes the speaker to conclude that the situation is worsening and so the cycle goes until the speaker is unable to control these responses.

When you have the right attitude, however, the whole process is altered. As soon as the first physiological changes occur, if you have an understanding of these reactions and the proper attitude toward performance apprehension, you interpret these changes as an indication that you are going to be ready for this speech, that these changes will increase your power of concentration, improve your thinking ability, and render more acute your perceptive processes. With this reaction, no further messages go out from the central nervous system to the emergency organs and the physiological changes remain at a beneficial and controllable level.

Get as Much Experience as Possible

The second means that enables you to control performance apprehension is experience. This experience does not have to be limited to public speaking occasions but can come from speaking in a broad variety of situations. Low and Sheets, in comparing students with the most performance apprehension to those with the least, found that the former—

1. Have not engaged in as much platform speaking activity.
2. Have not participated as much in extracurricular and social activities.
3. Have difficulty in making an adequate social adjustment.
4. Have less linguistic ability.
5. Have less interest in activities which involve self-expression in verbal activities and in work involving judgment and the supervision of others.[21]

The more experience you have, the more confidence you develop in your ability to perform successfully. Every successful speaking effort reinforces your belief that you can cope with future assignments. This is especially true in speaking since no speaking situation is the same as another. The wider and more varied the experience, therefore, the more confident you will be that you have been confronted with a situation in some way comparable to the present assignment. After studying students in a college speech course, Henrikson wrote that his study agreed "with previous investigations in indicating that speech training promotes confidence in the speaking situation." According to those students he studied, the most important factor in alleviating performance apprehension was *practice* (68.8 percent).[22] Knowing you have spoken successfully in past situations reduces the uncertainties about the outcome of the anticipated performance, resulting in less complicated anxiety and less performance apprehension. Researchers have also discovered through measurements of physiological reactions that experienced sport parachutists have greater emotional control than novices,[23] and experienced divers in underwater exploration develop an increasing ability to cope with the stresses of their environment.[24]

Jensen reports that " 'experience' is the important variable to be used in the prediction of self-report speech anxiety." An extremely important finding of his study is that a person's perception determines what is experience. "Thus, if a subject perceived working with Boy Scouts or singing in a choir as a kind of experience related to giving a speech in public, his perception of the relationship of that kind of experience to public speaking appears to have affected his score for self-reported speech anxiety."[25]

Figure 3.2
Thorough preparation is a strong antidote for performance apprehension.

Third, good preparation aids in controlling performance apprehension. If you have to worry about what you are going to say, how you are going to say it, and what the outcome will be, you will surely have more emotional tension than if you have to worry only about the outcome. Select your topic with care, do any necessary preliminary thinking, complete your research, organize the materials logically and psychologically to achieve your purpose and to suit this particular audience, and practice your speech. Kniseley reported that, among the prominent speakers in his study who experienced some form of apprehension, 70 percent said their primary method of coping with it was through thorough preparation.[26]

Prepare Well for the Speech

There is good evidence that you should practice your speech until you overlearn it. University of Illinois psychologists discovered that actors who overlearned their parts found apprehension helpful, whereas actors who underlearned their parts found apprehension harmful.[27] For the speaker, of course, overlearning refers to ideas, not to a particular sequence of words.

Thorough preparation will give you confidence in knowing that you have something to say and know how you want to say it. Anxiety about the outcome, then, will not be complicated by concern about various facets of preparation.

Use Bodily Action

Once in the speaking situation, bodily action can become a fourth means of controlling performance apprehension. Many speakers interpret shaking of the hands and trembling of the knees as evidence of fear. It is not fear, however, but merely the homeostatic process of the body dissipating excess energy that causes the trembling of certain limbs. Recall for a moment some time when you have narrowly averted a serious accident. You might have been driving down a main thoroughfare when another car suddenly darted in from a side street. Successfully maneuvering your car to avert an accident, you found your hands trembling so much you could hardly clutch the steering wheel. This is the same (homeostatic) process in both instances. The body attempts to maintain a constant balance. Just as the body perspires to cause a cooling process when there is danger of body temperature increasing above 98.6 degrees, so the body dissipates excess energy that is not being used. When the emergency organs prepare the body for a superhuman physical effort and no physical exertions are necessary, the body is left with this excess energy which it must dissipate. This dissipation takes the form of trembling muscles.

Many speakers, interpreting these reactions as fear, grab the sides of the speaker's stand and hold on like a freshman clutching his first letter from home, or shove their hands into their pockets hoping clenched fists will help stop the trembling. But these are the very things the speaker should not do. Inhibiting the dissipation of excess energy in one set of muscles simply means that another set will have to do the job. This often means greater trembling of the knees or a more tremulous vocal tone.

The best solution is to use this excess energy in a constructive way—use it for gestures and bodily movement. This not only rids the body of excess energy, but also aids in effective communication. With respect to this point, Lomas has made a trenchant observation: "If bodily action is to have therapeutic value for stage fright, that value must come through training received *before* speaking, not from anything the student may do *while* speaking."[28] In other words, you must have practiced the use of gestures and body action so that their use will occur automatically in a meaningful way during the speech. If you have to stop and think about using gestures and body action because of your emotional tension, the complexity of the situation is increased, which may in turn increase your excitement.

Concentrate on Communication

Fifth, a speaker gains control over performance apprehension by concentrating on communicating with the listeners. Talk to almost any athlete and he will tell you the "butterflies" disappear as soon as the game begins—when he makes the first tackle or block, when the ball is tipped off, when the pitcher throws the first pitch to him, when the starter's gun sounds. He does not have time to think about himself because he is too busy playing the game. Evonne Goolagong, the sensational Australian tennis player who won the Women's Wimbledon Cup in 1971 at the age of nineteen, reported to newsmen after the finals that she was nervous before the match began. "But," she said, "as soon as I got out there I forgot my nerves and started playing."[29]

This is what you must do—play the game. As soon as you begin speaking you must begin observing the reactions of your listeners and making efforts to adapt to their reactions. Look for friendly faces. They can reassure you, but avoid the appealing temptation to talk predominantly to the genial ones. You want to communicate with all the listeners. You should be asking yourself, "Are these people hearing and understanding what I am saying? Are they responding in the ways I desire?" If you are concentrating on communication in this fashion, you have no time for yourself. Wrenchley's study of apprehension in thirty experienced speakers revealed that "seventy percent of those interviewed" forget performance apprehension reactions as they get involved in speaking. Let the speakers themselves describe the process:

Speaker #27: Yes, I generally lose the feeling after I get started in my speech. I have learned to concentrate on my subject rather than on myself. Experience has also helped.

Speaker #28: Yes, I overcome it as I proceed. I'm completely relaxed when I get into my subject. Concentration and thinking about the content relaxes me.[30]

Sixth, performance apprehension can be controlled by remembering that the physiological upheavals taking place are internal and cannot be perceived by most listeners—at times not even by expert listeners. Dickens, Gibson, and Prall studied the overt manifestations of speaking apprehension and concluded that "analysis of individual ratings revealed such gross inaccuracies as to suggest that a speech teacher can place little faith in her unsupported judgment as to the emotions felt by a given student in a given speech."[31] Further substantiating this point of view is Clevenger's survey of research on speaking apprehension. He concluded that "the consistency with which judges' ratings ran below introspective accounts of speaking apprehension suggests that *a group of observers tends to notice less disruption in the speaker than the speaker reports having experienced.*"[32]

Remember that Physiological Reactions are Unseen

A number of years ago a southern university had an intercollegiate debater whose poise, coolness, fluency, and skill were always remarkable and impressive. Several years later his colleague, in reminiscing, revealed that this superb debater had become literally sick to his stomach before almost every round of debate. Yet neither the judges nor the opponents were ever aware of this debater's performance apprehension. Most of the time he made his opponents sick because of their inability to cope with his debating skills.

Among the best debaters with whom this writer has worked was one who found it difficult to eat at any time during a debate tournament, sometimes for as many as three days. At mealtime while his colleagues ate, he busied himself with several glasses of water. On the way home, however, he made up for all the meals he had missed. Yet no judge ever commented on his emotional tension; on the contrary, many commented on his confident and poised skill in debating.

So, as a beginning speaker, remember, the only way a listener can become aware of your emotional tension, or anxiety, is if you tell him in some way, either verbally or nonverbally. Since most listeners place greater reliance in a speaker who appears confident, poised, unruffled, and at ease (the means for developing these attributes are explained in chapter 12), you should refrain from commenting on your emotional tension unless some overt behavior makes it obvious you are suffering from this problem. Speakers have frequently begun talks with a reference to their nervousness when none of the listeners had any inkling of the problem. Such references distract the listeners from the main subject to be developed in the speech and diminish the listeners' estimate of the speaker's skill, experience, and confidence.

Of course, if you are holding notes and the trembling of your hands obviously reveals emotional tension, you can often relieve the tension by referring to it humorously. But remember: do not mention it unless it is obvious, and then do not apologize for it.

Remember that Listeners Want You to Succeed

A seventh means of controlling performance apprehension is to realize that the listeners are friendly people who generally want you to succeed. Knowing the audience is not hostile to you and your ideas should give you greater confidence in presenting your speech. An outward demonstration of confidence will not only make you feel better, it will also increase your credibility with the listeners.

Summary

Five main ideas should be remembered from this discussion of performance apprehension. 1. Stage fright is a misnomer. Although some authors imply or say directly that stage fright is a form of fear, this book presents the view that it represents an increase in tension caused by heightened drive or motivation as one approaches the performance situation. When one considers reports by trained professional athletes, musicians, and actors, it seems clear that apprehension in these individuals is more a reflection of high drive than of disorganizing fear. As we approach the critical situation, drives increase and are often experienced as tension. 2. Performance apprehension is not peculiar to certain individuals or groups of people but is a normal form of anxiety, or emotional tension, occurring in anyone confronted with a situation in which the performance is important and the outcome uncertain. 3. Performance apprehension causes helpful physiological reactions that can prepare you for more effective mental and physical efforts. 4. Performance apprehension can be harmful if you fail to understand it properly and control it. 5. Performance apprehension can be controlled by developing a proper attitude toward it, by getting much experience in a broad variety of speaking situations, by preparing well for any speaking effort, by using effective body action in presenting the speech, by remembering that the physiological reactions are unseen by listeners, and by remembering that listeners generally want to see you succeed.

Notes

1. *The Opelika-Auburn News,* March 17, 1985, p. A–4.
2. T. Clevenger, Jr., "A Synthesis of Experimental Research in Stage Fright," *Quarterly Journal of Speech* 45 (1959):135.

3. Ibid., pp. 135–38.
4. L. F. Shaffer and E. J. Shoben, Jr., *The Psychology of Adjustment* (Boston: Houghton Mifflin Co., 1956), p. 49.
5. "Pro Basketball: All the Credentials," *Time*, April 29, 1966, p. 106. Reprinted by permission from *TIME, The Weekly Newsmagazine;* Copyright Time Inc.
6. "Tarantula from Cabin Creek," *Time*, February 8, 1960, p. 49. Reprinted by permission from *TIME, The Weekly Newsmagazine;* Copyright Time Inc.
7. B. Thomas, "Hollywood Helps Comedian Enjoy Himself," Richmond *News Leader*, July 17, 1962. By permission of Associated Press.
8. "Ronstadt: The Gamble Pays Off Big," *Family Weekly*, January 8, 1984, pp. 5, 7.
9. Jim Martin, "Golf," *The Birmingham News*, September 29, 1985, p. 17B.
10. "Teaching: To Profess with a Passion," *Time*, May 6, 1966, p. 83. Reprinted by permission from *TIME, The Weekly Newsmagazine;* Copyright Time Inc.
11. F. H. Knower, "A Study of Speech Attitudes and Adjustments," *Speech Monographs* 5 (1938):131.
12. G. M. Low and B. V. Sheets, "The Relation of Psychometric Factors to Stage Fright," *Speech Monographs* 18 (1951):271.
13. E. D. O. Wrenchley, "A Study of Stage Fright Attacks in a Selected Group of Experienced Speakers," M.A. thesis, University of Denver, 1948, p. 36.
14. W. A. Kniseley, "An Investigation of the Phenomenon of Stage Fright in Certain Prominent Speakers," Ph.D. diss., University of Southern California, 1950, p. 90.
15. Wrenchley, "Study of Stage Fright Attacks," pp. 36–39.
16. *Birmingham News*, January 26, 1983.
17. I. A. R. Wylie, "I Enjoy Myself Most When I'm Scared," *The Reader's Digest*, March 1953, p. 18.
18. "1986 British Open," July 21, 1986. © 1986 Associated Press. Used by permission.
19. R. C. McCall, "Harry Emerson Fosdick: Paragon and Paradox," *Quarterly Journal of Speech* 39 (1953):289.
20. E. R. Robinson, "What Can the Speech Teacher Do about Students' Stage Fright?" *Speech Teacher* 8 (1959):10.
21. Low and Sheets, "Relation of Psychometric Factors to Stage Fright," p. 271.
22. E. H. Henrikson, "Some Effects on Stage Fright of a Course in Speech," *Quarterly Journal of Speech* 29 (1943):491.
23. S. Epstein, "Toward a Unified Theory of Anxiety," in *Progress in Experimental Personality Research*, ed. B. A. Maher (New York: Academic Press, 1967), p. 31.
24. R. Radloff and R. Helmreich, *Groups under Stress: Psychological Research in Sealab II* (New York: Appleton-Century-Crofts, 1968), p. 87.
25. K. Jensen, "Self-Reported Speech Anxiety and Selected Demographic Variables," *Central States Speech Journal* 27 (1976):107.
26. Kniseley, "Investigation of the Phenomenon of Stage Fright," p. 106.
27. "Eureka," *Theatre Arts*, July 1956, p. 11.
28. C. W. Lomas, "Stage Fright," *Quarterly Journal of Speech* 30 (1944):482.
29. AP dispatch, *Durham Morning Herald*, July 3, 1971.
30. Wrenchley, "Study of Stage Fright Attacks," pp. 57–60.
31. M. Dickens, F. Gibson, and C. Prall, "An Experimental Study of the Overt Manifestations of Stage Fright," *Speech Monographs* 17 (1950):47.
32. Clevenger, "Synthesis of Experimental Research," p. 137.

4

RESPONSIBILITIES OF SPEAKERS: ETHICAL DIMENSIONS

*I*t is not easy today to discuss ethical responsibilities. "Extenuating circumstances" are used to defend and explain unethical, immoral, and even illegal behavior. Yet the nature and role of oral communication demand that attention be paid to ethical considerations. The skilled and prominent public speaker exerts a greater than normal influence on the conduct of human affairs. An unprincipled, irresponsible speaker can cause erroneous and harmful decisions to be made.

As we turn our attention to ethical problems in communication, however, we find that it is almost impossible to get anyone today to think seriously of absolute, legalistic, or "natural law" rules of ethical responsibility. Most people accept the relativistic philosophy that each instance must be decided on its own merits, that the situation must be taken into consideration in evaluating the ethical principles involved. This creates problems for the theorist trying to define the ethical responsibilities of a public speaker.

Amorality of Speech Communication Principles

Further complicating the speaker's task is the fact that speech communication principles are amoral principles—they can be used for either good or evil purposes. Because these principles *are* sometimes used by speakers to achieve immoral ends, some have criticized and condemned the principles themselves. But this is no more valid than the criticism that automobiles are evil because drunken drivers use them to destroy property and kill human beings. It is the user of speech communication principles who determines the ethics: you may use the principles in irresponsible ways to attain some evil purpose or in moral ways to attain a generally accepted good purpose.

Before going any further, we should define the terms ethics. Ethics is concerned "with questions about the meaning of 'good' and 'bad,' 'right' and 'wrong,' and 'moral obligation.' "[1]

Does this book acknowledge the amoral nature of communication principles? Yes. Does it assume an amoral attitude toward their use? Definitely not! Communication professors cannot ensure that their students will use principles learned in their course for honest purposes, but the aim of this book and most speech teachers is to instill in students the habit of speaking responsibly. Speakers have ethical responsibilities which must be accepted if rhetoric is to play its most meaningful role in communication.

Some have argued that the freedom to speak in a democratic society ensures that false statements will be revealed by competing speakers; the unethical speaker will be detected and rejected. This point of view overlooks two important factors. First, it places the responsibility for one's actions on someone else. The speaker can thus justify the use of bad logic or invalid evidence by rationalizing that it is the opponents' responsibility to recognize and publicize it; if no one identifies it, the speaker's conscience is clear. Second, this position

Ethics and the Freedom of Speech

assumes that competing points of view will be presented equally well by sources that are equally prestigious. Yet we know only too well that these two criteria are rarely met. A message from the president generally receives far greater attention than one from a senator. And a private citizen has little chance against a public official. We are all too familiar with the false charge of a public official against a citizen blazoned across the front page of a newspaper only to have the retraction, a week later, buried in a brief paragraph well inside the newspaper. In a democratic society speakers must assume responsibility for their communicative efforts.

Lack of trust in public officials has already become a serious problem in our society. The ordinary citizen, who has little access to the actual facts of most controversies, is in a state of confusion over the charges and counter-charges presented. Whom should we believe? If this situation continues, the lack of trust could become so enormous that no speaker will be free of it. When that happens, information and persuasion as means of problem-solving in a democratic society will have lost much of their force.

Furthermore, a democratic society is based on the assumption that, given the information, the majority of people can make better decisions for the general welfare than can a single individual or a small group of individuals. When the public receives inaccurate or inadequate information, however, decisions no longer relate to reality. In such cases, the basic premise on which democracy rests ceases to function. If people are led to wrong decisions too often because of faulty information or fallacious reasoning, there is clear danger they will become disillusioned and either stop participating in the voting process or begin making decisions on irrelevant bases such as ethnic background or personality. With too many wrong decisions there is the tragic possibility that people will lose faith in the democratic process itself and reject it for what they believe are more reliable methods: dictatorship, oligarchy, anarchy.

Ethical Bases

What are the bases for determining the ethical nature of oral communications? Some will be considered in the remainder of this chapter.

Ends and Means

Some maintain that the end justifies the means. In other words, if a speaker attempts to persuade others to adopt a course of action deemed honorable, just, or desirable, then that speaker may use whatever means are available: distorting evidence, concealing motives, twisting reasoning, and making emotional appeals that prevent the rational thought processes of listeners from operating. The leaders of the Inquisition were convinced that the "truth" of Christianity was so indisputable that heretics should be identified, forced to admit their guilt, and recant their heresies. To achieve that "good end," they used the rack and other forms of torture to ensure that heresy was discredited. In this century Hitler used the "big lie" to persuade the German people to accept the programs of the Third Reich. Hitler justified the use of any means to achieve what he considered good social ends.

Unfortunately, this approach is based on one highly questionable assumption: that a given speaker has either the ability or the right to decide for others what is a good end. For example, some are so concerned about the danger of lung cancer and heart disease from cigarette smoking that they justify any means to discourage or prevent others from smoking. Yet some doctors have pointed out that smoking actually relieves nervous tension and anxieties for some people, thus possibly allowing them to live longer, healthier lives than if they did nothing to alleviate their tensions or turned to other means such as alcohol or hard drugs. Other doctors, however, have recently noted the harm that is done to children and other bystanders who inhale secondary tobacco smoke. This knowledge must certainly inhibit the freedom of others to smoke. Except in those instances where the choice is harmful to other members of society, however, who, other than the affected individual or individuals, has the right to determine what is a good end? The purpose of persuasion is to convince others that the speaker's objective is a good one. The only ethical method would be to present the strongest legitimate case possible and let each individual decide if the end is good.

The speaker who follows the philosophy that the end justifies the means may hold one of three attitudes: (1) "The opposing side is stronger and cannot be defeated unless deceit is used." If that is true, something must be wrong with the end sought. The solution is for the speaker to reconsider her position, not to attempt to sell the weaker side by means of deception. (2) "Advocates of the opposing position are more skillful in persuading." Aristotle observed that truth would prevail if presented as skillfully as falsehood. If it is true that opposing speakers are more skillful, an advocate should improve her speech skills instead of compensating with duplicity. (3) "The people to be persuaded are too stupid, too ignorant, or too motivated by baser emotions to be affected by truth." If this is the case, a speaker might make a more significant contribution to their welfare by engaging in an educational, informative effort. Then the listeners will have the ability to draw valid conclusions, and their commitment to the speaker's purpose will probably be longer lived. Moreover, if a speaker persuades through deceit because the listeners are stupid, ignorant, or motivated by base emotions, then the next skillful con artist to pass through the community may undo all the speaker's work.

Advocates should strive only for good ends. What, after all, can be said for a speaker who supports evil ends—even through ethical and legitimate means? If we condone the use of unethical and illegitimate means for good ends, we are confronted with a society whose advocates either propose evil ends or use evil methods, hardly a society one would cherish living in.

As an oral communicator, always be concerned about the ends you advocate, but not for the purpose of deciding the means to be used. Rather, you want to be certain in your own conscience that your ends are justifiable, supported by the best evidence and reasoning you can bring to bear on the problem. You want to be sure that your proposals will not seriously harm others. And you want to know that your ends are consistent with the highest values of your society, for as Thonssen, Baird, and Braden observe, "Speech is justified only if it betters society."[2]

Social Utility

Another means sometimes proposed for determining what is acceptable is the concept of social utility, which Brembeck and Howell say is ultimately concerned with "the *survival potential* of the group . . . involved."[3] The speaker determines which proposals to promote on the basis of which will do the most good for the group concerned. Certainly an advocate must consider, as one criterion, whether a proposal will contribute to the benefits of the specific group. One of the difficulties in applying this standard is defining the group. Is it all humanity? Is it one nation? Is it one geographical section of a nation? Is it an ethnic group? But even after the group has been defined, the social utility approach can never be used as the sole criterion for selecting a position. Under the guidance of the greatest good for the survival potential of the group, one could justify Hitler's policy of exterminating Jews, or the policy of suppression of individual freedom in Poland, or the current segregation policies in South Africa. The speaker must be concerned, therefore, about more than what is the greatest good for the group. Some policies and programs must be rejected because of the negative effects they have on a minority or another group, whereas others are desirable because of the good they do for a minority or another group.

Situation Ethics

Situation ethics, whose most noted proponent today is Joseph Fletcher, is predicated on the belief that there are no natural laws to be followed absolutely—each individual situation must be examined to determine what is the good thing to do. Although some assume that the individual making the decision has no principles to guide behavior except the situation in which he finds himself, Fletcher makes clear that "the situationist enters into every decision-making situation fully armed with the ethical maxims of his community and its heritage."[4] From the framework of these ethical principles, whether they be Judeo-Christian, Moslem, or whatever, the individual decides what is the most loving thing to do, for (says Fletcher) "Loving actions are the *only* conduct permissible."[5] The love he is talking about is an attitude, not sentiment or emotion. It is the agapeic love, which "is neighbor-concerned, outgoing, not self-concerned or selective."[6] Four factors must be taken into consideration by the situationist in making a decision. (1) What is the *end* desired? (2) What are the *means* to be used to attain that end? (3) What is the *motive* behind the act? (4) What will be the *consequences* of the action?[7]

On the surface, situation ethics seems a reasonable, rational approach to the problem of determining ethical behavior, and some examples of situation ethics in action evoke little opposition from most people. For example, if an individual is confronted by an escaped convict who wants to know the home address of an intended murder victim, the situationist says the individual would do a good, loving thing by lying. Few would argue with this analysis.

But as the situation becomes more complex, situation ethics seems less clear-cut in its appropriateness and its rightness. One of Fletcher's examples is that of two mothers on different wagon trains going west. Because the wagons are being trailed by Indians, the cries of each mother's infant child pose a danger to the entire wagon train. One mother copes with this problem by choking her baby to death with her own hands, thus allowing the wagon train to arrive safely at the fort. The other mother simply tries to quiet the baby's crying, but is unsuccessful, and the Indians wipe out the entire group. Although asking the rhetorical question, "Which woman made the right decision?" Fletcher clearly implies that the one who saved the train at the expense of the baby's life did the most loving thing because only one life was lost to save many. Many people would argue, however, that the mother who refused to murder her innocent, defenseless infant did the most loving thing. And many adults would not want their own lives saved in such a manner.

As a matter of fact, Fletcher himself provides a contradictory example when he refers to the expedition of Scott to the South Pole. When the men encountered trouble and had to return in haste to the coast, one of them was injured. Because carrying the stretcher slowed them down, Scott was faced with the choice of abandoning the injured man to save the others or continuing to carry him and risk all their lives. Scott chose the latter course, and all died. And Fletcher praises Scott, provided he "was not simply legalistic in his decision. . . ."[8]

It appears, therefore, that situation ethics has an unsettling ability to justify diverse decisions. It is not difficult to see how situation ethics can be used to rationalize, consciously or unconsciously, decisions and actions that stem from selfish and deceitful reasons.

An extremely vulnerable aspect of situation ethics is that it requires a high degree of sophistication in reasoning, objectivity in analysis, and an unusual breadth of perspective to exist in combination within a single individual. These attributes rarely occur singly in human beings.

Credibility Centered Ethics

This is the ethical standard that this book recommends that speakers adopt. In credibility-centered ethics, listeners hold you responsible for what you say and do in your messages. Anything that lowers your credibility can either nullify or minimize the impact of your speech on others. Approach your communicative efforts with the objective of demonstrating, by the methods used, your competence and trustworthiness.

In 1986 it was discovered that President Ronald Reagan, who for several years had been critical of other nations for selling military arms to Iran, had been doing that very thing. People then rejected his argument that Iran's size and location made it an important and critical country in the Middle East because Reagan's actions suggested that his arguments had been used for deceitful purposes. As a result of the contradiction of his words and his actions, Reagan's credibility was damaged.

To enhance the chances that your messages are accepted by listeners, avoid any possibility that they won't believe you. Because the following principles are approved by most societies, and because they result in the most valid ideas, observe them in developing and presenting messages to other people.

1. Formulate programs and policies only after a thorough examination of the available evidence. From all the available evidence, construct and present a rational basis for whatever policies and programs you advocate. If you have been unable to scrutinize some important

relevant data, admit it and avoid implying that you have investigated evidence that you have not. Examine the empirical evidence that exists, but do not ignore the evidence of experience, recognizing that experience adds a dimension unavailable from any other source.

2. Avoid fabricating or distorting evidence to make it support your position. If the evidence will not support your position, honest thinking demands that you alter that position to be consistent with the available evidence. Reject the counsel of those who justify the use of falsehoods in persuasive speaking because society condones such practices as a doctor's not telling a patient he has a fatal disease. Such situations are not analogous to a communicator trying to persuade others to adopt a policy or a program.

3. Do not knowingly use fallacious or unsound reasoning. If you innocently make an error in reasoning, your ethics should not be criticized. Since it is more difficult to assess ethical responsibilities in the use of reasoning than in the use of evidence, you should be given every benefit of the doubt before you are accused of unethical reasoning. But do not take advantage of this consideration by consciously using unsound reasoning and then, after you are detected, claiming that it was an innocent mistake.

4. Do not conceal an association with a group whose activities you are evaluating or advocating. Evaluating the activities of an organization without acknowledging an attachment to it creates an image of objectivity that distorts your statements and deceives your listeners.

5. Give credit to the sources of evidence. Do not present ideas that originated with others as though they are your own.

6. Do not abandon your own sincerely held convictions to say something pleasing to your audience. Understand that adaptation is an important ingredient of effective communication, but adapt to listeners only in whatever appropriate ways you legitimately can. Do not distort evidence or misrepresent your position or that of any group you represent in order to gain favor with particular listeners.

7. Do not imply or claim knowledge or experience that you do not have. Sometimes you must acknowledge that your information is incomplete and your experience limited on a topic.

8. Do not simplify a subject to such an extent that listeners fail to comprehend its complexities. Obviously, in any communication on a complicated topic a certain amount of simplification results from selecting some ideas and materials to present while eliminating others. But you should never leave the listeners unaware of any aspects germane to the policy or program under discussion.

9. Do not arouse emotions on irrelevant bases to get listeners to accept or reject a proposal. Emotions are legitimately involved in decision making when they pertain to the topic being discussed but not when they are irrelevant. It is appropriate for those who support busing to integrate schools to arouse emotions by referring to the harm done to children who receive an inadequate education. It is also appropriate for those who oppose busing of children away from their neighborhood schools to arouse emotions by referring to the harm done to children who have to spend unnecessary time riding a bus each day. It is *not* appropriate for opponents to arouse emotions toward busing by calling it a "communist plot," *unless* they have definite evidence that it is.

If you follow these principles of credibility-centered ethics, you should find your reputation growing as a responsible, ethical communicator, and people will turn to you more and more for advice and leadership. Later chapters will explain the principles of speech communication that will enable you to develop the full potential of your reputation for credibility.

Summary

Since speech communication principles are amoral, they may be used for good or evil purposes. Because the power of speech in a free society is so awesome, however, speech communication teachers cannot tolerate an amoral attitude toward its use. Anyone who uses communication must be concerned about its technical nature.

We have seen in this chapter that it is not easy to establish a base on which to judge the ethical nature of communication. Judging on the basis of ends and means creates problems that are not avoided with the bases of social utility and situation ethics. In the final analysis, credibility-centered ethics seems to offer the best means of establishing a dependable basis for promoting ethical communication.

1. Write an essay describing the ethical conduct you deem appropriate for a speaker on your campus. How does that conduct contribute to the creation of credibility?
2. Name a contemporary speaker whom you consider credible. How do his or her ethics contribute to credibility?
3. Name a contemporary speaker whose credibility you question. What role do his or her ethics play in your judgment?
4. Name a political speaker who has, in your judgment, demonstrated a responsible attitude. Describe particular speeches or portions of speeches that caused you to think this person responsible.
5. You are the administrative assistant to a congressional representative from a district in which the state university is located. Your boss recently voted against a bill providing for federal support of higher education. You have been assigned to go to the campus to explain your chief's action. How would you do this in a credible and ethical way?
6. You are the information officer for the Pentagon. The United States is at war with another nation and an important campaign is now under way. An element of the army has been badly beaten. Although unaware of the extent of the damage, the enemy would be aided significantly, both militarily and psychologically, if they knew of it. Since a newspaper reporter has reported rumors of the defeat, the news media are now clamoring for a reply from you. What do you do?

Notes _____

1. T. R. Nilsen, *Ethics of Speech Communication* (Indianapolis: Bobbs-Merrill, 1966), p. 1.
2. L. Thonssen, A. C. Baird, and W. W. Braden, *Speech Criticism* (New York: Ronald Press, 1970), p. 452.
3. W. L. Brembeck and W. S. Howell, *Persuasion* (New York: Prentice-Hall, 1952), p. 455.
4. J. Fletcher, *Situation Ethics* (Philadelphia: Westminster Press, 1966), p. 26.
5. Ibid., p. 51.
6. Ibid., p. 103.
7. Ibid., pp. 127–28.
8. Ibid., p. 136.

5

RESPONSIBILITIES OF RECEIVERS: EFFECTIVE LISTENING

*I*n the movie *Oh God,* George Burns, as God, admits about prayers, "I can't help hearing, but I don't always listen." This statement recognizes that there is a difference between hearing and listening and that responsibility for effective communication rests on the listener as well as the speaker. Listeners must share responsibility with speakers if effective communication is to occur. A receiver's refusal to listen stops communication as effectively as the refusal of a source to speak. This is not to deny that each of us has the right to refuse to listen to any speaker or any message. We do not have to communicate with any speaker.

The importance of listening in overall communicative effectiveness is underscored when one considers the amount of time we devote to listening behavior. Approximately 70 percent of our waking hours are spent in some form of communication. Rankin's pioneer study revealed that our communication time is divided roughly as follows: 15 percent reading, 11 percent writing, 32 percent speaking, and 42 percent listening.[1] A recent study of college students revealed that they devoted 52.5 percent of their communication day to listening, 16.3 percent to speaking, 17.3 percent to reading, and 13.9 percent to writing.[2] Although the largest part of our communicative activity involves speaking and listening, our formal educational training from kindergarten through high school focuses on developing reading and writing skills. Consequently, it is not surprising that the average person can recall only about 50 percent of the information heard—even when tested immediately after receiving information orally.[3] Thus, even when we are highly motivated to listen, we are frequently "poor" or inefficient listeners because we have little training in how to meet our obligations as listeners. In this chapter we will consider the act of listening, what the speaker can do to aid listening, and what the listener can do to improve listening.

The Act of Listening

The act of listening involves four distinct processes: receiving, perceiving, interpreting, and responding.

Receiving

The first listening process, receiving, consists of two aspects: seeing and hearing. Seeing, says one scholar of vision, "is, first and foremost, an information-processing task."[4] That precisely defines the role of vision in listening. Seeing is important to listening because it enables us to observe the nonverbal forms of communication: facial expression, gestures, bodily movement. It is also important in recognizing sounds and words. Visual cues such as movement of the lips and tongue assist in identifying some sounds, such as *f, th, t, p,* that are not readily distinguished without observation of the facial cues.

Effective receiving involves good eyesight. Anatomical processes operate the pupils and eyelids. The optical process changes the shape and focus of the lens so that near and distant objects are brought into focus. A photochemical process converts the light that strikes the retina into nerve impulses that are transmitted by a neurophysiological process through the optic nerve to the brain to be analyzed. Recent research indicates that some of the information is processed in the visual system itself; however, most of the processing occurs in the brain.

Receiving also involves hearing, a neurophysiological process that also requires a working mechanism. If a person is deaf, listening is thwarted because hearing cannot occur. Sound is produced when something is caused to vibrate in a medium such as air. When a person vibrates the vocal folds, sound waves are created that carry to the outer ear of another person, where they travel down the external auditory canal to the tympanum, a thin membrane stretched tight across the opening into the middle ear. The tympanum vibrates in consonance with the air waves and transmits these vibrations, by means of three tiny bones (the malleus, incus, and stapes), to the oval window. The membrane covering the oval window moves in and out in concert with the tympanum, causing fluid in the inner ear to move. The movement of this fluid generates nerve signals that are transmitted by the eighth cranial nerve to the brain where they are interpreted as sounds. In this manner we "hear" all sounds that make their way to our outer ear, although we are not consciously aware of all of them.

Perceiving

That brings us to perceiving, the second process involved in listening. When we are listening to one set of vibrations striking our eardrum, we are generally not conscious of other vibrations also striking it. When we sit in our homes and watch the evening news, we listen to the commentator by focusing our attention on the vibrations from her voice and not the vibrations coming from voices in the next room even though they strike our eardrums. We can listen to those voices, however, simply by shifting our attention to them. It is not enough to hear sounds in the environment, we must perceive them by focusing attention on the ones we want to listen to. Of course, there are some stimuli that are so dominant we cannot avoid perceiving them.

How can we control attention? By external factors (characteristics of the stimulus) or by internal factors (attitudes, expectations, desires of the individual). What do we mean by attention? "The essence of paying attention is simple," say Carver and Scheier. "It is noticing something, mentally picking it up, processing it." They then admit, however, that defining attention is not easy.[5] Although there is currently much controversy about the nature of attention and exactly how it works and when it begins, we can profitably use the definition given by Wolvin and Coakley: attention is "the focused perception of stimuli."[6]

Interpreting

Once we have received and perceived the visual and aural symbols, we then begin the third listening process: interpreting. We interpret the meaning of sounds as best we can. We recognize them as belonging to some category, such as music, noise, or speech. If we interpret the sounds as speech, we next interpret the meaning of those speech sounds. We may be unable to interpret the meaning, however, if the speech includes words we do not know or if it is in a foreign language we do not understand. If it is language we understand, we attempt to discern the intended meaning. We must interpret not only the language, however, but also the meaning of the nonverbal communication.

Because communication is a transactional process—one in which all communicators are actively involved—the fourth process, responding, is important and necessary. F. H. Ernst, a psychiatrist, defines listening as "that moving of a person made . . . in response to . . . the spoken word of another person." He requires that a person responding to the speech communication of others manifest listening "by an organized set of movements." It is these responses that cause speakers to be affected by listeners.[7] What kind of listening does Ernst prescribe? It is an active, involved process. It is listening that communicates with the speaker, that involves overt responses and necessitates active processing of the ideas being received. Ernst's listener cannot be a human recorder simply repeating the words of a speaker. You must not only go further and interpret the meaning of the words, you must also respond internally and externally to them. Unless you do, the transactional nature of communication cannot be achieved. Once you have responded, you have completed the act of listening.

Responding

Receiving messages, therefore, is largely an involuntary process, whereas perceiving, interpreting, and responding are predominantly voluntary processes.

What happens in the cognitive processing of oral messages? We do not clearly understand. Based upon his research, C. M. Kelly concluded that listening was primarily a function of general mental ability.[8] Bostrom and Waldhart concluded that, while lecture-comprehension listening is "more closely related to measures of general mental ability," short-term listening ability "seems more closely related to measures of oral performance."[9] Bostrom and Bryant suggest that we do not yet understand how the processes involved in listening operate.[10]

What, then, can the speaker do to improve listening? Consider the possibilities. A person's receiving ability cannot be changed except by artificial means. The third process, interpreting, consists of cognitive processing, which Bostrom and Bryant say we do not understand. Probably the most that a speaker can do to aid interpretation is to be sure that the message is organized clearly, stated in accurate language, developed adequately with credible supporting materials, and delivered effectively. We are left, then, with the second and fourth listening processes, perceiving and responding. Here is where we can control our own listening habits and efforts and can influence those of others. Speakers can assist listeners in perceiving the message, and listeners can improve their perception of and response to messages. In the next two sections, we will look first at what the speaker can do to improve listening and then at what the receiver can do to improve listening.

How the Speaker Can Improve Listening

To talk about affecting the listening of others is to talk about attention. You can improve listening, therefore, by increasing listeners' attention. What are the factors that affect attention?

Under most conditions, we have the ability to decide what we listen to, what we focus on, how we interpret it, and how we respond to it. There are certain factors, however, that make it easier for us to listen to certain stimuli.

Movement

All things being equal, a moving object attracts attention away from a nonmoving object. On a clear night, for example, which captures your attention, a falling star or all the apparently stationary ones? In a wooded area, on the other hand, you can stand near a rabbit for several minutes and not see it unless it moves.

Movement is also important psychologically. It brings change to the situation. "Normal consciousness, perception, and thought can be maintained only in a constantly changing environment." Unless there is change, "the capacity of adults to concentrate deteriorates, attention fluctuates and lapses, and normal perception fades."[11]

You can use this principle to assist your listeners in attending to your speech rather than other stimuli in the environment. You can achieve movement in the speech by having it well organized and keeping that organization readily apparent to the listeners. Making clear the progression through the main ideas gives a sense of movement to the speech. Use stories that have movement in them to develop your ideas. In addition, you can use physical movement: reflect your ideas with appropriate facial expressions; gesture; walk about the podium in a meaningful way. Walk over and talk to the listeners on your left, then to those on your right, then return to the lectern and talk from there.

Repetition

We are attracted to a stimulus we have experienced a number of times because of its repetition and familiarity. Stimuli we have experienced before attract our attention. Do you find yourself singing the words or humming the tune of the advertising jingle you have heard repeatedly?

You can capitalize on this principle by previewing your main points, stating them when you develop each of them, and summarizing them at the end. You can restate your main points or important ideas. You can repeat them as you stated them initially or restate them in different words. You can also restate them by using testimony from someone who has said the same thing. If that person happens to be a highly credible source, the impact of the restatement is increased. You can also use repetition by choosing words that are familiar to your listeners; this has the effect of restatement.

Size

The larger a stimulus, the more likely we are to be attracted to it. Have you had a loud noise literally jerk your attention away from something you were engrossed in?

You can take advantage of this factor by at least occasionally using the largest gestures that are appropriate. You can also use a loudness level that makes your speech the dominant sound in the situation, and you can increase the loudness level to indicate more important information or ideas.

You can also utilize the concept of size by demonstrating or referring to the enormity of the problem you are discussing. Describe how widespread the problem is, how many people are affected by it, the large amounts of money that have to be spent on it, the many harmful effects that result from it.

Intensity

We are prone to attend to those stimuli that exhibit great energy, strength, or vehemence. Any object, activity, thought, or feeling whose characteristics are extreme in degree possesses intensity.

You can achieve intensity in speeches by exhibiting the emotions that are appropriate to your words. Maintaining physical alertness and using crisp, energetic gestures will communicate intensity. Your language can convey a feeling of intensity. Use active sentences, rather than passive ones, and use action verbs. Since a slow rate conveys a relaxed feeling, speak at a fairly rapid rate.

Novelty

A stimulus is unusual or unique if it stands out in comparison to others, is rare or unusual, has no equal, or is the only one. A small object in the midst of large objects attracts our attention because of its unusual size. An object we have never seen before gets our attention because of its novelty.

How can you achieve novelty in a speech? Present a new or original analysis of the topic. Phrase your ideas in colorful and memorable ways. Tell your listeners things they do not know. Use variety in supporting materials, language, and delivery.

Personal Needs and Interests	Attention is drawn to those stimuli that affect our personal needs and specific interests to a greater degree than to stimuli in which we have no interest.

To create greater interest in your speech, show how your proposal will affect the personal needs and interests of your hearers. Show that what you are advocating will improve economic conditions in the community, enlarge educational facilities, provide additional cultural opportunities, or promote racial harmony and cooperation.

You can enhance the benefits of your proposal by showing how the present situation or one advocated by others will not meet the personal needs and interests of your listeners as well as your plan will. |
| **Conflict** | People seem naturally attracted to conflict. Our interest is piqued and we want to know the outcome.

Identify opponents of your proposal and show why they oppose it and how they would profit from failure to adopt it. Then show how most people would gain from your proposal. This will establish direct conflict between you and your opponents. Since personal conflict is most attention-getting, challenge your opponents to answer criticisms. |
| **Uncertainty** | We are attracted to those situations involving uncertainty. Have you ever lost interest in going to a football game because you felt that your team was undermatched or overmatched with an opponent? But if you feel that either team can win, you want to be there to resolve the uncertainty. |
| **Color** | Bright colors attract us more than dull colors. Notice how the appearance of a redbird gets your attention while that of a sparrow generally does not.

Female speakers can use bright colors in their dress much more easily than males can. Males can generally use bright colored ties but not suits. On one occasion a visiting professor at a university arrived at his lecture wearing a bright, luminous green suit. The next day a student said, "When the speaker first came in yesterday, I thought he was a used car salesman." Keep in mind that you do not want to attract unfavorable attention.

Can color be used in other ways? Yes, if you are using visual aids with your speech, they can be made attractively appealing by using colors to differentiate the parts. |

How the Listener Can Improve Listening

Does the full responsibility for communication have to be assumed by a speaker? No, but even a cooperative listener can impede communication with poor listening habits. The following suggestions, therefore, should help you meet your communicative responsibilities as a listener.

Purposeful Listening	Just as a speaker approaches a communicative situation with a purpose in mind, you should approach listening with a purpose. Otherwise, you will not know what type of behavior is appropriate. When you go to a classroom lecture, you go to be informed. That means you will probably want to take notes

on the lecture. When you go to a nightclub to hear a comedian, or when you sit down with friends for a pleasant evening of conversation, you listen for entertainment and enjoyment. Wherever you go, you should go with a listening purpose in mind. In that way, you know how to react to the information and how to process it. You do not take notes when your purpose is to be entertained or inspired. You do take notes when you want to be instructed or to recall the information.

Communicating a message to a receiver is not like transferring water from one bottle to another. You cannot sit passively and let a speaker "pour" a message into your brain. Listening is an active process. You must receive, perceive, interpret, and respond to what the speaker is saying. What do the speaker's statements mean to you? to others? As an active listener, you must listen "with more or less your total self—including your special senses, attitudes, beliefs, feelings, and intuitions."[12]

Active Listening

Can you create mental images of what the speaker is saying? As the speaker describes the scarred and barren land resulting from strip mining, can you visualize it? Can you envision the oncoming car as the speaker describes the experience of a head-on collision? Can you empathize with the speaker's anger at the cruel abuse of children by disturbed parents?

Active listening is not easy. It requires physical, mental, and emotional involvement. Active listening can be considered work. The extent of our physical and mental involvement is evidenced when we are sick with a cold or tired from losing a night's sleep. Then we discover that it is difficult to listen with a high degree of concentration.

You should capitalize on the difference between the speaking rate and the thinking rate in a constructive way. Although the speaking rate may vary from about one hundred to almost three hundred words per minute, the average speaking rate is about 125 to 150 words per minute. Our thinking rate, however, is approximately four times that. This means we have about four hundred words per minute to play around with while listening to the normal speaker. If we are not careful, those extra thinking words will be used to go off on tangents, even to entirely new topics. This extra thinking time can be used constructively, however, by elaborating on what the speaker is saying. This can be accomplished in a number of ways. Look ahead to what the speaker is going to say (although you must be careful not to get so far ahead of the speaker that you lose track of what is being said and get lost). Summarize frequently in your mind what has been said. Keep the central idea in mind and relate the speaker's words to it. Identify the main points and the speaker's organizational pattern. Evaluate the evidence. (1) Is it accurate? (2) Is it current? (3) Are the sources objective ones? (4) Does the evidence presented give a complete analysis of the subject? But keep moving with the speaker. Do not permit your attention to focus too long on one topic, or you may suddenly discover that you have not been listening to the speaker. Then you may find you can no longer understand what is being said.

Respond to the speaker and what is said. Smile when the speaker says something pleasant; frown when something is unclear; nod your head to indicate agreement; applaud to show approval. Whatever the type of response, the presence of some response reveals that you are actively involved.

Objective Listening

As you already know, and as we will discuss in greater depth later, we selectively perceive the stimuli around us. Do we want to perceive selectively? Not necessarily, but we are forced to because we cannot simultaneously perceive multiple stimuli. Consequently, we perceive certain stimuli and disregard others because of our background, attitudes, interests, previous experiences, values, and other factors. Although our perceptions are necessarily selective, we must, in our role as receivers in the communicative process, consciously strive to avoid misperceiving or misinterpreting information we receive.

The first step in avoiding communication problems caused by selective perception is to identify your attitudes toward the speaker and the subject. Do you admire the speaker a great deal? If so, then resolve that your admiration will not prevent your listening carefully and impartially to the ideas and evidence. Do you approach a communicative situation with a preconceived attitude? Do not assume that you will hear nothing worthwhile because the speaker is going to speak in favor of an idea, such as labor unions, that you oppose. Listen to what the speaker has to say. You may learn something that will give you a new perspective on labor unions. Are you aware that your attitude on the subject is opposed to that of the speaker? Then resolve that you will not reject unheard the ideas and evidence presented. Apply the same standards of evaluation that you would to a speech supporting a position you favor: Are the sources valid ones? Is the evidence consistent with familiar information? Is the evidence up-to-date?

Avoid letting your emotions get overly aroused by anything the speaker says. Do certain terms, such as "male chauvinist," "redneck," "abortion," four-letter words, or religious and racial epithets, cause you to explode emotionally? Are you then unable to respond rationally to what the speaker has said previously? Are you also unable to listen effectively to what follows? The objective listener guards against an emotional overreaction to these "signal" words.

Don't let other people around you have an effect on your listening. The process of listening changes in the presence of others. Their inattention may cause you to do a poor job of listening. Their negative responses can cause your listening to be more critical, or their positive responses may make your listening less critical. Maintain as much objectivity as possible in evaluating the speaker's ideas.

Constructive Listening

It is often easy to listen destructively. Have you made fun of an occasion? Have you criticized a speaker's dress, pronunciation, hometown, or organization? Have you sneered at a speaker's failure to use effectively the principles of communication? As deplorable as these things may be, we cannot let them cause us to overlook important information. Peer behind the external factors and evaluate what the speaker is saying. Overcome noise and distractions by attempting to discover personal value in what is being said. Ask yourself, "How is this information relevant to me? What can I gain from listening?"

Have you found it difficult to keep an open mind about a speaker's idea because of his personal commitments or prejudices? Instead of closing your mind to the speaker or focusing on areas of disagreement, look for points of agreement and emphasize them. Then you do not permit a closed mind to prevent expansion of your knowledge of a topic.

Try to pick out the central idea and organizational pattern of the speech. Not all speakers will clearly identify their central idea for you. Some will not do so because they are unfamiliar with basic principles of communication, some because they want to obscure their true purpose. Decide whether you need to listen for general ideas or specific details. In some cases it is imperative that you get the specific details. If someone is giving you complicated directions about how to use a home computer, you will need to listen carefully for the specific details. In other instances it will be easy to get lost in a maze of facts if you focus too much on specifics, then you will miss the general ideas as well as the details. In many communicative situations, the general ideas are more important than the details.

Attentive Listening

We filter the external world into our system by directing our attention to particular stimuli in our surroundings. When we want to filter out a stimulus, we simply direct our attention elsewhere. In a communicative situation, unless we direct our attention to the speaker we effectively filter out the message. Some people are skillful at faking attention. They assume an alert posture, look in the direction of the speaker with an attentive expression, shift the brain

into neutral, and let it roam off on other topics. Daydreaming may be a pleasant diversion, but it interferes with communication. Do you tend to daydream during speeches or conferences? It may help to take a pencil and pad with you even though you do not actually need the notes. Taking a few notes can keep you concentrating on the communication. When you take notes, do you insist on outlining them? Don't! Some messages are not organized so they can be outlined. If you insist on imposing order on disorganized messages, you will not only be frustrated, you will also get hopelessly lost and miss what the speaker has to say.

Avoid behavior that is distracting to you and others. Do you whisper to friends around you? You may miss an idea that is crucial to understanding the message. Do you work on other projects while involved in a communication activity? Do you avoid eye contact with the speaker? Eye contact improves the communication process for both speaker and listener.

Learn to cope with distractions that occur. Concentrate on the speaker and thus filter out the stimuli coming from noisy neighbors, crying babies, or creaking water pipes. Whether or not these stimuli disturb us is frequently a matter of attitude. If we are annoyed by a crying baby, we have difficulty filtering out the noise. But if we do not get annoyed, it is fairly easy to shut out that disturbance. Most people can read a newspaper with a radio or television on. Similarly, with practice, you can learn to overcome distractions in a communicative situation.

Basic Considerations

Listening attentively means attending not only to the verbal cues of the speaker, but to the nonverbal ones as well. Observing the speaker's various nonverbal clues will increase the understanding of the message. Sometimes the speaker does not communicate the true message verbally. On those occasions, the nonverbal cues—a frown, a smile, a vocal inflection, a pause, a nervous gesture—may reveal the true message. These nonverbal methods of communication are discussed in detail in chapter 12.

Very little motivates a speaker as well as an attentive listener, even if the listener is hostile. The reward of knowing someone is receptive to the message frequently provides the needed incentive to continue the communicative effort.

Meet your obligation by attending to the speaker. Only in this way can you broaden your horizons, and only in this way can the speaker have an opportunity to communicate.

If you are unenthusiastic about listening to a message, your mind is free to wander. You will have difficulty maintaining the kind of interest necessary to achieve good communication. If you are unenthusiastic about the person speaking, forget who is talking and focus on the topic. Examine the credibility of the content; do not allow your low regard for the speaker to interfere with your reception of the ideas. If you are unenthusiastic about the subject, make an effort to discover its relevance to you. Think of ways you can apply the information in your own activities. Can you use the information in one of your college courses? Can you use it in the part-time job you now have? Will you be able to use it in your future work? Is the speaker saying anything that you can use to enjoy life more? In some instances you may want to create enthusiasm by focusing on a negative feature. For example, because you oppose the speaker's position, you will want to know what she is saying in order to be able to counter that position. Sometimes you may just have to remember that even unpleasant tasks need to be finished.

Summary ⎯⎯⎯⎯⎯⎯⎯⎯⎯⎯⎯⎯⎯⎯⎯⎯⎯⎯⎯⎯

Listening is a necessary component of communication. The act of listening involves four distinct processes: receiving, perceiving, interpreting, and responding.

Both the speaker and the listener can take action to improve listening. The speaker can improve listeners' perception by utilizing factors that affect attention: movement, repetition, size, intensity, novelty, conflict, uncertainty, and color.

The listener can improve the process by listening purposefully, actively, objectively, constructively, attentively, and enthusiastically.

Exercises

1. Attend a lecture on campus with another member of the class. Sit in different parts of the room. Without conferring with one another, report what you heard to the class.
2. Divide the class into dyads (two-person units). Let one member of each dyad tell about a recent trip. The other member of each dyad should avoid listening to the speaker. After several minutes, the instructor should bring the class back together and let the members discuss the experience.
3. Assign three class members to listen to student speeches. Let one concentrate on the effectiveness of the speakers, one on the ineffectiveness of the speakers, and one on whatever seems appropriate. Let each student report to the class.
4. Attend a lecture and observe the behavior of listeners. Describe both positive and negative behavior that you witness.

Notes

1. P. T. Rankin, "The Measurement of Ability to Understand Spoken Language," Ph.d. diss., University of Michigan, 1926, *Dissertation Abstracts* 12 (1952):847–48.
2. L. Barker, R. Edwards, C. Gaines, K. Gladney, and F. Holley, "An Investigation of Proportional Time Spent in Various Communication Activities by College Students," *Journal of Applied Communication Research* 8 (1980):104–06.
3. R. G. Nichols, "Do You Know How to Listen? Practical Help in a Modern Age," *Speech Teacher* 10 (1961):120.
4. D. Marr, *Vision* (San Francisco: W. H. Freeman and Co., 1982), p. 3. Used by permission of W. H. Freeman and Co.
5. C. S. Carver and M. F. Scheier, *Attention and Self-Regulation* (New York: Springer-Verlag, 1981), p. 33.
6. A. D. Wolvin and C. G. Coakley, *Listening* (Dubuque, Iowa: Wm. C. Brown Company Publishers, 1982), p. 40. Used by permission.
7. F. H. Ernst, Jr., *Who's Listening?* (Vallejo, Calif.: Addresso'set, 1973), pp. 27, 37. Used by permission.
8. C. M. Kelly, "Listening: Complex of Activities—And a Unitary Skill," *Speech Monographs* 34 (1967):464.
9. R. N. Bostrom and E. S. Waldhart, "Components in Listening Behavior: The Role of Short-Term Memory," *Human Communication Research* 6 (1980):226.
10. R. N. Bostrom and C. L. Bryant, "Factors in the Retention of Information Presented Orally: The Role of Short-Term Listening," *Western Journal of Speech Communication* 44 (1980):145.
11. M. D. Vernon, *The Psychology of Perception,* 2nd ed. (London: Pelican Books, 1971), p. 173. © M. D. Vernon, 1962, 1971. By permission of Penguin Books, Ltd.
12. D. Barbara, "On Listening—The Role of the Ear in Psychic Life," *Today's Speech* 5 (1957):12.

PART 2

PREPARATION

6

CREATING CREDIBILITY

Columnist Patrick J. Buchanan was amazed that Pope John Paul II was "clasped to America's bosom" when he visited the United States in the fall of 1979.

Answering his own question, "How is it that a man with a message so unacceptable to the many—on contraception, abortion, divorce—can be so welcomed in the heart of the nation?" Buchanan wrote, "One answer can be found in the character of the man."[1] Columnist Charles Bartlett observed that "One thing is clear: the Pope has a gift for inspiring trust."[2] Character and trustworthiness—these are the qualities that develop credibility. As the credibility theme of this book indicates, ethos is particularly important to effective public speakers.

Definition of Ethos

Ethos, according to Aristotle, is the impression the speaker makes with his communication. Today we refer to it as the image of the speaker held by a particular listener. Aristotle considered ethos the most powerful factor in persuasion.[3] Modern research supports Aristotle's observation. Experimental studies have consistently revealed that although persuasive messages attributed to sources with low ethos produce opinion change, these same messages generally produce more attitude change when attributed to a source with high ethos.

Does ethos exist in you? No, it is in the eyes of the beholder. Ethos does not exist independently of you, however. Listeners' attitudes interact with your attributes to determine their attitude toward you. A university professor may be a nationally recognized scholar in a particular field, but in a city where university professors are held in low esteem, personal attainments as a scholar contribute nothing to ethos, and may in fact lower it. In another community, however, where university professors are held in high esteem, scholarly achievements enhance ethos. The same speaker, therefore, may have high ethos with some audiences and low ethos with others.

Not only does ethos vary from audience to audience, but, as shown in figure 6.1, it is a dynamic process. Your ethos varies every time you make an intelligent or unintelligent statement, a temperate or intemperate statement, or a selfish or unselfish statement. Consequently, you must be aware that everything you say or do in a speaking situation has an effect on your ethos.

Brooks and Scheidel showed clearly how a speaker's ethos can change during a speech. They measured the ethos of Malcolm X before, several times during, and after a speech to a predominantly white college audience. Of the eight measurements taken during the speech, the first—taken just after an opening prayer—showed a highly significant favorable shift. In remaining measurements, however, Malcolm X's ethos first went down, up twice, then consistently downward until the measurement taken after the speech was significantly lower than the first one made at the beginning of the speech.[4]

Figure 6.1

Ethos is not a static phenomenon, as revealed by this graph of the relationship between different events and Nixon's changing popularity.

From The Gallup Opinion Index, *Report 111 (September 1974), p. 12. Used by permission.*

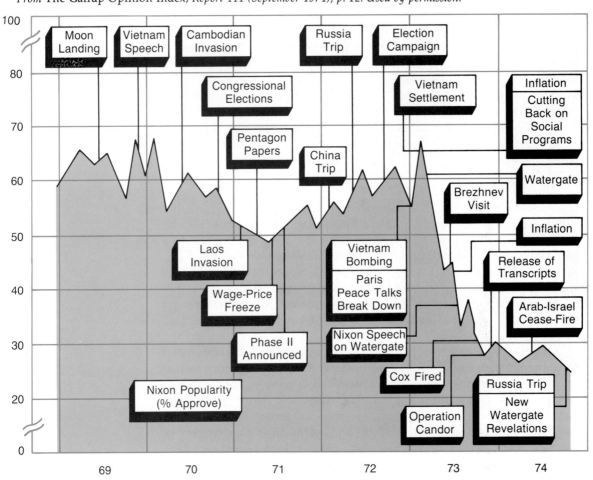

The change in the image of Jack Nicklaus demonstrates the dynamic nature of ethos. Early in his career he was called "Fat Jack" by golf spectators, and his wife lamented that it seemed she was the only one at a tournament pulling for "Fat Jack." With a slimmed-down physique, youthful clothes, a mod haircut, and a winning record, he suddenly became the "Golden Bear," and sports writers reported that he had become a sex symbol for females. His ethos was definitely enhanced!

Aristotle required that ethos "be created by the speech itself, and not left to depend upon an antecedent impression that the speaker is this or that kind of man."[5] Although it is certainly true that you should employ available

techniques in speech to enhance your ethos, it is unrealistic to attempt to divorce the listeners' reaction to your communicative effort from their prior attitudes toward you. Most speakers are known for something—efficiency or inefficiency, wit or humorlessness, concern for others or disregard for others, emotional maturity or immaturity, intellectual superiority or inferiority—and that produces an image in the minds of others. Whatever your image, you bring it to the communicative situation, and it either contributes to or detracts from your effectiveness. By bringing positive ethos to the speaking occasion, you help to build credibility for your ideas and make them more easily accepted by the listeners.

Not only can you use your ethos to get your ideas accepted, you can also use speech to improve your ethos. As McCroskey has pointed out, politicians have been using speeches to increase their ethos for a long time. They make statements on issues favored by their constituents, thus putting ethos in the bank. Then, when they have to take stands antithetical to their constituents on other issues, they draw on this reserve.[6]

McGinnies demonstrated that speakers improve their ethos in the speech itself by saying things that listeners like. He used the same speaker to present six different tape-recorded persuasive communications to students at four Japanese universities: a pro-American and pro-Soviet communication on the cold war; a pro-American and a pro-Soviet communication on the Cuban missile crisis; a communication favoring American submarine visits to Japanese ports; and a communication presenting arguments both for and against such visitations. Following the message, the students completed a questionnaire revealing their attitudes toward the speaker. The results showed that the message affected what they thought about the speaker. Although it was the same speaker delivering each message, one group of students thought the speaker, defending the role of the United States in the cold war, was significantly "more honest, sincere, interesting, strong, informed, and intelligent" than the speaker presenting the pro-Soviet argument.[7] The statements reflected their pro-American thoughts and caused the students to think more highly of the speaker.

Is ethos affected by the presence or absence of communication skills in the presentation of a speech? Miller and Hewgill say it is. They tape-recorded nine versions of a speech with various numbers and types of nonfluencies occurring in each. Each student rated the credibility of the speaker in each of the versions. The results showed that increases in nonfluencies decreased the speaker's credibility.[8]

A speaker's ethos contributes to and is affected by a speech's impact. If your prespeech ethos is high, it should favorably influence the listener to accept your ideas. If, however, your speech contains statements that are obviously absurd, or if your ideas are opposite to those of the listeners, then the negative reaction may be so strong among the listeners that your postspeech ethos will be lowered. Even in this case there is generally a positive effect on listener attitudes toward the ideas. If you have positive ethos and you speak on an issue toward which the listeners are negative, there is a tendency for the listeners' attitudes to become less positive toward you and less negative toward your ideas. On the other hand, if you have negative ethos and you discuss issues toward which the listeners are positive, there is a tendency for the listeners' attitudes to become less negative toward you and less positive toward the issue.[9]

Sources of Ethos

If you are to take advantage of your existing ethos—use it when possible, build it when necessary, ignore it when feasible—you must understand the sources of ethos. "There are three things that gain our belief," wrote Aristotle, "namely, intelligence, character, and goodwill."[10] Present-day researchers have identified from two to twenty-one factors as the sources of ethos.[11]

Admittedly, determining the sources of ethos is complex, and there is also interaction among the speaker, the audience, the occasion, and the speech itself. In fact, after studying listeners' perceptions of the sources of ethos in

three different situations—a lecture in a classroom, a speech to a social organization, and a sermon in a church—Applebaum and Anatol concluded that the sources of ethos are not the same over different situations.[12] Nevertheless, experimental evidence, supported by observation, indicates five main sources from which a speaker may derive ethos: *competence, trustworthiness, similarity, attraction,* and *sincerity.* It should be stressed that these dimensions may not be mutually exclusive—they may overlap—but it is helpful to approach ethos from different focuses.

Competence refers to those factors indicating that the speaker is a source of valid information. Included are experience, age, any leadership offices or titles, educational background, and other significant factors. It is sufficient that you seem to know what you are talking about. Evidence indicates that you do not have to be an actual expert in order to be considered competent.[13]

Competence

In the classic study on ethos, Haiman measured the attitudes of a group of college students toward compulsory health insurance on a nationwide basis. Dividing the students into three sections, he presented a recorded speech in which the speaker was identified first as the surgeon general of United States, second as the secretary general of the Communist party in the United States, and third as a sophomore speech major (which the speaker in all three cases truly was) at Northwestern University. Attitude scales administered after the speech found a significant positive shift of opinion for those who thought they were hearing the surgeon general. There was a positive, less than significant, shift for those who thought they were hearing the sophomore student. Those who thought they were listening to a communist made a negative, though not significant, shift from the position advocated in the speech.[14] Although other factors were involved, undoubtedly one of the important factors influencing those who believed they were hearing the surgeon general was the belief that he was qualified to speak on this subject.

Competence as a specific source of credibility was accidentally identified by Hovland and Weiss. Establishing levels of credibility for various sources by pretests, they then presented assorted persuasive messages from the different sources. They found that opinion change in the direction advocated occurred significantly more often with the high-ethos source than with the low-ethos sources. One exception stood out. The message, arguing that TV would cause a decline in the number of movie theaters, was attributed to *Fortune* magazine in the high-credible situation and to a movie gossip columnist in the low-credible situation. Surprisingly, the subjects changed their attitudes more when the message was attributed to the movie columnist than when it was attributed to *Fortune*. Apparently, the subjects generally considered *Fortune* to be a more credible source, but when faced with the specific topic, they felt that the movie columnist would be more competent to gauge the impact of TV on movie theaters.[15] You should attempt to establish your knowledge on the matter under discussion if you are going to be a most effective speaker.

Since expertise or competence is probably the most important dimension of ethos,[16] avoid topics which you do not know. Of course, for you, the student, this is a particular source of difficulty. In a beginning speech class, you must generally develop your competence through the acquisition of information on your topic, for rarely will you have the experience and status for your peers to perceive you as an expert. Not only must you develop competence on your subjects but you must skillfully make the auditors aware of that competence.

Even speakers with high ethos recognize that they must make listeners aware of their competence. The Surgeon General of the United States, C. Everett Koop, made his audience aware of his competence to deal with the specific problem of violence in children.

. . . I believe the pediatrician has a unique relationship with children and with parents. You gain certain insights about individuals and families that other physicians may not have the chance to see.

I base that opinion, by the way, on the reflections of my own career of 35 years in pediatric surgery. Dealing with the young children who were my patients I saw firsthand the stresses of childhood and was aware of both the strengths and weaknesses of children trying to cope. I also had to understand the families of those children. I had to gain their confidence and win them as allies in the battle to help their children.

In the process, I think I began to understand a great deal about the contemporary family.

I tried to absorb that information and then focus it upon the problem to be solved by surgery. Sometimes, when it was clear to me that I was gaining insights into a serious family problem not directly related to the surgery, I would be open and available to that family, just in case they wanted to talk it through. But, I knew that I lacked a clear understanding of the need for me to become involved and to what extent I should become involved and what I might hope to accomplish.

Now, after looking at the data from my new vantage point as surgeon general, and appreciating the special access to and relationship with the American family that pediatricians do enjoy, I think my message to you today on violence in our society and its effects on children and families is appropriate and necessary.[17]

James B. Conant, former president of Harvard University and a critic of the system of secondary education in the United States, revealed his competence to discuss education by referring to his experiences and his accomplishments. Early in his speech he called attention to his experiences when he said,

There has been a good deal of talk in recent years about the need for a national educational policy. As I have studied public education in this country at all levels. I have become more and more convinced that the phrase a national educational policy is misleading.

Later he called attention to his accomplishments:

In a book published last year entitled *Shaping Educational Policy,* I answered this question in the affirmative. I suggested that the states enter into a compact or agreement to establish a commission which would be a planning commission with no administrative authority and thus differ from some of the regional boards.

In referring to statistics concerning dropout rates from school Conant said, "I have referred to these in my book *The Education of American Teachers,* and would merely like to repeat here what I have written in that book."[18]

Few college students have written books to which they can refer to increase ethos, but you can refer to books you have read to demonstrate your competence to talk on the subject of your speech.

These are some methods—referring to knowledge, experiences, and accomplishments—you can use to call attention to factors that establish your competence to be heard on an issue. You should always be careful, however, that you do not seem to be boasting, for the adverse effects of boasting can

destroy the beneficial impact of your positive attributes. You may provide information about your competence to the person who will introduce you, allowing that person to present it in what will seem a more objective manner. However, information establishing your competence has greater impact if provided at the point in the speech at which it is pertinent.

Trustworthiness

A second source of ethos is *trustworthiness,* or the appearance that the speaker gives of being honest, just, and objective. You must seem to be free from any self-interest in the outcome of the speaking effort. Most people are suspicious of a speaker whose self-interest will be served by the proposal advocated. Clear objectivity on your part will enhance your ethos. This fact was clearly demonstrated by Walster, Aronson, and Abrahams, who presented a message to subjects from a convicted criminal. When the message advocated greater individual freedom and opposed greater power for police, little attitude change occurred. When the message advocated greater powers for police, there was a large attitude change. Clearly, in the latter instance, the subjects perceived the source of the communication as arguing against his own self-interest and changed opinion in the direction he favored even though he was originally a low-ethos source. The researchers conclude that when a low-prestige source argues against his own self-interest, he is "even more effective than a high-prestige communicator presenting the same argument."[19]

A study of the impact of orientation films, such as "The Battle of Britain" and "Prelude to War," for servicemen in World War II, indicated that the serviceman's estimate of the objectivity of the film affected his response to it. Those who thought the films were shown for propaganda purposes were less likely to accept their attitudes than were those who thought the films were shown for informational purposes.[20] You may increase your ethos by making listeners aware of your objectivity or lack of self-interest.

By making clear his candidness and implying his lack of hypocrisy, Attorney General Robert F. Kennedy demonstrated his trustworthiness in a speech to faculty and students at the University of Georgia during the time when civil rights was a particularly sensitive issue in the South.

> I have many friends in the United States Senate who are Southerners. Many of these friendships stem from my work as counsel for the Senate Rackets Committee, headed by Senator John McClellan of Arkansas for whom I have the greatest admiration and affection.
> If these Southern friends of mine are representative Southerners—and I believe they are—I do not pretend that they believe with me on everything or that I agree with them on everything. But, knowing them as I do, I am convinced of this:
> Southerners have a special respect for candor and plain talk. They certainly don't like hypocrisy. So, in discussing this third major problem, I must tell you candidly what our policies are going to be in the field of civil rights and why.[21]

In a 1961 speech to the National Association of Broadcasters, Newton Minow, then the new chairman of the FCC, made obvious his objectivity and his lack of self-interest:

> It would not surprise me if some of you had expected me to come here today and say in effect, "Clean up your own house or the government will do it for you."
> Well, in a limited sense, you would be right—I've just said it. But I want to say to you earnestly that it is not in that spirit that I come before you today, nor is it in that spirit that I intend to serve the FCC.
> I am in Washington to help broadcasting, not to harm it; to strengthen it, not weaken it; to reward it, not punish it; to encourage it, not threaten it; to stimulate it, not censor it.
> Above all, I am here to uphold and protect the public interest.[22]

A recent study of American values in the 1980s asked people to identify the least admired leader. Ranking Nixon first, respondents named dishonesty as the quality "they least admire in him." When asked to identify the quality of a leader they consider most important, the public overwhelmingly cited honesty.[23]

On the basis of his study of trustworthiness and ethos, Smith concluded that despite other qualities, a speaker considered untrustworthy is viewed as a questionable source.[24]

Similarity

A *similarity* of attitudes or other factors between you and the audience in related and even nonrelated factors increases your ethos and makes it easier to gain acceptance for your ideas. During the Vietnam War, some protestors complicated their persuasive efforts by flaunting attitudes and behavior that alienated the very people they wanted to persuade. In the eyes of many Americans, the ethos of some protestors was tarnished by their waving of Viet Cong flags, disrespect for the American flag, use of foul language, disregard for others' rights, nudity, public participation in sexual activity, and other actions. These actions clearly emphasized the *dissimilarity* between certain protestors and those Americans who did not approve of their beliefs and actions. Fully aware of this loss of ethos, many politicians in the 1970 elections refused to let young people who had become identified with the protest movement go out and campaign among the general public. They simply relegated them to doing clerical tasks in the back rooms.

It is difficult to overcome differences between yourself and your auditors on an issue you want to discuss. If, at the same time, you must overcome differences on a number of other related or unrelated factors, you have little chance to succeed in changing listeners' attitudes. Find and stress all the similarities with your listeners that you can. Thus you will be able to build credibility for your ideas.

Successful politicians and other speakers have known and used for hundreds of years the "common ground" approach—the stressing of the similarities between speaker and audience. Kenneth Burke emphasized this point when he noted that, "You persuade a man only insofar as you can talk his language by speech, gesture, tonality, order, image, attitude, idea, *identifying* your way with his."[25] In the 1980 presidential campaign, both Carter and Reagan attempted to establish their similarities to southern voters. Carter tried to create a bond of similarity with southern audiences when he opened his campaign in Alabama on Labor Day, telling his audience: "It's good to be home." Then he further stressed his similarity by saying he was happy to be with friends "who don't talk with an accent." On the other hand, Reagan stressed his similarity in political attitudes. His campaign argued that there was greater philosophical similarity between southerners and Reagan than between them and Carter, even though Carter was from the South.

Although unrelated points of similarity are effective in increasing the ethos of the source, related items of similarity are the most effective. Berscheid presented a speaker to one audience as having attitudes similar to theirs in the field of education and dissimilar to theirs in the field of international affairs. To another audience she presented the speaker as having dissimilar ideas to theirs in the field of education and similar attitudes to theirs in the field of international affairs. Half of each audience then received a message on education and half received a message on international affairs. The results showed that the most effective message for changing attitudes was the one in which the similarity was in the same area as the subject matter of the message.[26] You should attempt to establish similarities in areas closely relevant to the subject of your speech.

As a persuasive speaker you do not have to rely on information given before the speech to develop common ground with your listeners; you may develop the similarities in the speech itself. Examining the attitudes of college students on a number of topics, Weiss discovered that most of them were for water fluoridation, but were not strongly in favor of it. He also discovered that they were almost unanimously in favor of academic freedom. Consequently, he prepared a communication opposing water fluoridation and favoring academic freedom. One group of students was exposed to the message favoring academic freedom before they were given the message opposing water fluoridation. A second group was exposed to a neutral communication before receiving the message opposing water fluoridation. Attitude scales collected immediately after the fluoridation speeches revealed that those students who were first exposed to the message on academic freedom accepted the attitudes against fluoridation more than did those who were first exposed to the neutral message.[27]

Any similarity between the speaker and audience may be used to build ethos for the speaker. Notice how the president of the Pharmaceutical Manufacturers Association, speaking to representatives at an annual meeting of the American Land Title Association, undoubtedly enhanced his ethos by focusing on a similarity between his professional group and that of his audience:

Perhaps I ought to confess that when I first received the invitation to appear here, I was somewhat daunted. I wondered why an organization whose wide interests lie in real estate development and underwriting title insurance would want to hear from a representative of the manufacturers of pharmaceuticals. Then I learned that your industry may be the object of a Congressional investigation in the foreseeable future.

This, of course, is something with which the pharmaceutical industry has had long and painful experience, and the scars to prove it. We have been investigated, on and off, for ten solid years and the end is not in sight.

There may be one or two exceptions which do not come readily to mind but I believe we are probably the most thoroughly investigated industry in the country today.

My subject "The Congressional Hearing" allows me to review this decade of inquiry, and to offer you some comments and thoughts based on our experiences which may prove helpful to you at some later time.[28]

Attraction

Attraction refers to the orientation of one person toward another person. Newcomb observes that although it is normal to consider attraction equivalent to "liking," he prefers to think of it "in somewhat broader terms. Thus respect, admiration, and dependence all refer to positive person-to-person orientation, and yet any of these may be associated with either positive or negative liking." *Attraction,* then, refers to any relationship with another person that causes "approach rather than avoidance, moving toward rather than against or away from."[29]

One source of negative or positive attraction seems to be racial prejudice or the absence of it. Aronson and Golden had four speakers—a white engineer, a black engineer, a white dishwasher, and a black dishwasher—discuss the worth and significance of arithmetic with white fifth-grade students. Questionnaires designed to reveal any change in attitude toward arithmetic were completed following the speech. The results showed that the white engineer and the black engineer were equally persuasive, and both were significantly more persuasive than the black dishwasher. While neither was significantly more effective than the white dishwasher, the latter was more effective than the black dishwasher. When the experimenters divided the subjects into "prejudiced" and "unprejudiced" categories, they discovered that there was not only a "tendency for prejudiced individuals to be undersusceptible to the influence" of a black communicator, "but there was also a tendency for unprejudiced subjects to be oversusceptible to the influence of a" black communicator.[30]

A second source of attraction is appearance. Support for this conclusion comes from a study by Mills and Aronson. In front of a group of subjects who were being asked to fill out a questionnaire, the experimenter called for a volunteer to reply to the questionnaire aloud. A female confederate, who had already been coached, "volunteered." In one condition of the experiment, she "was made up to look extremely attractive. She wore chic, tight-fitting clothing; her hair was modishly coiffured; she wore becoming makeup." In the other condition, "the same confederate was made up to look repulsive. She wore loose, ugly, ill-fitting clothing; her hair was messy; her makeup was conspicuously absent; the trace of a moustache was etched on her upper lip; her complexion was oily and unwholesome looking." The results showed that the attractive communicator was more effective in changing the attitudes of the subjects.[31]

A third source of attraction is recognition by another person of positive aspects of one's self-concept. If a person considers himself to be intelligent and another person compliments his intelligence, the first person tends to be attracted to the other. In other words, we like those who like us for what we consider to be the right reasons. A clear distinction must be made, however, between flattery and liking. We frequently hear the statement "Flattery will get you everywhere." Not necessarily—only if the compliments are perceived as genuine.

A fourth source of attraction is fulfilling attributes. If a woman plays a violin, a man who likes violin music but doesn't play the instrument may be attracted to her. The man is fulfilled by listening to the music, and the woman is fulfilled by having someone listen while she plays. In other instances, opposites may attract one another. A woman who is forceful and domineering and a man who is meek and mild may be attracted to one another because each finds the relationship fulfilling.

Factors that will cause the listeners to like or be attracted to you may be stressed in order to increase your ethos.

Sincerity

Although listeners are not always able to differentiate between genuine and feigned sincerity on the part of the speaker, they do respond more favorably to what they *perceive* as sincerity on the part of the speaker. Hildreth had speakers present speeches on topics in which they believed and on topics in which they did not believe. Listeners were asked to determine the sincerity of each speaker and to rate his or her effectiveness. Although they were unable to distinguish between sincere and insincere speakers, the hearers rated as most effective those speakers they perceived as sincere.[32]

In practical as well as experimental situations, a speaker who seems to mean what he says is found by listeners to be more credible. Following the presidential debates in 1960, listeners were asked who won the debate, then they were asked why they thought Kennedy or Nixon was better. One of the three main reasons respondents cited was the speaker's sincerity.[33]

During World War II, the late Kate Smith, a popular singer noted for her rendition of "God Bless America," conducted a radio marathon to sell war bonds. In one day's broadcast she sold $39 million worth. In studying the reasons for her success, Merton discovered that sincerity was considered her outstanding quality.[34]

An admirer of Abraham Lincoln reported that she had long been interested in what had been the most important element of Lincoln's "success as a speaker." Finally, she addressed the question to Paul Angle, a noted authority on Lincoln. He replied that, "Lincoln's transparent honesty and sincerity was the impressive characteristic of his oratorical style. I believe he created the impression of sincerity by complete honesty in dealing with his opponent."[35]

Recent evidence demonstrates the importance of sincerity in obtaining a favorable response from others. Psychologist Norman H. Anderson presented a list of 555 trait names to subjects with instructions "to think of a person being described by each word and to rate the word according to how much they would like the person." The word receiving the highest likeableness rating was *sincerity.* [36]

The late President Harry S Truman, recognizing the immense importance of this quality to a speaker, declared that "Sincerity, honesty, and a straight-forward manner are more important than special talent or polish."[37]

Without undermining in any way the importance of sincerity or the veracity of Mr. Truman's testimony, let it be noted that it does not have to be an either/or situation. The polished speaker can be sincere, honest, and straightforward, and the sincere, honest, straightforward speaker can develop polish.

In the early seventies Ralph Nader was popular with young college audiences despite the fact that he wore his hair and sideburns short and dressed in suits whose coats had extremely narrow lapels. One important reason he was well accepted by these listeners was that he exuded sincerity.[38]

When you are *perceived* as sincere, you lend credibility to your ideas. And you have an ethical responsibility to *be* sincere.

Summary

Ethos is the listener's perceived image of the speaker. It is a function not only of who you actually are, but also of the listeners' attitudes toward your attributes. Thus you have only partial control over your ethos. In the final analysis, it is not your abilities, accomplishments, and attributes that determine your ethos, but the estimate of those factors made by listeners.

You should recognize that ethos plays an important role in the degree to which your speaking will influence listeners. Although the accumulated evidence seems to indicate that a well-developed speech can change the attitudes of listeners despite the low ethos of the speaker, it also quite clearly shows that the same speech will have a more significant impact if presented by a speaker with high ethos. The development of ethos will do much to create credibility for your ideas.

The sources of ethos are many and complex, but research indicates that five main sources are *competence* of the speaker, *trustworthiness* of the speaker, *similarity* between the speaker and listeners, *attraction* of the speaker to the audience, and perceived *sincerity* of the speaker.

Exercises

1. Analyze the speaking of a contemporary politician. In what ways does he or she use ethos to retain or improve credibility? What does this person do that makes you believe that he or she (a) knows what he or she is talking about, (b) is trustworthy, (c) is similar to you, or (d) has traits that are attractive to you?

2. Attend a lecture on campus. Describe the ways in which the lecturer attempted to develop similarities between the listeners and himself or herself. Did this affect the speaker's credibility? Why or why not?

3. Select one of the sources of ethos discussed in this chapter and explain in detail how you can use it in your next speech to increase your credibility.

4. Discuss the practice of responding to the speaker's "image." In what ways is this an unfair method of determining a speaker's credibility? In what ways a fair method?

5. List three contemporary speakers who evince sincerity in speaking. Explain what causes you to think they are sincere.

Notes

1. Patrick J. Buchanan, "The Dividing Line," *Birmingham News,* October 12, 1979. Used by permission.

2. Charles Bartlett, "News Focus," *Birmingham News,* October 2, 1979. Used by permission.

3. L. Cooper, *The Rhetoric of Aristotle* (New York: D. Appleton-Century Co., 1932), pp. 8–9.

4. R. D. Brooks and T. M. Scheidel, "Speech as Process: A Case Study," *Speech Monographs* 35 (1968):1–7.

5. Cooper, *Rhetoric of Aristotle,* pp. 8–9.

6. J. C. McCroskey, "Ethos, Credibility and Communication in the Real World," *North Carolina Journal of Speech* 4 (Spring 1971):24–31.

7. E. McGinnies, "Studies in Persuasion: V. Perceptions of a Speaker as Related to Communication Content," *Journal of Social Psychology* 75 (1968):21–33.

8. G. R. Miller and M. A. Hewgill, "The Effect of Variations in Nonfluency on Audience Ratings of Source Credibility," *Quarterly Journal of Speech* 50 (1964):36–44.

9. C. E. Osgood and P. H. Tannenbaum, "The Principle of Congruity in the Prediction of Attitude Change," *Psychological Review* 62 (1955):42–55.

10. Cooper, *Rhetoric of Aristotle,* p. 92.

11. C. I. Hovland, I. L. Janis, and H. H. Kelley, *Communication and Persuasion* (New Haven: Yale University Press, 1953), chap. 2; D. K. Berlo, J. B. Lemert, and R. J. Mertz, "Dimensions for Evaluating the Acceptability of Message Sources," *Public Opinion Quarterly* 33 (1969–70):563–76; J. C. McCroskey, "Scales for the Measurement of Ethos," *Speech Monographs* 33 (1966):65–72; J. L. Whitehead, Jr., "Factors of Source Credibility," *Quarterly Journal of Speech* 54 (1968):59–63; D. Schweitzer and G. P. Ginsburg, "Factors of Communicator Credibility," in *Problems of Social Psychology,* ed. C. C. Backman and P. F. Secord (New York: McGraw-Hill, 1966), pp. 94–102; W. J. McGuire, "The Nature of Attitudes and Attitude Change," *The Handbook of Social Psychology,* ed. G. Lindzey and E. Aronson (Reading, Mass.: Addison-Wesley Publishing Co., 1969), 3:179.

12. R. F. Applebaum and K. W. E. Anatol, "The Factor Structure of Source Credibility as a Function of the Speaking Situation," *Speech Monographs* 39 (1972):216–22.

13. Whitehead, "Factors of Source Credibility," p. 60.
14. F. S. Haiman, "An Experimental Study of the Effects of Ethos in Public Speaking," *Speech Monographs* 16 (1949):190–202.
15. C. I. Hovland and W. Weiss, "The Influence of Source Credibility on Communication Effectiveness," *Public Opinion Quarterly* 15 (1951):635–50. See also Kelman and Hovland, " 'Reinstatement' of the Communicator," pp. 327–35; E. Aronson, J. A. Turner, and J. M. Carlsmith, "Communicator Credibility and Communicator Discrepancy as Determinants of Opinion Change," *Journal of Abnormal and Social Psychology* 67 (1963):31–36.
16. D. G. Bock and T. J. Saine, "The Impact of Source Credibility, Attitude Valence, and Task Sensitization on Trait Errors in Speech Evaluation," *Speech Monographs* 42 (1975):235.
17. C. Everett Koop, "Violence and Public Health," Owen Peterson, ed., *Representative American Speeches, 1982–1983* (New York: The H. W. Wilson Co., 1983), pp. 210–11.
18. J. B. Conant, "The Role of the States in Education," *Vital Speeches of the Day* 31 (1965):686–88.
19. E. Walster, E. Aronson, and D. Abrahams, "On Increasing the Persuasiveness of a Low Prestige Communicator," *Journal of Experimental Social Psychology* 2 (1966):325–42.
20. Hovland et al., *Communication and Persuasion,* p. 24.
21. R. F. Kennedy, "Law Day Address—University of Georgia," from *Rights for Americans: The Speeches of Robert F. Kennedy,* ed. Thomas A. Hopkins, copyright © 1964 by Thomas A. Hopkins, reprinted by permission of The Bobbs-Merrill Company, Inc., pp. 17–26.
22. N. N. Minow, "The Vast Wasteland," from Newton N. Minow, *Equal Time: The Private Broadcaster and the Public Interest,* ed. Lawrence Laurent (New York: Atheneum Publishers, 1964), p. 50. Used by permission of Atheneum Publishers.
23. *The Connecticut Mutual Life Report on American Values in the '80s: The Impact of Belief* (Hartford: Connecticut Mutual Life Insurance Co., 1981), pp. 193–95.
24. R. G. Smith, "Source Credibility Context Effects," *Speech Monographs* 40 (1973):309.
25. K. Burke, *A Rhetoric of Motives* (New York: Prentice-Hall, 1950), p. 55. See also E. Burnstein, E. Stotland, and A. Zander, "Similarity to a Model and Self-Evaluation," *Journal of Abnormal and Social Psychology* 62 (1961):257–64.
26. E. Berscheid, "Opinion Change and Communicator—Communicatee Similarity and Dissimilarity," *Journal of Personality and Social Psychology* 4 (1966):670–80.
27. W. Weiss, "Opinion Congruence with a Negative Source on One Issue as a Factor Influencing Agreement on Another Issue," *Journal of Abnormal and Social Psychology* 54 (1957):180–86.
28. C. J. Stetler, "The Congressional Hearing," *Vital Speeches of the Day* 36 (1969–70), 53–56.
29. T. M. Newcomb, *The Acquaintance Process* (New York: Holt, Rinehart & Winston, 1961), pp. 6–7.
30. E. Aronson and B. Golden, "The Effect of Relevant and Irrelevant Aspects of Communicator Credibility on Opinion Change," *Journal of Personality* 30 (1962):135–46.

31. J. Mills and E. Aronson, "Opinion Change as a Function of the Communicator's Attractiveness and Desire to Influence," *Journal of Personality and Social Psychology* 1 (1965):173–77.

32. R. A. Hildreth, "An Experimental Study of Audiences' Ability to Distinguish between Sincere and Insincere Speeches," Ph.D. diss., University of Southern California, 1953.

33. S. Kraus, ed., *The Great Debates* (Bloomington: Indiana University Press, 1962), p. 198.

34. R. K. Merton, *Mass Persuasion: The Social Psychology of a War Bond Drive* (New York: Harper & Brothers, 1946), pp. 80–85.

35. M. F. Berry, "Lincoln—The Speaker: Part II," *Quarterly Journal of Speech* 17 (1931):187.

36. N. H. Anderson, "Likeableness Ratings of 555 Personality-Trait Words," *Journal of Personality and Social Psychology* 9 (1968):272–79.

37. E. E. White and C. R. Henderlider, "What Harry S Truman Told Us about His Speaking," *Quarterly Journal of Speech* 40 (1954):39.

38. *Time,* May 10, 1971, p. 18.

7

UNDERSTANDING AND ADAPTING TO LISTENERS

*A*ttitudes are the wellsprings from which behavior flows. This is not to contend that the development, arousal, or holding of an attitude will result in a specific behavior related to that attitude. Other factors may intervene. A person may believe strongly in the necessity of saving gasoline, but the fear of flying and a desire to take a vacation 2,000 miles away may motivate that individual to drive that distance, using many gallons of gasoline. Or a person who believes drugs are harmful may not express that attitude when everyone in the group begins smoking marijuana. Consequently, you may arouse an old attitude or develop a new one and still not produce the behavior desired. Nevertheless, the existence of an attitude does create pressure within the individual to behave in a manner consistent with that attitude. With an effect similar to that of credibility, activating an attitude in a listener enhances enormously your chances of causing the desired behavior. To understand how to actuate attitudes, you must know what they are and how they operate.

Definition of Attitude

Many definitions of attitudes have been offered. In this book, an attitude will be considered to be "an evaluation or feeling reaction."[1] As Sherif, Sherif, and Nebergall explain,

Attitudes refer to the stands the individual upholds and cherishes about objects, issues, persons, groups, or institutions. The referents of a person's attitudes may be a "way of life"; economic, political, or religious institutions; family, school, or government. We are speaking of the individual's attitudes when we refer to his holding in high esteem his own family, his own school, his own party, his own religion, with all the emotional and affective overtones these terms imply. We refer to his attitudes when we say he holds other groups, other schools, other parties or religions in a less favorable light or at a safe distance (as "safe" is defined by his attitudes).[2]

An attitude differs from a motive in that an attitude persists, while a motive comes and goes, and its strength depends on a drive state. Thus a person may have a favorable attitude toward the eating of rabbit. Though the attitude remains constant, the person will not ordinarily eat rabbit until the hunger motive occurs. Another individual may have an unfavorable attitude toward the eating of rabbit. If this person has been in the forest for several days without food, however, the hunger motive may be cause to overlook this attitude in order to satisfy the hunger. Nevertheless, unless eating the rabbit causes some change, the original unfavorable attitude toward the eating of rabbit will persist.

An attitude is also different from a belief in that a belief is more cognitively oriented. A belief is based, or seemingly based, on factual information. That the United States has a universal system of free education is a belief.

That the universal system of free education in the United States is worthwhile is an attitude. That the United States has a democratic form of government is a belief. That the democratic form of government in the United States is beneficial is an attitude. Thus an attitude involves judgment, evaluation, feeling.

An opinion may be defined as the verbalization of an attitude. It may or may not accurately reflect the attitude underlying it, but in many instances it is the only index we have to a person's attitudes. At least the opinion constitutes what the individual wants the world around her to think her attitude is.

Components of Attitude

An attitude has three components: the cognitive, the affective, and the behavioral. Its *cognitive* aspect consists of the perceptions, thoughts, and beliefs a person has about a particular class of objects. It does not matter whether these perceptions, thoughts, and beliefs are accurate or inaccurate. For the person who has them, they constitute "knowledge." If the athletes you have known have been dumb, then for you athletes are dumb. If someone has lived in a community where businessmen have been corrupt, then for that person businessmen are corrupt. What can you do to change attitudes? You can provide information. It can be very important in changing and forming attitudes, especially if it is credible information previously unknown to the listener.

The *affective* component consists of the feelings that an individual has about a particular object. Those feelings may be favorable or unfavorable, and they may be measured physiologically. Cooper had college students listen to complimentary or derogatory statements about ethnic groups while he measured their galvanic skin response (GSR). The GSRs of most students were greater while they were hearing a derogatory statement about a group they liked than while hearing a derogatory statement about a group toward which they were neutral. Moreover, the GSRs were greater when the students were listening to complimentary statements about groups they disliked than when listening to complimentary statements about groups toward which they were neutral.[3] After determining the attitudes of a group of university students toward the church, Dickson and McGinnies measured the students' GSRs while letting them hear recorded statements praising or criticizing the church. Regardless of the individual student's attitude toward the church, the GSR was greater when the statement heard contradicted the student's attitude than when the statement agreed with it.[4] On the basis of this evidence and everyday observation, McGinnies concluded "that attitudes do have emotional support, and that the emotional component is more apparent when someone's attitudes are attacked than when they are supported."[5] Speakers who attack objects or concepts cause a greater emotional response among their hearers than speakers who make positive statements about their proposals.

The *behavioral* component refers to the actions that a person adopts in relation to an object or concept because of an attitude or group of attitudes. Although no person's behavior is going to correlate directly with attitudes, there is good evidence now that behavior and attitudes are more positively

related than had been previously thought. For example, when people are reminded of their experience with an object, there is a greater tendency for behavior to be related to their attitude toward that object. In one study, for example, subjects were asked about their attitudes toward religion. Prior to being asked, however, some of the subjects were asked to complete a ninety-item checklist describing their religious behavior in the past year. Approximately thirty days later, all the subjects were requested to describe their recent religious behavior. Those who had completed the checklist revealed generally higher correlations between attitude and behavior. Those who had not filled out the checklist had significantly lower attitude-behavior correlations. Thus, it appears that attitudes and behavior are more closely related if subjects are reminded of their past behavior.[6]

Well-conducted public opinion polls, by virtue of their accuracy in predicting what actions people will take on such issues as voting, have demonstrated an impressive correlation between attitudes and behavior.

Several factors affect the consistency between attitudes and behavior. First, the strength of the attitude is important. The greater the strength, the more likely is a person's behavior to reflect that attitude. Second, the way in which the attitude is formed affects the correlation between it and behavior.

Attitudes created by direct experience tend to correlate more highly with behavior than those developed by indirect experience ("reading or being told about the attitude object").[7] Third, the social acceptance of an attitude influences whether behavior will reflect it. A person who is prejudiced against a particular group of people will be less likely to reflect that prejudice in behavior if the people with whom he is currently associating are opposed to that particular prejudice.[8]

There are two factors that sometimes give the impression that behavior is not related to attitudes. First, time may have elapsed between the expression of an attitude and its expected behavioral component, and the attitude may no longer be held at the time of the expected behavior. Second, an expected behavior does not necessarily follow from one specific attitude. For example, you may like college football, but that does not mean you will support the relaxing of academic standards to make an all-American player eligible. If it is concluded that your behavior does not reflect your attitude, it is because a behavior was expected that doesn't necessarily follow from your attitude.[9]

Characteristics of Attitudes

Attitudes have distinctive characteristics. First, the *intensity,* or strength, of an attitude may vary, since it involves a judgment, an emotional reaction, which may be strong or mild, or varying degrees in between. The person who evaluates nuclear weapons as dangerous may hold that attitude strongly, moderately, or mildly. The intensity of the attitude may well be reflected in that person's behavior. Citizens who join in marches against the use of animals for experimental research probably have stronger attitudes against cruelty to animals than those who stay home.

A second important characteristic of attitude is its *centrality* to the whole attitude system. It may be peripheral, or it may be a vital part of the person's attitude system. If a person who has a favorable attitude toward athletics is a football coach, then that attitude will lie close to the center of his attitude system. To disturb that attitude would be to disturb many other attitudes. If the person is a businesswoman advising high school athletes, that attitude will be important to her but not as vital as to the coach. A disturbance of this attitude would probably not affect many of her attitudes. Other attitudes will play a more important role in determining her behavior.

Third, attitudes may be *salient* or nonsalient. An attitude is salient if the immediate situation causes you to be aware of it. For example, you may dislike intensely a professor on your campus. But, on most occasions that attitude is not salient and you are not consciously aware of it. If someone begins to talk about that professor, however, or you are forced to take a class from her, then the attitude becomes salient and you become aware of it.

Fourth, attitudes have *direction*—they may be positive or negative. An individual may have a favorable or unfavorable attitude toward the Strategic Defense Initiative (SDI or Star Wars). The positive attitude will cause him to "approach" SDI—for example, to support higher taxes for military spending. The negative attitude will cause him to "avoid" SDI—to oppose higher taxes for military spending.

Fifth, attitudes have differing levels of *stability*. They tend to grow more fixed the longer they are held. Since young people have held most attitudes only a short time, they are more flexible, as demonstrated in their greater willingness to accept new proposals or new concepts. Older persons, having held attitudes a longer time, are generally less willing to change from what they have been accustomed to. Accumulated evidence clearly shows this to be true for political affiliation, in which the increasing rigidity of attitudes affects behavior. Campbell found that there is a decline in the probability that a person will change his political party as he gets older.[10]

Sixth, attitudes have varying degrees of *clarity*. We define the clarity of an attitude as the width of a person's latitude of acceptance. An attitude with a high degree of clarity reduces the number of positions a person finds acceptable. An attitude with a low degree of clarity increases the number of positions a person finds acceptable.

The six characteristics of attitudes—intensity, centrality, salience, direction, stability, and clarity—are important to the oral communicator. You will need to know how these characteristics apply to the attitudes held by your listeners if you are to deal meaningfully with them and to establish credibility for your ideas. Only a careful, intensive analysis of your listeners prior to the communicative effort can provide this important information.

Formation of Attitudes

Within the past two decades a number of theories have been developed to account for and predict the formation and mutation of attitudes. None has proved wholly satisfactory. After a careful scrutiny of the various theories, Insko concluded that "none of the theories . . . is perfect or even near perfect. Subsequent research will undoubtedly make these theoretical orientations appear more and more inadequate."[11]

On the assumption that attitude formation and change are complex processes dependent on individual differences as well as on contextual factors, this book argues that attitudes may be formed or changed at any age from a variety of causes. Without getting involved in the dispute over which theory is best, it will be maintained that most attitudes stem from one or more of the following three causes: (1) one's environment, (2) one's self-interest, and (3) one's desire for cognitive consistency.

Our environment plays an important role in determining the attitudes we will have. Communication, both verbal and nonverbal, is a prime vehicle in the process. As children we begin early to adopt attitudes from those around us. Newcomb and Svehla discovered, for example, a strong correlation between the attitudes of children and their parents.[12] A 1968 national survey of high

Environment

school seniors disclosed that when both parents held the same political beliefs, 76 percent of the seniors held those same beliefs.[13] Other attitudes are acquired by imitation, either conscious or unconscious. We like the people around us and want to be like them, and one important way to be like them is to adopt their attitudes.

Some attitudes are the result of deliberate cultivation, primarily through oral communication. Religious attitudes are consciously taught in synagogues, temples, and churches. New recruits into military service undergo training to develop specific attitudes toward discipline, fighting, and being shot at. The Boy Scouts and the 4-H Clubs in the United States, the Komsomol in the Soviet Union, the pioneer youth movements in Israel, though different in a number of respects, have a common concern: they aim, in part, to challenge adolescents to give a high priority to the performance of public service roles. This includes the performance of acts of good citizenship, the discussion of social issues and consideration of the idea that, in an emergency, they should volunteer for difficult and dangerous assignments. They offer an organizational framework for young people to play approved adult-like roles, to acquire self-confidence, and to undergo a rite of passage into a more mature status. The program includes work and adventure, indoctrination and self-expression, study and instruction which the sponsoring adult-making agency views as relevant preparation for becoming a reliable person.[14]

Self-Interest

Our self-interest causes many attitudes to develop. A child learns many attitudes through being rewarded for some behaviors and punished for others. Adults also develop and hold attitudes as a result of rewards and punishments. An employee changes political affiliation to conform to that of the boss because it removes an area of discord between them and will likely mean quicker promotions and larger salary increases.

One of the reasons young people in the mid–1980s support the present system is that they perceive that the system operates in their self-interest. The more material possessions people have, the more they stand to lose by a destruction of the established order. It is no accident that most of the radical revolutionaries are among those who have "dropped out" of society, since they have few material possessions—little self-interest at stake—they have little to lose by destruction of "the system." Reference groups—those whose standards or norms influence a person's attitude—exert enormous pressure on a person's attitudes because self-interest demands conformity to group values in order to remain a member in good standing with peers.

Our desire for cognitive consistency causes many attitudes to be formed or altered. This process is known by a number of names: dissonance theory, congruency theory, balance theory.[15] It is nothing more than homeostasis (automatic efforts of the body to maintain a constant, normal state) on the cognitive level, similar in type to the homeostasis that takes place on the physiological level. Just as the body attempts to restore balance to the bodily temperature by sweating in a hot environment, so we attempt to restore balance to our attitudinal system when two or more attitudes become imbalanced. Significantly, when an imbalance occurs in a person's attitude system, it generally means that "some *new state of balance* will come about—not just any old change, at random, but a change that is orderly because it follows the principle of balance."[16]

Cognitive Consistency

For example, if a person whom we admire makes a statement praising an object we detest, we are faced with a cognitively inconsistent situation. To restore the consistency, we have a number of alternatives. We may decide we were in error in our judgment of the individual and develop a negative attitude toward that person. We may decide we were in error about the object and develop a positive attitude toward it. We may decide we were in error about our judgment of both the individual and the object and develop a less positive attitude toward the person and a less negative attitude toward the object. Another alternative is to deny the reality of the situation, which in this instance would be to deny that the person made the statement. This allows us to maintain our cognitive consistency. This alternative is not available, however, unless there is ambiguity about the reality of the situation. In 1964 many lifelong Republicans found themselves unable to support their presidential candidate because their attitudes differed from his. One of the most devastating campaign tactics of the Democrats attempted to remove any ambiguity about the candidate's attitudes by focusing on statements by Republican leaders opposing the attitudes of their party's candidate. You may effect attitude change simply by removing the ambiguities of a situation so that a listener's cognitive inconsistency becomes obvious.

Another alternative is to acknowledge that the inconsistent reality exists, but to deny its importance. For example, you may know that a person for whom you have a favorable attitude has made a positive statement about an object for which you have a negative attitude. You simply maintain that your different attitude toward that object is insignificant and unrelated to your relationship with that person. So you quit thinking about the imbalanced attitudes. You may be able to effect attitude change, therefore, by bringing cognitive inconsistency to a conscious level and setting forth its significance.

A final alternative is that the imbalance persists and no attitude change occurs. This is possible, but unlikely because it makes most people uncomfortable. In fact, the imbalance motivates most people to eliminate the factors causing discomfort.[17]

Audience Analysis

An important advantage of human communication is that you can adapt your message to the specific situation and the particular receiver. The message thus acquires greater credibility because it is more appropriate.

In order to adapt your speaking to particular listeners, you must understand not only the theoretical bases of attitudes but also what specific attitudes are held by your listeners. For this reason, a careful audience analysis must be made for each speaking occasion. *Audience analysis is the identification of those characteristics of the listeners—including their needs, wants, beliefs, attitudes, experiences, knowledge, and values—that influence the way they will probably respond to the speaker's message.*

Analyzing the Attitudes of Potential Listeners

In the ideal situation, you would analyze the attitudes of each member of an audience, developing a thorough knowledge of each person. Except in a classroom situation, you will only rarely know beforehand precisely who will be in the audience. At best, you will generally know only that the listeners will come from certain areas of the city, county, state, or nation. Even if the exact composition of an audience can be determined, it is normally impractical to meet all listeners in advance to discover their attitudes regarding the speech topic.

When the exact membership of an audience is unknown, you can still find information to draw inferences about the population from which the audience will be drawn. The validity of those inferences will determine the value of the audience analysis. Clevenger has suggested that, to make a careful analysis of an anticipated audience, the speaker may use one of two methods: a demographic analysis or a purpose-oriented analysis.[18]

Demographic Analysis

In a demographic analysis you consider important and salient characteristics of the potential hearers to enable you to derive inferences about their attitudes. You can then use these inferences to make strategic choices about subjects, materials, and methods to be used in the specific communicative situation. Some of the more common questions used in making a demographic analysis are discussed below.

Age What is the *age* of the listeners? Age affects an individual's interests, motivations, values, attitudes and other factors. In the last few years, some commentators have talked about a "generation gap" as though it were a new phenomenon. In fact, it has existed as long as human beings have, although some periods draw more attention to it than others. Some 2,500 years ago, Aristotle described the characteristics of people in their youth, middle age, and old age. His descriptions are amazingly apt even today. Note, for example, his description of youth:

Young men have strong desires, and whatever they desire they are prone to do. Of the bodily desires the one they let govern them the most is the sexual; here they lack self-control. They are shifting and unsteady in their desires, which are vehement for a time, but soon relinquished; for the longings of youth are keen rather than deep— are like sick people's fits of hunger and thirst. The young are passionate, quick to anger, and apt to give way to it. . . . They love both honor and victory more than they love money. Indeed, they care next to nothing about money, for they have not yet learned what the want of it means. . . . The young think no evil [are not cynical], but believe in human goodness, for as yet they have not seen many examples of vice. They are trustful, for as yet they have not been often deceived. . . . They live their lives for the most part in hope [anticipation], as hope is of the future and memory of the past; and for young men the future is long, the past but short. . . . They are high-minded [have lofty aspirations]; first, because they have not yet been humbled by life, nor come to know the force of circumstances; and secondly, because high-mindedness means thinking oneself fitted for great things, and this again is characteristic of the hopeful. In their actions they prefer honor to expediency; for their lives are rather lives of good impulse. . . . All their mistakes are on the side of intensity and excess. . . . They carry everything too far; they love to excess, they hate to excess—and so in all else. They think they know everything, and are positive about everything; indeed, this is why they always carry their doings too far.[19]

On the other hand, notes Aristotle, the characteristics of elderly men "for the most part are the opposite of these."[20] As he did for all subjects, Aristotle applied the principle of the golden mean to this topic of age when he said: "As for men in the prime of life, their character evidently will be intermediate between these two, exempt from the excess of either young or old."[21]

An important fact to note is that age has a significant effect on the stability of a person's attitudes. Young people's attitudes are more likely to be unstable simply because, in general, they have been held for a shorter period of time. Since older people generally will have held their attitudes for a longer time, theirs will generally be more stable.

Sex What is the *sex* of the listeners? This information will be needed primarily to determine whether your audience includes both men and women or just one sex. Just a few years ago, researchers reported that women succumbed to group pressures more than men, were less willing to express their views on public affairs than men, and were more persuasible than men; that married women tended to accept the political affiliation of their husbands when it conflicted with that of their parents, and that women were less interested than men in the economy, business, sports, and politics. These statements may have been generally valid at one time, but their validity is highly questionable today.

Currently women do most things men do. They are enrolled in all the service academies; they participate in intercollegiate athletic programs; they are active in mass communication; they seek and win political office; they hold leadership posts in education and business. Undoubtedly these role models have altered the attitudes of many women, especially young girls. In the future, the speaker will have to look more at other factors, such as the group involved, than at the sex of the listeners.

Education What is the *educational level* of the listeners? The amount of education people possess influences their interest and participation in politics and community affairs. It affects the amount of knowledge they have about current events and world affairs, their expectations for the future, the amount of confidence they have in their ability to control events, and the consistency of their stated beliefs in democratic principles with actions involving those principles. It affects tolerance for others in the general population and influences the stability, intensity, and consistency of attitudes. People's educational level will influence whether changes in attitude will come primarily because of new information, or whether group pressures and authoritative opinions will be the major factors. Critical thinking ability and vocabulary level are affected by educational level. Finally, educational level influences people's awareness of the political system, their detachment from it, the degree of alienation resulting from policies of the system, and their place in it.

Political philosophy What is the *political philosophy* or ideology of the listeners? Does this refer to the political party the listeners belong to? Not at all! There are in both major political parties individuals with differing political philosophies. Two political observers concluded: "Conservatives are only somewhat more likely to be Republican than Democrat, and Democrats are not much more likely to be liberal than conservative."[22] Almost equal numbers of independents are liberal, conservative, and moderate. The political philosophy or ideology of an individual affects attitudes toward government spending, restrictions on business, national defense, individual freedom, busing to achieve integration, public work programs, abortion on demand, and a more relaxed relationship with Communist nations.

Audience homogeneity How *homogeneous* are the listeners? If the people are greatly similar, it will be easier to find speech content that is acceptable to the majority. If all the listeners are farmers, they will be a rather homogeneous group. If half are farmers and half are urbanites, there will be considerable heterogeneity. If a third are farmers, a third urbanites, and a third suburbanites, there will be a great deal of heterogeneity. In a college speech course, the classroom audience to which you speak is relatively homogeneous. The students are all about the same age, have essentially the same level of education, come from the same general geographical area, and are generally motivated to achieve. Although a classroom audience certainly has heterogeneous features, the number of homogeneous factors provides ample areas in which you can adapt the message.

Cultural interests What are the *cultural interests* of the listeners? Is this related to the educational level? In many ways it is; in others, it is not. People in two areas with the same general educational level can have entirely different cultural interests. Are the people of the area interested in the arts—Is there a symphony orchestra in the area? A museum of fine arts? An art gallery? Or are the people of the area strongly interested in sports—Are there professional teams in various sports? A stock car racetrack?

Are there a number of bookstores in the area, indicating that the people read frequently? What kind of books sell best in the area? What kind of magazines do the people read: *Reader's Digest, Harper's, Atlantic, People, The Wilson Quarterly, Sport?*

Are the people of the area widely traveled, or do few travel outside the area? Are they familiar with cultural activities in other areas, or are they predominantly provincial in their knowledge and interests?

All these aspects of cultural interests will affect the attitudes of the people who might be in an audience.

Ethnic background What is the *ethnicity* of the listeners? Until recently it was considered un-American by some to have a sense of cultural identity. The United States was supposed to be the great "melting pot," which took in immigrants and produced Americans. In the last few years, however, it has become acceptable and popular to recognize that various ethnic groups do in fact exist and retain particular cultural traits.

There are many different ethnic groups in the United States, including Arab, Chinese, French, German, Greek, Scandinavian, Japanese, Turkish, Vietnamese, and Indian (or, as some would say, "Native Americans"). The six major ethnic groups now identified in the United States are (1) black Americans, who are about 11 percent of the population; (2) Hispanic Americans (including Cubans, Mexicans, and Puerto Ricans), who make up about 5 percent; (3) Jewish-Americans, who constitute approximately 2.9 percent; (4) Irish Americans, who amount to about 6.5 percent; (5) Slavic-Americans who make up about 2.5 percent; and (6) Italian Americans, who constitute about 3.5 percent.[23] The ethnicity of individuals influences their political philosophy, political party affiliation, voting habits, occupation, economic status, assimilation into the general population, and attitude toward other American groups.

Economic status   What is the *economic status* of the listeners? Economic level has a definite impact on the programs and policies in which a person is interested. Attitudes toward the government, political philosophy, and the like are affected. Someone who is just eking out a subsistence level of existence is not interested in the fluctuations of the stock market. A low-income person's attitudes toward welfare programs are different from those of a high-income individual. Economic level affects attitudes toward labor unions, business, religion. People with lower incomes tend to be less motivated and feel more alienated and powerless than those with higher incomes. Whether these psychological feelings are a cause or an effect of poverty is not entirely clear, but they are a factor with which you must deal.

Religion   What is the *religious affiliation* of the hearers? Protestants, Catholics, and Jews have strikingly different attitudes toward government, divorce, the Middle East, abortion, and other public issues. Do all or most of the members of the audience hold the same religious beliefs? How strong or intense are their religious commitments? You must determine whether there are members of the audience who hold no religious beliefs. Unless you have this information, you may make comments or include data that will offend some or most of your audience.

Group interest   Is there a common *group interest?* Some groups are held together by a common bond even though in many other respects the members are dissimilar. A group such as the Sierra Club, for example, may be made up of homemakers, students, doctors, lawyers, businesspersons, and laborers who have a multiplicity of attitudes about many subjects. As members of the Sierra Club, however, they all have a strong interest in, and positive attitudes toward, the conservation of natural resources. This will influence their reaction to any topic, idea, or proposal that affects the use of natural resources.

Audience occupations   What is the *occupation* of the listeners? White-collar workers have different attitudes and interests from blue-collar workers. Educators do not hold the same attitudes as lawyers. Businesspeople differ from

farmers. Truck drivers' attitudes and interests differ from those of police officers. People who are employed may have different concerns from those who are full-time students. An argument that might be highly persuasive with one of these occupational groups might be self-defeating with another group. An idea in a speech may be better comprehended and accepted if it is related to some aspect of the listeners' occupations.

Residence What is the *place of residence* of the listeners? Do they reside in the city, in suburban areas, or on farms? Do they live in the south, the northeast, the middle west, or the far west? Each of these different areas of residence affects a person's attitudes and interests. A farmer in the south and one in the middle west will have a number of attitudes in common because of their occupation. But a farmer in the middle west will probably have little knowledge of or interest in growing cotton and tobacco, whereas a farmer in the south will have little interest in or knowledge of growing wheat. A farmer and a city dweller in the south will have a number of attitudes and interests in common because they both live in the south. But they will also have a number of differences because of the place where they live within that region.

Understanding and Adapting to Listeners

Listener knowledge What *knowledge* do listeners have about the topic to be discussed? The amount of information possessed by the listener, both in general and on the speech topic, will determine the intellectual level at which you can effectively function. A speech on mathematics given to a group of high school students will be geared to a much lower level than one given to a group of Ph.D.s in mathematics.

Obviously, there can be interrelationships or overlapping of these various demographic factors. Sometimes one demographic trait will cancel out another. To seek the answers to all these questions about any one audience will provide much duplicative data. Nevertheless, it is better to have several pieces of information that duplicate one another than to be missing a vital bit of data that might make the difference between success and failure as a speaker. The more thorough the demographic analysis, the more complete your information will be and, consequently, the more accurate the inferences you make about the audience.

Purpose-Oriented Analysis

As Clevenger points out, this method of audience analysis begins from a totally different perspective. Instead of seeking answers to a number of questions about various traits of listeners, the purpose-oriented analysis asks the question: *What about my audience is important to the purpose of my speech?* Purpose-oriented analysis can be viewed as an extension or specific application of demographic analysis that focuses on the interactive effects of a particular speech topic and relevant attitudes of a particular group of receivers. Rather than attempting to understand listeners in general, purpose-oriented analysis attempts to assess the receivers' potential reactions to a particular speech topic and speaking purpose or goal. If you are going to speak on tax reform, for example, you would want to ask a number of questions related to your listeners and taxes. What is the income level of the listeners? What is their attitude toward taxes? What is their attitude toward government? How much do they know about present income tax laws? What is their interpretation of the term *tax reform?* What is their concept of the purpose of income taxes—to pay for government or to redistribute wealth? The answers to these and other such questions will tell you where to begin development of the topic and how best to present it.

Listeners' motivations An important question you must ask is *How does my purpose in this speech relate to the motivations of my listeners?* A quick review of Maslow's hierarchy of needs as motivating factors may help reveal the relevance of this question. Maslow sets forth five different levels of needs: (1) physiological needs—hunger, thirst, sex; (2) safety needs—security, stability, protection, freedom from fear; (3) belongingness and love needs—friends, sweetheart, wife, children; (4) esteem needs—strength, achievement, adequacy, competence, reputation, status, fame, recognition; (5) self-actualization need—necessity to be what one can be. Maslow observes that people are not necessarily motivated by only one of these needs; there can be a multiple-need motivation of behavior.[24] In Maslow's scheme, human needs and motivations are thought to be arranged in a hierarchical order.

That is, listeners will not generally be influenced by appeals to esteem or self-actualization unless other more basic drives such as physiological or safety needs are already satisfied. Whether listeners are motivated by single or by multiple needs, you must consider the speech purpose in relation to their motivations.

Listeners' emotions Another important question to ask is *How does my purpose in this speech relate to the emotions of the listeners?* One psychologist has classified emotions into four categories: (1) goal-related emotions—joy, anger, grief, and fear; (2) emotions related to sensory stimulation—pain, pleasure, disgust, revulsion, and delight; (3) emotions related to the self-concept—shame, guilt, pride, satisfaction, and self-abasement; (4) emotions directed toward other people—love, hate, resentment, affection, and jealousy.[25] Obviously, these categories are not mutually exclusive; anger and fear, for example, may be directed at other people. Nevertheless, the categories are reasonable and make it easier to understand the origin of emotions. To be well-prepared, you must know whether your purpose will allay or aggravate any of these emotions.

The occasion Finally, you will want to answer the question *How does the purpose of my speech relate to the occasion?* The listeners' states of mind are affected by the occasion and the time. If the occasion is a festive one, it will certainly affect the attitudes and behavior of the listeners. If the audience is convening to commemorate Lincoln's birthday, the hearers will expect you to relate the speech to that event. If a speech is scheduled for midmorning, hearers generally will be alert and attentive. Consequently, it will be easier to get them to respond behaviorally, if that is the purpose. In addition, listeners will be able to follow carefully constructed and complex chains of reasoning more easily than at other times. After a banquet, on the other hand, listeners will be less alert because of the physiological processes taking place; they will have more difficulty attending to closely reasoned arguments than would the morning audience. You need to understand, then, all the ways in which the speech purpose and the occasion may or may not be related.

The purpose-oriented analysis continues throughout the development of the speech. For every idea and piece of supporting material that is considered, you must ask the question: *What* about my audience is important to my purpose in using this?

The ability to obtain data about a specific group of listeners is affected by two main factors: (1) The greater the geographical area from which the listeners are drawn, the more difficult it is to obtain data. (2) The more unfamiliar you are with the area in which the speech is to be given, the more difficult it is to accumulate data.

With these difficulties in obtaining data in mind, it should be understood that the following sources are not always available to you. Nevertheless, make use of whatever sources you can to learn as much as possible about potential listeners.

Obtaining Data about Listeners' Attitudes

Mass Media

One of the most important mass media sources of general information is the newspaper(s) of the area in which the speech will be given. The front page provides data about major events. The editorial page gives interpretations of major events and issues, and generally, by the way the editorials are written, reveals whether the writer is in accord with or in opposition to majority opinion. The business section and the classified section give important clues about the economic activity of the community, and the entertainment section tells a great deal about its cultural level. Most newspapers also include a "Letters to the Editor" section, which often can offer important clues to public opinion. This section must be used cautiously, however, as the letters can also be misleading. Sometimes special interest groups organize letter-writing campaigns, so that what looks like a spontaneous outpouring of community sentiment is in fact a small, well-organized effort. Another problem is that every community produces habitual letter writers whose attitudes are not typical of the community. Newspapers themselves create a potential booby trap for anyone trying to infer community attitudes from letters to the editor. While many newspapers print letters for each position on an issue according to the ratio of letters received, other newspapers follow what they consider an evenhanded policy and print an equal number of letters for each position, regardless of the number they receive. Used with care, however, newspapers are an important and valuable source of information about a community and its people. Newspapers provide greater detail and in-depth coverage than any other mass media source.

If you are going into a new community to speak, it is wise to order a subscription to a local newspaper approximately a month before the speech. This will inform you of what is happening in the area and allow you to add "local color" to your speech by referring to pertinent events.

Radio and television are also important mass media sources of information. Local news programs offer insight into the interests and problems of an area. Local talk shows give a hint of the attitudes of the region.

Find out about the nature of the organization to which you are to speak. If it has a publication, read some copies of it to learn what goals and values the members cherish. Determine the issues the organization is concerned about. Try to discover the nature of the people who belong to the group. If possible, attend a meeting to get a feel for the group's interests and attitudes.

The Organization

Much can be learned through conversations with local people who are familiar with people and events in the area. If you live in the area in which the speech is to be given, you will have many opportunities to talk with local people. Business leaders, educators, and ministers, for example, can give vital insight into prevalent attitudes. If you are speaking in an area other than your home community, do not overlook the most important source of information: the person or committee that invites you to speak. Interview them in great depth. Using both demographic and purpose-oriented analyses, devise as many questions as you possibly can to learn as much as they can tell you. If you can talk to others who have spoken to the group, they may be able to provide important insights into the audience's attitudes and beliefs. Finally, do not forget taxi drivers; most have a wealth of information.

Conversations

Scientific methods for ascertaining public opinion were first utilized by George Gallup. Using those procedures, he has amassed an amazing record of accuracy in predicting the results of political campaigns since 1936.[26] One of the major reasons for the success of both the Gallup and Roper organizations in polling public opinion is that neither has ever accepted a job as pollster for an organization or political candidate. They take polls on public issues and sell the results to whatever person or agency is interested. Some pollsters, on the other hand, have assisted or worked for particular groups or specific political candidates. The danger in this practice is that the pollster's conscious or unconscious desire to please the employer may bias obtained results or conclusions.

Public Opinion Polls

Caution must be observed in using polls. Polls provide valid results only if the questions are carefully designed, the respondents are randomly chosen, and care taken to avoid nonverbal cues that may slant carefully designed questions.

Important information can be gleaned from well-conducted polls. Politicians and advertisers frequently use polls to plan their campaigns. Analysis of their target group by polls enables them to make vital decisions.

Two important problems confront many speakers who want to use polls to aid in obtaining information about an audience: (1) there may not be a poll available on the specific issue for the particular group; and (2) the cost of conducting a valid poll may be prohibitive.

Some important sources of polls are the following: (1) *Public Opinion Quarterly,* a periodical which publishes polls from various sources; (2) *The Gallup Report,* which contains results of Gallup polls; (3) *Public Affairs Information Service,* which indexes various polls under the heading "Public Opinion Polls"; (4) *Gallup International Public Opinion Polls, France, 1937–1975;* (5) *Gallup International Public Opinion Polls, United Kingdom, 1937–1975.*

Audience Adaptation

Audience adaptation may be defined as the actions taken as a result of audience analysis, in order to develop maximum credibility. The practice of adapting messages to specific hearers has long been an important part of human communication. Does this mean that you should say what you think the receivers want to hear, regardless of your own beliefs and convictions? Critics point out that many leaders in all fields wait for the most recent public opinion poll to tell them what a majority of people think, then rush out to advocate those policies. Do not compromise your principles by making statements you do not believe. In fact, to do so would ultimately destroy your credibility. Effective audience adaptation does not involve a compromise of principles. It does require a concern for listeners and a sensitivity to their needs, wants, and values.

After investigating an issue and collecting and analyzing all available evidence (including public opinion), you should form whatever conclusions are valid, *regardless of public opinion.* In deciding what ideas to use and the order in which to present them, you should be sensitive to the beliefs, attitudes, interests, mores, wants, values, and desires of an audience. Thus, you use all the information obtained from audience analysis to help in preparing and presenting the most effective message for the particular receiver.

Cast your ideas in the form most acceptable to the particular persons you are addressing. Audience adaptation should occur at three times: *before* the speech, when audience analysis helps you select the subject and prepare the message in certain ways; *during* the speech, as you interpret audience feedback and adjust your presentation accordingly; and *after* the speech, when—with a view toward future speechmaking—you revise and change the speech on the basis of all available final impressions of successes and mistakes.

Figure 7.1
Continuum of audience attitude.

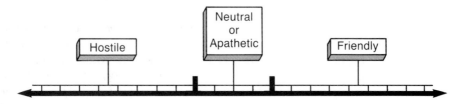

Adaptation to the audience begins immediately after the commitment to speak has been made.

Adaptation before the Speech

The subject chosen for a speech should be one that will be appropriate to the speaker, the occasion, and the audience. In the 1976 presidential campaign, Jimmy Carter displayed consummate skill in speaking to various audiences. His subjects were matched with great "care to the particular audience—Navy talk in Norfolk, parochial school aid in Pittsburgh, Arab boycotts to B'nai B'rith."[27]

Selection of Subject

Once the subject has been chosen, a specific purpose can be determined and adapted to the particular listeners. One of the first things you will need to know is the attitude of your listeners toward the particular topic you are considering. Members of an audience may be generally classified as hostile, neutral or apathetic, or friendly toward your subject. Obviously, there are degrees within each of these categories, so we may range the members along a continuum similar to that in figure 7.1.

You may be considering a speech expressing your belief that subsidized intercollegiate athletics should be abolished. On your campus, however, you know there is overwhelming support for subsidized athletics. Moreover, research indicates that the members of your speech class reflect the campus opinion. If you give a speech advocating the abandonment of a subsidized athletic program, it will obviously be received with considerable hostility. Instead of advocating abolishment of subsidized athletics, therefore, you may change your topic to the cost of a subsidized intercollegiate athletic program. In developing this topic, you would refrain from criticizing a subsidized program and focus on factual data that would prevent personalities or attitudes—yours or your listeners'—from becoming involved. You would use as much evidence as you could from sources respected by your listeners. In this way, you identify a problem for your listeners, but do not offer a solution. This approach would be consistent with research findings that have revealed that as the opposition of an audience increases, the effective speaker uses "fewer solution arguments" and "more problem arguments."[28]

Supporting Materials Once the specific topic has been chosen, you can select particular supporting ideas or arguments on the basis of their compatibility with the specific listeners. For example, a controversy may be raging in your area about where to locate a new highway. In speaking in favor of a particular route to a group such as the Sierra Club, focus the speech on the fact that the route you favor would disturb the natural environment less than others. On the other hand, if the hearers are members of an economics club, focus on the fact that the proposed route would be less costly.

The listeners' attitudes and knowledge can help you shape the supporting evidence used in the speech. Select testimony from experts whom the listeners respect and admire. If you are talking to a group of union members about the need for the United States to maintain a strong defense, cite someone like George Meany, the late president of the AFL-CIO. Choose examples relevant to the audience's interests, knowledge, and experience. If you are talking to a group of business leaders about the need for honesty in everyday affairs, use illustrations (detailed examples) or specific instances (undetailed examples) of people in business who have practiced the kind of honesty you are talking about. Develop statistics showing the percentage of businesspeople who have been identified as being dishonest. Make comparisons with the number of dishonest people in other occupational groups. Use restatement of key points or important information to make sure the listeners remember that supporting material.

Organization Frequently, you can make a message more acceptable to listeners by adapting the order of the ideas to their predispositions. When addressing a hostile audience, it is advisable to employ an *indirect* organizational pattern, that is, begin with ideas and arguments based on values and premises that the speaker and listeners share before introducing potentially objectionable issues.

Your purpose may be to argue for an increase in defense spending. The audience, however, may be hostile to defense spending. In this instance, you may want to prepare them by beginning with a discussion of the need for a balance of power between the Communist bloc of nations and the rest of the world. Next, you may discuss the spending of the Communist bloc to show that the balance of power is being tilted away from the non-Communist bloc. Finally, you can argue that world peace will be jeopardized unless the United States increases its defense spending sufficiently to maintain a balance of power. The hostility of the listeners toward increased defense spending may then be lessened enough to permit them to consider in a more unbiased way your arguments for it.

To a friendly audience, you should adopt a more *direct* organizational plan and begin with the argument that world peace will be jeopardized unless the United States increases its defense spending sufficiently to maintain a balance of power. There will probably be no need to discuss the need for a balance of power between the Communist and non-Communist nations. The fact that the listeners are favorable toward defense spending indicates that they have probably already accepted that argument.

Adaptation during the speech is just as important as that prior to the speech. Sometimes it is more so.

Feedback begins as soon as you appear in front of the audience. Perceive it and adapt to it.

Certain nonverbal cues may indicate that the listeners are having difficulty understanding your ideas. A puzzled expression on the faces of some listeners may denote a need for clarification of what you mean. You may offer another example, explain more fully an example that has been used, define a technical term, use new vocabulary, or shift to a different pattern of organization.

Facial expression, eye contact, and bodily action provide nonverbal cues about the audience's acceptance or rejection of the ideas. If you perceive rejection, you should adapt by offering additional supporting material that will make it easier for the listeners to agree with your position. In some instances opposition to your ideas may be so strong that the audience provides verbal cues. Sometimes you can cope with this by lowering the volume of your voice until it becomes difficult for the listeners to hear you. Wendell Phillips, the great antislavery agitator, used this technique effectively on one occasion.

Adaptation during the Speech

Verbal and Nonverbal Cues from Listeners

Often called before howling mobs, who had come to the lecture-room to prevent him from being heard, and who would shout and sing to drown his voice, he never failed to subdue them in a short time. . . . One illustration of his power and tact occurred in Boston. The majority of the audience was hostile. They yelled and sang and completely drowned his voice. The reporters were seated in a row just under the platform, in the place where the orchestra play in an ordinary theatre. Phillips made no attempt to address the howling audience, but bent over and seemed to be speaking in a low tone to the reporters. By and by the curiosity of the howling audience was excited; they ceased to clamor and tried to hear what he was saying to the reporters. Phillips looked at them and said quietly:

"Go on, gentlemen, go on. I do not need your ears. Through these pencils I speak to thirty millions of people."

Not a voice was raised again. The mob had found its master and stayed whipped until he sat down.[29]

You should note any feedback that indicates the attention of the listeners is lagging. Adaptation can regain their attention. Make sure you are talking with them, not at them. Use more nonverbal behavior—more physical action, more varied vocal behavior. It may be necessary to move closer to the listeners, even to the point of moving among them. Sometimes an unmalicious interruption may direct attention away from the speaker. A witty, caustic, ironic, or similar comment may sometimes be just the thing to return attention to the speaker. A noted Civil War historian visiting a southern university was addressing a class of students on the defeat of the southern forces. One student suddenly called out: "I am so proud of the southern effort that I keep the Confederate flag with me." He then held up his foot to reveal his socks into which had been woven a Confederate flag. Without a moment's hesitation, the lecturer replied: "That just goes to prove my point, that ultimately the Confederate flag went down to 'de' feet." The lecturer's quick retort mastered the brief interruption and held the attention of his hearers so that he had no difficulty in continuing his lecture. Not everyone has such a quick wit, but if you have it, use it.

Changes in the Occasion

Sometimes changes in the occasion demand that you adapt in some way. Several years ago, as the commencement exercises began in an outdoor amphitheater on a college campus, lightning began to play on the horizon, the distant rumble of thunder could be heard, and the wind began to blow. The president of the college, analyzing the situation and adapting to the changed conditions, decided to reverse the order of events and award the diplomas before the commencement address was given. By the time the main speaker was introduced, lightning could be seen clearly overhead, thunder claps had become distinct, and the wind smelled of fresh rain. The speaker announced that he was as afraid of lightning as anyone and that if it got closer he would cut his speech short and run for cover with everyone else. With that he plunged into his prepared manuscript, and one listener whispered to another: "That means we're here for the duration." As the impending storm drew nearer, the members of the audience became increasingly apprehensive and began to grow restless and noisy. An almost steady line of people moved from their seats to the exits and hastily departed. Despite these changed conditions and the obvious inattention of the listeners, the speaker read doggedly through page after page of his manuscript until he literally reached the last word on the last page. This was a situation that cried out for the speaker to present quickly the main points of his address, develop each briefly, summarize, and sit down. The listeners would then have departed with admiration and affection for the speaker because of his ability to adapt to the changed conditions of the situation and his willingness to be sensitive to the fears and concerns of others. As it was, those who remained until the end were caught in a downpour on the way to their cars. They left with only negative attitudes toward the speaker.

Sometimes the room may become overheated during the speech. You may need to ask someone to open some windows or turn down the thermostat. A sudden loud noise in the vicinity of the speech may require a comment or an explanation from you.

Adaptation after the Speech

Adaptation does not end with the speech; it is a continuing process. Why would you want to adapt *after* giving a speech? Because, even though you may not give the same speech twice, you frequently speak on the same topic a number of times. Consequently, you want to know what you can do differently the next time to make a speech on that subject more effective. In addition, you will want to improve your speech-making ability in general. Several sources of feedback provide information to aid in better adapting a speech to the next audience.

Analyze Your Own Perceptions

The most obvious source of feedback is your own perceptions of what did and did not work as expected. Knowing that something did not work is not sufficient, however. After the speech, try to find out why it did not work. Consider all possibilities and try to deduce as accurately as possible the cause or causes for the success or failure of any part of the speech.

Consult Other People

Listen to the comments of family and friends. They can provide constructive criticism on the basis of their observations and what they heard others saying. If you can, find out the reactions of opponents of your position. Their comments may not be unbiased, but they cannot be ignored. Consideration of the valid ones can yield useful insights and possibly valuable results for future speaking situations.

Other students and the instructor are important sources of feedback after a classroom speech. Listen to the comments of fellow students, even those that hurt. What do they say about the subject of your speech, the organization, the supporting materials used to develop the subject, the language, the nonverbal presentation? Do not take the criticism personally and resolve not to be upset by negative comments, even those that seem to be maliciously motivated. In a friendly way, ask the critic what you could have done to eliminate the perceived faults.

If your instructor fills out a rating sheet for each speech, analyze it. In which areas did you get your highest ratings, in which the lowest? For your next speech, remember to continue doing what you did in the area where you got your highest rating. If the rating can be improved, use the instructor's comments as a basis for changes. Analyze the instructor's comments to find ways of improving the area of lowest rating. Concentrate on making improvements in that area. After each speech, compare your rating with that of previous speeches. In that way, you can see where your strengths are, where your weaknesses are, and where your possibilities for improvement are.

Consider Media Reactions

A third source of feedback after the speech may be the comments and criticisms of reporters in some of the mass media. Since the efforts of most students and many other speakers do not merit attention from the media, this is not generally a source of feedback. If such feedback is available, however, you certainly must evaluate whatever appraisal is made.

Summary

You must have an understanding of attitudes to take full advantage of the available means of persuasion in building an aura of credibility. An attitude is defined as a tendency to respond favorably or unfavorably to a class of objects or a concept.

An attitude is composed of three ingredients: the *cognitive,* consisting of the perceptions, thoughts, and beliefs a person has about a particular class of objects or concepts; the *affective,* consisting of the feelings an individual has about a particular object or concept; and the *behavioral,* consisting of the behavior of an individual with respect to a class of objects or concept because of the attitude.

Six characteristics of attitudes seem apparent. An attitude may be weak or strong; it may be central or peripheral to the individual's attitude system; it may be salient or nonsalient; it may be positive or negative; it may be stable or unstable, and it may have a high or low degree of clarity.

Although a number of theories attempt to account for the formation and change of attitudes, you would be wise to take the position that such development can be attributed to one or more of three causes: an individual's (1) environment, (2) self-interest, (3) desire for cognitive consistency.

Using either a demographic analysis or a purpose-oriented analysis, analyze an audience in order to identify those characteristics of the listeners that influence their probable response to your message.

The media, conversations with other people, the organization to be addressed, and public opinion polls are four important sources of information about the attitudes of potential listeners.

The information obtained from the audience analysis is used to prepare and present the most effective message for the particular receiver. An on-going process, audience adaptation occurs before, during, and after the speech.

Exercises

1. You are planning a speech to a group of listeners who are opposed to your point of view. What can you do to make your position credible to them?
2. Describe one of your classmate's attitudes in terms of the characteristics of an attitude discussed in this chapter.
3. Name one of your classmate's attitudes that you must consider in the next speech you give. In what ways will that attitude determine what you say? What you do not say? How can you use that attitude to improve your credibility?
4. Select one of your attitudes and describe in detail how you think it was formed.
5. Prepare a written description of the demographic characteristics of your classroom audience.
6. Attend a lecture on campus. Write a description of the ways in which the speaker adapted and failed to adapt to the audience.

Notes

1. L. Berkowitz, *A Survey of Social Psychology,* 2d ed. (New York: Holt, Rinehart and Winston, 1980), p. 275. Reprinted by permission of Holt, Rinehart and Winston, CBS College Publishing.
2. C. W. Sherif, M. Sherif, and R. E. Nebergall, *Attitude and Atittude Change* (Philadelphia: W. B. Saunders Co., 1965), p. 4.
3. J. B. Cooper, "Emotion in Prejudice," *Science* 130 (1959):314–18.
4. H. W. Dickson and E. McGinnies, "Affectivity in the Arousal of Attitudes as Measured by Galvanic Skin Response," *American Journal of Psychology* 79 (1966):584–89.
5. E. McGinnies, *Social Behavior: A Functional Analysis* (Boston: Houghton Mifflin Co., 1970), p. 302.
6. M. P. Zanna, J. M. Olson, and R. H. Fazio, "Self-Perception and Attitude-Behavior Consistency," *Personality and Social Psychology Bulletin* 7 (1981):252–56.
7. R. H. Fazio and M. P. Zanna, "Direct Experience and Attitude-Behavior Consistency," in *Advances in Experimental Social Psychology,* ed. L. Berkowitz, vol. 14 (New York: Academic Press, 1981), pp. 163–65.
8. D. W. Rajecki, *Attitudes: Themes and Advances* (Sunderland, Mass.: Sinauer Associates, Inc., 1982), p. 77.
9. Ibid.
10. A. Campbell, P. E. Converse, W. E. Miller, and D. E. Stokes, *The American Voter* (New York: John Wiley & Sons, 1960), pp. 160–67.
11. C. A. Insko, *Theories of Attitude Change* (New York: Appleton-Century-Crofts, 1967), p. 348.
12. T. M. Newcomb and G. Svehla, "Intra-family Relationships in Attitude," *Sociometry* 1 (1937):180–205. The correlation coefficients were war, .44; communism, .56; religion, .63.

13. M. K. Jennings and R. G. Niemi, "The Transmission of Political Values from Parent to Child," *American Political Science Review* 62 (1968):169–84.

14. J. W. Eaton, *Influencing the Youth Culture* (Beverly Hills, Calif.: Sage Publications, 1970), pp. 21–22.

15. For a discussion, analysis, and evaluation of the various cognitive consistency theories, see Insko, *Theories of Attitude Change.*

16. T. M. Newcomb, R. H. Turner, and P. E. Converse, *Social Psychology* (New York: Holt, Rinehart & Winston, 1965), p. 130.

17. Ibid., p. 131.

18. T. Clevenger, Jr., *Audience Analysis* (Indianapolis: Bobbs-Merrill Co., 1966), pp. 43–48.

19. Lane Cooper, trans., *The Rhetoric of Aristotle* (New York: D. Appleton-Century Co., 1932), pp. 132–34.

20. Ibid., p. 134.

21. Ibid., p. 136.

22. W. H. Flanigan and N. H. Zingle, *Political Behavior of the American Electorate* (Boston: Allyn and Bacon, 1975), pp. 114–15.

23. M. R. Levy and M. S. Kramer, *The Ethnic Factor* (New York: Simon & Schuster, 1972).

24. A. H. Maslow, *Motivation and Personality* (New York: Harper & Row, Publishers, 1970), pp. 35–58, 149–80.

25. R. B. Levy, *You and Your Behavior* (Boston: Holbrook Press, 1975), p. 189.

26. G. Gallup, *The Sophisticated Poll Watcher's Guide* (Ephrata, Pa.: Science Press, 1972), p. 215.

27. D. S. Broder, "Computer Telling Carter What to Say," *Opelika-Auburn News,* September 15, 1976. Used by permission.

28. M. D. Hazen and S. B. Kiesler, "Communication Strategies Affected by Audience Opposition, Feedback and Persuasibility," *Speech Monographs* 42 (1975):59.

29. Major J. B. Pond, *Eccentricities of Genius* (New York: G. W. Dillingham Company, 1900), pp. 7–8.

— 8 —

SELECTING THE SUBJECT AND THE PURPOSE

You will be tempted to say, as other students have, "Professor, if you'll just assign me a topic for my speech assignment, it'll give me more time to work on this speech, and I'll be happy to speak on whatever you tell me to." Your professor will have to decline your request because no person—no matter how informed about speech communication principles—can tell another person what topic to speak on. Your professor can assist in selecting a subject, though, if you simply ask some pertinent questions. As these questions are answered, you will become aware of potential subjects and can then select one.

In this chapter you will learn what questions to ask so that you do not burden your professor with helping you make that decision. Moreover, after you finish this course, you will no longer have ready access to help from your professor.

Sometimes the topic for a speech is supplied by the group inviting the speaker. They wish to hear that person because he has some information or a particular point of view. In other instances, a speaker is invited because of her position or renown as a speaker, but no natural subject suggests itself. Faced with this situation, some speakers simply reach into their mind and pull out a subject, with little or no thought about its appropriateness for the particular speaking engagement. In some instances such methods result in successful speeches, but the odds of selecting an effective subject are enhanced if the selection process is more methodical.

In preparing any speech, carefully select the subject, determine the general purpose, and choose the specific purpose.

The Speech Subject

Generally, the first opportunity to take positive action to establish your credibility occurs when you select a subject for your speech. That choice determines whether you develop credibility at the outset or labor through the speech with the handicap of an inappropriate subject. Making an effective choice of subject requires considering three factors: (1) the speaker, (2) the occasion, and (3) the audience.

The Speaker

Begin by considering yourself. The answers to a series of questions will be helpful in selecting an appropriate subject.

What are you interested in? The things you are interested in are those things you like to do, such as playing tennis, backpacking, making handmade jewelry, visiting Civil War battlefields, working with Boy Scouts. Make a list of these interests. By drawing on these topics, you will make speaking more fun. Not only is it more enjoyable to talk about topics in which you are interested, but you are then presenting genuine feelings and convictions. That is what listeners are interested in—your attitudes, your perceptions, your point of view. In addition, the enthusiasm you feel when discussing a topic you are concerned about is conveyed to the listeners who, in turn, become more interested in the speech.

What experiences have you had? There are two kinds of experience: actual and vicarious. Actual experience refers to things you have done. Vicarious experience is that which you obtain indirectly, as through reading a book, seeing a movie, hearing a speech. Vicarious experience can be enjoyable, but actual experience provides knowledge and insights not found in a book or any other source. Take the list you prepared of the things you are interested in and underscore those on which you have had actual experience. These will be the best subjects on which you can speak.

Speaking from personal experience has several advantages. You can express the material in your own words, and you do not have to worry about trying to interpret the meaning of another person's statement. The material has a freshness because the listeners will not have heard it before, at least not from your point of view. Almost any subject can be made interesting if you draw materials from your own experiences.

What knowledge do you have? Unfortunately, some speakers ask only the first two questions and do not ask this one. But interest and experience are not enough without knowledge. William Norwood Brigance, an outstanding speech professor for many years, asserted that a speaker "must earn the right to give every speech."[1] What he meant was that you have a responsibility to learn everything you can about any subject on which you plan to give a speech. It is a waste of the listeners' time for you to talk on a subject about which you know so little you are unable to offer anything useful or new. For that reason, interest and experience are not enough. For example, you may have become a skydiver only recently. You have much interest in your new hobby and some brief experience, but you simply haven't had time to acquire much information. This is not yet a topic for a speech. It will be in time, so be patient. Don't think these last remarks mean that you must know everything or nearly everything about a topic in order to use it in a speech.

Research is essential to provide knowledge for your speech. When you do not yet know enough to speak, or the specific topic chosen covers an aspect of the subject about which you know relatively little, or the subject is one on which new information is currently being developed, research is necessary. Before speaking on a subject, you should be able to put your current information or any new information into perspective.

In considering your knowledge, do not forget the other college courses you have had or are taking. A topic you have studied and discussed in sociology or psychology, for example, may be *developed* into a subject for a speech assignment. A term paper in political science may be *transformed* into a speech. Notice that in each of these examples the emphasis is on changing whatever information you possess into appropriate form for a speech. A term paper is not a speech; neither is an essay. You must make the necessary changes and additions to produce a speech. You will also probably have to do additional research.

Do not overlook groups or organizations to which you belong. You may be a member of the Pershing Rifles, the marching band, the foreign relations club, or some other group. Few nonmembers know much about any of these groups. A speech about some phase of such a group may not only be interesting and informative, it may also create potential new members.

What does your audience know about you? What expectations will they have? They may anticipate that you will speak on a certain subject. If you do not, they may be disappointed. On some occasions, therefore, your range of choices will be severely limited because the listeners are aware of your interests and knowledge. Consequently, they desire and expect you to speak on a subject within your known expertise. In most such instances, you will not want to disappoint your audience. If your audience knows that you are an expert on China and have visited there, they will probably expect you to speak on some aspect of China. Give them what they want.

Occasionally, however, you can delightfully surprise your listeners by speaking on an unexpected subject. In one college speech class, for example, a tall, burly basketball player created instant attention for his first speech when he began: "I know that athletes are supposed to be interested only in athletics. Since I am a member of the basketball team, you probably expect me to talk about some phase of the game. I won't deny that basketball is one of the two major interests that I have. I have great love for two activities: basketball and art. And art is what I want to talk to you about this morning."

The Occasion

A second factor you must take into consideration in selecting a subject is the occasion. People are not the same in all places; they are not even the same at different times in the same place. Unless you consider the occasion in selecting a subject, you minimize your chances of communicating effectively. The answers to the following five questions will help in choosing a subject appropriate to the specific occasion.

What is the nature of the occasion? Put another way, *why* are these people coming together on this day, at this time, in this place, to hear me speak? You may discover, for example, that there is nothing special about the occasion. The listeners may be convening simply because this is a regular meeting of their service club—Kiwanis, Lions, Rotary—and they always meet at the same time and place. And except for a few meetings when special activities occur, they always have a different speaker, one of whom is you. In other instances, the audience may be gathering for a special occasion. It may be Veterans Day or Martin Luther King's birthday. You may have been invited to speak to the local Democrats because it is Thomas Jefferson's birthday or the local Republicans because it is Abraham Lincoln's birthday.

What kind of mood will the occasion encourage? If the occasion is one to celebrate the final payment on the debt of a church, the mood will be happy and the subject should be one that matches the joy of the occasion. If the occasion is to commemorate the death of some person who was a member of the group or was associated with it, the mood will be somber. Again, the subject should be one that matches the sadness of the occasion.

If the subject of the speech is inconsistent with the mood of the occasion, the listeners will have difficulty shifting their mood to coincide with that of the speech. Think, for example, of a time when you had been looking forward to an important social event. Anticipation had been increasing daily. Then suddenly the afternoon of the event, you were informed that your host had become ill—nothing so serious that you needed to worry about his welfare, but serious enough to prevent his giving the party. But your mood was set to have fun, even though you had some studying to do, you could not really concentrate on it because your mood was set to be carefree and happy. This is the difficult kind of shift required of listeners when a speaker's subject is inconsistent with their mood.

What are the time limits of the speech? Some program planners will voluntarily tell you of important time limitations, but many will not unless you ask. Never make any assumptions. Insist that the person in charge of the program give you precise time limits. Beware of the program planners who are very cavalier about time limits. When asked how long the speech should be, they will reply: "Oh, about twenty minutes," or "Oh, whatever you need." But time limits are extremely important. You cannot rationally select a subject unless you know how much time you are to have. A subject that is excellent for a five-minute speech may be unsatisfactory for a twenty-minute speech. Unobserved time limits can ruin a speech, even one that is otherwise very good. Some organizations are extremely conscientious about the length of their meetings and adjourn promptly at the appointed time. Service clubs that hold luncheon meetings, for example, have members who must be back to work on time. Any speaker who goes past the adjournment time will be looking at the backs of members as they depart. You must select a subject, therefore, that you can develop clearly and thoroughly in the time allotted. Some students get angry at professors who strictly enforce time limits on classroom speeches. But this is a discipline you must develop; therefore, you should be appreciative of the professor's help.

What will the program consist of? There are a number of reasons for asking this question. A most important one is that it provides a check on the time limits suggested by the program planner. Some program planners, like some speakers, are poor organizers and assign too little time for each program activity. Since the speaker is generally the last activity, any deficit of time will come from the speech. If you have seen a copy of the entire program beforehand, however, you may realize that the time limits for the speech appear to be unrealistic, and you can select a subject that can be developed in a shorter

time or expanded through additional supporting material if the promised time materializes. Being aware of the entire program also allows you to prepare appropriate adaptations and references. Sometimes, in fact, the rest of the program or some part of it may suggest a subject that will enhance the effectiveness of your speech. And it may be a subject that would not otherwise have occurred to you.

What is the nature of the place where the speech will be given? Will the speech be inside or outside? Will the audience be sitting or standing? Will the members of the audience be free to come and go? If so, you may have to avoid a subject that would be more challenging and select one that will be more interesting in order to hold the listeners in the audience. Will there be a place to display visual aids? If not, that may eliminate some topics from consideration. Are the seats comfortable or uncomfortable? Will you have to use a microphone? If so, will there be one available? What kind of lectern is available? Will you be able to use notes? If not, some subjects may not be practicable for that situation.

The Audience

The third factor to be considered in selecting a subject is the audience. Four questions can provide information about the audience that will significantly improve the selection of a subject.

What are the important demographic features of the listeners? We have already discussed in chapter 7 the methods of analyzing an audience. That information will be vitally important in selecting a subject. You will need to know the age, sex, educational level, political philosophy, homogeneity, ethnicity, economic status, religious affiliation, group interest, occupation, and place of residence of your expected auditors. A knowledge of important demographic factors allows you to determine, through inference, what topics or subjects the audience will consider interesting and worthwhile.

Why are the listeners present for the speech? You will need to know why your listeners are present to hear your speech. Have they come voluntarily or were they compelled to come? If the listeners have attended voluntarily, that indicates interest on their part in some aspect of the situation. Careful analysis may reveal that motivation, which in turn may suggest an appropriate subject. Listeners who attend involuntarily, on the other hand, may have a certain amount of hostility that will make it more difficult for you to develop rapport with them. Any subject that might increase that hostility should be avoided.

What are the listeners interested in? You will need to know the concerns of your potential listeners. What issues are important to them at the moment? In what ways will those issues affect them, politically, socially, economically, religiously, educationally?

If your hearers are bankers, they will probably be interested in hearing a discussion of the effects of manipulating the money supply. Farmers will be interested in hearing about new fertilizers on the market or improved ways of getting their products to market. Law enforcement officers will be interested in innovative methods of tracking fugitives. Members of a photography club will be interested in learning about a new film-processing method.

Obviously, in many instances you will attempt to choose a topic in which your listeners will be interested. On other occasions, however, you may choose a topic precisely because the audience is not interested in it. For example, the potential audience may have little or no interest in participating in political activities, but your analysis indicates that their self-interest would be better served if they became involved in political activities. Consequently, you may select a subject that will encourage your listeners to become active politically.

What do the listeners know? You cannot expect to know more about the subject you choose than *every* member of the audience. But you must certainly know more than most. If you don't, you will probably lose the interest and attention of the listeners in a short time. When selecting a topic and deciding on your development or treatment of that subject, you should consider the general level of knowledge of the audience as well as their knowledge of the particular topic on which you are speaking.

One thing you must never do is talk down to or treat an audience condescendingly by choosing a subject that is too elementary for them. Choose a subject that respects the listeners' intellectual ability. It is better to aim too high than too low. Such a subject will challenge your listeners and will also be a challenge to your ability as a speaker to present the subject so they can understand and appreciate it.

The General Purpose

Once you have chosen a subject, you must determine the general purpose of the speech, in other words, the general response you want the listeners to make. You may choose from among three general purposes: to entertain, to inform, and to persuade.

If your purpose is to entertain, you simply want the listeners to relax and enjoy the occasion. The speech may also make your listeners aware of some idea, but that is a supplementary effect. The main function of the speech is to amuse, enthrall, or divert. Many different methods can be used to entertain. The vivid description of an interesting place can be entertaining. The suspenseful narration of an exciting adventure can be entertaining. One of the most frequently used methods of entertaining is humor. **To Entertain**

    Most people enjoy humor, provided it is appropriate to the occasion and the subject. Humor must be used with care, however. It should never be offensive to any of the listeners. If it is directed toward people, ideas, or anything that the audience respects, it should poke fun gently and in a conciliatory way, rather than with biting satire or a derogatory attitude. It should be perceived as humorous; few things are more deadly to a speaker's cause than humor that is unappreciated.

    Almost any subject can be made entertaining if the speaker uses ingenuity and creative thinking. The speech to entertain is especially appropriate in after-dinner situations where members of the audience are less than alert and are not interested in following closely reasoned arguments. They just want to be amused.

If your purpose is to inform, then your main goal is to make clear to your listeners the material you are presenting and enable them to comprehend the ideas. A central or primary requirement of an informative speech is that it must present new information to the listeners. An informative speech can, and probably should, be entertaining, but it should never pursue amusement as its main objective. You will have failed as an informative speaker if the listeners cannot recall at least the main ideas of the speech. **To Inform**

You generally have one of four objectives in mind with a persuasive message: to create a new belief or attitude, to change the direction of an existing attitude, to increase the intensity of an existing attitude, or to obtain a behavioral response. **To Persuade**

Creating a New Attitude	First, you may want to create a new attitude on the part of your listeners. For example, you may want to develop an awareness of the neglect of elderly people in many nursing homes.
Changing an Existing Attitude's Direction	Second, you may want to change the direction of an existing attitude. This means changing an attitude from positive to negative, or vice versa. You might change the direction of an existing attitude by persuading your classmates that "big time" football is an anachronism, or that taxes should be increased to provide greater support for education.
Changing an Existing Attitude's Intensity	Third, you may want to increase the intensity of an existing attitude, such as making a positive attitude more strongly positive, a negative attitude more strongly negative, or a neutral attitude more strongly neutral. In the 1984 presidential election both political parties used this technique. Democrats attempted to increase the intensity of the negative attitudes among the general populace toward the Reagan administration's inability to reduce the budget deficit. Republicans attempted to increase the intensity of the positive attitudes toward progress in reducing inflation and unemployment.
Obtaining a Behavioral Response	Finally, you may try to persuade an audience to behave in some way. In an election, politicians attempt to persuade the electorate that it will be advantageous for them to go to the polls on election day. A speech with this purpose attempts to go beyond mere intellectual agreement and influence the audience's overt behavior in some way. Two questions must be answered before you prepare a speech seeking a behavioral response: (1) Does the audience have the capability to act on this subject? It would be unrealistic, for example, for you to attempt to persuade your classmates to dismiss the president of your school. Your classmates do not have that capability. You could persuade them, however, to sign a petition to be presented to the Board of Trustees or Regents asking that they replace the president. The members of the audience have the capability to sign the petition; the Board of Trustees has the capability to dismiss the president. (2) Is the proposed action practicable? A petition to the Board of Trustees or Regents asking that each faculty member be given a 30 percent increase in salary would not be practicable for most schools; even though the board has the authority to make such a decision, the money is not available.

It should be noted that the distinction between an informative and persuasive speech is not always clear-cut. In the first place, informative speeches can be persuasive. Learning new information is frequently sufficient to cause a change in attitudes and behavior. When people were told that there was a relationship between smoking and lung cancer, some stopped smoking. Others began to use less salt in their food when they learned that salt may cause high blood pressure. In the second place, persuasive speeches do use information to persuade. In fact, the methods of presenting information are the same, whether the purpose of the speech is to persuade or to inform. The methods of informing are not exclusive to informative speaking. This explains why an intended persuasive speech may succeed in informing an audience but fail to persuade them, while a speech designed primarily to inform may, indirectly, have persuasive effects. In the third place, some informative speeches are given to accomplish covert persuasion. Some companies, such as public utilities, conduct advertising campaigns and maintain a speakers' bureau to inform interested groups about company programs and activities. Their ultimate purpose, however, is to develop goodwill for the company. In other words, their underlying purpose is subtly or indirectly to increase public approval of the company.

The persuasive speech generally must also be informative to be effective, and it may also be entertaining. Nevertheless, the persuasive speaker uses these other methods simply as means to an end.

The Specific Purpose

Once the general purpose has been determined, you must turn your attention to the specific purpose of the speech.

Whereas the general purpose identifies the type of general response you want the listeners to make, the specific purpose identifies the particular objective of a given speech. The specific purpose should then be transformed or cast into an appropriately worded and precise thesis sentence. The following examples may help to clarify the difference between the two kinds of purpose:

Subject: Voting
General Purpose: To entertain
Specific Purpose: To describe the reactions of voters who supported losing candidates

Subject: Voting
General Purpose: To inform
Specific Purpose: To explain how to cast an absentee ballot in California

Subject: Voting
General Purpose: To persuade (actuate)
Specific Purpose: To persuade the local Democrats to vote a straight ticket

A specific purpose ensures that you have narrowed the subject sufficiently for the specified time limits. Some think they can prepare a speech and then expand or contract simply by adding or omitting supporting materials. It is true that this method can be used for slight changes in the length of a speech. But a significant change in length cannot be achieved in this way. To reduce a twenty-minute speech to a five-minute speech by eliminating supporting materials will generally result in a skeleton of a speech. To make a length change of this magnitude, you must change the specific purpose to one encompassing one complete segment of the twenty-minute speech. For example, your specific purpose for a twenty-minute speech might be to explain the factors that produce a successful golf shot. Your main points might be these:

A. The grip
B. The stance
C. The swing

If you reduce this speech to five minutes and retain all these main points, you will be able to present very little worthwhile information. But if you narrow the speech by making your specific purpose to explain just one of those three main points, you can still say approximately as much about that one point as you could in a twenty-minute speech devoted to all three main points. (This example also clearly illustrates the importance of determining the time limits for your speech well in advance.)

Deciding on the specific purpose is also important because it aids you in preparing the speech. As soon as possible after selecting the subject, you should decide specifically what you intend to discuss in that particular speech. This will eliminate much unnecessary work from the preparation of the speech. For example, shortly after you begin working on a speech, you will probably go to the library to do research. In reading an article, you may discover an extremely interesting piece of information. Unfortunately, every piece of interesting information will not be relevant to your purpose. If you have determined your specific purpose, you will know immediately whether you should take time to transfer the information to a note card for use in the speech. If you have not decided on your purpose for the speech, all you can do is record the information in the hope that it will be relevant to whatever specific purpose you ultimately decide on. Once you determine your purpose, you may find that a significant number of your notes are irrelevant and must be discarded. Much valuable time will thus have been wasted that could have been spent in gathering pertinent data if the specific purpose had been clear in your mind.

Researching the Topic

As you do research on your speech topic, you should collect the information on four-by-six or five-by-eight index cards. Record on each card information from only one source and pertaining to only a single topic. Figures 8.1 and 8.2 show sample note cards with information recorded from a book and a periodical article. Do not put the headings on the cards when you record the information on them. Wait until you have collected most of your evidence. In that way you will have a better idea of what the headings ought to be.

Figure 8.1

A sample note card: information taken from a book.

```
EDUCATION:  Focus on False Values

"As evidenced by their conspicuous and wholesale absence
from virtually every one of these reports and proposals,
we have obviously relegated all the moral and civic (read
"civilizing") values of education to the very back seat
of the big yellow bus--if indeed they are still being
allowed to ride at all--while prominently seated up front
are the real necessities, those which give primacy to our
economic needs, our escalating technological needs; in
short those that are unabashedly utilitarian." p. 81
Author:  Jeffrey R. Holland
Title: "A 'Notion' at Risk:  The Greater Crisis in
American Education," in Representative American Speeches,
1984-1985
Publisher:  The H. W. Wilson Company, 1985
```

Figure 8.2

A sample note card: information taken from a periodical article.

```
SPORTS:  Drug Use by Athletes

The pileup of revelations about drugs in sports raises
issues beyond the propriety of testing.  Big time univer-
sity athletic programs have come under fire for allegedly
placing sports competition--and the revenue it garners--
ahead of educational ideals.  In professional sports, the
big leagues may be in danger of alienating fans permanent-
ly if the perception grows that players are unable or
unwilling to tackle the drug problem.  "We have to restore
public confidence in the game," says Don Shula, head
coach of the Miami Dolphins.  "We must do everything
possible to show fans that the game is drug free.  This
is a battle we have to win, and the players, coaches,
and owners must join together to win it."  pp. 52-53
Author:  Jacob V. Lamar Jr.
Title:  "Scoring off the Field"
Periodical:  Time, August 25, 1986
```

Suggested Speech Topics

Listed below are some suggested topics for informative and persuasive speeches. Some of the topics listed under one heading could just as easily be listed under the other heading. Some of the topics will need to be narrowed to fit the time limits available. At the least, these few topics will provide a starting point for finding a subject for your speeches.

Informative Speeches

Découpage
Rappelling
Clog dancing
Racketball
Using a microscope
Karate
The Bermuda Triangle
Transcendental meditation
Repotting a plant
Warming up for jogging
Bypass heart surgery
Cooking crepes
Gripping a golf club
Swinging a tennis racket
Skydiving
Pruning a peach tree
Skinning a frog
Magnet schools
Values clarification

How the instant camera works
Card tricks
Selling real estate
Laser beams
Soccer
Handmade jewelry
Arts and crafts fairs
Rummage sales
Selecting a tennis racket
Caring for a hi-fi stereo record
Home smoke detectors
Astrology
Home computers
Stock market
The Marsh Arabs
The diadem butterfly
The flat tax
A co-op program

Persuasive Speeches

Strip mining
Teenage alcoholism
Child abuse
Wife abuse
Abortion
Gun control
Reinstatement of the military draft
Vegetarianism
Fuel shortage
Poverty
Crime
Zoning restrictions
Crime victims' rights

Railroad passenger service
Pollution
Fishing rights
Overcrowded national parks
Energy crisis
Divorce
Airbags for automobiles
Mandatory seatbelt laws
Athletic scholarships for women
Academy Awards
Violence on television
Sex on television

Summary

Selecting a speech subject is one of the most important decisions you can make. The subject is frequently the determining factor in the success or failure of a speech. Making an effective choice of subject requires the consideration of three factors: (1) the speaker, (2) the occasion, and (3) the audience.

Begin with yourself, considering your interests, experiences, and knowledge, and the audience's expectations of you.

A more effective subject will be selected if you also determine the nature and mood of the occasion, the time limits of the speech, the other events on the program, and the nature of the place where the speech will be given.

The chances of selecting a subject appropriate to the audience will be enhanced if you ascertain the important demographic features of the listeners, why they are present for the speech, what they are interested in, and what they know.

After choosing the subject, decide upon the general purpose (to entertain, to inform, to persuade) and the specific purpose (the particular objective for the speech).

Exercises

1. Prepare a list of topics in which you are interested. Prepare a list of topics in which your classmates are interested. On the basis of knowledge possessed by you and your classmates, identify from the two lists three common topics on which you could speak to the class.
2. For each of the three topics identified in exercise 1, determine a specific purpose for a speech for each of the three general purposes.
3. Phrase a specific purpose and list the main idea to develop it for a twenty-minute speech. Then, using the same topic, phrase a specific purpose and list the main ideas to develop it for a seven-minute speech.
4. Identify two or three areas of the topic in exercise 3 that you need to research for a speech. Collect evidence on five four-by-six index cards to be turned in.
5. Explain how a speech subject you choose for a classroom speech could create credibility for you.

Notes

1. W. N. Brigance, *Speech: Its Techniques and Disciplines in a Free Society,* 2d ed. (New York: Appleton-Century-Crofts, 1961), pp. 35–37.

9

UNDERSTANDING METHODS OF PRESENTATION

You can use one of four methods in presenting a speech to an audience. Each has certain strengths and certain weaknesses; each is more appropriate in specific situations; and one method may be better suited to an individual than the others. You have the responsibility of assessing the circumstances, evaluating the methods of presentation, and determining which is more effective for your specific occasion, your audience, and yourself.

Extemporaneous Speaking

Extemporaneous does not mean speaking without preparation. Extemporaneous speeches result from a carefully prepared effort. Select your topic carefully, limit it to an idea that can be developed in the time available, phrase a statement of purpose, decide on the main points needed to develop the purpose, gather and select supporting materials for the main points, think about the language to use, and prepare an introduction and conclusion. Then practice the speech a number of times. Does this mean that you will couch your thoughts in the specific sequence of words to be used in presenting the speech? No, you will make the exact choice of words and construction of sentences largely during the act of communicating directly with your listeners.

The extemporaneous method of presentation has distinct advantages. It is generally the most effective method of delivering a speech and is usually preferred by experienced speakers. In an interview with two speech communication scholars, the late President Harry Truman said

Advantages of the Extemporaneous Method

If I had my choice, I would always speak extemporaneously. However, as President I was compelled to read most of my speeches. While I feel less strained than I used to, I'm still not completely at home when I have to read from a text. Like almost everyone else, I talk more effectively than I read. As I have said, sometimes I try to get away from the formality of a text by inserting ad-libbed comments. Even in formal Presidential addresses I often strayed from the official copy.[1]

The extemporaneous speech leaves you free to develop and maintain direct contact with listeners. Since only occasional glances at notes are necessary, you can look directly at listeners the rest of the time. You can utilize the same behavior apparent in good conversational speech. Speaking extemporaneously also leaves you relatively free to use body action and gestures. You can move away from the lectern because you are not tied to a written manuscript.

You generally have a greater tendency to use an oral style when you speak extemporaneously. Norman Thomas, perennial Socialist candidate for president during the first half of the twentieth century, evidenced an awareness of this:

It cannot be too strongly insisted that the written and spoken word, while they have much in common, are by no means the same. The speaker is concerned with the particular group before him; he is not speaking to a scattered group of readers or to posterity. Sometimes he can communicate more effectively by repetition, intonation, gesture, unfinished sentence. I have often winced at stenographic reports of speeches which had gone over well enough to receive much applause. But I am convinced that I would have made a mistake to have read a smoother speech.[2]

Having to think about the ideas as you phrase them usually causes you to talk in a more direct, conversational style. And you may still get some of the advantages of preparation by committing to memory precisely stated portions of the speech. Some speakers, for example, prepare their introduction and conclusion and learn it thoroughly in order to begin and end the speech smoothly and effectively. William E. Borah, senator from Idaho from 1907 to 1940 and an effective speaker, is reported to have "memorized choice sentences" he wanted to use while speaking extemporaneously.[3]

The most important advantage of the extemporaneous method is that you are better able to adjust and adapt to the audience and the situation. You don't have to worry about being unable to break into a specific sequence of words that you are giving from memory or reading from a manuscript. You find it easier to restate your ideas in different words if it appears the listeners do not understand, to offer additional supporting material if what you have given appears inadequate, to comment on some unexpected occurrence in the speech situation. Norman Vincent Peale reported: "I prepare only a pattern or sequence of ideas and leave the exact expression of those ideas to the inspiration of the moment. I find that reading or memorizing a speech injures spontaneity. Without spontaneity there can be little rapport between the speaker and his audience."[4]

Disadvantages of the Extemporaneous Method

Does the extemporaneous method have any weaknesses? Yes, the language can be less precise. Frequently the most apt word to communicate an idea does not occur to you, so a synonym is taken that has a slightly different meaning. Phrases and sentences may be less polished because you cannot study the construction and rewrite for clarity and aptness of expression.

Speaking extemporaneously makes it a bit more difficult to observe the time limits in a speaking situation. Since no practice session is the same as the actual speaking situation, you can never be sure you are going to use the same number of words and the same amount of time. With practice, however, your timing can be close.

You can get so emotionally involved in the speaking situation that you get carried away and say things you don't intend to. The give-and-take between you and the audience may induce you to make remarks that calm deliberation would tell you were inappropriate and ill-advised. Against the counsel of his advisers, President Andrew Johnson spoke extemporaneously and let his audiences guide and influence his speeches in his ill-fated "Swing Around the Circle" in 1866. He found himself responding to listener's reactions with replies that created ill will and established the impression of a reckless, egotistical individual.

Preparing to speak extemporaneously can give you a false sense of security. Since you do not have to labor to develop the speech into a written form, you may decide there is little to worry about. You may rely too heavily on the inspiration of the moment and not make the preparation that is necessary for an effective speech. If the language is to be adequately precise and colorful, there must be a sufficient number of practice sessions to allow you to work out major problems of awkwardness and inexactness.

Speaking extemporaneously can result in a jerky, halting, nonfluent speech instead of a smoothly fluent rate. You may find yourself hesitating in order to think of the best word to communicate your meaning. Too much of this, especially if filled in with "uhs" and "and-uhs," can disrupt the communicative process and cause the listener to lose interest in what you have to say.

Using Notes

Is it permissible to use notes when you speak? Your professor will set the policy for your class. If you are permitted them be sure they do not interfere with communication.

One of the best ways to use notes is to prepare them on note cards, preferably four by six inches, which can be held easily in the hand and slipped into a coat pocket or handbook. Not only are they easier to get to the speaking situation, but they can then be held unobtrusively in your hand if there is no lectern, and if there is a lectern you can move away from it if you desire. If holding the cards in your hands interferes with your ability to gesture, you can slip them into a pocket, or you may gesture with the cards in one hand.

Note cards should be held to a minimum. This means you put only an outline of key words and phrases on the cards. If you include more, you will spend most of your time shuffling note cards and looking at them instead of at the listeners.

Material on the cards should be printed, written clearly, or typed. Having to decipher notes in front of an audience can be both disconcerting to you and distracting to the listener. Only one side of the cards should be used; unless you flip the card the right way when you use both sides, it will be upside down, in which case you must flip it again before it can be used. This can cause some awkward and distracting moments.

Number note cards clearly to minimize the chances of getting them out of order. Also, should you drop them, only a few seconds will be needed to return them to their proper sequence.

Reading from a Manuscript

In this method of presentation the speech is written out in its entirety and read to the audience. One of the most common errors you must avoid is the tendency to write an essay. Even though the speech is completely written, it must conform to all the principles of good speechmaking. One of the best ways to prevent a speech from sounding like an essay is to use an oral, conversational style, not a written style. Former television news commentator David Brinkley advised aspiring news broadcasters, "In writing news for broadcasting, it's important to remember that what you're writing is conversation—not words to be printed but words to be spoken, and there is a great difference. The most important requirements are clarity, simplicity and brevity. It's harder to do it that way, but the results are worth the effort."[5]

Your instructor will tell you which type of presentation you are to use in your classroom speeches. As a general rule, however, it is best not to prepare a speech to be read from a manuscript until you have mastered the extemporaneous method of presentation. Most students have been trained in writing much more than in speaking. As a result, you will be prone to use a written style if you write a speech early in your public speaking course. After you have mastered the extemporaneous method and have developed an oral style that has become habitual, you will find it much easier to write a speech that will retain the spontaneity of conversational speech. The absence of this quality is a frequent fault of written speeches.

Principles of Reading a Speech

Using a manuscript in the speaking situation can be more effective if certain guidelines are followed. The manuscript must be clearly legible. It should be typed with either double or triple spacing. Most people find that triple spacing makes for easier reading at the lectern. The typescript is also more easily read if nothing but capitals are used. This prevents you from having to squint at the manuscript or bend over the lectern in order to read the speech.

A speech that is to be read from a manuscript must be practiced diligently. Avoid thinking that because the speech is written and is to be read you have little to worry about. If the speech is to be read effectively, you need to develop a strong familiarity with it so you can read it with the proper meaning and establish direct eye contact with your listeners.

When reading the speech, avoid bending your head to look at the manuscript. Learn to glance at the page so the audience will not be distracted by the constant bobbing up and down of your head.

Avoid sounding as if you are reading the manuscript; sound as if you are talking to the listeners. One important way to achieve a conversational style is to avoid the type of reading in which every sound is accented. Children read in this manner: The—boy—was—playing—with—the—marbles. In normal conversation, however, only rarely would more than three words in that sentence be accented; generally the sentence would be divided into two thought units: Thə boy—wəz playing wi-thə marbles. Learn to accent the sounds and words that merit emphasis and let those that do not remain unaccented. Get the same kind of elision in your speech as in your conversational speaking.

Turning the pages of the manuscript can be distracting if you are not careful. As a general rule it is best not to turn the pages as they are completed. In terms of communication of ideas this a purposeless and distracting action. You can accomplish the same objective by simply sliding the top page across the lectern to the other side. With practice this can be done unobtrusively. If you slide each page over when you are about half through that page, you will be able to accomplish the movement from page to page with a minimum of disturbance.

Are gestures needed in reading a speech from a manuscript? Yes, just as much as in giving a speech extemporaneously or from memory. Make a conscious effort to use gestures and avoid letting the manuscript set up a barrier between you and the audience.

Advantages of Reading a Speech

Reading a speech has several advantages. The language of the speech can be much more precise than in an extemporaneous presentation. Sentences can be recast as often as necessary to develop clarity. A dictionary and thesaurus can be consulted to select the precise word to communicate intended meaning. The fireside chats of Franklin D. Roosevelt, noted for their clarity and felicity of expression, went through numerous drafts before they achieved the qualities that characterized them in their actual presentation.

Not only can language be made delicately precise, it can also be polished to express ideas more vividly and felicitously. You can consciously manipulate language to take advantage of stylistic devices such as alliteration and periodic sentences. You can also avoid sequences of sounds and words that are difficult to pronounce. It is not always possible to accomplish these in an extemporaneous delivery.

Reading a manuscript permits you to conform to the time limits with much greater precision and ease than when you are speaking extemporaneously. You can time the speech during practice sessions and edit it to within a few seconds of the prescribed time limit.

Finally, reading a speech from manuscript frees you from worrying about what you are going to say or how you are going to say it. The speech is completely prepared, except for the adaptations to be made during the speech. Although you must be sufficiently familiar with your speech to be able to maintain direct contact with the listeners, you never need worry about forgetting material.

Disadvantages of Reading a Speech

Despite its advantages, there are some distinct weaknesses in manuscript reading that hamper it as an effective speaking method. The speaker reading a manuscript finds it extremely difficult to adapt to changing conditions in the situation. Senator Borah "felt that a manuscript gave him a sense of restriction and rigidity."[6]

This is not to say that adjustments cannot be made. A comparison of Franklin D. Roosevelt's reading text with the actual recorded speech reveals many interpolations made during the presentation of his speeches. Crowell counted "172 instances of spontaneous alteration" in one speech and she reported that this was not atypical.[7] An example of Roosevelt's ability to deviate from the prepared text is demonstrated in the following example. Those words in italics were added in delivery; those in parentheses were in the prepared text but omitted in delivery:

Secretary Ickes, Governor Hoey, Governor Cooper and our neighbor, Governor Maybank of South Carolina, and my friends from all the states: I have listened with attention and great interest to the thousands of varieties of plants and trees and fishes and animals that Governor Cooper told us about, but he failed to mention the hundreds of thousands of species of human animals that come to the park.

Here in the Great Smokies, we (meet today) *have come together* to dedicate these mountains, and streams and forests, *the thousands of them,* to the service of the *millions of* American people. We are living under governments (which) *that* are proving their devotion to national parks. The Governors of North Carolina and of Tennessee have greatly helped us, and the Secretary of the Interior is so active that he has today ready for dedication *a number of other great National* (two more) parks—*like* Kings Canyon in California and the Olympic National Park in the State of Washington, *the Isle Park up in Michigan and, over here, the Great Cavern of Tennessee,* and soon, I hope, *he will have another one for us to dedicate* (a third,) the Big Bend Park *away down* in Texas, *close to the Mexican Line.*[8]

Franklin D. Roosevelt was a man of unusual speaking ability, however, and many speakers find it difficult to make even the relatively minor changes in a manuscript speech that Roosevelt made. To make major changes and adaptations becomes, for many speakers, a monumental task.

One of the most harmful aspects of reading a speech from manuscript is that it interferes with direct communication between speaker and listener. No matter how familiar you are with the manuscript, it is obvious that your eye contact is more limited than if you were speaking extemporaneously. It is extremely difficult to maintain eye contact and keep your place in the manuscript at the same time.

Moreover, you are more definitely bound to the lectern and your manuscript; consequently, your freedom to gesture and to move at will about the podium or around the lectern is seriously hampered. If you perceive the necessity of moving to one end of the platform to talk more directly to a particular segment of your audience, you must either ignore that need or resort to the rather awkward solution of picking up your manuscript and carrying it with you.

Finally, unless you are skilled at reading aloud, you will find it difficult to read a speech from manuscript in a conversational manner.

Comparison with Extemporaneous Method

Despite the several obstacles in effectively reading a speech from manuscript, evidence indicates that the two methods are equally effective in imparting information to an audience. You should note, however, that this is different from holding the interest of an audience and developing credibility for a speaker. Investigators did discover, however, that one speaker was more effective with one method than with the other. Consequently, they caution against indiscriminately recommending one method over the other. "As common sense perhaps should have suggested all along, the statement in textbooks that the extemporaneous method is superior to reading should be revised to read *Some speakers are more effective extemporaneously than they are when using a manuscript, and some use both methods with equal effectiveness.*"[9] Since only skilled speakers were used in this experiment, however, the conclusions cannot be extended to beginning speakers.

Speaking from Memory

The memorized speech differs from both the extemporaneous and the manuscript speech. It differs from the extemporaneous speech because it is written out completely prior to the speaking engagement. It differs from the manuscript speech because it is entirely committed to memory and no copy is brought to the speaking situation.

Advantages of the Memorized Presentation

The memorized speech offers several advantages. You are free to roam about the platform and to use as much body action and as many gestures as you deem necessary. Since you use no notes or manuscript, you are freer to use body action in delivering the memorized speech than with any other method of presentation.

The absence of notes or a manuscript allows you to maintain the most direct communication of any method of presentation. You can look at listeners all the time because you have no notes to read from. You can move to any part of the platform for better contact with some or all of the listeners without worrying about notes that would normally be on the lectern.

Like the manuscript speech, the prior preparation of the memorized speech enables you to achieve a more precise use of language, to be more accurate and more colorful. This is especially helpful when you want to be sure you do not accidentally use a word that would give the wrong impression to the listeners.

Also, as in the manuscript speech, the memorized speech permits you to conform more precisely to the time limits. The length of a memorized speech will vary by only a few seconds from one occasion to another.

Disadvantages of the Memorized Presentation

Despite the advantages of the memorized speech, you must accept and cope with several weaknesses. Those who have heard schoolboy orators with memorized pieces know how artificial and unmoving those efforts can be. The spontaneity that results from thinking about your ideas and phrasing them as you talk is sometimes lacking in a memorized speech. Your mind is focused on a particular sequence of words rather than on the ideas themselves; this is frequently reflected in your voice and manner.

Probably the greatest objection to memorization arises from the obstacles it raises against adaptation to the specific situation. Once a sequence of words has been learned, it is extremely difficult for many people to insert additional words. Consequently, if anything happens in the situation that demands a spontaneous response, it is difficult to alter the memorized material. Yet some speakers can. Although Rufus Choate and Chauncy M. Depew, outstanding lawyers of the nineteenth century, "wrote their speeches, neither of them . . . used notes in their delivery. Both reproduced what they had written with fidelity and were" skillful at making their speeches seem spontaneous "by witty and appropriate interjections, obviously inspired by the occasion."[10]

Another weakness, which also occurs in the manuscript speech, is the danger that the ideas will be presented in a written rather than oral style. This is not a direct result of the speech being memorized, however; it is the result of the speech being written beforehand. Consequently, when using the memorized method, pay special attention to style and make a conscious effort to write in an oral style.

A final and sometimes prohibitive weakness of memorization is that some individuals have great difficulty in memorizing material. Although techniques are available to aid a person's memory, these methods do not always produce the results claimed by their proponents. Susan B. Anthony, foremost advocate of women's rights, temperance, and other causes in the nineteenth century, found memorization difficult. The first time she was to make a major speech for woman's suffrage, "She paced up and down for hours trying to commit the speech to memory, but all in vain. It was impossible for her, then or later, ever to memorize exact words. For this reason most of her speeches were given from notes, never being presented in quite the same way."[11] If you have difficulty in memorizing exactly, avoid this method of speech presentation.

Impromptu Speaking

A truly impromptu speech is one for which the speaker has had no prior warning. No specific preparation has been made and no previous planning of the speech was possible, although this does not mean the impromptu speech is unorganized. If the topic for the speech is also one on which the speaker has had little or no experience and has little or no knowledge, it will not be much of a speech. The speaker would better serve himself, and speechmaking in general, if he gracefully declined the opportunity to speak.

On occasion, impromptu speeches may be unavoidable. In a meeting, for example, an unexpected discussion of a topic may call for an informed member of the group to speak on some phase of the topic. Or, occasionally, a

person may be intrigued by some unanticipated event about which he has information and decide to talk about it. This happened to poet Robert Frost on one of his lecture tours:

Once, at a midwestern college, just before he was to begin a lecture, someone piqued him by a reference to Plato's "Republic," and he launched off on a remarkable impromptu excursus on Plato. Yet what appears to be impromptu usually has a long foreground. A longtime reader of Plato who puts down no notes, keeps no journal, he was ready, and the occasion was right.[12]

With quick thinking and application of certain principles in such instances as these, an acceptable speech can be made.

Organizing an Impromptu Speech

The organization of an impromptu speech should begin the same way as for any other speech: phrase the central idea in a clearly worded, simple, declarative sentence. In many instances, choosing a statement of specific purpose for an impromptu speech will be easier than for any other type because the request or need for an impromptu effort will be an outgrowth of a specific discussion and a specific request. On rare occasions you may receive a general request for an impromptu speech, and must choose and word the statement of purpose yourself.

Once you have decided on the thesis sentence, divide the topic into some logical sections to be used as the main points of the speech. If called upon to discuss, for example, politics in the state of Indiana, you might decide to use as your thesis "The changing political structure in Indiana is beneficial." You might decide to show that the changes are beneficial by using a syllogistic development with the following three points:

1. The political changes occurring across the United States are beneficial.
2. Similar political changes are occurring in Indiana.
3. Therefore, the political changes in Indiana are beneficial.

Whatever logical divisions are used can be developed with the appropriate supporting material that can be recalled. Technical or strange terms should be defined. Attempt to cite at least one example for each main point, and if you can recall any testimony, statistics, or humorous anecdotes, these can be used to develop your ideas more fully.

Starting an Impromptu Speech

Like any other speech, most impromptu speeches need an introduction to get the attention of the hearers, gain their goodwill, and start them thinking about the subject. In many instances, however, an impromptu speech does not need an introduction. Any discussion that leads to a request for an impromptu speech is, in effect, an introduction to the speech. Since the people present have indicated their interest in the topic, demonstrated their goodwill toward the speaker by asking her to speak, and have their attention focused on her, all she needs to do is launch immediately into the statement of purpose and begin her development of it. On other occasions the request to make an impromptu speech will be completely unexpected. In such an instance an introduction of the speech is much more necessary, even if it serves no other purpose than to give you a moment longer to organize your thoughts.

A number of means are available in introducing this kind of impromptu speech. You may relate to what a previous speaker has said, to something the presiding officer has said, or to what an authority has said. You may begin by repeating a question that was asked or with a brief anecdote or some pertinent statistics. The one thing you must not do as an impromptu speaker is to begin with an apology for your lack of preparation. An apology sounds as though you are begging for sympathy.

Ending an Impromptu Speech

The conclusion of an impromptu speech will rarely be as polished as the conclusion of a prepared speech. Nevertheless, attempt to focus your listeners' thoughts for a final time on the central idea of the speech. You may simply summarize the main points, restate the original question, explain the significance of your ideas to the listeners, or repeat and amplify the main idea with authoritative testimony.

Anticipating an Impromptu Speech

Not all impromptu requests have to result in impromptu speeches; many times you can successfully anticipate the request and be prepared for it. A person who is known to give speeches frequently must realize that if someone is going to be singled out for an impromptu speech, there is a strong likelihood she will be that person. Knowing this, she will go prepared. As a matter of fact, some known speakers never go anyplace without an "emergency" speech in mind.

Even if you do little public speaking, though, you can analyze the situation beforehand to determine if there is any likelihood you will be asked to speak. If you are attending a going-away dinner for a close personal friend of many years, you can anticipate being asked to make a few remarks about your friend. Before leaving home, therefore, select two or three main ideas you would like to emphasize about your friend and recall one or two interesting anecdotes to illustrate each point. Then, if you are asked to speak, you will not be unprepared.

Advantages of an Impromptu Speech

It is difficult to talk about advantages of the impromptu method. Ordinarily this method is used because the speaker is unexpectedly asked to speak and has no other choice. Most speakers caught in this predicament will verify that there are few advantages. At first glance, the impromptu speech may seem to have all the advantages of the extemporaneous method—direct contact with listeners, free use of body action and gestures, easy adaptation to situations, and increased tendency to use an oral style. A closer look reveals, however, that the impromptu speaker is so involved in determining what he is going to say and how he is going to organize it that he has little time or attention to devote to these factors.

If used in the educational situation carefully and discriminatingly, however, the impromptu speech can have value. It can teach you to think quickly on your feet, which hopefully, will be transferred to other speaking occasions when you are called on to think quickly.

Disadvantages of an Impromptu Speech

Although the impromptu method has a number of disadvantages (absence of careful selection of main ideas, lack of research to develop ideas, lack of thoughtful choice of language), there is one basic cause for a poor speech: the lack of careful preparation for the speech.

Summary

This chapter has presented the strengths and weaknesses of four methods of presenting a speech. The different methods have been developed as though they are largely discreet and mutually exclusive. In fact, however, any speech may use more than one method. The extemporaneous speaker frequently has committed to memory or written on a note card a choice way of stating a particular part of the speech. Speakers using a manuscript or giving a speech from memory frequently make extemporaneous adaptations to the particular audience or situation. The truly effective speaker, therefore, must be capable of using all three of these methods.

Finally, each of the methods of presentation has both advantages and disadvantages. The advantages of extemporaneous speaking are that it permits direct contact with listeners, encourages free use of body actions and gestures, allows easy adaptation to the situation, and invites use of an oral style. The disadvantages are that the language may be less precise, time limits are more difficult to observe, the speaker may say something unintended, the speaker may rely too heavily on the inspiration of the moment and not prepare properly, the speaker's fluency may be adversely affected.

The advantages of reading from a manuscript are that language can be more precise, language can be more polished, time limits can be conformed to more easily, and there is no worry about what is going to be said. The disadvantages of reading from a manuscript are that it makes adaptation difficult, can interfere with direct communication, requires a skilled reader, and encourages use of a written style.

The advantages of speaking from memory are that it permits complete freedom in body action, direct communication, precise use of language, and easy conformance to time limits. The disadvantages of speaking from memory are that it tends to sound memorized, makes adaptation difficult, encourages use of a written style, and it is difficult for some people to memorize.

The only advantage of impromptu speaking is that it teaches the ability to think quickly on one's feet. Impromptu speaking has many disadvantages, but the basic one is a lack of careful preparation.

Notes

1. E. E. White and C. R. Henderlider, "What Harry S Truman Told Us About His Speaking," *Quarterly Journal of Speech* 40 (1954):39.
2. N. Thomas, "Random Reflections on Public Speaking," *Quarterly Journal of Speech* 40 (1954):149.
3. W. W. Braden, "The Bases of William E. Borah's Speech Preparation," *Quarterly Journal of Speech* 33 (1947):29.
4. E. E. White and C. R. Henderlider, "What Norman Vincent Peale Told Us About His Speaking," *Quarterly Journal of Speech* 40 (1954):414–15.
5. David Brinkley, *Richmond News Leader* May 22, 1956. Used by permission.
6. A. E. Whitehead, "The Oratory of William Edgar Borah," *Quarterly Journal of Speech* 32 (1949):296.
7. L. Crowell, "Word Changes Introduced Ad Libitum in Five Speeches by Franklin Delano Roosevelt," *Speech Monograms* 25 (1958):230.
8. E. Brandenburg, "The Preparation of Franklin D. Roosevelt's Speeches," *Quarterly Journal of Speech* 35 (1949):219–20.
9. H. W. Hildebrandt and W. W. Stevens, "Manuscript and Extemporaneous Delivery in Communicating Information," *Speech Monographs* 30 (1963):372.
10. H. W. Taft, *Kindred Arts: Conversation and Public Speaking* (New York: Macmillan Publishing Co., 1929), p. 91. Used by permission.
11. E. E. McDavitt, "Susan B. Anthony, Reformer and Speaker," *Quarterly Journal of Speech* 30 (1944):176.
12. Reginald L. Cook, "Notes on Frost the Lecturer," *Quarterly Journal of Speech* 42 (1956):129.

PART 3

THE SPEECH

10

STRUCTURING THE SPEECH

S ome evidence indicates that the element of organization is a more important factor than content in a listener's evaluation of a speech.[1] Obviously no one is going to advocate giving speeches without supporting materials, but content alone is insufficient. You can improve your chances of developing credibility for your ideas by putting them into some meaningful form.

The Value of Organization

The ability of organization to affect the credibility of a speaker's ideas has been revealed by experimental evidence. Four main values of organization have been identified, any one of which is sufficient to justify the time and labor necessary to produce a well-organized speech.

Organization makes a significant impact on the listener's comprehension of information included in a speech. Studies show that you must be careful about the placement of all organizational elements of a speech. Taking a well-organized speech and randomly changing the order of the sentences, Thompson then revealed that listeners comprehended the unaltered version significantly better than the altered one.[2] Darnell found that rearranging the "thesis sentence, two major contentions, two subcontentions for each, and two assertions for each subpoint" of an organized speech, adversely affected the listeners' comprehension.[3] Kulgren randomly rearranged the paragraphs of a well-organized speech and found that those who heard the unaltered version comprehended it significantly better than those who heard the altered form.[4] Spicer and Bassett altered the chronological pattern of rules explaining the game of *Risk,* and revealed that subjects hearing the organized message scored significantly higher on a recall test than those listening to the disorganized version.[5] Varying the order of three basic parts of a speech—attention, need, satisfaction—Miller found that comprehension was significantly higher for those who heard the correct version.[6]

Affects Listeners' Comprehension of Message

You must be concerned not only about the order of major parts of a speech but also about placement of paragraphs and sequence of sentences.

Does organization aid only listeners with low levels of ability in comprehending orally communicated messages? On the contrary, a number of studies have revealed that organization is most beneficial to listeners with high levels of ability. Thompson determined the organization ability of his subjects and discovered that organization increased the comprehension of subjects with high organization ability more than those with low.[7] Parker measured the linguistic ability of his subjects before presenting material in organized and disorganized form. He found that "clear organization increased comprehension more among [subjects] with high linguistic ability than among those with middle linguistic ability."[8] Thistlethwaite, de Haan, and Kemenetzky discovered that communications with clear organization resulted in better comprehension, which was clearly related to the intellectual ability of the listener.[9]

Thus you cannot evade responsibility for organizing a message with the excuse that listeners are highly intelligent and can organize the material themselves.

Affects Ethos of the Speaker

A second value of organization is that it increases your ethos or credibility. Using Thompson's organized and disorganized speeches, Sharp and McClung found that subjects who heard the disorganized speech thought significantly less of the speaker afterwards.[10] Baker had a speaker deliver two forms of the same speech, the only difference between them was that one included eighteen disorganization cues. Although the inclusion of the cues did not significantly lower the speaker's credibility, "there was a significant increase in speaker credibility in the *absence* of speaker disorganization cues."[11] Good organization will not necessarily increase your credibility, but its absence will reduce it.

Although it appears that organization by itself is insufficient to cause a change in attitude, evidence indicates that organization is a necessary ingredient if a speech is to significantly shift attitudes. McCroskey and Mehrley presented to subjects four versions of a speech: organized and fluent, organized and nonfluent, disorganized and fluent, disorganized and nonfluent. Only one version, the organized and fluent, caused a significant shift in the attitudes of the listeners.[12] Smith developed a speech that was divided into six main parts: attention, need, satisfaction, visualization, refutation, and action. He varied the organization by transposing one or two parts and also by randomizing the order of the parts. His results showed a negative audience reaction when all parts of the speech were randomized.[13]

Affects Attitude Change

To maximize your chances of changing listeners' attitudes, organize your speech.

Clear organization prevents listeners from becoming frustrated, especially those with high cognitive need, defined by Cohen "as a need to structure relevant situations in meaningful, integrated ways." After measuring the cognitive need of subjects, he presented to half of them an ambiguous story; to the other half he presented the same story in structured form. The results revealed that the subjects with high cognitive need experienced significantly more frustration in the ambiguous situation than they did in the structured situation. Those with medium and low cognitive need did not differ in the two conditions. "Thus," concluded Cohen and his colleagues, "the degree of structure becomes more crucial for the individual as the strength of his need for cognition increases."[14]

Affects Listeners' Frustration

Avoid frustrating listeners with high cognitive need; organize your speech.

With these values in mind, let's consider the organization of a speech. It includes three distinct processes: (1) selecting the ideas to be used in a particular speech, (2) developing the entity we call a speech, and (3) ordering the main ideas in the body of the speech.

Selection of Ideas

When you analyze a subject, you frequently find many different ideas you can present sincerely and develop with valid evidence and reasoning. Some of these ideas will be more acceptable to one group than to another. For example, many different ideas can be used to support increasing efforts to curtail the crime rate in the United States: The high crime rate (1) makes streets unsafe for defenseless citizens, (2) increases prices for consumers, (3) increases the economic burdens of small businesses, (4) increases personal danger to owners of small businesses, (5) causes loss of revenue to cities by deterring tourists and shoppers from coming into the downtown area, and (6) increases the complexities and hazards of police work.

Assuming that you could support all these arguments with equal sincerity, you would use the ones that would be most persuasive to a particular group of listeners. If you were talking to a group of elderly citizens, you would contend that the high crime rate makes our streets unsafe for citizens and increases prices for consumers; to a group of business owners, you would argue that the high crime rate increases the economic burden of small businesses and increases the personal danger to their owners; to a group of city officials and politicians, you would assert that the high crime rate causes a loss of revenue to cities by deterring tourists and shoppers from coming into dangerous areas; to a group of law enforcement officers, you would maintain that the high crime rate increases the complexities and hazards of police work.

An important phase of organization is selecting the arguments you are going to use with a particular audience. This selection of appropriate arguments can be made only after you have carefully analyzed the attitudes and characteristics of the potential hearers.

Development of the Speech

Can the entity we call a speech be created in a number of different ways? Definitely! Aristotle suggested that there were only two necessary parts to a speech: (1) state your case (what we call the thesis), and (2) prove it. However, he also observed that because of the sorry nature of audiences it was frequently necessary to add two other parts, an exordium (introduction) and a peroration (conclusion). These four basic parts—introduction, thesis, body, and conclusion—make up the entity we call a speech. There are other ways to divide a speech, but we will limit our discussion to these four parts, plus a fifth optional part—the preview.

Although experienced and skillful speakers find it appropriate and desirable on a given occasion to omit one or more of these basic parts, proceed on the assumption that each is absolutely necessary. Once these fundamental procedures have been deeply ingrained in your speaking behavior, they can be altered to deviate from the pattern suggested here. However, in the vast majority of speaking situations you will find these four fundamental parts to be appropriate elements of a speech.

Purposes and types of introductions and conclusions are discussed in the next chapter. At this point we will consider the thesis and the body of the speech. The thesis is discussed first because until it is precisely stated there can be no meaningful development of the other parts of a speech.

Thesis

The thesis sentence—also called the statement of central idea, purpose sentence, statement sentence, or the subject sentence—normally comes at the end of the introduction, after you have the attention of the listeners. In unusual instances where the listeners' attention is already riveted on the subject or the speaker, the speech may open with the thesis. Otherwise, to begin with a statement of the thesis, as some speakers do, is to invite those hearers who have not begun to attend to the speech to miss this most vital part. In some unusual circumstances, the thesis may not be stated until later in the speech, sometimes not until the end. And in some rare cases, the thesis may not be stated at all, even though you have it framed for your own purposes. As we shall see, however, this latter practice creates both practical and ethical problems.

The thesis sentence identifies the topic you want your listeners to focus on in this particular speech. The focus may be on any one or all of several things: (1) It may simply focus on what the topic of the speech will be: "This morning I want to explain three disadvantages of the government reorganization bill." (2) It may focus on the meaning you want your listeners to obtain from the material presented in the speech: "This morning I want to show that the present government reorganization bill pending before Congress should be defeated." (3) It may focus on the behavioral response you want your listeners to make: "This morning I want to show why you should write your congressman to oppose the government reorganization bill pending before Congress." In all these instances, you would discuss the three disadvantages of the government reorganization bill.

The thesis sentence must be explicitly identified so that listeners recognize it. For example, one's thesis sentence might be: "There are three actions the United States can take to improve educational opportunities." In this form, however, many listeners can fail to recognize it as the thesis sentence. Therefore, you can present your thesis more explicitly by stating it in a manner similar to this: "This morning I would like to call your attention to three actions the United States can take to improve educational opportunities." Be sure your thesis is stated as a complete sentence.

Why should a speaker be so obvious in presenting the thesis? Isn't this an insult to the listeners' intelligence? Isn't the speaker talking down to the listeners? The answer to these questions is that you must be obvious, not because you belittle the intelligence of hearers or because you are talking down to them, but because this is one method of adapting to the oral mode of communication.

Value of the Thesis

A writer can provide many cues that will aid in the communication of ideas. Many of these cues are not available to a speaker. On these pages, for example, the punctuation marks help in determining what words go together in thought units. The period shows that one group of words is related in a sentence. An indentation at the beginning of a sentence indicates that the next group of sentences is going to develop a specific theme. Headings over a group of paragraphs reveal that those paragraphs are related to the idea expressed by the heading.

Since none of these visual guides is available to you as a speaker, you must use others to provide similar information to listeners. Since you cannot put a thesis sentence in visual italics, one of the ways you can emphasize it is to put it in *aural italics*. The statement, "This morning I would like to call to your attention," constitutes the speaker's aural italics. It informs the listeners that this sentence is more important than others around it, that it contains an important idea not to be missed. As writers put main ideas in large, bold print to make them stand out for readers, so speakers should put main ideas in words that make them stand out for listeners.

We have accepted without question the need for visual cues to help readers with written material. Surely we must grant speakers the freedom to use aural cues since listening is a much more difficult task than reading.

The thesis sentence is important not only because it provides significant aural cues for communication, but it is also useful in establishing the listeners' *set,* which is a predisposition to focus on specific stimuli and to respond in a particular way.[15] You ask listeners to perceive the data in such a way that they will draw the same conclusions from the data that you do. We know, from both personal observation and experimentation, that individuals do not always perceive data in like ways. Consequently, without a clear thesis sentence, listeners may draw conclusions different from those desired by the speaker.

People's perception may be influenced by a number of factors: attitudes, mental and physical condition at the moment, ability to perceive, knowledge, and recent experiences. The impact of recent experience was clearly demonstrated in a classroom experiment. One group of subjects was told that they were going to be shown words related to boats; a second group was told they were going to be shown words related to animals. The letters SAEL and WHARL were then flashed briefly before them. The first group perceived them as SAIL and WHARF; the second as SEAL and WHALE.[16]

Another experiment demonstrated that value judgments can also be influenced by the *set* of the listeners. The following narrative was presented to three groups of subjects:

A middle-aged man, his wife, and teenage son live in a public housing development. Their house is adequate for their needs and is superior to anything that they could obtain on the open market at the same price. This development was built by the government to provide housing for underprivileged families and, in order to assure that this low-cost housing is properly used, the regulations require that the resident families have an income under the figure of $2,900.

The man mentioned above has an income just under this amount and his entire income is used in running his household. He has, however, a strong desire to send his son to college and finds that he can obtain a job on weekends with a relative, which would provide enough money for his son's education.

This additional income, however, would require his moving from the housing development and the increased rent would absorb most of his increased income. To provide for his son's education, he takes the job but makes arrangements for this additional income not to be reported. Thus he is able to stay in the low-cost housing and also secure the desired education for his son.

Prior to hearing this narrative, the first group of subjects was told they were going to hear about an ethical issue, the second was told they were going to hear about a social issue, and the third was told they were going to hear about an economic issue. The experimenters discovered that the ethical set "produced a significantly greater negative attitude toward the situation than either the economic or social sets."[17] In other words, the experimenters, by labeling the material to be presented, established a *set* in the listeners which caused them to perceive the stimuli in a manner consistent with the labels.

Use the thesis sentence to create a *set* in listeners toward your ideas and supporting materials. Once this set is established, it is easier for hearers to listen to the material because they have a frame of reference in which to place it. Instead of wondering why certain statements are being made, the listener has a perspective from which to view them. Omitting a thesis sentence or failing to state it clearly leaves the door open for a speech to be perceived differently than desired.

The thesis sentence is also important because, in stating explicitly what you are trying to do, it aids in changing the attitudes of listeners. Tubbs compared the use of explicit and implicit conclusions with the degree of commitment of listeners. He found "that the speech with the explicit conclusion elicited significantly more attitude change than the speech with the implicit conclusion."[18] Further, he found that the explicit conclusion was significantly effective in changing the attitude of both noncommitted and highly committed subjects, while the implicit conclusion was more persuasive only to those who were strongly committed to the topic. There was a tendency for the neutral and less committed members of the audience to boomerang (change opinion in the opposite direction from that advocated by the speaker) when the implicit conclusion was used. On the basis of this study, Tubbs concluded that an explicit conclusion is more effective in causing attitude change when members of the audience are heterogeneous in their degree of commitment.[19]

Even more important is the finding that direct statement of purpose does not alienate those opposed to the purpose. A series of experiments testing the effectiveness of various methods revealed that explicit refutation does not necessarily diminish a speech's persuasiveness for listeners who are opposed.[20]

The explicitly stated conclusion is also more effective with the less intelligent members of an audience. Cooper and Dinerman presented an antiprejudice film to adults and high school students. They hoped that an important message implicitly stated would be detected by the audience. The more intelligent members of the audience were influenced by the message, but the less intelligent ones were not. Cooper and Dinerman concluded that the implicit form of the message may well have caused it to be inaccessible to the less intelligent members of the audience. Further, they claimed that the only parts of the message that made any lasting impression were the explicit and specific details.[21]

Finally, the thesis sentence aids in delivering a speech because it gives coherence and unity to the ideas and supporting materials selected for presentation. Numerous experiments by psychologists have demonstrated that organized material is learned more easily and remembered longer than unorganized or disorganized data. Thus, you will have less need for reliance on notes when the material is coherent and unified.

Once you have determined the thesis and gathered the materials you are going to use in the speech, you may begin to think about how you are going to express that sentence in the speech itself. It may be presented in many different forms; you should not assume that only one, rigid, inflexible way of focusing on the central idea of the speech is appropriate or desirable. One way in which the statement of purpose may be developed is to first tell the listener what the speech is not going to do, then what it is. President Woodrow Wilson used this

Statement of the Thesis

technique in the speech he gave at the ceremony on July 4, 1913, commemorating the fiftieth anniversary of the Battle of Gettysburg. Since the nature of the occasion demanded little in the way of an introduction, Wilson moved swiftly to a statement of his purpose.

Friends and Fellow Citizens:—I need not tell you what the Battle of Gettysburg meant. These gallant men in blue and gray sit all about us here. Many of them met upon this ground in grim and deadly struggle. Upon these famous fields and hillsides their comrades died about them. In their presence it were an impertinence to discourse upon how the battle went, how it ended, what it signified! But fifty years have gone by since then, and I crave the privilege of speaking to you for a few minutes of what those fifty years have meant.

Another way of presenting the thesis sentence is to introduce it as a question. John C. Calhoun, in the last speech that he gave in the U.S. Senate, used just this method to make clear what his speech was about:

I have, senators, believed from the first that the agitation of the subject of slavery would, if not prevented by some timely and effective measure, end in disunion. Entertaining this opinion, I have, on all proper occasions, endeavored to call the attention of both the two great parties which divide the country, to adopt some such measure to prevent so great a disaster, but without success. The agitation has been permitted to proceed, with almost no attempt to resist it, until it has reached a period when it can no longer be disguised or denied that the Union is in danger. You have thus forced upon you the greatest and the gravest question that ever can come under your consideration: How can the Union be preserved?

Like all phases of a speech, the thesis sentence should be adapted to the specific situation. On occasion this will mean phrasing a thesis sentence which is clear to those who are present when the speech is given, but which does not explicitly delineate the scope of the speech for someone not present. Such an example is found in a speech made by John Marshall in the Virginia convention called to ratify the Constitution. In the debate that ensued, Marshall and Patrick Henry found themselves on opposite sides. Following one of Henry's speeches, Marshall took the floor:

Mr. Chairman:—I conceive that the object of the discussion now before us is, whether democracy or despotism be most eligible. I am sure that those who framed the system submitted to our investigation, and those who now support it intend the establishment and security of the former. The supporters of the Constitution claim the title of being firm friends of the liberty and rights of mankind. They say that they consider it as the best means of protecting liberty. We, sir, idolize democracy. Those who oppose it have bestowed eulogiums on monarchy. We prefer this system to any monarchy, because we are convinced that it has a greater tendency to secure our liberty and promote our happiness. We admire it, because we think it a well regulated democracy: it is recommended to the good people of this country; they are, through us, to declare whether it be such a plan of government as will establish and secure their freedom.

Permit me to attend to what the honorable gentleman, Mr. Henry, has said.

Those unfamiliar with Patrick Henry's speech have little idea of the arguments to be covered by Marshall, but those delegates in the convention who had just heard Henry speak needed no more specific information. The thesis sentence need be no more specific than is required by the particular conditions.

Skillful speakers may use a thesis sentence that does not explicitly tell what they are going to do in the speech but instead merely implies the scope and purpose of the speech. As a general rule, you should avoid using this particular method until you have learned to use thesis sentences well and have gained the ability to make implicative statements that are unambiguous. Nevertheless, the implicative method is a valid one and should be understood. William Jennings Bryan used this technique in his famous lecture "Prince of Peace." After several introductory paragraphs, he came to the one in which he stated, in implied form, his thesis sentence:

There are honest doubters whose sincerity we recognize and respect, but occasionally I find young men who think it smart to be skeptical; they talk as if it were an evidence of larger intelligence to scoff at creeds and to refuse to connect themselves with churches. They call themselves "Liberal," as if a Christian were narrow-minded. Some go so far as to assert that the "advanced thought of the world" has discarded the idea that there is a God. To these young men I desire to address myself.

Although Bryan does not state his purpose explicitly, it is practically impossible to misinterpret his intentions. If you choose to imply your statement of purpose, it must be done in a manner as unambiguous as that used by Bryan.

The Preview

An optional part of a speech is the preview, an extension of the thesis sentence telling the listeners precisely what main points will be included in the development of your main purpose. The preview may be included as a part of the thesis sentence: "I wish to speak to you this morning about the changes in the educational, recreational, protective, and economic functions of the family during the past century." Or it may be presented in a sentence or two immediately following the thesis sentence: "This morning I'd like to give you a brief outline of a model reading program. Such a reading program includes four elements: one good book each week, a newspaper daily, a magazine of interpretation weekly, and a book review monthly."

What are the advantages of a preview? It enables listeners to see in advance where the speech is going and to interpret supporting materials as they are presented. It also permits listeners to perceive movement in the speech as you progress from one main point to another. Knowing that there are only four main points can often give hearers the fortitude to continue listening when, in a long speech, they hear the third or fourth point introduced.

Research on speeches of different organizational quality may have revealed the most important value of a preview: it significantly improved comprehension.[22]

The Body

Once you have settled on a thesis sentence and selected the main ideas to develop it, you then have to decide in what sequence to present those ideas. The ideas and development constitute the body of the speech.

Organizing Main Points According to a Stock Pattern

One alternative is to use a stock pattern for ordering the ideas. A number of these are available; six will be discussed on the following pages.

Chronological pattern In this instance the ideas are put together according to their relationship in time. For example, if you decided to speak on the topic "Population Growth," you might assemble the materials in a chronological pattern.

A. Prior to the seventeenth century, population growth was relatively slight.
1. The food supply was inadequate to support large increases in population growth.
2. The death rate was high.
3. The birth rate was not high enough to overcome the death rate.
B. From the seventeenth century to the twentieth century, there was a substantial increase in the world's population.
1. Medical advances drastically lowered the death rate.
2. The food supply increased sufficiently to support large increases in population growth.
3. The birth rate increased.
4. Normal pressures of population growth were relieved by the immigration of the people of many countries to newly discovered and unsettled lands.

C. During the twentieth century, population growth has begun to create problems.
   1. The food supply has failed to keep pace with the increases in population growth.
   2. The continually declining death rate has created social problems.
   3. Normal pressures from population growth are now being experienced because immigration is no longer a viable means of siphoning off people from overpopulated areas.
D. The prognosis for population growth beyond the twentieth century is discouraging.
   1. At present growth rates, the food supply will be insufficient to provide most people with an adequate diet.
   2. Present population growth rates will create a population density so great that living will be uncomfortable.
   3. Present methods for controlling population growth have not proved to be widely effective.

As you can see, the chronological development of the subject provides an understanding of the problem that cannot be attained with any other pattern of organization. Instead of moving from past to future as the above example does, it sometimes is more effective to reverse the order of the main points and move from future to past.

Spatial pattern The spatial pattern assembles materials in terms of their relationship in space. An analysis of population growth around the world could be organized in a spatial pattern.

A. There has been population growth in the European nations.
   1. Most European countries have low rates of population increase.
   2. All European countries have low death rates.
   3. Most European countries have a moderately high population density.
B. There has been population growth in the African nations.
   1. Most African countries have high rates of population increase.
   2. All African countries have high death rates.
   3. Most African countries have a low population density.
C. There has been population growth in the Asian nations.
   1. Most Asian countries have high rates of population increase.
   2. The death rate in Asia varies from country to country.
      a. About half of the Asian countries have a low death rate.
      b. About half of the Asian countries have a high death rate.
   3. The population density in Asia is extremely varied.
      a. Some Asian countries have a very low population density.
      b. About half of the Asian countries have a high population density.
      c. Some Asian countries have a moderate population density.

D. There has been population growth in the American nations.
1. Most American countries have high rates of population increase.
2. The death rate in America varies from country to country.
   a. Most American countries have a low death rate.
   b. A few American countries have a high death rate.
3. Most American countries have a relatively low population density.

As you can see from this example, the spatial pattern may order the parts in various ways; any one of the main points may be put first, second, or third. You are free to present them in the order that will best meet your purpose with a particular audience.

Topical pattern The topical pattern groups ideas according to some classification of natural or conventional parts. If you wanted to discuss the disadvantages of the various methods of deterring population growth, you could use a topical pattern.

A. Deterring population growth by contraception has disadvantages.
1. It is too expensive for many groups.
2. It requires voluntary cooperation.
B. Deterring population growth by sterilization has disadvantages.
1. Most methods are irrevocable.
2. It requires voluntary cooperation.
3. It can be used selectively if a compulsory program is adopted.
C. Deterring population growth by abortion has disadvantages.
1. It violates the religious principles of many.
2. It can be dangerous to the mother unless performed early in pregnancy.
3. It uses medical personnel needed for other purposes.
4. It uses medical facilities needed for other purposes.
5. It uses medical services needed for other purposes.
D. Deterring population growth by infanticide has disadvantages.
1. It is repugnant to humanitarian ideals.
2. It would brutalize the people.
E. Deterring population growth by euthanasia has disadvantages.
1. It is repugnant to humanitarian ideals.
2. It would brutalize the people.

In most cases the topical pattern is more effective if the number of topics in the body of the speech exhausts the divisions of the subject. One of the advantages of the topical pattern, however, is that you may develop in a speech only a few selected topics from a longer list. It permits you to avoid discussion of areas of the subject that you deem irrelevant and insignificant for you, the audience, or the occasion. In the preceding example, you might omit D and E, since infanticide and euthanasia are not commonly suggested methods of deterring population growth. An important consideration is that the principle for determining the topics must be consistent. In other words, points A, B, and C cannot discuss methods of deterring population growth while points D and E discuss methods of getting people to accept controls on population growth.

Causal pattern The causal pattern organizes materials according to their cause-and-effect relationship. A causal relationship may be concerned with discussing why a particular thing occurred, that is, the factors that caused a particular effect. This is an effect-to-cause relationship. Looking at the factors that have contributed to population growth gives an effect-to-cause pattern.

A. A lowered death rate has contributed to population growth.
   1. Advances in medical science helped to produce a lowered death rate.
   2. The advent of industrialization helped to produce a lowered death rate.
   3. Improvements in the physical environments helped to produce a lowered death rate.
B. Increasing birth rates have contributed to population growth.
   1. Early marriages have increased the birth rates.
   2. More women living through a greater proportion of their child-bearing years has increased the birth rates.
C. An increased food supply has contributed to population growth.
   1. The development of agriculture made possible a greater food supply.
   2. Technological developments increased the food supply.
   3. Machine production made possible an increased food supply.

Or a causal relationship may be concerned with a discussion of the results or predicted results of a particular factor. This is known as a cause-to-effect relationship. Consideration of the problems arising from population growth gives a cause-to-effect pattern.

A. Population growth retards economic advances.
   1. Population growth depletes savings.
   2. Population growth decreases capital formation.
   3. Population growth hampers investment.
B. Population growth hinders social development.
   1. Population growth increases the percentage of dependent children.
   2. Population growth strains medical services.
   3. Population growth results in inadequate funds for development of transportation.
   4. Population growth results in inadequate funds for the development of communication facilities.
   5. Population growth results in inadequate funds for education.
   6. Population growth results in inadequate funds for recreational facilities.

Before proceeding to the next pattern of organization, it should be pointed out that all symbols of the same type in an outline must use the same pattern. If A and B are parts of a topical analysis, then C and D must also be of the same topical analysis. If 1 and 2 under A are of a time sequence analysis, then 3 and 4 must be of a time sequence analysis.

There is a simple method to help you be sure you are following the same principle in assembling the materials. Assume that you have a helper who has the outline of your points, while you have the supporting materials that are to be fitted into their appropriate places in the outline. To determine where each piece of information goes, the helper will ask a question that will be different for each pattern of organization. If a chronological pattern of organization is being used, the question will be—*when* did it happen? For a spatial pattern, the question will be—*where* is it located? For a topical pattern, the question may take several forms—*what* is it? *which* is it? *how* did it happen? For a causal pattern, the question will be—*why* did it happen? If more than one of these questions can be asked to locate materials under several points headed by similar symbols, you know you have mixed two different patterns of organization.

Problem-solution pattern In the problem-solution pattern you discuss a problem facing a particular group of people, then advocate what you think is the most viable solution to that problem. This can be an effective method of organizing a persuasive speech. Beginning with an analysis of the problem gives listeners the framework from which you arrived at your conclusions. It also indicates that you have made a careful study of the situation and have based your position on an objective, rational analysis. The outline of a speech using the problem-solution pattern might resemble the following:

A. Problem
   1. Historical background of problem.
   2. Nature of problem.
   3. Causes of problem.
   4. Effects of problem.
B. Solution
   1. Explanation of solution.
   2. Explanation of how solution eliminates problem.
   3. Explanation of practicability of solution.
   4. Explanation of advantages of solution.

In a given speech, you might cover only a few of the subtopics in this outline. If your audience has had long experience with the problem, there will be no need to discuss the historical background. In some instances, it might be impossible to isolate specific causes of a problem; obviously, then, you cannot discuss them. You must weigh all factors and decide which of these subtopics can and should be included in any particular speech. Although common sense tells us that the order of problem-solution would be preferable to solution-problem, Cohen confirmed this with experimental data.[23]

Motivated sequence Developed by Alan H. Monroe,[24] the motivated sequence has five main divisions: *attention, need, satisfaction, visualization,* and *action.* Monroe's motivated sequence is a variant of the problem-solution pattern with the *need* step presenting the problem and the *satisfaction* step developing the solution.

The *attention* step is self-explanatory; it simply involves doing something appropriate to get the favorable attention of the listeners directed to your topic. It is in reality the introduction of the speech, and suggestions for purposes and types of introductions can be found in chapter 11. The *need* step in a persuasive speech describes the problem either by discussing evils in the present system that need to be eliminated or by showing that the present system should be retained. In an informative speech, the *need* step demonstrates the listeners' need for information on the subject. The *satisfaction* step in a persuasive speech offers a plan that will eliminate the evils presented in the *need.* In an informative speech it presents the information. Monroe recommends only these first three parts for informative speeches. This has the unsettling effect of either stopping with no conclusion or including it as a part of the *satisfaction* step, which creates logical outlining problems. I do not recommend the motivated sequence for an informative speech.

The final two parts of the motivated sequence are used only in a persuasive speech. The *visualization* step describes the conditions that will prevail once the plan is instituted and the evils of the present system have been abolished. This allows listeners to perceive themselves enjoying the satisfaction of doing, believing, or feeling what you are advocating. The *action* step shows what specific acts should be taken to implement the plan offered in the *satisfaction* step and requests listeners' approval. It is the conclusion of the speech.

The motivated sequence is an excellent pattern of organization for a persuasive speech. Its progression involves the listeners psychologically and moves them naturally to the final phase calling for action. Following is an outline of a speech using the motivated sequence.

A. [*attention*] People are the world's most important product. Planet Earth now has over 4 billion people living on it.
B. [*need*] Overpopulation leads to problems in the world.
   1. Population growth has caused food deficits in the world.
      a. Many countries cannot produce sufficient food for their citizens.
      b. Other countries are not always able to make up the deficits.
   2. Population growth has created social problems.
      a. Many overpopulated countries have crime problems.
      b. Many overpopulated countries have housing problems.
      c. Many overpopulated countries have health problems.
C. [*satisfaction*] A decrease in birth rate can help solve the problems of overpopulation.
   1. Population growth can be reduced by a decrease in the birth rate.
      a. The United States has brought population growth to almost a zero growth level.
      b. Canada has brought population growth to almost a zero growth level.
      c. Most European countries have brought population growth to almost a zero growth level.
   2. The highly overpopulated nations need to adopt birth control measures.
      a. India needs to curtail the birth rate.
      b. Many African nations need to curtail the birth rate.
      c. Many Asian nations need to curtail the birth rate.
D. [*visualization*] Imagine a world where population growth is curtailed.
   1. With a decrease in population growth, the world can produce sufficient food to eliminate hunger.
   2. With a decrease in population growth, many of the social problems of overpopulated nations can be reduced.
E. [*action*] The time to act is now.
   1. The UN should adopt a worldwide plan for decreasing population growth.
   2. The plan should be financed by a proportional tax levied on all nations.

Transitions

Organization may exist in your mind and may even have been transferred to paper in the form of a preparation outline of your speech, but to be effective that organization must be clear to those who hear the speech. Transitional devices can be used to give unity and coherence to the ideas, to give a sense of movement to the speech, and to emphasize important ideas.

An effective transitional technique which you may use is to provide signposts to guide listeners through the ideas. Number main points: "My first point is. . . ." "A second option is. . . ." "Third, let's consider. . . ." The main points can be labeled: "The economic consequences of this program. . . ." "Let's look at the social effects of this proposal. . . ." "This analysis would be deficient if it did not also discuss the political ramifications." You can sometimes give main points a more striking impact by phrasing them in parallel form: "When government officials are corrupt, the efficiency of the government is diminished. . . . When government officials are corrupt, the confidence of the citizens in their government is destroyed. . . . When government officials are corrupt, the moral fiber of society is subverted." Speakers are frequently heard introducing main points with "another reason," "another factor." It is generally best to avoid the use of "another" to introduce main points: it lacks both the movement and specificity provided by numbers or labels. Subpoints can be numbered or labeled, but different terms should be used to designate main points and subpoints. Otherwise, listeners may become totally confused trying to find their way among the various ideas.

Almost as bad as unclear organization is organization so stark as to seem skeletal, mechanical, or artificial. To overcome this problem, use transitional words and phrases to make ideas and supporting materials flow easily from one to another. Single words can readily serve as transitional elements: *therefore, nevertheless, furthermore, since, although, however, moreover, consequently, finally, also*. Avoid overuse of these terms. Be especially sensitive to the tendency to overuse "also." Phrases and sentences can be used as transitional bridges from one segment to another: "More than that," "In addition to," "On the other hand," "As a result of this analysis," "Now that we have seen the causes of this problem, we can next look at the consequences," "The economic features, which we have just examined, have a direct bearing upon the social impact of this problem." One of the most thought-provoking transitional methods is the rhetorical question: "What do the political ramifications of this proposal have to do with us?" "How will this problem affect us in the next ten years?" "What can we do to prevent the recurrence of these social ills?" Questions of this nature cause listeners to begin to think along the lines you desire. Internal summaries give an opportunity to signal the end of one unit, as well as to focus listeners' attention on the main thoughts just developed: "Economically we have seen that this proposal will affect our balance of payments in international trade adversely and will necessitate an increase in deficit spending in domestic affairs. Now let's examine the social impact of this proposal on the nation."

It is imperative that you use variety in transitions. Especially to be avoided are repetitious transitions. They are self-defeating because they call attention to themselves, and so lose the ability to unify, emphasize, or give a sense of movement to the ideas.

The Preparation Outline

The preparation outline is an important aid. It enables you to plan the major parts of a speech and to check the logical relationship of ideas and supporting materials. Until you have assigned outline symbols to the various parts and ideas, it is frequently difficult to detect logical deficiencies.

The preparation outline must be understood for exactly what it is, however. It is not necessarily—and generally is not—the complete speech, or the speech as it will be delivered. It may or may not include the transitions you use. It may or may not include internal summaries. It generally will not include restatements of ideas or evidence. It should be viewed as little more than the skeleton of the speech, which will be fleshed out when you actually communicate with listeners.

Not only is the preparation outline not the finished speech, it is also not a straitjacket binding your efforts to what is in the outline. You should adapt the material in the outline to the response of the particular listeners. As you develop point one of the speech, for example, you may decide that it would be more effective to present the planned third point next rather than the one you had put in the outline as the second one. Then you may introduce that second point as the third one, or decide that this audience is not ready for that second point and so omit it altogether. Supporting materials may be handled differently. Testimony that is quoted verbatim in the preparation outline may be paraphrased in the speech.

Even though the preparation outline is not the complete speech, it still should contain all the ideas and supporting materials that you plan to include in the speech. Unless they are all included, errors in analysis may not be detected. But keep in mind, all materials in the outline do not have to be used in the speech.

The preparation outline also should not be confused with the notes to be taken to the communicative situation. These two aids exist for totally different purposes. The preparation outline is to logically analyze all ideas and supporting materials involved in the speech. Notes you take to the lectern are intended to remind you of key ideas and supporting materials. Such notes may be unintelligible to anyone but you. The preparation outline, however, should be clear to others.

Following are some suggestions that may make easier and more beneficial the production of the preparation outline.

1. It should have four parts: *introduction, thesis sentence, body,* and *conclusion.* If a *preview* is to be used, it may or may not be included in the outline.
2. These parts should be numbered in sequence: I, II, III, IV. This will continually remind you that these are not independent parts, but are interrelated units of a totality—the entity we call a speech.

3. A consistent set of symbols should be used to represent each part.
   a. Roman numerals usually represent the major parts.
   b. Capital letters indicate the main ideas of each part.
   c. Arabic numerals signify the subpoints of main ideas.
   d. Small letters identify divisions of the subpoints.

   Most outlines will not go beyond this level of division, but if it is necessary to do so, Arabic numerals in parentheses can be used next, followed by small letters in parentheses. Beyond that you can make up your own system!
4. Each succeeding level of symbols should be indented from the previous level:

   I.
     A.
        1.
        2.
     B.
   II.

   This permits you, or anyone else, to perceive at a glance the relationships between the various parts of the outline.
5. Complete sentences should be used for all *main points*. Since the main points are such vital parts of the speech, this helps to ensure that you have spent some time in phrasing them clearly and concisely.
6. The introduction and conclusion may be either written out completely or outlined.
7. Put only one idea after each symbol. Unless this practice is followed, great confusion can result. When two ideas are placed after one symbol, the outline cannot demonstrate which of the succeeding subpoints supports each idea. The outline, therefore, will have failed in one of its most important purposes—demonstrating logical relationships.
8. If transitions and summaries are included in the outline, they should be labeled as such. To assign them a symbol destroys the logical framework of the outline.

Many scholars caution that no head in an outline should be supported by only one subhead. This principle does not apply, however, when symbols are used to indicate evidence. Some avoid the problem by not using outline symbols before evidence. I prefer the use of symbols, however, because they indicate the relationship of the evidence to the point it supports. Since there are times when only one piece of evidence is necessary or desirable, the speech preparation outline will have only one subhead under some heads.

A Sample Outline

I. Introduction

"Since the late 1960s, and especially since the 'oil crisis' of 1973, coal . . . has once more moved onto center stage of the energy scene. Projections of long-term availability and costs of alternative fossil fuels, and better appreciation of technical options for interchanging gas, oil, and coal, have not only led to a consensus that coal will again become an increasingly important component of future energy supplies, but also persuaded many that it will become a preeminent primary energy resource before the end of the century." N. Berkowitz, *An Introduction to Coal Technology* (New York: Academic Press, 1979), p. xi.

II. Thesis Sentence

Today, I want to explain why coal is an important source of future energy in the U.S.

III. Preview

Coal is important for three reasons: (1) It is abundant in the U.S.; (2) It can be converted to other usable forms. (3) It would provide economic advantages to the U.S.

IV. Body

  A. Coal is abundant in the U.S.

    1. "Coal is the most abundant energy resource in the U.S. . . . At current demand levels, we have enough coal reserves to last at least 300 years and, at . . . projected 1985 production levels . . . coal reserves could last 150 or more years." *U.S. Energy Demand and Supply 1976–1985: Limited Options, Unlimited Constraints,* March 1978, p. 49.

    2. ". . . estimates of coal resources published by the U.S. Geological Survey established a resource base of 3.2 trillion tons, about half of which . . . is usually considered recoverable." James E. McNulty and Clayton G. Bell, "Coal Reserves—Estimates," *Energy Technology Handbook,* 1977, 1–35.

    3. "The U.S. Bureau of Mines estimates that 437 billion tons are in deposits that are mineable with current technology at today's prices." W. R. Hibbard, Jr., "Policies and Constraints for Major Expansion of U.S. Coal Production and Utilization," *Annual Review of Energy* 4 (1979):149.

    4. An international group, The Workshop on Alternative Energy Strategies, concluded: "Coal has the potential to contribute substantially to future energy supplies. Coal reserves are abundant, but taking advantage of them requires an active program of development by both producers and consumers." James Lust and Lester Lave, "Review of Scenarios of Future U.S. Energy Use," *Annual Review of Energy* 4 (1979):529.

  B. Coal can be converted to other usable forms.

    1. ". . . there is no technical barrier to immediate gasification of coal or production of methanol from coal." J. R. Bowden, "Prospects for Coal as a Direct Fuel and Its Potential through

Application of Liquefaction and Gasification Technology," *Energy Sources—An Interdisciplinary International Journal of Science and Technology* (1976):6.

2. "The Navy has actually run some ships on synthetic fuel created from coal; they found that some adjustments were required but that it could be done." *The National Energy Plan Options under Assumptions of National Security Threat,* Congressional Research Service, Library of Congress for the Subcommittee on Energy and Power, April 1978, p. 44.

3. Airplanes can use fuel from coal. "In 1976 a T-63 engine was operated on JP-5 fuel derived from coal. Engine performance for this test . . . was equivalent to that using JP-5 refined from crude oil." *National Energy Plan Options,* p. 45.

4. Coal "can be gasified to produce a low Btu gas or subsequently modified to synthetic natural gas. Alternatively, the low Btu gas can be improved through removal of the nitrogen to a medium Btu gas, believed by many to be the most suitable and economic form as a feedstock to the chemical industry." Charles Simeons, *Coal: Its Role in Tomorrow's Technology* (New York: Pergamon Press, 1978), p. 142.

C. The greater use of coal would provide economic advantages for the U.S.

  1. Coal can reduce the balance of payments.

    a. Oil imports send billions of dollars out of the U.S.

      (1) Currently we are importing 45 percent of the oil we use. *Birmingham Post-Herald,* February 8, 1980.

      (2) It is estimated that imported oil cost the U.S. $74 billion in 1979. *Wall Street Journal,* December 21, 1979.

      (3) The outflow of this huge sum of money has an adverse effect on the U.S.

        (a) It contributes significantly to a deficit in our balance of payments, which fuels inflation.

        (b) Our balance of payments deficit for 1979 was approximately $23.5 billion. *Wall Street Journal,* December 31, 1979.

    b. The substitution of coal for oil in the generation of electricity would help to decrease the amount of oil to be imported.

      (1) Coal can be substituted for oil in producing electricity. Harvey Brooks and Jack M. Hollander, "United States Energy Alternatives to 2010 and Beyond: The Conaes Study," *Annual Review of Energy* 4 (1979):32–33.

(2) "If all public utility boilers were to convert to coal . . . we could save 1.8 million barrels a day; if every industrial boiler converted to coal, we could save more than 3.5 million barrels a day. These two steps alone could save more than half of the oil we now import." Armand Hammer, "Our Dependence on Foreign Imports," *Vital Speeches of the Day* 46 (1979):47.

2. Increased use of coal would create new jobs.

a. "U.S. mines are producing more than 750 million tons of coal a year. But they could probably be bringing out 100 million tons more—if the coal could be used." Charles J. Dibona, "U.S. Energy," *Vital Speeches of the Day* 46 (1979):106.

b. ". . . it would help to revitalize our domestic coal industry and help to put some thirteen thousand unemployed coal miners back to work and create many thousands of new jobs." Armand Hammer, "Our Dependence on Foreign Imports," *Vital Speeches of the Day* 46 (1979):48.

V. Conclusion

The Workshop on Alternative Energy Strategies, an international study, concluded: "The supply of oil will fail to meet increasing demand before the year 2000, most probably between 1985 and 1995, even if energy prices rise 50 percent above current levels in real terms. Additional constraints on oil production will hasten this shortage, thereby reducing the time available for action on alternatives." Simeons, *Coal*, p. 528.

Coal is a realistic alternative energy source for the U.S. because coal is abundant in the U.S., it can be converted to other usable forms, and its use would provide economic advantages.

The Speech as Presented

"Since the late 1960s, and especially since the 'oil crisis' of 1973, coal . . . has once more moved onto center stage of the energy scene. Projections of long-term availability and costs of alternative fossil fuels, and better appreciation of technical options for interchanging gas, oil, and coal, have not only led to a consensus that coal will again become an increasingly important component of future energy supplies, but also persuaded many that it will become a preeminent primary energy resource before the end of the century." That is the conclusion of Professor Berkowitz of the University of Alberta.

I believe Professor Berkowitz is correct in his analysis, and today I want to explain three reasons coal will be an important future source of energy in the U.S.

Coal will be important because: (1) Coal is abundant in the U.S. (2) Coal can be converted to other usable forms. (3) The use of coal would provide economic advantages to the U.S. Because of these factors, the U.S. will be able to decrease its dependence on foreign oil and improve its economic status at home and abroad. Now, let's consider each of these reasons.

First, the U.S. has large supplies of coal. Concluding that, "Coal is the most abundant energy resource in the U.S.," a congressional study projected that coal will last "at least 300 years" at the current level of use. At expected demands in 1985, we have enough coal to last "150 or more years." The U.S. Geological Survey estimates we have "3.2 trillion tons" of coal resources. About half "is usually considered recoverable."

Even more optimistically, Dr. W. R. Hibbard, University Distinguished Professor of Engineering at Virginia Tech, reports that "437 billion tons can be mined by today's methods at today's prices." Even an international group, the Workshop on Alternative Energy Strategies, believes that coal can become an important future energy source if both producers and consumers undertake an active program of development and use in order to take advantage of the abundant coal reserves.

It seems clear, therefore, that the U.S. has ample supplies of coal, that the coal is recoverable, and that it can play an important role in meeting the energy needs of this country. Nevertheless, both consumers and producers will have to adopt more aggressive policies with respect to coal if its potential as an energy source is to be realized.

A second reason that coal is an important source of future energy in the U.S. is that it can be converted to other usable forms. J. R. Bowden, Vice President of Conoco Coal Development Co., argues that "there is no technical barrier to immediate gasification of coal or production of methanol from coal." Supporting that contention are some specific examples of the use of coal-converted fuels. A congressional study revealed that, though some adjustments were necessary, some Navy ships have operated on synthetic fuel made from coal. The same study also disclosed that one type of fuel made from coal ran an airplane jet engine as efficiently as the same type of fuel made from crude oil.

Not only can coal be converted to a liquid fuel, but Charles Simeons, a British industrial consultant and author of the book, *Coal: Its Role in Tomorrow's Technology,* claims that coal can be converted to different forms of gas, one of which can be used by the chemical industry to create other products.

Thus, by testimony and example we have evidence that coal can be converted to other usable forms of energy.

A third reason that coal is an important source of future energy in the U.S. is that it would provide economic advantages. Increased use of coal would keep billions of dollars in the U.S. Currently, we are importing 45 percent of the oil we use. The *Wall Street Journal* of December 21, 1979, estimated that imported oil cost us $74 billion in 1979. The outflow of this huge sum of money fuels inflation because it contributes significantly to a deficit in our balance of payments. The *Wall Street Journal* reported on December 31, 1979, that our balance of payments deficit for 1979 was $23.5 billion. In other words, if we could have cut our oil imports by one-third in 1979, we would have had no deficit in our balance of payments. Think of the effect that would have had on inflation in this country.

The substitution of coal for oil in the generation of electricity would help to decrease the amount of oil to be imported. Professors Harvey Brooks of Harvard University and Jack Hollander of the University of California contend that coal is a practicable substitute for oil in producing electricity. Armand Hammer, chairman of Occidental Petroleum Corporation, has pointed out that "If all public utility boilers were to convert to coal . . . we could save 1.8 million barrels a day." He goes on to say that "if every industrial boiler converted to coal, we could save more than 3.5 million barrels a day." As a result of these two steps alone, says Mr. Hammer, we "could save more than half of the oil we now import." Thus, we could not only eliminate our balance of payments deficit, we could create a balance of payments surplus.

Not only would an increased use of coal have a positive impact on our balance of payments, it would also provide economic advantages by creating new jobs. Charles J. Dibona, president of the American Petroleum Institute, says that though we "are producing more than 750 million tons of coal a year," we "could probably be bringing out 100 million tons more—if the coal could be used." Mr. Hammer believes that increased use of coal "would help . . . our domestic coal industry" by putting "some thirteen thousand unemployed coal miners back to work and" creating "many thousands of new jobs."

In this speech I have explained three reasons that coal is an important source of future energy in the U.S. The Workshop on Alternative Energy Strategies has concluded that "The supply of oil will fail to meet increasing demand before the year 2000, most probably between 1985 and 1995, even if energy prices rise 50 percent above current levels in real terms. Additional constraints on oil production will hasten this shortage, thereby reducing the time available for action on alternatives."

We need not despair about our energy future, however; we only need to take positive action. Coal is a realistic alternative energy source for the U.S. because it is abundant, it can be converted to other usable forms, and its use would provide significant economic advantages.

Differences between Sample Outline and the Speech as Presented

It is obvious there are a number of significant differences between the sample outline and the speech as presented. You should not conclude, however, that all these differences must always exist, or that these are all the differences that may occur. This example is just to give you an idea of the relationship between a preparation outline and the speech as presented. Another factor

you must keep in mind is that there is no adaptation in this speech to a particular audience. It is written for a general audience. In presenting it to a specific audience, however, adaptation would be made wherever appropriate. In this example, the following differences may be noted:

1. The outline has no transitional words or phrases; the speech does.
2. The outline has no internal summaries; the speech does. Notice that the summary at the end of point 1 is longer and more detailed because point 1 is more complex than points 2 and 3. Point 2 has only a brief one-sentence summary because the point itself is easily understood and remembered. There is no summary after point 3 because of the brevity of the speech and the inclusion of a summary of the three main points in the conclusion.
3. The outline has detailed bibliographical information for the evidence used; the speech omits much of the bibliographical data and focuses instead on the sources and their qualifications. If someone asked you about some of your information after the speech, however, you would have the complete bibliographical information in the preparation outline.
4. The symbols in the outline identify the main points; the speech converts those symbols to verbal forms, such as "the first reason."
5. The outline cites evidence in the precise form in which it appears in the original source; the speech paraphrases much of the evidence and presents some in abbreviated quotations. This has two advantages: (a) It presents the evidence in the words of the speaker. (b) It eliminates the need for excessive reliance on note cards in the presentation of the speech.

Summary

Organization, which some evidence reveals as more important than content, is valuable for four reasons: (1) It significantly increases the listener's comprehension of the information. (2) It affects your ethos. (3) It aids in shifting the attitudes of listeners. (4) It prevents some listeners from becoming frustrated.

Organizing a speech involves three processes: selecting the materials to be used in a particular speech, developing the entity we call a speech, and ordering the main ideas in the body of a speech.

The entity we call a speech usually has four divisions: an introduction, a thesis, a body, and a conclusion. Not infrequently, a fifth optional part, a preview, is also included.

The thesis sentence, telling the audience specifically and explicitly what you want them to focus on in this particular speech, has three values: it provides necessary aural cues for the listener, it establishes the set of the listeners, and it aids you in preparing and delivering your speech. An effective thesis sentence can be stated in various ways.

The main ideas in the body of a speech may be ordered according to stock patterns (chronological, spatial, topical, causal, problem-solution, or motivated sequence). Transitional devices help to make the organization of a speech clear to the listeners by giving unity and coherence to the ideas, conveying a sense of movement to the speech, and emphasizing important ideas.

Exercises

1. Attend an intercollegiate debate. Write a critique of the organization of the speeches. How did it affect the credibility of the debaters?
2. Attend a public lecture on campus. Discuss the speaker's organization. What did this speaker do that made it easier for the listener? What could he or she have done? How did the organization affect the credibility of the ideas?

Notes

1. K. B. Olson, "Content and Form in Public Address: An Analysis of the Relative Influence of the Major Components upon the Listener," M.A. thesis, University of the Pacific, Calif., 1965.
2. E. Thompson, "An Experimental Investigation of the Relative Effectiveness of Organization Structure in Oral Communication," *Southern Speech Journal* 26 (1960):59–69.
3. D. K. Darnell, "The Relation between Sentence Order and Comprehension," *Speech Monographs* 30 (1963):97–100.
4. J. A. Kulgren, "The Effects of Organization upon the Comprehension of a Persuasive-Type Speech," M.A. thesis, Fresno State College, Calif., 1960.

5. C. Spicer and R. E. Bassett, "The Effect of Organization on Learning from an Informative Message," *Southern Speech Communication Journal* 41 (1976):298.

6. F. R. Miller, "An Experiment to Determine the Effect Organization Has on the Immediate and Delayed Recall of Information," M.A. thesis, Miami University, Ohio, 1966.

7. Thompson, "An Experimental Investigation."

8. J. P. Parker, "Some Organizational Variables and Their Effect upon Comprehension," *Journal of Communication* 12 (1962):27–32.

9. D. L. Thistlethwaite, H. de Haan, and J. Kemenetzky, "The Effects of 'Directive' and 'Nondirective' Communication Procedures on Attitudes," *Journal of Abnormal and Social Psychology* 51 (1955):107–13.

10. H. Sharp, Jr., and T. McClung, "Effect of Organization on the Speaker's Ethos," *Speech Monographs* 33 (1966):182–84.

11. E. E. Baker, "The Immediate Effects of Perceived Speaker Disorganization on Speaker Credibility and Audience Attitude Change in Persuasive Speaking," *Western Speech Journal* 29 (1965):148–61.

12. J. C. McCroskey and R. S. Mehrley, "The Effects of Disorganization and Nonfluency on Attitude Change and Source Credibility," *Speech Monographs* 36 (1969):13–21.

13. R. G. Smith, "An Experimental Study of the Effects of Speech Organization upon Attitudes of College Students," *Speech Monographs* 18 (1951):292.

14. A. R. Cohen, E. Stotland, and D. M. Wolfe, "An Experimental Investigation of Need for Cognition," *Journal of Abnormal and Social Psychology* 51 (1955):291–94.

15. P. L. Harriman, *Handbook of Psychological Terms* (Paterson, N.J.: Littlefield, Adams & Co., 1959), p. 168.

16. E. Siipola, "A Group Study of Some Effects of Preparatory Sets," *Psychological Monographs* 46: no. 210 (1935).

17. F. J. Di Vesta and P. Bossart, "The Effects of Sets Induced by Labeling on the Modification of Attitudes," *Journal of Personality* 26 (1958):379–87. See also D. Sears and J. L. Freedman, "Effects of Expected Familiarity with Arguments upon Opinion Change and Selective Exposure," *Journal of Personality and Social Psychology* 2 (1965):420–26.

18. S. L. Tubbs, "Explicit versus Implicit Conclusions and Audience Commitment," *Speech Monographs* 35 (1968):14–19.

19. S. L. Tubbs, "An Experimental Study of an Explicit versus an Implicit Conclusion in a Persuasive Speech, and Degree of Commitment in the Audience," M.A. thesis, Bowling Green State University, Ohio, 1966.

20. D. L. Thistlethwaite, J. Kemenetzky, and H. Schmidt, "Factors Influencing Attitude Change through Refutative Communications," *Speech Monographs* 23 (1956):14–25.

21. E. Cooper and H. Dinerman, "Analysis of the Film 'Don't Be a Sucker': A Study in Communication," *Public Opinion Quarterly* 15 (1951):243–64.

22. J. E. Baird, Jr., "The Effects of Speech Summaries upon Audience Comprehension of Expository Speeches of Varying Quality and Complexity," *Central States Speech Journal* 25 (1974):124–25.

23. C. I. Hovland, *Order of Presentation in Persuasion* (New Haven: Yale University Press, 1961), p. 135.

24. A. H. Monroe and D. Ehninger, *Principles and Types of Speeches* (Glenview, Ill.: Scott, Foresman & Co., 1967), pp. 264–89.

11

BEGINNING AND ENDING THE SPEECH

Opening and closing remarks are the crucial points of a speech. In the beginning listeners form their initial judgment of the speaker; in the ending they obtain their final impression. If the introduction creates a poor image, the listeners may become prejudiced toward the ideas presented in the body of the speech. If the conclusion leaves a bad final impression, it may nullify the impact of the ideas presented earlier. Most speakers cannot afford to communicate a bad impression either at the beginning or end of their speech. For this reason, introductions and conclusions should be prepared with great care and presented well.

When Aristotle said that an introduction and a conclusion were needed in a speech because of the sorry nature of audiences, he was not so much denigrating humankind as acknowledging that the communicative situation makes certain demands on listeners which require adjustments and adaptations on the part of the speaker. This chapter considers the nature of introductions and conclusions and the ways in which they can be used.

Introductions

Three concerns should dominate the preparation of an introduction for a speech: Will the introduction (1) attract the attention of the listeners; (2) either improve your ethos with the listeners or at least not damage the ethos you already have; (3) assist the listeners in beginning to think about the topic you are going to develop in this particular speech?

An important objective of the introduction is to attract the listeners' attention. When you arrive at the lectern, you are not faced with a group of automatons whose attention you obtain by punching a button. Many members of the audience will be engaged in other activities before you arrive at the lectern. Some will be daydreaming; some will be worrying about problems; some will be musing over recent or anticipated experiences; some will be actively engaged in conversations with their neighbors. These activities do not end abruptly when you begin to talk. Those listeners engaged in other thought processes only gradually come to an awareness of the speaker. A member of the audience carrying on a conversation rarely stops in the middle of a sentence. Generally he finishes his sentence and may even complete the thought. Not infrequently, his neighbor replies before they both settle down to listen to the speaker. Obviously, then, you need to do something that will attract the attention of all listeners, something that will make your listeners consider it more important to listen to you than to do these other things. Quite obviously, also, whatever you do must be something that is not vital to the development of the specific purpose of the speech, because some of the hearers are going to miss at least part of it. This is the reason you should not normally begin with the thesis sentence. Only when the audience's attention is already fixed on you or on the subject can the speech be opened with the thesis; in such situations the speech needs no introduction.

The introduction should also safeguard or enhance your ethos. If you come to the occasion with high ethos, then you must avoid doing anything in the introduction that will decrease it. Making statements that sound rash or unwise will offend the listeners or cause them to think that you cannot provide valid information and advice. If your ethos is either low or neutral, avoid doing anything that will further damage your image. Instead, do something that will enhance your ethos.

We have seen in chapter 6 that five major sources of ethos are competence, trustworthiness, similarity, attraction, and sincerity. So if you want to increase your ethos, attempt to establish one or more of these qualities for yourself. You can call attention to your qualifications, your concern for the best interests of the listeners, your lack of self-interest, attributes you hold in common with the listeners, personal characteristics that will make you attractive to the listeners, or your sincerity.

Finally, the introduction should cause the listeners to begin to think about the topic you are going to develop in the speech. This requirement places some limitations on what you can do to attract the attention of the listeners or what you can do to enhance your ethos. You may have a humorous anecdote that is a proven attention-getter, but if it is irrelevant to the topic, you cannot use it. Whatever you do to achieve the other purposes of the introduction must be something that enables the listener to make a smooth transition to the thesis sentence and then to the body of the speech.

The length of an introduction will depend on several factors. Normally an introduction constitutes only about 10 percent of the total speech; in some instances it might be as little as 1 percent and in others as much as 38 percent.[1] If your ethos is low and the topic is an unfamiliar one, you might have to spend nearly a third of the speech on the introduction. In some cases, you might want to develop background material before you get to your main purpose; this could necessitate spending a longer time on the introduction. On the other hand, if you have high ethos and the topic is important to the listeners, you might actually begin to lose the attention of the audience by spending too much time in the introduction. A few brief statements may suffice to get to your thesis sentence. In some rare instances, an introduction might even be detrimental. If the preceding speakers have discussed the topic of your speech, and the listeners are deeply involved in that discussion, you may want to begin immediately with your thesis sentence; to do otherwise may cause the listeners' attention to wane.

Generally any apology should be avoided in the introduction. Do not tell the listeners that you "did not have time" to make adequate preparation unless that is a clearly legitimate reason for not having prepared properly; that not only insults the hearers by indicating that you did not esteem them highly, but also damages your ethos. Do not apologize for your ability as a speaker. Let the audience evaluate your efforts without prejudice. They might decide you are skilled and well prepared.

You should not prepare the introduction until after you have phrased the thesis sentence and developed the body of the speech. Only then can you know exactly what you want to introduce and what method will best achieve it. If the introduction is prepared before the purpose is clearly formulated and the body developed, the result may be a speech that lacks purpose and significance because the body was suited to the introduction rather than vice versa. When the body of the speech has been completed, you know approximately what you are going to say and can choose an introduction that best prepares the listeners for your remarks.

A number of different types of introductions are available. In the following discussion, the different introductions will be organized by type instead of by purpose, since a good introduction may accomplish the three purposes of attracting your listeners' attention, improving or at least not damaging your ethos, and helping your listeners start to think about your speech topic.

You may find that a reference to the listeners and their interests will be an effective way to achieve your purpose. Notice how Arabella Martinez, assistant secretary for Human Development Services, made the members of the University of Connecticut's School of Social Work feel both important and appreciated.

Begin with Reference to the Audience

It is a pleasure to be with you today in a school of social work which has—and deserves—both a regional and a national reputation for excellence. In your course work, field placements, training, research, and evaluation you are contributing to the progress of social work in this country, extending your influence on a daily basis far beyond the classroom right into the lives of people who need help.

You are to be commended for the role you play in the cause of child welfare, and especially in the area of child welfare training. HEW's Office of Human Development Services is pleased to have provided funds for some of your outstanding training programs, including your current project to train foster care workers in working with biological parents.

I applaud your selection by our own Children's Bureau within the Office of Human Development Services as one of the ten regional child welfare training centers in the country.

HDS is also pleased to have been a part of other social work funding to the school and to the university, including the multidisciplinary center of gerontology and teaching grants in rehabilitation services and counseling.[2]

In contrast to the serious reference to the audience is the humorous reference to the listeners. Harold Howe II, commissioner of education, alluded humorously to his previous association with his listeners when he addressed the College Entrance Examination Board.

It is very pleasant for me to realize that this evening I have the members of the College Entrance Examination Board temporarily at my mercy. I know that this heady monopoly won't last long, but as a former vice chairman and a longtime committee member I hope you will forgive me for enjoying the opportunity to speak to you at some length, on a subject of my own choosing, without fear of interruption.

I do this, of course, by virtue of my present office. Though I am no more learned and not any wiser than I was as a member of this group, being Commissioner of Education does give me a certain leverage I didn't have before.[3]

A reference to the audience may emphasize hardships its members have undergone. If you have experienced those hardships as well, the introduction also serves to stress a point of similarity, to establish a bond between the listener and the speaker. In speaking to the 62nd Annual NAACP Convention, the Rev. Leon H. Sullivan, pastor of the Zion Baptist Church of Philadelphia, used this method to develop rapport with his listeners and to start them thinking about his topic, the steps the black man must take in the future.

First, let me thank you for this Award. I am aware this is among the highest honors a black man can receive. I want to thank you for considering me and for this presentation. One hundred years ago the black man began the journey towards full emancipation in America. The journey has been long and hard. A full century has gone by, and three generations have passed off the scene since the journey began, but we still have not reached our goal. The attainment of full emancipation, equal opportunity and first class citizenship is still a distance away.

To be sure, giant strides have been made. Never in the history of the world have a people, starting with so little, gone so far. The road has been rocky and rigorous. As James Weldon Johnson put it in that stirring anthem "Lift Every Voice and Sing":

"We have come over a way that with tears has been watered,
We have come treading our path thro' the blood of the slaughtered."

Somehow, though, in spite of it all, with God's help, we have survived. We have endured. We have come this far.[4]

Begin with Reference to the Subject

On some occasions the subject of your speech may be so vital and immediate to the listeners that you will want to develop the introduction around a reference to that topic. Beginning with a reference to the subject should be used as an introduction only when the listeners have a strong interest in the topic. Fully aware of his listeners' enthusiasm for his topic, Lowry Wyatt, senior vice-president of Weyerhaeuser, thrust immediately to his subject in a speech to the students at Washington State College.

The "Environmentalist Movement," which I have been asked to view today, is a modern phenomenon—an issue which, like no other, has quickly caught the attention of the public. It may be the healthiest influence for the good of the country in our history.

On the other hand, it has the potential to destroy much of the social progress which the nation has made in the past few decades.

And today, there are definite signs in many parts of the country that the movement is in imminent danger of falling flat on its face.

As one "industrialist," I will say right now that that must not be allowed to happen.[5]

Begin with Reference to the Occasion

When the occasion for the speech is an unusual or important one, you may begin the speech by pointing up the significance of the event.

Sargent Shriver, former director of the Peace Corps, alluded to the importance of the occasion for his audience.

It's a joy for me to be here this day with you. Thanks to all of you for coming to this splendid 20th Anniversary celebration; thanks for your service as Peace Corps Volunteers and staff members; thanks to our distinguished visitors whose presence has dignified this occasion; thanks to the Congress and Executive Branch members who have kept the Peace Corps alive and prospering; but thanks most of all to every Senator and Congressperson who just this week voted for the independence and freedom of the Peace Corps! From now on a new Independence Day will be celebrated every June 16th in Peace Corps precincts around the world![6]

In beginning his speech to the Kent State University faculty and students, Alton W. Whitehouse, Jr., chairman of the board of the Standard Oil Company of Ohio, referred to the occasion.

Thank you for this chance to keynote Kent State's honors week events. We gather this week to recognize academic achievement. Oddly, the theme of these proceedings is the approach of 1984, the year George Orwell made a metaphor for totalitarianism. I say "oddly" because the central feature of Orwell's 1984 was the mass mind—whole populations thinking in state-imposed uniformity. Such uniformity strikes me as the antithesis of the individual intellectual excellence that we gather to honor this week, the excellence that René Descartes celebrated in saying, "I think, therefore I am."[7]

If you have qualifications that enhance your expertise, have had experiences that equip you to discuss the topic, or have had previous association with the audience or the topic, you may use a personal reference to introduce the speech. This particular introduction can be especially effective in building your ethos. Recalling her efforts in opposing the "excesses on the extreme right" during the McCarthy era of the 1950s, Senator Margaret Chase Smith seemed to justify her right to speak in the U.S. Senate against "excesses of dissent on the extreme left."

Begin with Personal Reference

Twenty years ago on this June 1 date at this same desk I spoke about the then serious national condition with a statement known as the "Declaration of Conscience." We had a national sickness then from which we recovered. We have a national sickness now from which I pray we will recover.[8]

When Alan Rosenthal, director of the Eagleton Institute of Politics at Rutgers University, addressed the Public Affairs Council of Atlanta, Georgia, he apparently felt the need to enhance his credibility. Consequently, he referred to his expertise on the subject of his speech.

The justification for my addressing you here today is that I've just written a book about American state legislatures and am presumed to know something about these peculiar institutions. I should, since I've been at it over the course of fifteen years, during which period I've been able to visit with legislatures and legislative staff in three-quarters of the states. I've observed these people in their natural habitats, listened to them speak their native tongues, and tried to understand their customs and their folkways.[9]

In his address to the conference of the Academy of Religion and Mental Health and the Metropolitan Applied Research Center, the noted black psychologist Kenneth B. Clark surely did no harm to his ethos with his reference to his own experience.

In terms of what has happened to the country—and to me—in the interim, it seems a very long time ago that I agreed, as a young graduate student, to work with my former teacher, Ralph Bunche, and Gunnar Myrdal on the project that was to result in *An American Dilemma.*

Much of the data in that report is now superseded; many of the findings may seem naive in terms of our new realism about the depth of American racism. But the basic truths of that study have not been superseded and there is still an American dilemma, more frightening now than it seemed even then—and still unresolved.[10]

Begin with a Startling Statement or Startling Analysis

A speech begun with a startling statement will often jerk the listeners to attention. For this reason it can be very effective. Unfortunately, after the use of a particularly startling statement, the rest of the speech may seem anticlimactic; it may never quite rise to the heights of the beginning. The listener then goes away feeling let down by a speech that would otherwise have seemed effective. The introduction that presents startling information or an unusual analysis can also be effective in attracting the attention of the listeners and has the advantage of being less stark in contrast with the rest of the speech.

Terry Sanford, then president of Duke University and former governor of North Carolina, opened his speech to the 1983 graduating class of Emory University with startling information.

Communicating with college students is always somewhat of a challenge. It is not that I have too much difficulty understanding your changing expressions and attitudes. It is that I forget what you never saw. I recently read in a church magazine that when preparing a sermon, one should remember to assume that ten is the age at which an event creates an impression, which means that of today's 200 million Americans:

- 86% cannot recall Charles Lindbergh's solo flight to Paris;
- 68% cannot recollect Hitler;
- 65% cannot remember life without television;
- 58% cannot remember Senator Joe McCarthy (so listen when I mention him later);
- 53% cannot remember a Studebaker or think it is a German pudding.

And 64,345,092 people don't know what a church key is; they started life with Coca-Cola's pop-top cans.

I started my speech aware that 100 percent of you keenly know that I am the last, big obstacle between you and your diploma, and that a diploma, even after all your work, doesn't come without pain. So stick with me. I am not going to give you all the advice there is. I will try to make only one point, that ought to be enough for one commencement.[11]

Begin with an Example

You can use an example to call the listeners' attention to a principle or principles you plan to develop. The advantage of the example at the beginning is that it makes your idea more concrete and specific for your hearers. James B. Reston, *New York Times* columnist, in a speech honoring fellow newsman Walter W. (Red) Smith at the University of Notre Dame, began with an example.

What we have just heard from Terry Smith tells us a lot about his father and his mother, who didn't get a Pulitzer Prize but got Terry and Terry's sister, Kit, who are with us this evening. Red once delivered a brief eulogy at the funeral of a colleague. "Dying is no big deal," he said. "The least of us can manage it. Living is the trick." He knew the trick. And the proof lies at the end, when your children become your friends, and sons can talk about their fathers as Terry talked about Red.[12]

William E. Gibson, Chief Economist and Senior Vice President, Republicbank Corporation, began his speech to the Canadian Conference Board with an example.

I was asked this morning to tackle the United States economic outlook for you—we certainly picked a good day for an economist to tackle such a subject. After all, this is the birthday of two of the greatest economists ever: Adam Smith's (the first one) as well as John Maynard Keynes. So it must be preordained that you would have an economist here.

Traditionally, we economists approach such a task in a manner reminiscent of a story told about our late chief justice of the Supreme Court, Oliver Wendell Holmes. Although in his 90s, he maintained an active schedule, and the famous jurist was on a train enroute to a speaking engagement one day. The conductor approached, asking for his ticket. The jurist patted one pocket. No ticket. Another pocket. No ticket. The conductor, who recognized him, said, "That's alright, Mr. Chief Justice. Just hand in your ticket when you get off the train." Holmes looked up. Quite annoyed, he snapped back, "The problem, young man, is not 'Where is the ticket;' the problem is—'Where am I going?' " Choosing how to set an agenda for 'where we are going' would actually predict what kind of answers I would give you. As I said, traditionally, we would look to where standard indices are at a fixed point in time—say January 1, 1984—then looking ahead to where they might be at a similar date in the future, the end of this year, or next year, or this decade.[13]

Begin with Humor

If you can cause listeners to laugh at the outset of your speech, it does much to develop rapport between you and the audience, especially if you can avoid "canned" humor.

Dianne Feinstein, the first woman mayor of San Francisco, in her role as the closing keynote speaker at a conference entitled "Impact 84: A Leadership Conference for Democratic Women," used humor to begin her speech.

About thirty years ago, Senator Margaret Chase Smith was asked by *Time* magazine what she would do if one day she woke up in the White House? She replied that she would apologize to Bess Truman and leave immediately.

Women in politics, particularly in positions of major authority, have carried that kind of gender burden traditionally in our country. There is an incredulity and improbability that has surrounded women's rise to the top of the political ladder. I suggest to you that times and traditions have changed, and that women have changed, too.[14]

In his address to the audience at Harvard Class Day, Mario M. Cuomo, Governor of New York, used humor to begin.

It's an honor to share this day with you.

And since this Harvard and your motto is "Veritas"—truth—let me be completely truthful with you. I know I wasn't your first choice as a speaker here today. Nor your second. Nor your third.

You invited three of America's funniest men . . . then, when Larry and Curley and Moe all declined, you invited me.

I can only think of two reasons why you'd do so.

Either you decided that instead of enjoying yourself here today, you'd invite someone who'd help you get some sleep before tomorrow's ritual; or, along with millions of other Americans, you decided there's no bigger joke than a politician.

Still, whether you invited me here as a politican or a comedian—or on the assumption that one is as good as the other—it's an honor for me to be here, to be allowed to be part of the Harvard tradition.[15]

Begin with a Quotation

A speech begun with a quotation can attract attention because of the pleasing quality of the wording of the quotation itself, because of the reputation of its author, because of the timeliness or relevancy of the quotation, because of the humor of the quotation, or because of all or several of these.

Charles W. Parry, the Chairman and Chief Executive Officer of the Alcoa Aluminum Corporation, began his speech to the Carlow College Ethics Seminar with a quotation.

Winston Churchill once remarked that, "Some see private enterprise as a predatory target to be shot, others as a cow to be milked, but few are those who see it as a sturdy horse pulling the wagon." Long after Churchill's death, we still find ourselves to be in a period of diminishing public trust toward the standards and behavior of the business community. Yet the "wagon" moves on, steadily increasing the wealth of the nation. America's ambivalence toward its own prosperity results from a continuing struggle to understand the relationship between business, ethics and society. While not hoping to master this mystery, I would like to share with you a few thoughts on this relationship and discuss the direction our enterprise is pulling us.[16]

The president of The College Board, George Hanford, in a speech to the City Club of Cleveland, began with a quotation.

Among his many other wise observations Aristotle, we are told, once remarked that education is ". . . an ornament in prosperity, but a refuge in adversity." That principle certainly seems to apply to American education, which is left pretty much to itself when times are good, but becomes a major source of concern when things are not going so well.[17]

Quotations used in the introduction should be concise. A long quotation may at first get the attention of the listeners but then cause them to become inattentive before you get to the topic of your speech.

Providing at the outset of your speech a clear definition of the main idea of your speech can insure that listeners understand what you are trying to say and do not quit listening because they fail to understand what you are trying to do.

Begin with a Definition

The surgeon general of the United States, Dr. C. Everett Koop, in his keynote address to a conference sponsored by the National Coalition on Television Violence, began with a definition.

I'm pleased to be your keynote speaker today. As you well know, this topic of violence on television is as much a part of the Office of Surgeon General as the flag and the uniform. And violence is every bit a public health issue for me and my successors in this century, as smallpox, tuberculosis, and syphilis were for my predecessors in the last two centuries.

And it is understandable, especially when we apply the term "epidemic." And I think it is fair to do that. Violence in American public and private life has indeed assumed the proportions of an epidemic. Assaults, child and spouse abuse, homicides and suicides among young adults, these indicators of violence in our population are still climbing. They are occurring at a rate "beyond what is normally expected," to use the phrase used by epidemiologists to define the term "epidemic." The occurrence of a case or an illness *beyond what we might expect, based upon past experience,* is an epidemic.[18]

Begin with a Justification of the Speech

An effective type of introduction for both an experienced and an inexperienced speaker is to open with a justification for the speech. The justification may take several forms. It may explain (1) why you have elected to speak on this topic, (2) why you are qualified to speak on this topic, or (3) why the topic is important to the listeners.

Credibility is created more easily by this type of introduction because listeners are more interested in information that seems to touch them personally. Moreover, they more readily believe statements from a speaker qualified to speak on the topic. A word of warning, however—your qualifications must be presented in such a way that you do not appear to be bragging. The qualifications must appear to be an integral part of the total narrative, included to clarify other points. For example, a speaker who is going to discuss three basic first aid techniques that any person might use could begin his speech in the following manner:

Last summer while working with the Henderson Rescue Squad, we were called to an accident on Interstate 85. In my five years of working with the Rescue Squad, I have never seen an accident as bad as that one. Four people were killed and three were seriously injured. Turning our attention to the injured, we were able, in a few minutes, to stop the severe bleeding of one victim, treat another for shock, and place a splint on the broken leg of another. Because of those measures, the victims were in better condition when they arrived at the hospital. The basic first aid techniques that we used are simple ones and can be used by anyone who understands them.

Notice how the information—five years of working with the Rescue Squad—which establishes the qualifications of the speaker on this topic is introduced indirectly and seems to be a natural part of the narrative.

Obviously, then, there are many effective methods to introduce a speech. It is clear also that not all introductions achieve equally well all three purposes of the introduction. Some will attract the attention of the listeners more effectively, some will enhance your ethos to a greater extent, some will start the listener thinking about the subject matter more easily. As a matter of fact, you will not always want these purposes achieved equally; it will frequently be more important to attain one more than the others.

Once the preparation of the introduction is completed, you can begin to think about how to conclude the speech. Whenever possible, you should return in the conclusion to a theme initiated in the introduction.

Conclusions

The primary purpose of the conclusion is to direct the attention of the listeners for the last time to the main purpose of the speech. You may focus on your central idea by restating the thesis, summarizing the main ideas, appealing for action or behavior consistent with the main purpose, presenting a quotation that expresses the main purpose eloquently or vividly, giving an illustration that exemplifies the central purpose, issuing a challenge to the listeners to think about or accept the main thought, or stating your intention to follow the ideas developed in the speech. If the conclusion is successful, listeners leave with the main purpose of the speech firmly fixed in their minds.

A second purpose of the conclusion is to leave the listeners with a favorable image of you. In most instances, you begin with high ethos, the speech either increases the ethos or does nothing to decrease it, so the conclusion simply has to avoid arousing any negative reactions. On other occasions, however, you may be forced to present ideas that will decrease your ethos with the audience. When this occurs, you must make a special effort in the conclusion to reestablish a favorable image in the minds of the listeners. Otherwise, your ideas may be rejected.

The third purpose of the conclusion is to give a sense of completeness to the speech, to avoid an abrupt ending that leaves listeners wondering if they heard all the speech. If you quit on your last main idea, you run a risk of leaving the listeners frustrated and dissatisfied by a feeling that the task was not completed. A conclusion gives the impression that there are no loose ends remaining; everything has been tied up in a nice neat bundle. You can often enhance this impression by returning in the conclusion to a theme or a reference developed in the introduction. In fact, one of the best ways to achieve this is to restate your thesis and summarize your main ideas. The speech then appears to have come full circle. The listener leaves with a sense of completeness; the speech had a beginning, a middle, and an end.

Ordinarily the conclusion should be rather brief, generally no more than 5 percent of the total speaking time, and frequently even less than that.[19] Once you have finished the discussion of your ideas, you should quickly move through the conclusion.

A number of different methods of ending a speech are available. Some of the most frequently used ones will be discussed.

End with a Quotation

If you can find an effective statement of your main purpose authored by someone else, especially someone whom the listeners know and respect, you not only focus the minds of the listeners on the main theme, but add weight to it as well.

In a speech to the convention of the National Association for the Advancement of Colored People, Vice President George Bush closed his speech with a quotation from a speech given by Roy Wilkins ten years before to the NAACP convention.

It was exactly ten years ago, at your convention in Indianapolis, that Roy Wilkins spoke of black people having an investment in America, as he put it, "an investment in blood and tears, in lives dead and revered, and in lives which are triumphant over insults and barriers and persecution. . . . This is our land," Roy Wilkins said, "For good or bad, it owns us, and we own it. We bought it and our futures here with sacrifices and heroism, with humility and love. It belongs to us and we shall never give up our claim and run away."

So spoke a great black leader a decade ago. As followers in his tradition, you aren't going to run away from the challenges and problems facing black and minority Americans and, speaking for the Reagan administration, neither are we.

That's why I'm here today. And that's why the doors to the White House are open and will remain open to those who, whether they vote for us or not, seek a dialogue to help meet the challenges and solve the problems that affect America's black community.[20]

William French Smith, former Attorney General of the United States, closed his speech to the Town Hall of California with two quotations, one from former Secretary of State Stimson and one from Mark Twain.

Too frequently in a democracy, the pendulum of public policy swings in an excessively wide arc. Some fifty years ago Secretary of State Stimson observed: "Gentlemen do not read each other's mail." As we have learned since then, however, the real world is not peopled by gentlemen. In making intelligence gathering more effective and in protecting the rights guaranteed to all Americans by the Constitution, we must keep the balance true and realistic. Many years ago Mark Twain wrote:

"We should be careful to get out of an experience only the wisdom that is in it—and stop there; lest we be like the cat that sits down on a hot stove lid. She will never sit down on a hot stove lid again—and that is well; but also she will never sit down on a cold one either."

Keeping that balance true is one of the major challenges of our intelligence community. At the same time that community has an awesome responsibility for our national security and deserves the fullest support of the American people.[21]

End with a Challenge

One of the most frequently used type of conclusions is that which attempts to challenge the listeners in some way. The challenge differs from an appeal. Whereas the appeal asks the listeners for a behavioral commitment, the challenge attempts to stimulate listeners to a mental or spiritual commitment.

In a speech to the College Board, Dr. Harry Edwards, a black associate professor of sociology at the University of California at Berkeley, challenged black athletes to meet the requirements that Proposition 48, then newly passed by the NCAA, had placed on all college athletes.

And, finally, it must be made unequivocally clear that in the last analysis, it is black student-athletes themselves who must shoulder a substantial portion of the responsibility for improving their own circumstances. Education is an activist pursuit and cannot in reality be "given." It must be obtained "the old-fashioned way"—one must earn it! Black student-athletes, therefore, must insist upon educational discipline no less than athletic discipline among themselves, and they must insist upon educational integrity in athletic programs rather than, as is all too often the case, merely seeking the most parsimonious academic route to maintaining athletic eligibility. The bottom line here is that if black student-athletes fail to take an active role in establishing and legitimizing a priority upon academic achievement, nothing done by any other party to this American sports tragedy will matter—if for no other reason than a slave cannot be freed against his will.[22]

Dan Angel, President of Austin Community College, used a challenge to close his speech to the 1985 graduating class of the college.

This is a great place to work on those rainbows I mentioned. Your future is in your hands. Just choose your couplets carefully:

1. Be optimistic.
2. Make yourself knowledgeable and prepared.
3. Look for opportunities in problems.
4. Remember to stretch yourself.
5. Be competitive, but offer cooperation.
6. And remember, you can, you really can make a difference.

When you look up into our sky of opportunities, you will see why there are so many songs about rainbows. You will have the choice in painting those rainbows, giving them color and depth, brightness and brilliance. That opportunity is what your life is going to be all about. Find your rainbow connection.

Looking at the future, I can say to you graduates tonight that I feel like John Naisbitt when at the end of his book *Megatrends* he wrote, "My God, what an exciting honor to be alive!"[23]

End with an Appeal   When you want the listeners to take some specific action, an effective conclusion is to specifically ask them to do whatever is desired. If the speech has been effectively organized, supported, and presented, they should be ready to act in the desired manner. Wendell Chino, president of the Mescalero Apache Tribe, issued the following appeal to the National Congress of American Indians:

Finally—I say to our Indian Leaders and our Indian people, let *your* people see *you* take an active part in Indian affairs, and be involved in salvaging the ideals of our people, the traditions of our people. Fight the non-Indian values that would destroy our culture, and *oppose* the platitudes of our time and of the dominant society. Our mutual concern and protection will preserve and sustain our Indian heritage and culture for generations to come.[24]

In a speech to the Round Table at Lincoln, Nebraska, William J. Aitken, attorney, used a quotation to sum up his speech and to lead into an appeal for action on the part of his listeners.

In conclusion, the National Panel of Consultants on the Conquest of Cancer said:
While it is probably unrealistic at this time to talk about the total elimination of cancer within a short period of time or to expect a single vaccine or cure that will eradicate the disease completely, the progress that has been made in the past decade provides a strong basis for the belief that an accelerated and intensified assault on cancer at this time will produce extraordinary rewards and the committee is of the view that an effective national program for the conquest of cancer should be promptly initiated and relentlessly pursued.
Within our own group, I hope you may be willing to devote the few moments of time required to write Congressman Charles Thone, and express your approval of his Resolution (HCR 28) and to Senators Carl Curtis and Roman Hruska to exert your influence, and request their support at this time, of a massive funding of cancer research by the federal government as recommended by the National Panel of Consultants on the Conquest of Cancer.[25]

End with Startling Information   Like the introduction that provides startling information, the conclusion that does so vividly grabs the listeners' attention. Coming as it does, in the final moments of the speech, it sends the listeners away with a graphic impression of the speaker's main thoughts.

In her address to a College Convocation at Central University, Iowa, Dr. Anita Taylor, Professor of Communication at George Mason University, Virginia, concluded with startling information.

In the final analysis, you are responsible for your own education. Your college years, if they succeed, only help you learn how to learn. In no other way will you be prepared to cope with the future. Half of the "facts" you learn in college will be obsolete within ten years of your graduation. There will be facts to know then that no one has even dreamed of yet.

Your education must prepare you to keep learning, and if it is a quality education, it will hone your ability to think, write, talk and listen. In short, real education teaches you how to solve problems. Learn that, and you will not be one of the terrified of whom Toffler speaks. You will not succumb to future shock nor futureshlock, and you will not engage in a desperate, futile flight into the past. You will, instead, ride the crest of the Third Wave into the future.[26]

One of the easiest and most effective methods of concluding a speech is to summarize the main points. Not only is the repetition effective in helping listeners remember the main points, but if any listeners happened to miss a point during the body of the speech, this gives them an opportunity to hear it.

End with a Summary

In a speech to the Humanities Society of the University of Iowa, Dr. Carolyn Stewart Dyer, an assistant professor in the School of Journalism and Mass Communication, used a summary to remind her listeners of her main ideas.

In summary, then, economic factors affecting all three groups of media as I have described them define freedom of the press. The ordinary local media don't use it or define it because it's too costly. The media at the fringes of radical politics and social propriety use all the freedom they can get, but risk litigation, the cost of which can destroy them and diminish the breadth of debate on public affairs. And the First Amendment Club members which use freedom modestly and to engage in litigation to extend it define the parameters within which the law is developed, and those parameters do not extend as far as they might. The consequence is an impoverished debate on public affairs.[27]

A particularly interesting, unusual, or vivid example which demonstrates clearly the main theme of the speech can be used effectively as a conclusion. It has the virtue of peaking the attention of the listeners at a crucial moment and calling attention to the central purpose of the speech in an indirect, interesting way.

End with an Example

Speaking to the City Club of Cleveland, Ohio, George Hanford, President of the College Board, used an example to focus on the main theme of his speech.

In a way what I am talking about is imbedded in a story that one of my predecessors at the board, Sidney P. Marland, liked to tell.

It took place while he was superintendent of schools in Winnetka, a prosperous north shore suburb of Chicago, and involved an irate father, an MIT graduate, who complained that his son's school counselor was giving him bad advice. "My son wants to go to MIT, and the counselor said he shouldn't try," the father said.

Sid looked up the boy's record. "I'm sorry to say I have to agree with the counselor," he told the father. "Your son's grades are just not good enough. He's in the bottom half of his class. He'd never have a chance."

"Bottom half of the class," the father said. "Why that's just ridiculous. With the school taxes we pay here, nobody should be in the bottom half of the class."

In a way, that expectation is what I suggest we need to work toward: an educational system and program that has no losers. It may be statistically impossible to put everyone in the top half of the class, but we strive to make sure that those in the bottom half still have what they need to succeed.

It's been said that the trouble today is that the future isn't what it used to be. That may be true, but we can change it. We have the opportunity today to educate the ones who will determine the future of this country in the twenty-first century. Let's make the most of it.[28]

End with Humor

A humorous ending may be used to focus your listeners' minds on the main theme in an easy, painless way. Moreover, the humor will generally leave them in a good frame of mind, thus enhancing your ethos and encouraging acceptance of your ideas. John S. Reed, president of the Santa Fe Railway, in a speech to the Chicago Traffic Club, used a humorous anecdote to help in changing the mood of his listeners following a negative analysis of the condition of the railroads.

I started by asking if anyone was listening and you have been a good audience. The difficulty in talking about railroads today is that one almost has to stress the negatives, whereas our natural instinct out in this part of the country is to accentuate the positives. I hope this talk hasn't sounded too much like the conversation that one old henpecked codger had with his wife. Even on his deathbed he was being nagged. As he was taking his last gasps, the old gal pursued a line of lugubrious questioning. "Now George, which side of the cemetery plot do you wish to be buried in? What flowers do you wish to have placed at the headstone on Memorial Day?" And so it went. And so finally her last question was "George, which way do you want your coffin in the procession—head first or feet first?" The old boy had just enough strength left to say, "I'll leave that up to you—surprise me."

No, gentlemen, your railroads are not dead, we are not going to any funeral. There may be some surprises, but we are going to solve those problems. To use a baseball expression, we will be coming in feet first and with our spikes high. With your assistance we can keep our railroads out of nationalization and out of political control. Then when we sing, "I've Been Working on the Railroad," we can say, "I've been working for the railroad" and really mean it.[29]

No matter what type of conclusion you use, avoid making false stops. Nothing is more irritating to the listener than to hear the speaker reach a logical place to stop and then continue on. Some speakers seem to be unwilling to quit and even continue past several good stopping places.

A final word on conclusions: Try to end your speech on an accented, strong vowel. Language authority James J. Kilpatrick advises writers "to end a piece of writing on an accented syllable. If you can work it with a long vowel or a diphthong, so much the better." Kilpatrick offers some examples: "*The Wall Street Journal* had a piece on Ohio's bank holiday. The final paragraph poses a series of rhetorical questions. This is the last word: 'Will we have . . . a full explanation of what went wrong?' "

Kilpatrick gives another example: "*The Washington Post* comments that industrial democracies need to keep their economies safely and prosperously dull: 'That's never so easy as it looks.' "[30]

If this prosodic device is effective in writing, it should be even more so in speaking where the strong, accented vowel will make its full impact on the ear.

Summary

Introductions and conclusions are important because they provide the initial and final impression that you make on your listeners. Although not always required parts of a speech, they become necessary under certain circumstances in order for a speech to have its maximum impact on the listeners.

An introduction is necessary when you must get the attention of some or all of your hearers, when you need to enhance your ethos with these particular listeners, and when you want to get them started thinking about the topic of your speech.

Many different methods may be used to introduce a speech. Ten of the most commonly used ones were discussed: (1) begin with a reference to the audience, (2) begin with a reference to the subject, (3) begin with a reference to the occasion, (4) begin with a personal reference, (5) begin with a startling statement or startling information, (6) begin with an example, (7) begin with humor, (8) begin with a quotation, (9) begin with a definition, and (10) begin with a justification of the speech.

A conclusion is used to focus the listeners' attention on the central idea of the speech, to leave those listeners with a favorable image of you, and to give a sense of completeness to the speech.

Among the many types of conclusions that might be used, the seven following were discussed: (1) end with a quotation, (2) end with a challenge, (3) end with an appeal, (4) end with a startling statement or startling information, (5) end with a summary, (6) end with an example, and (7) end with humor.

Exercises

1. Prepare three introductions for your next speech. Choose one that you will actually use and explain why you made that decision.
2. Analyze the introduction of one of your classmates' speeches. Which of the purposes of an introduction were achieved? How? Which purposes were not achieved? Why not?
3. Choose a topic toward which your classmates are hostile. For a speech opposing their attitudes, prepare an introduction that would overcome hostility and gain you a favorable hearing from your listeners.
4. Analyze the conclusion of one of your classmates' speeches. What was the speaker trying to do? Did the speaker achieve his or her purpose? How? If not, why not?
5. For your next speech, prepare the following conclusions: (1) one that will challenge your listeners, (2) one that appeals for some action on the part of your listeners, (3) one that leaves them well disposed toward you.

Notes

1. E. Miller, "Speech Introductions and Conclusions," *Quarterly Journal of Speech* 32 (1946):181–83. This study analyzed fifty speeches from *Vital Speeches of the Day* over a three-month period in 1943.
2. Arabella Martinez, "Listen to the Children," *Vital Speeches of the Day* 46 (1979):18.
3. Harold Howe II, "Changing the Pecking Order," in *Representative American Speeches: 1967–1968,* ed. Lester Thonssen (New York: H. W. Wilson Co., 1968), p. 113. Used by permission.
4. Leon H. Sullivan, "Steps We Must Take," *Vital Speeches of the Day* 37 (1971):676. Used by permission.
5. Lowry Wyatt, "Economy & Environment," *Vital Speeches of the Day* 37 (1971):509. Used by permission.
6. Sargent Shriver, "The Peace Corps," *Vital Speeches of the Day* 47 (1981):700. Used by permission.
7. Alton W. Whitehouse, Jr., "The Misinformation Society," *Vital Speeches of the Day* 47 (1981):506. Used by permission.
8. Margaret Chase Smith, "Declaration of Conscience—Twenty Years Later," in *Representative American Speeches: 1969–1970,* ed. Lester Thonssen (New York: H. W. Wilson Co., 1970), pp. 133–34. Used by permission.
9. Alan Rosenthal, "The Pressure-Cooker World of the State Legislator," *Vital Speeches of the Day* 47 (1981):733. Used by permission.
10. Kenneth B. Clark, "Beyond the Dilemma," in *Representative American Speeches: 1969–1970,* ed. Lester Thonssen (New York: H. W. Wilson Co., 1970), p. 169. Used by permission.

11. Terry Sanford, "Is America a Leader?," in *Representative American Speeches, 1983–1984,* ed. Owen Peterson (New York: H. W. Wilson Co., 1984), p. 46. Used by permission.
12. James B. Reston, "Sport and Politics," *Representative American Speeches, 1983–1984,* ed. Owen Peterson (New York: H. W. Wilson Co., 1984), p. 114. Used by permission.
13. William E. Gibson, "The United States Economic Outlook," *Vital Speeches of the Day* 51 (1985):658. © City News Publishing Company. Used by permission.
14. Dianne Feinstein, "Women in Politics: Time for a Change," *Representative American Speeches, 1983–1984,* ed. Owen Peterson (New York: H. W. Wilson Company, 1984), pp. 99–100. Used by permission.
15. Mario M. Cuomo, "Your One Life Can Make a Difference," *Vital Speeches of the Day* 51 (1985):581–82. © City News Publishing Company. Used by permission.
16. Charles W. Parry, "My Company—Right or Wrong?," *Vital Speeches of the Day* 51 (1985):632. © City News Publishing Company. Used by permission.
17. George Hanford, "An Educational System That Has No Losers," *Vital Speeches of the Day* 51 (1985):595. © City News Publishing Company. Used by permission.
18. C. Everett Koop, "An Epidemic of Violence," *Representative American Speeches, 1983–1984,* ed. Owen Peterson (New York: H. W. Wilson Co., 1984), p. 164.
19. Miller, "Speech Introductions and Conclusions," pp. 181–83. Miller found that the length of conclusions in the fifty speeches studied ranged from 1 to 15 percent of the total length of the speech, with the mean length being approximately 5 percent.
20. George H. W. Bush, "A Wall of Misunderstanding," *Representative American Speeches, 1983–1984,* ed. Owen Peterson (New York: H. W. Wilson Co., 1984), p. 98. Used by permission.
21. William French Smith, "Intelligence and National Security," *Vital Speeches of the Day* 51 (1985):680. © City News Publishing Company. Used by permission.
22. Harry Edwards, "Black Student-Athletes Taking Responsibility," in *Representative American Speeches, 1983–1984,* ed. Owen Peterson (New York: H. W. Wilson Co., 1984), p. 132. Used by permission.
23. Dan Angel, "The Rainbow Connection," *Vital Speeches of the Day* 51 (1985):623. © City News Publishing Company. Used by permission.
24. Wendell Chino, "Indian Affairs—What Has Been Done and What Needs to Be Done," in *Representative American Speeches: 1969–1970,* ed. Lester Thonssen (New York: H. W. Wilson Co., 1970), p. 187.
25. William J. Aitken, "Cancer: The Problems and Progress," *Vital Speeches of the Day* 37 (1971):556. Used by permission.
26. Anita Taylor, "Talk, Future Shock, and Futureshlock," *Vital Speeches of the Day* 51 (1985):683. © City News Publishing Company. Used by permission.
27. Carolyn Stewart Dyer, "The Costs of Freedom of the Press," in *Representative American Speeches: 1983–1984,* ed. Owen Peterson (New York: H. W. Wilson Co., 1984), p. 152. Used by permission.
28. Hanford, "An Educational System That Has No Losers," p. 597–598.
29. John S. Reed, "Is Anyone Listening?" *Vital Speeches of the Day* 37 (1971):572.
30. James J. Kilpatrick, "The Writer's Art," *The Birmingham News,* May 26, 1985, p. D-3. Used by permission.

12

NONVERBAL PRESENTATION

*I*n an international weightlifting tournament in Manila in 1975, the Russians had been complaining about the slippery surface of the floor. When the Russian came out to attempt the lift that would give him the championship, he kicked rosin away as he reached for the weights. The announcer observed that this was probably his silent way of criticizing the conditions. This illustrates the meaning that can be communicated through nonverval behavior.

Mehrabian and Ferris demonstrated the importance of nonverbal communication by asking subjects to infer communicator *attitudes* on the basis of words presented with positive, neutral, and negative vocal attitude and on the basis of photographs of models with positive, neutral, and negative facial expressions. They concluded that "simultaneous verbal, vocal, and facial *attitude* communications" account for 7 percent, 38 percent, and 55 percent, respectively, of the total communication.[1] Although this study demonstrates the importance of vocal and facial cues in communicating attitudes, we must not draw the erroneous conclusion that these cues communicate information. In fact, the use of single words in the experiment held the communication of information to a minimum. If we could communicate 93 percent of information and attitudes with vocal and facial cues, it would be wasteful to spend time learning a language. What we must remember, as Hart and Brown point out, is that "natural speech content conveys information primarily through the combination of words and sentences rather than through the communication of single isolated words."[2]

Nevertheless, the study by Mehrabian and Ferris clearly demonstrates that we cannot ignore the effect of nonverbal stimuli on a communicative effort. Observation and experimental research indicate that skillful use of vocal and physical behavior helps to develop credibility.

Skillful Use of Nonverbal Forms of Presentation

In the last few decades empirical research has verified what rhetoricians have been teaching for thousands of years: nonverbal forms of communication—physical and vocal behavior—are important contributors to the effectiveness of a speech. They help to make the speaker's ideas more credible to the listeners. As a matter of fact, if they contradict the verbal message, hearers tend to place more credence in the nonverbal communicators.

In an early study Henrikson asked 256 students to give speeches on the best and poorest speaker they had ever heard. After analyzing these speeches, he asked 54 additional students to give speeches on the best and poorest speakers they had heard and to rank nine categories of characteristics revealed by analysis of the previous speeches. Henrikson found that the best speaker was generally identified "as one who *spoke without notes* and in an optimistic mood with good speech material, *good delivery, a good voice,* and a good personality." The poorest speaker, on the other hand, was usually recalled "as the one who spoke with notes or reading his speech in a factual or pessimistic mood with poor material, poor delivery, a poor voice, and a poor personality."[3]

Beighley investigated the effect of organization and vocal skills on the comprehension of "hard" and "easy" material. He concluded that vocally skilled speakers "helped the audience achieve higher comprehension test scores than did the vocally unskilled ones" when the material was hard or disorganized.[4] Vocal skills made the "hard" material more understandable and thereby more credible.

Vohs presented a well-delivered or a poorly delivered (referring to use of voice) speech to four groups of subjects. Following the speech, each group completed a retention test of fifty multiple-choice questions. Those who heard a well-delivered speech retained more information than those who heard a poorly presented one.[5]

Bettinghaus presented four persuasive speeches on different topics—two positive and two negative—by different speakers to four different groups. Each speaker gave his speech in the following forms: (1) effective delivery with strong content, (2) effective delivery with weak content, (3) ineffective delivery with strong content, (4) ineffective delivery with weak content. Following each speech the subjects indicated their evaluation of the speaker, his topic, his delivery, and his development of the speech. After analyzing the results, Bettinghaus concluded that "the speaker with better delivery is more persuasive than the speaker with poorer delivery."[6]

McCroskey found that good delivery made a speech with evidence significantly more effective in changing the attitudes of listeners than a speech with evidence and poor delivery, one with good delivery and no evidence, or one with poor delivery and no evidence.[7]

In a series of experiments, Mehrabian and Williams found that facial expression and speech rate, volume, and intonation were significantly related to intended and perceived persuasiveness.[8]

Effective delivery is important in developing credibility for your ideas, thus enabling them to have their maximum impact. Effective delivery by itself will not change attitudes, but it is necessary for the effective rhetorical message to exert its potential influence upon a receiver. You must not only become familiar with the principles of physical and vocal behavior, but you must become skilled in their use.

Physical Behavior

Since communication is your goal, anything that interferes with it must be eliminated. Physical behavior can play either a beneficial or a detrimental role. Physical behavior resulting from an outgrowth of your urge to communicate and suited to your purpose, personality, and physical vitality will be most effective with your listeners.

Speakers are frequently advised to *be natural* in their physical behavior. Unfortunately, many people do not use effective bodily action naturally. We are all familiar with individuals who are naturally awkward, who cannot make a movement that has any grace or is effectively communicative. For these people to be natural in a speaking situation simply means they are going to appear awkward in front of an audience. Telling most beginning speakers to be natural is tantamount to telling them to use ineffective physical action. As a general rule, effective physical behavior for the specific skill must be learned and practiced. The polished grace of the skilled ballet dancer is admired by those watching who may forget it has replaced the lumbering movements of a novice only after long hours of hard and dedicated practice. It is important that effective physical behavior be practiced until it *is* natural.

An understanding, then, of the types of physical behavior that may be used is necessary. You need to understand and use effective principles of posture, platform movement, eye contact, facial expression, and gestures.

Posture

Posture influences the listeners' reaction because it reflects your alertness and poise. Don't slump in a chair on the platform; sit comfortably erect. While speaking, avoid such motions as collapsing on the lectern, shifting your weight from foot to foot, swaying from side to side, or rocking back and forth. Don't stand in a militarily stilted position or become so relaxed that you appear to be unconcerned.

Distribute your weight equally on both feet, stand poised on the balls of your feet, and you will give the impression of a person vibrantly aware of the circumstances and able to move immediately to react to any contingency. If your weight is on your heels you are not fully alert; you are not capable of reacting swiftly and you show it. Notice, for example, how an alert infielder on a baseball team gets poised on the balls of his feet just before the pitcher throws the ball to the batter. It is obvious he is alert to the situation and is ready to respond quickly. The infielder standing with his weight on his heels cannot react as quickly and his lack of alertness is apparent to the spectators. In the same way listeners can detect the degree of alertness by the way your weight is distributed on your feet. Listeners may not be consciously aware of how your weight is distributed, but the muscular tone of your body will reflect it. As a result, nonverbal stimuli from your muscular tone will influence their impression of you.

Find the posture that is most effective for you. Let it convey an appearance of relaxed alertness. Make it appropriate to the situation. In a more formal setting your posture must have a certain rigidity to it. In an informal situation you can appropriately assume a more relaxed posture.

Avoid standing at arm's length from the lectern with elbows unbent and hands on the lectern. If you are going to place your hands on the lectern, stand close enough so your elbows can be bent. This position looks more relaxed and makes listeners feel more comfortable.

Beginning speakers are often worried about what to do with their hands. There are a number of things you *can* do with your hands, but whatever you do should seem comfortable and be effective. Some speakers let their hands hang easily at their sides. So long as the hands are not moved about randomly, this is an acceptable position for the hands. Other speakers like to rest their hands lightly on the lectern. So long as the hands are not moved about unpurposefully, this too is an acceptable position. Still others find it comfortable to put one hand in a pocket and let the other one hang easily at the side or rest lightly on the lectern. So long as the hand is not put in and taken out frequently and is not used to jingle keys or coins in the pocket, this is an acceptable position if it does not interfere with the gestures. Most gestures can be anticipated sufficiently, however, to remove the hand in time to use it effectively for gesturing. On rare occasions you may even find it desirable to put both hands in your pockets. Although this is acceptable if done infrequently, you should be careful not to let this position interfere with desirable gestures. Some speakers prefer to clasp their hands behind their back. As a general rule, this is a less acceptable position and should be avoided. It is a position rarely used except by soldiers standing at parade rest and it gives the appearance of trying to hide your hands.

Remember that those appendages at the ends of your arms do not look as big or as awkward to listeners as they feel to you.

Movement

Increasing attention in recent years to *kinesics*—the study of body motion and its role in communication—has intensified awareness that movement is a significant form of nonverbal communication.

Your movement begins to influence the listeners' reaction to you even before you arrive at the podium. Your approach communicates nonverbally your attitude toward the situation. Approaching the lectern in an alertly relaxed manner gives the impression that you have something to say, know you can say it, and want to say it to this particular audience. As a result, your credibility is enhanced.

Movement on the podium is important for a number of reasons. It is effective in getting and holding attention. An often proved psychological principle is that, other things being equal, a moving stimulus attracts attention away from a nonmoving stimulus. If you stand immobile in one position you provide an opportunity for other stimuli in the situation to become stronger and attract the attention of the listeners. Animation may be used at the beginning of a speech to capture attention. Movement can also be used to recapture attention.

To gain and hold attention effectively, however, movement has to be meaningful. Unpurposeful movements attract attention but they are detrimental because they distract the attention from what you are saying or doing in a purposeful way. If you shift your weight from foot to foot, it is an unpurposeful movement and distracts attention from your purpose. Swaying from side to side or rocking back and forth distracts attention because it is unmeaningful. Buttoning and unbuttoning your coat, pulling an ear, scratching your forehead, rubbing your chin, tapping the fingers on the lectern, running

your hands around the edges of the lectern, playing with note cards, continually putting hands into and taking them out of your pockets, rubbing your hands together, straightening your tie, fingering a bracelet, brooch, or watch— all of these, and other similar actions are distracting and detrimental. Because of the movement they attract attention, but because they are irrelevant and unpurposeful, they distract from your main purpose and interfere with effective communication.

Concentration

These irrelevant movements are also indications that you are not concentrating on the act of communication. Observe a golfer preparing to hit a shot or putt. Every muscle is focused on the task at hand; there are no irrelevant movements and the golfer is unaware of events around her. If the golfer feels an itch, she knows she has not concentrated sufficiently. In the same way, if you are concentrating on the act of communication every muscle in your body will be focused on the task. If you feel an itch, then you have failed to concentrate sufficiently on the act of communication. Of course there are times when you are unable to concentrate because of some mental or physical problem. If you have a case of hives, the intense itching may prevent concentration on anything. Under ordinary conditions, however, if you are concentrating, you will be unaware of minor irritations.

Use movement to emphasize transition from one point to another. At the conclusion of a point you may pause and move to another position on the platform before beginning the next point. This movement serves figuratively as a bridge between the two points and emphasizes to the listeners that you have moved to a new idea.

Use movement as a means of physical relief for listeners. The muscles in the human body cannot stay in one position too long; they become fatigued if they do. One set of muscles normally will be tensed for a while, then relax while another set becomes tensed. This is a constant action on the part of the muscles in the body. Recent studies have shown this takes place even while we are sleeping. As a matter of fact, there is movement by at least one set of muscles at some place in the body all the time a person sleeps. In an audience situation where people are crowded close together and where the space between rows of seats is limited, there is restricted opportunity for listeners to move different parts of their body for relaxation.

Empathy

The primary means by which listeners can achieve needed muscular change is through *empathy*—the feeling of being a part of whatever we are observing. The empathic response is natural to all people, more to some than others. We sit in front of a television set in our homes watching the marshall stalk the outlaw in the inevitable gunfight. As the two men approach one another the muscles in our bodies tense. When they grab for their guns, the muscles in our arms twitch and jerk involuntarily as we feel ourselves pulled into the action we are watching. When you move in front of an audience, listeners are able to flex their muscles through empathy, thus avoiding the restlessness resulting from unused muscles.

By the same token, avoid too much movement so that you do not physically exhaust listeners. If you constantly pace back and forth, you fatigue your listeners since their muscles never get a chance to relax. You must strive for the proper balance by using neither too much nor too little physical movement.

Use empathy to help get desired audience reactions. Listeners tend to feel the emotions and attitudes being displayed. If you display anger, listeners tend to feel anger; if you display sadness, listeners tend to feel sad.

In all movements strive to appear relaxed, comfortable, confident. Only then can listeners really feel relaxed and comfortable. If you appear to be ill at ease, listeners, through empathy, feel ill at ease. It is difficult to get people to listen carefully to what you are saying if they feel uncomfortable.

Build rapport with listeners by communicating directly with them; this requires direct eye contact, looking directly into their eyes, just as you would in a small face-to-face conversation. Eye contact in a speech should be similar to that which you have when you are deeply involved in a conversation with a group of friends. Eye contact is an important nonverbal means of obtaining a favorable response from hearers. Exline and Eldridge concluded on the basis of their study "that the same verbal communication" was interpreted as "being more favorable" by a listener when it was accompanied by "more eye contact than when it was presented with less eye contact."[9]

Direct eye contact with the audience significantly increases credibility. Comparing the effect of three levels of eye contact—none, moderate, and high—Beebe found that high eye contact created significantly higher credibility for the speaker's competence and trustworthiness than no eye contact.[10]

Research has also indicated that in the course of an interview, when two people are communicating on topics that are neutral or generally positive, subjects like the interviewer significantly more and have more positive reactions to the interview itself when that person looks them in the eyes. On the other hand, when an interview is "indirectly but persistently critical of the subject," subjects like the interviewer significantly less and have more negative reactions to the interview itself when the interviewer looks them in the eyes.[11] Unless you are being critical of your listeners, therefore, you should look directly at them.

Of course you cannot look at all members of the audience simultaneously; you must look at one person at a time, letting your eyes move easily around the room from one person to another. Eye contact should never become mechanical as it does when speakers sweep alternately from one side of the room to the other. Don't be reluctant to look at some of the listeners more than others; in fact, in a large audience you will be unable to look at every listener. Some hearers will respond more actively and more overtly to what you are saying. Their favorable response can be highly stimulating. It is perfectly all right to talk to these people more than you do to the others, but be sure you do not let the speech develop into a private conversation between you and the few who are responding more favorably.

Avoid looking at distractions that occur outside the speaking area unless the distraction is so great that you cannot possibly ignore it. Remember that the movement of your eyes to an object outside the speaking area serves to focus the eyes and attention of the hearers on that object. Most extraneous noises will go unnoticed unless you call attention to them.

Eye contact permits perception of the interaction of listeners. You cannot communicate directly with listeners if you are unaware of and fail to respond to their behavior and reactions. Frowns, smiles, nodding of heads, shaking of heads, applause, hisses, and whispering are all overt responses that tell something of what the listener is thinking. You must learn to respond to these reactions in desirable ways.

Facial Expression

Reveal your communicative attitude through facial expression. When you look at listeners with an alert, expressive face and an occasional smile, you tell them nonverbally more effectively than you ever could verbally that you are happy to be there talking to them. A frown at the mention of something unpleasant reinforces the words in a way that nothing else can. A contemporary of Tom Corwin, stump orator and senator from Ohio in the 1840s, claimed that "his wonderful effect upon an audience depended more upon his marvelous facial expression than upon anything he said."[12] A number of reporters have claimed that one of the prime reasons for Arnold Palmer's enormous popularity with golf fans is his wonderfully mobile facial expression which reflects visibly the nuances of his successes and struggles while golfing.

Facial expression is an important determinant of the impact of a message on a listener. Mehrabian found that the nonverbal message conveyed by facial expressions accounted for more than 50 percent of the impact of the total message when the verbal and nonverbal messages were inconsistent.[13]

Experimenters have found a high degree of reliability in interpreting facial expressions of emotional tendencies and attitudes.[14] The deadpan speaker not only loses this valuable nonverbal assistance in communication but also gives the impression of being uninterested in talking to these people and of being a "cold fish," a detached person who is insensitive to what goes on about him. Most people are unwilling to place their confidence in and submit their decisions to a person who is unable or unwilling to sympathize with them and their problems.

There are some facial expressions that are detrimental, however. You should avoid grimacing when you make a mistake, for it just calls greater attention to the error. Especially detrimental are facial expressions not coordinated with what you are saying.

Gestures

Gestures are those movements of the head, shoulders, hands, and arms used to assist in communicating ideas. They may serve one or more of three purposes: (1) to clarify or describe, (2) to reinforce or emphasize, (3) to get and hold attention.

The most effective gestures seem to be an integral part of communication. They do not appear to be made simply for the sake of making a gesture. Each has a definite communicative purpose. Even when they are purposeful, however, they need to appear to be integrated with what you are saying. To achieve this, gestures ought to be made in the listener's focal area of vision. In most small audience situations, gestures are more effective if made above the waist, somewhere in the area of the chest, and fairly close to the body.

Gestures made below the waist are in the peripheral area of the listeners' vision and become distracting. Occasionally listeners are not consciously aware of these movements even though they are subconsciously distracting. Once listeners become aware of them, they must shift their vision from your face in order to see the gestures. This becomes distracting because the gestures now seem unrelated to your words; they do not seem to be an integral part of the total communicative process.

If gestures are made in the line of vision, listeners can see them without shifting their line of vision since they appear to be integrated with what you are saying. Generally, listeners perceive gestures and respond to them without thinking of them in isolation as gestures.

The larger the place in which the speech is being given and the farther the listeners are from you, the more of you that is included in the focal area of vision. In these instances you can expand the area in which you gesture since there is less likelihood of the gestures occurring outside the line of vision.

Timing Gestures

Gestures timed to correspond with what you are saying assist the communication of ideas. If you say, "My first point this morning, . . ." and raise your hand with the index finger extended on *this,* the lack of coordination between action and words will minimize the effect of the gesture. To be coordinated the action of the gesture begins before the word it accompanies so that the gesture will reach its climax precisely at the moment the word is spoken. The upward movement of the hand in this example should begin slightly before the beginning of the word *my,* then the hand with the extended forefinger should reach the top of the stroke just as the word *first* is said. However, you cannot expect to achieve perfect results on the first try; you may not get perfection even on the tenth effort. Remember that athletes spend hours practicing the development of fine coordination. Don't expect to develop coordination with little practice. The important thing is to start practicing gestures and using gestures in speaking. In time the coordination will develop. Keep in mind that the classroom is your laboratory; this is the place to experiment with gestures in front of an audience. Your instructor will not criticize you adversely for lack of coordination; she will be pleased you are making the effort.

Completing Gestures

When you gesture in a speech, make it complete. Don't start it and then inhibit it. A half-completed or limply executed gesture becomes a meaningless, distracting movement instead of an effective, purposeful aid to communication. Inexperienced or unskilled speakers often produce weak gestures of this type. If you gesture while your hands are resting on the lectern, do not leave the heel of your hands in contact with the edge of the lectern and simply raise your fingers—the only part of the body involved in the gesture. If you decide to gesture while your hands are hanging down by your side, don't just bend your hand upward at the wrist. Again, the hand is the only part of the body involved in the gesture. These gestures not only lack a dynamic quality, they are distracting and meaningless. They contribute nothing to communication.

A dynamic gesture involves the whole body. The body prefers to work as a whole; let it. If you want to gesture while your hand is lying on the lectern, pick it up, make the gesture decisively and energetically, then return your hand to the lectern. Your entire body then becomes involved in the action and seems to be an integral part of the total act of communication.

If your hand is hanging at your side and you decide to gesture, raise your entire arm, bend the elbow, let the elbow swing slightly away from your body, bring the hand slightly toward the center of the body, and make the gesture. When the gesture is completed, the hand is returned to your side. Again the entire body will be taking part in the action. And because the body likes to work as a whole, you may even find that making the gesture encourages you to take a step in the direction of the listeners.

The most effective gestures are suited to you, the audience, and the occasion. They are suited to your personality and to what you are saying. If you talk at a slow rate, you will appear ludicrous if your gestures are fast and choppy. On the other hand, if you are talking fast, you will not be effective using slow-paced hand movements.

Making Gestures Appropriate

Make gestures appropriate to listeners. If you are talking to people who normally lead a sedentary life, fewer and less energetic gestures will be necessary since these people are not accustomed to much physical activity. They don't want it, they generally don't like it, and they are quickly fatigued by it. If you are talking to people who lead a physically active life, more and larger gestures can be used. It takes more action to prevent their muscles from getting restless from lack of use. The empathic response is insufficient for these people if your gestures are too infrequent or too small physically.

Gestures should be appropriate to the occasion. On a serious, solemn, sad occasion you will be expected to gesture less. A funeral oration, for example, is delivered with almost no gesturing. If gestures are used on such an

The Speech

occasion, they should be slow and dignified. When the people are in high spirits, more gestures are appropriate. Observe the vigorous, almost continuous actions of a cheerleader at an athletic event. Speaking at midmorning or at night, you can expect listeners to be fully alert. Consequently, gestures are less important in holding the attention of listeners than if you are speaking just after lunch or a banquet. The drowsy inattention of the listeners resulting from the digestive processes taking place in their bodies can be overcome only by rather frequent and vigorous physical activity.

Gestures are also adapted to the times. At some periods in the past listeners have accepted as normal behavior windmill-like movements of the speaker's hands and arms. Today speakers are expected to be more restrained in their actions. The widespread use of television and public address systems has done much to establish less expansive movements as the norm for speakers.

Ideally, gestures should stem from a specific desire on the part of the speaker to gesture at that precise moment. If this were followed rigidly, however, some speakers would never gesture. Some people are simply not accustomed to using physical action and others inhibit all desire to gesture when they are in front of an audience.

Many times, therefore, the desire to gesture has to be cultivated. Seek places where you can gesture as you practice and think about the speech. Try to devise gestures that will help in communicating the ideas. If there are two contrasting ideas at some point in the speech, for example, you can gesture with the left hand on one idea and the right hand on the other idea. In the beginning a good method for using gestures is to number the main points with your fingers. These are effective gestures in aiding communication, they are easily executed, and most people look natural when making them. A word of caution, however: avoid overpracticing gestures so they look artificial and rehearsed.

Even though gestures that result from an urge to gesture are appropriate, dynamic, coordinated, and an integral part of the communication, they must be varied if they are to be truly effective. The same gesture used with different ideas and different feelings soon loses its meaning and its effectiveness.

Summary

Five types of physical behavior that the speaker must learn to use effectively are correct posture, movement, eye contact, facial expression, and gesturing.

Posture should be alert, with weight distributed equally on both feet. Hands may be placed in a number of acceptable positions but should not be allowed to move unpurposefully.

Movement is important to capture and hold attention, to emphasize transitions from one point to another, to offer physical relief for the listeners, and to help get desired audience reactions. All movement should be meaningful.

Direct eye contact helps establish rapport with listeners, obtain a favorable response from them, and perceive their interaction.

Facial expressions can be used to express meaning and to demonstrate an interest in talking to the hearers.

Gestures may be used to clarify or describe, to reinforce or emphasize, or to get attention. They should be an integral part of the communication, be coordinated, dynamic, appropriate, varied, and give the appearance of springing from desire.

Vocal Behavior

Use of voice is another extremely important nonverbal factor in determining how well the listeners understand, interpret, and believe what you say. There is even evidence to indicate that the way a thing is said is more important than what is said. Two investigators selected words that communicated positive, neutral, and negative content. Subjects were then asked to read each type of content word with a positive, neutral, and negative tone. Thus three of the readings had content and tone that were consistent, while six had content and tone that were inconsistent. Other subjects were then exposed to these readings and asked to interpret the reader's attitude. The investigators concluded that the tonal component contributes much more to the interpretation of a message than content.[15]

A number of factors affect the way we speak. One of the most important is physiological. The natural pitch level and range are determined by physiological characteristics. Physical defects in any part of the vocal mechanism will affect the speech. Even normal vocal mechanisms come in varying sizes and shapes, and these affect the production of speech.

Psychological factors also affect our speech. The energetic, confident speaker generally has a voice that sounds energetic and confident. The whining, complaining person is usually identifiable by the voice. The listless, bored personality reveals itself through the monotone. Obviously, voice and speech do not always give an accurate representation of the individual's personality, but in many instances they do.

Environment also helps shape our speech. Characteristics heard in the speech of one's family are reproduced. There is even a recorded instance of several children in a family speaking with the breathy, nasal characteristics of a person with a cleft palate, yet each child's palate was normal. Investigation revealed that the mother had a cleft palate and the children had just imitated what they heard. For them the defective speech of their mother was normal.

Educational level affects our pronunciations. The more education an individual has had, the more likely the pronunciations are to be standard because exposure to cultivated pronunciations will have been greater.

Unfortunately for some, environment and education combine to create speech that provides status cues for listeners. Harms classified sample speakers into three groups: high status (those with advanced degrees and in prestige occupations), middle status (those with at least a high school education or no more than one year of college and in a middle status occupation), low status (those with no more than an eighth grade education and in unskilled jobs). After recording "content free" samples of speech from these subjects, Harms presented the recorded speech to 180 adults and asked them to indicate the speaker's status and credibility. The listeners successfully identified the status of the speakers. Moreover, they judged "the high-status speakers to be the most credible and the low-status speakers to be the least credible."[16] With the right kind of speech, you can enhance the credibility of your ideas.

Fortunately, there is ample evidence that speech and voice can be changed. To be most effective, develop a pleasant voice and clear articulation and learn to communicate nonverbally with your voice the meanings to be conveyed with words. Use clear articulation, be aware of the characteristics of a good voice, and use effective emphasis and stress, an appropriate rate, meaningful pauses, and acceptable pronunciations.

Articulation

Articulation is an interference with the outward flow of air through the mouth and nose to create the sounds of the language. The principal articulatory organs are (1) the tongue, (2) the lips, (3) the teeth, (4) the hard palate, and (5) the soft palate, or velum. The sounds produced are classified as vowels, diphthongs, or consonants. The clarity and sharpness of the articulation determines the intelligibility of your speech. Free movement of the tongue, lips, and jaws is necessary if you are to articulate clearly. Lazy movements result in mumbled speech. The mumbler not only is difficult to understand, but also gives the impression of being a careless person. Such an impression will not contribute to credibility.

Articulation Problems

An avoidance of the articulatory problems of substitution, addition, and omission, which are generally considered substandard, is desirable. Substitution occurs in such instances as using *dat* for *that*. An example of addition is *athalete* for *athlete*. Saying *goverment* for *government* is an instance of omission. Proper articulation can contribute to the image of authoritativeness or competence. In this way you enhance your ethos with listeners. Clear articulation is required if you are to be correctly comprehended.

Assimilation

Another important aspect of articulation is assimilation. The way we pronounce words in isolation is often extremely different from the way we pronounce them in running speech. When words are strung together in sentences, some of the sounds change because of the influence of other sounds. This process is called assimilation. In extreme cases, the words may become unintelligible. For example, *jeet* is frequently heard, meaning *Did you eat?* One student recently asked, "Sapning?" meaning, "What's happening?" Although extremes like this are substandard and should be avoided, some assimilation is necessary and desirable to avoid an artificiality in speaking. The *how-now-brown-cow* school of articulation has fittingly been abandoned. Good conversational speech runs the sounds together so there is an easy flow of sounds without an accompanying loss of intelligibility. When a stop-plosive sound both ends one word and begins the next in a sentence, the sounds are produced as one. Consider the sentence, *The cook cleaned the fish*. The *k* is begun in *cook*, but is released as the *k* in *cleaned*. To release the *k* in *cook* and then begin another *k* in *cleaned* would cause an unnatural break in your fluency. The articulation would be so precise it would sound artificial.

Assimilation sometimes causes us to change a sound. If a voiced consonant is followed or preceded by a voiceless one, we frequently change one so that both sounds are either voiced or voiceless. In the sentence, *I have to go to school,* the *v* sound in *have* usually becomes an *f* because of the influence of the *t* sound in *to.* Normally, *used* is pronounced with a *z* sound, but in the sentence, *He used to be a good driver,* the *d* sound in *used* is usually dropped and the *z* sound changed to an *s* sound. So the sentence becomes, *He use to be a good driver.* When the *s* sound follows a voiced consonant, it becomes a *z* sound. Consider such examples as *cabs, pads, gags, pens.*

Assimilation causes sounds to be dropped from some words. In some instances words articulated with a sound omitted have become accepted as standard pronunciations. Users of standard speech pronounce *cupboard* without the *p* and *handkerchief* without the *d.*

Unwanted nasal resonance can be caused by assimilation. Sounds that immediately precede or follow the nasal sounds, *m, n,* or *ng,* may include nasal resonance because the velum cannot block and unblock the nasal passage abruptly enough in running speech to prevent the emission of air through the nose on sounds adjacent to the nasal sounds.

To contribute to your credibility, then, develop articulation that avoids the twin evils of overly precise articulation and excessive assimilation. Do not sound stilted and artificial, but avoid unintelligibility.

On the other hand, there are situations in which articulation must be as precise as possible without sounding affected. If you are conveying important information to another person, such as the flight dispatcher talking to the pilot of an airplane, you must use careful articulation. If you want to make a good impression on another, as when interviewing for a job, make sounds clear enough that the interviewer will not consider your speech sloppy. If you are talking to a large audience and the sounds must carry some distance, keep assimilation to a minimum in order for the sounds to carry distinctly to the most distant listeners.

Characteristics of Voice

There are five characteristics of voice: (1) pitch, (2) range, (3) loudness, (4) rate, and (5) quality. An understanding of these characteristics will help you achieve your full potential.

Pitch

The frequency of the vibrations is the physical characteristic of a vibrating object that produces what we call pitch, a psychological interpretation of those vibrations. We interpret a sound resulting from a rapidly vibrating object as having a high pitch and that from a slowly vibrating object as having a low pitch. A number of factors determine the frequency with which an object will vibrate. On a stringed instrument, such as a piano or guitar, three factors—length, mass, and tension of the string—affect the frequency of the vibrations. Notice on a piano that the strings that create the high-pitched sounds are shorter, tighter, and smaller, whereas those that make the low-pitched sounds are longer, looser, and larger. In the human voice, two other factors are important—the elasticity of the vocal folds and the amount of subglottal breath

pressure. The elasticity of the vocal folds enables them to change their mass and length whenever there is a change in tension. This feature gives the human voice a flexibility that musical instruments do not have.

Pitch can be used as an effective nonverbal means of communicating fine shades of meaning. Inflection, a change of pitch during the production of a syllable or word, can be used to convey delicate meanings to the listeners. A falling inflection gives the impression of confidence, determination, and assurance on the part of the speaker. It also indicates completeness of thought. Thus, the pitch should normally fall at the end of a sentence. Pitch should not normally be allowed to fall at commas or semicolons, otherwise the listener is given the impression that the end of the sentence has arrived. A rising inflection communicates a questioning attitude, hesitancy, doubt, indecisiveness, incompleteness of thought, and surprise. Skilled speakers are able to use double inflections which communicate irony, sarcasm, and subtle meanings. A double inflection is a movement both up and down, often on the same word.

The speech itself, however, is not the place to be thinking about varying your pitch or using a particular inflection. Whatever pitch changes occur should take place naturally as the result of an intellectual understanding or an emotional reaction. Practice sessions should be used to gain the ability to achieve maximum variation in pitch—then let nature take its course in the actual communicative situation.

Try to avoid falling into a "pitch pattern." Sometimes referred to as a "ministerial tone" because many ministers are guilty of employing it, this is a recurring rising and falling of pitch. The pitch rises in the same way at the beginning of each phrase or sentence and falls in the same way at the end.

The underlying emotion of a message can also be communicated with pitch. Fairbanks and Pronovost had an ambiguous message read with six different emotional states implied by the use of different pitch variations. Listeners consistently identified the emotional states communicated by the pitch characteristics.[17]

Range

The range of a voice is the interval between the lowest and highest tones that can be produced. The total range of the human vocal mechanism is approximately four octaves, extending from a low tone of approximately 70 cycles per second in the male to a high tone of approximately 1,024 cycles per second in the female. Most individuals have a range of only about one octave. Trained speakers and singers sometimes have a range of two octaves; it is a rare person who has a range of four octaves.

No matter where your range begins and ends, you will be more effective if you use a good part of it in speaking. Nothing is more deadly to effective communication than a monotonous pitch level. Few people normally have a monotonous pitch level, but some beginning speakers inhibit their reactions in front of an audience and become monotonous. The solution to the problem of monotonous pitch level generally is to become involved in communicating your ideas to the listeners—to forget yourself. Under these conditions, the monotony usually disappears and variety in pitch occurs. If this fails to eliminate the problem, you may want to practice reading and speaking into a tape recorder to listen to yourself and learn to recognize and produce variation in pitch.

Loudness

Loudness is the listener's psychological interpretation of the intensity or amplitude of a vibrating object. The farther the vibrating object moves from its original position, the greater the amplitude and thus the resulting loudness. The pressure of the breath stream, the efficiency with which the vocal folds vibrate, and the reinforcement of the sound by the resonating chambers determine the loudness of the human voice. Some speakers attempt to increase the loudness level simply by rubbing the vocal folds together more tightly. This will increase the loudness level, but it also irritates the vocal folds and can cause harshness or hoarseness. Continued action of this type can do serious damage, resulting in singer's nodes.

Speech sounds differ in their intensity level. The vowel sound in the word *saw* has an intensity value approximately seven hundred times greater than the weakest sound, which is the *th* sound in the word *thaw*. Among the weakest sounds in intensity are such consonants as *f, t, v, d, k,* which is why it is so difficult to hear these sounds in speech. Clear articulation of these sounds is required if communication is to occur.

Change in loudness level is one of the easiest methods of emphasizing specific ideas. Lewis and Tiffin studied six speakers' use of voice and reported that those evaluated as the better speakers used more variations in loudness. The better speakers tended to differentiate among the various grammatical elements by using lower loudness levels for conjunctions, articles, and prepositions than did the poorer speakers.[18]

Beginning speakers have a tendency to use only increased loudness as a means of emphasis. But in many instances a decrease in loudness level is a better means of emphasis. To lower your voice at a strategic point causes listeners to strain to hear what is being said; this causes closer attention to what is being said.

Suit your loudness level to the listeners and the situation. If the room is extremely small, lower the volume to an appropriate level. If there is noise present, increase the loudness level so that it is greater than the noise. Observation of the listeners in the back of the room can provide clues as to whether the loudness is adequate. If some of the listeners are leaning forward, turning their "good" ear to the front, or cupping a hand behind it, you can reasonably conclude that your loudness level is inadequate.

Rate

Rate is the number of words that are spoken in a given amount of time, usually a minute. The number of words per minute varies anywhere from about 90 to 230. The normal speaking rate for most people, however, is approximately 125 to 150 words per minute. But the efficacy of a particular rate depends upon a number of factors: your personality, your emotional state, the situation, the mood of the audience, the subject of the speech. A sports announcer describing a basketball game over the radio must use a fast rate or he will soon be hopelessly behind the action. A minister repeating the Lord's Prayer must use a slow rate in keeping with the solemnity of the moment. A speaker who cannot vary speech rate in accord with different occasions and purposes will be limited in effectiveness.

Although some are critical of a fast rate of speaking, so long as you can articulate sounds in a comprehensible way and it is appropriate to the situation, there seems little justification for antipathy to a fast rate. Ernest presented both historical and technical materials to listeners at rates of 120 and 160 w.p.m. and concluded that "listening comprehension is not significantly affected by rate of presentation."[19] On the other hand, another investigator found that both male and female speakers were thought to be more animated and extroverted as they increased their speaking rates.[20]

Quality   The characteristic of a sound that enables the hearer to recognize its source is the quality. If the same note is initiated at the same loudness level for the same time by a trumpet and a trombone, the factor that makes it possible to distinguish one instrument from the other is the quality. This is the attribute that enables us to recognize a person only by hearing his voice.

Quality is related to the complexity of the vibrations. Few objects vibrate in a simple motion; most vibrate as a whole and in segments. The frequency produced by the vibration of the entire vibrating object is the fundamental tone. The frequencies produced by the vibration of the segments—each of which is an equal division of the whole object—are the overtones. The quality of the sound is determined by the number of overtones, the relative loudness of the overtones, and the relationship of the pitch of the fundamental to that of the overtones.

As already pointed out, the amount and type of resonance also affects the quality of the voice. A rich, mellow quality results when the walls of the pharynx are relaxed and soft.

Improving speech quality involves practicing and listening to the voice until the most pleasing sound is produced. Work on the tape recorder offers an opportunity to choose the best sound.

Voice Projection   In these days of artificial amplification through public address systems, it seems of little value to talk of the necessity and importance of voice projection. Nevertheless, you cannot disregard this aspect of voice production because it is not simply a matter of increasing the loudness level. There will be occasions when the size of the room does not permit you to talk in a normal voice level and yet there will be no public address system available. If you are to be heard, you must not only project, you must also increase the loudness level.

Even when no public address system is needed, you must still be able to project your voice in order for the listeners who are farthest removed to be able to hear clearly. In order to develop good projection, speakers are sometimes advised to get the sound into the front of the mouth, out onto the tip of the tongue. Although this achievement is more psychological than physical, there is an exercise which helps in learning to project the voice and gives the feeling that the voice is coming from the front of the mouth. Practice whispering so that someone can hear you across the room; when you have achieved that, then practice so they can hear you down the hall. This will force you to use more air and to articulate the sounds more precisely. When you get to the point where others can hear your whisper clearly at a distance, you can restore sound to your speech. You should be surprised at the improvement of distinctness and increased projection of your speech. The result should be speech that is more distinct and carries much farther.

Another factor that can help in projecting the voice is to prolong syllables or vowel sounds. While most consonants cannot be prolonged, vowels can. The prolongation of syllables and sounds makes it easier for the most distant listeners to hear and understand you.

A pause is a meaningful moment of silence during speaking; it is not just any silence. The pause can be one of the most effective speaking tools. With it you can give the listener an opportunity to assimilate and digest what has been said. An extremely rapid rate of speech can be easy to listen to if you judiciously use the pause. With the pause you can emphasize important parts of the speech. It can serve the function that punctuation serves for the writer. The pause can also be used as a means of replenishing the breath supply, so you don't come to the end of a sentence with insufficient air to produce the final words or sounds.

Pause

Pauses should occur at the end of thought units, not in the middle of one. Examine the sentence, "The boy went to town." There are three thought units: "the boy," "went," and "to town." Normally in a sentence this short and simple, you would make no pauses, but if you desired you could legitimately pause both before and after the word "went." Try reading the sentence, however, with a pause following "the" or "to," and see how disjointed the thought becomes. That is because these pauses take place in the middle of thought units.

Some inexperienced speakers and readers believe that pauses should occur where commas appear. It is true that in many instances the place where a comma is inserted is a logical place to pause. But not always. Read the following sentence: "It has often been said that, in a tornado, the windows of a house should be left open." Pausing after "said" and after "tornado" results in a much more conversational tone than pausing after "that" and "tornado."

Probably one of the most difficult tasks for a beginning speaker is to learn to use the pause. Any period of silence at first seems like an eternity; with experience you learn what a short period of time it really is. It may be helpful at first to count silently during the pause in order to be aware of the short time period. Avoid inserting an "uh," an "and uh," or a "you know" to fill a period of silence.

Good speaking involves emphasizing and stressing certain sounds and words while leaving other sounds and words relatively unstressed. It would not only be boring to listen to a speaker who stressed every word, it would also be difficult to comprehend the meaning. One of the difficulties in fully understanding and appreciating written material is that we miss the vocal variations that stress some sounds and words and play down others. One of the problems in using pronunciations found in dictionaries is that the pronunciations given there are the ones used when the word is in a stressed position. Sometimes, however, the pronunciation of a word changes because of its occurrence in an unstressed position. A number of words such as *a, of, the, was* frequently occur in unstressed form in running speech. In the stressed position, these words are pronounced *ā, thē, ŏv, wäz;* but in the unstressed position they are pronounced *ə, thı* or *thə, əv, wəz.* These latter pronunciations are acceptable when the words are unstressed, but they become substandard when used in stressed positions.

Emphasis and Stress

Some words change meaning by shifting the stress on the syllables. A number of words have verb and noun forms, and the syllable stressed identifies which is being used. Thus reCORD becomes REcord, deSERT becomes DEsert, proCEED becomes PROceed, surVEY becomes SURvey.

Putting emphasis on the right sounds and words helps the speaker to communicate nonverbally the intended meaning. Saying, "He is a *good* professor," communicates an entirely different meaning from saying, "He is a good *professor.*"

Emphasis and stress may be achieved in a number of ways. Tiffin and Steer analyzed the methods by which skilled speakers emphasized words in sentences. They discovered that emphasized words were of longer duration, louder, either higher or lower in pitch, and involved larger shifts of inflection.[21]

Pronunciation

Pronunciation is determined by two factors: (1) the specific sounds used to represent a word and (2) the placement of stress on certain syllables. The spelling of English offers only a faint clue to the pronunciation you should use. There is no clue that in words like *palm, calm, calf, half,* the *l* sound is omitted. There is no clue that *ough* will be pronounced differently in *cough, bough, through,* and *rough.*

"Correct" vs. "Acceptable" Pronunciation

Some people talk about "correct" pronunciations. Unfortunately, this gives the impression that there is only one correct pronunciation of each word. It would be more meaningful and more accurate if the word "correct" were replaced by the word "acceptable." Although it is true that most words have only one pronunciation, a large number of words have several pronunciations that are acceptable. The word *data,* for example, can be pronounced dāta, dăta, däta. Any one of these pronunciations is acceptable. But if someone says the correct pronunciation is *dāta,* this not only implies that other pronunciations are incorrect but also that there is some absolute standard to which you can go to determine what pronunciations should be used. If we say, however, that a pronunciation is acceptable, that seems to give the desired impression that what is acceptable is not inflexible and immutable.

It must be understood, however, that even though we talk about acceptable pronunciations, that does not mean that there are no standards for determining what is acceptable. In recent years, some have maintained that there should be no "standard speech," that any speech used by a number of people should be acceptable. This book rejects that viewpoint, and insists, with *Webster's Third New International Dictionary,* that acceptable pronunciations are those that are "in use by a sufficient number of cultivated speakers."[22]

There are many dialects in the United States, some provincial, some substandard, some standard. In 1958, C. K. Thomas designated ten dialects of American English in his book, *An Introduction to the Phonetics of American English.* Nevertheless, most speech scholars think of American speech as consisting of three major dialectal patterns: southern, eastern, and general American, sometimes called the midwestern dialect.

A skilled linguist or phonetician can listen to the speech of a person and place him geographically within a relatively close proximity to the person's home, sometimes in the right county or city. Most of us, however, are able to recognize only the gross differences that identify the speech as southern, eastern, or general American. None of these dialects is superior to another, but many forces are at work today to eliminate the gross differences among them. The rise of mass education and the increasing number of people who complete higher levels of education mean that more and more of our citizens come into contact with more uniform standards. The development of motion pictures, radio, and television, along with the networks' adoption of the general American dialect as the standard for their announcers, have brought increasing numbers into direct contact with the general American dialect. The accelerating mobility of the population has also done much to introduce the speech of each region to the people of other regions. It is not illogical to expect that the major characteristics of southern and eastern speech will gradually disappear, to be replaced by the major features of general American speech.

Finding the Acceptable Pronunciation

The easiest and most practicable method of determining the acceptable pronunciations of words is to listen to the speech of those about you—in your own community, on the radio, on television. Listen especially to the speech of those who have some claim to knowledge of the English language, those who have at least a modicum of education, such as ministers, doctors, lawyers, educators, business leaders; in other words, listen to "the speech of those expecting to be completely understood by their hearers."[23] This is not to say that any one member of any of these groups will exemplify acceptable pronunciation of any single word or of all words, but if several members of a single one of these groups or a number of people from several of these groups all use the same pronunciation, the chances are good that that particular pronunciation is an acceptable one.

Of course, you will discover, in the course of reading, new words for which you desire acceptable pronunciations. If there is no one around to whom you can listen to learn an acceptable pronunciation, you need another way of finding a pronunciation. This is when a dictionary comes into use. In the dictionary, you may find one or several pronunciations listed for the word. If there is only one, you have no problem. But if there is more than one, you must decide which one you want to use. Some will tell you that you must use the first one, that it is the preferred one. Reject that advice. It is true that the first pronunciation listed in many dictionaries is the one most frequently used by cultivated speakers at the time the dictionary was compiled. Since the dictionary is simply a record of what has occurred, however, some listed pronunciations may be out of date shortly after publication; another pronunciation for the word in question may have become the most frequently used. But even assuming the dictionary's order of pronunciations has remained accurate, there is another problem: another listed pronunciation may be newer and may be gaining more acceptance every day. In time it may become the one most frequently used. If everyone followed the dictum that the first listed pronunciation must be used, however, no new pronunciation could ever get accepted.

Once a pronunciation got to the head of the list in the dictionary, all others would have to be abandoned since the preferred one would have to be used. The English language would soon lose its vitality because opportunity for change would be stifled.

If you have no other criteria for deciding which of a number of pronunciations in the dictionary to use, it is logical to adopt the first one listed since that tells you it is likely to be the most frequently used pronunciation. But attention to other criteria may cause you to make another decision. You are interested in the word *incognito,* for example. You go to the dictionary and find the first pronunciation listed is *in-KOG-ni-TO.* But as you become sensitive to this word and listen to its pronunciation in the community about you, you may discover that you never hear that particular pronunciation, even among the educated and cultured leaders of the community. The only pronunciation you hear is *in-kog-NE-tə.* There is absolutely no reason why you should adopt a pronunciation which is never used in your community when the one being used is acceptable.

Summary

In running speech, many sounds are dropped or modified. This process is called assimilation. You should attempt to have sufficient assimilation in your speech to avoid sounding stilted and yet not so much that your speech is unintelligible.

The voice has five characteristics: (1) Pitch is the psychological interpretation of the frequency of tones produced in the larynx. (2) Range is the interval between the lowest and the highest pitched tone that a speaker can produce. (3) Loudness is the psychological interpretation of the amplitude, or intensity, of the vibrations of the vocal folds. (4) Rate is the number of words a speaker can vocalize in a given amount of time. (5) Quality is the attribute that enables the voice of a person to be recognized.

You should strive to use only acceptable pronunciations of standard speech, that used by the majority of cultivated speakers in a community.

A final word of caution: Although you should strive to develop the most effective voice possible, you should never adopt a voice that is not yours. Develop your own style with as much flexibility as you can achieve, but leave the imitations for those who make fake diamonds.

Exercises

1. Attend a lecture on campus. Describe the physical behavior of the speaker. What aspects of this person's nonverbal communication contributed to the credibility of his or her ideas? What aspects detracted from the credibility of these ideas?
2. Observe a classmate practicing his or her next speech. Write an analysis of what this student can do to improve his or her physical behavior so that greater credibility is achieved.

The Speech

3. Listen to a speaker on the radio. Write a description of that person and explain why you developed the particular image that you did.
4. Go to an open area with several friends. Practice your next speech with one person approximately five yards in front of you, another approximately fifteen yards away, and another approximately thirty yards away. Describe your reactions to this experience.
5. Prepare an experience to relate to your class. Without using language, pantomime your message to communicate with your classmates.
6. Define the conversational mode. Describe what some member of your class does that makes you feel the conversational mode is being used. What does that student do that makes you feel it is not being used?
7. Analyze your own platform behavior in your last speech. What were its strengths? its weaknesses? What can you do to eliminate or minimize these weaknesses? What can you do to capitalize on the strengths? Which of these aid in establishing the credibility of your ideas?
8. Each member of the class should write on a slip of paper the name of a feeling and the part of the body to be used to express the emotion. After exchanging slips, each student should try to express with his or her body the emotion on this paper. The other students should try to guess what feeling was being expressed.
9. A class member is asked to stand in front of and express his or her feelings toward another class member in a nonverbal manner and with exaggeration, as in mime.

Notes

1. A. Mehrabian and S. R. Ferris, "Inference of Attitudes from Nonverbal Communication in Two Channels," *Journal of Consulting Psychology* 31 (1967):248–52. Italics added.
2. R. J. Hart and B. L. Brown, "Interpersonal Information Conveyed by the Content and Vocal Aspects of Speech," *Speech Monographs* 41 (1974):372.
3. E. H. Henrikson, "An Analysis of the Characteristics of Some 'Good' and 'Poor' Speakers," *Speech Monographs* 11 (1944):120–24. Italics added.
4. K. C. Beighley, "An Experimental Study of the Effect of Four Speech Variables on Listener Comprehension," *Speech Monographs* 19 (1952):249–58.
5. J. L. Vohs, "An Empirical Approach to the Concept of Attention," *Speech Monographs* 31 (1964):355–60.
6. E. P. Bettinghaus, "The Operation of Congruity in an Oral Communication Situation," *Speech Monographs* 28 (1961):131–42.
7. J. C. McCroskey, *Studies of the Effects of Evidence in Persuasive Communication,* Speech Communication Research Laboratory Report SCRL 4–67, Department of Speech (E. Lansing, Mich.: Michigan State University, 1967), p. 36.
8. A. Mehrabian and M. Williams, "Nonverbal Concomitants of Perceived and Intended Persuasiveness," *Journal of Personality and Social Psychology* 13 (1969):37–58.

9. R. V. Exline and C. Eldridge, "Effects of Two Patterns of a Speaker's Visual Behavior upon the Perception of the Authenticity of His Verbal Message" (paper presented at the meeting of the Eastern Psychological Association, Boston, April 1967). Reported in A. Mehrabian, "Significance of Posture and Position in the Communication of Attitude and Status Relationships," *Psychological Bulletin* 71 (1969):359–72.

10. S. A. Beebe, "Eye Contact: A Nonverbal Determinant of Speaker Credibility," *Speech Teacher* 23 (1974):23–24.

11. P. C. Ellsworth and J. M. Carlsmith, "Effects of Eye Contact and Verbal Content on Affective Response to a Dyadic Interaction," *Journal of Personality and Social Psychology* 10 (1968):15–20.

12. J. J. Auer, "Tom Corwin: 'King of the Stump,' " *Quarterly Journal of Speech* 30 (1944):53.

13. A. Mehrabian, *Silent Messages* (Belmont, Calif.: Wadsworth Publishing Co., 1971), p. 43.

14. D. Dusenbury and F. H. Knower, "Experimental Studies of the Symbolism of Action and Voice—1: A Study of the Specificity of Meaning in Facial Expression," *Quarterly Journal of Speech* 24 (1938):436.

15. A. Mehrabian and M. Wiener, "Decoding of Inconsistent Communications," *Journal of Personality and Social Psychology* 6 (1967):109–14.

16. L. S. Harms, "Listener Judgments of Status Cues in Speech," *Quarterly Journal of Speech* 47 (1961):164–72.

17. G. Fairbanks and W. Pronovost, "An Experimental Study of the Pitch Characteristics of the Voice during the Expression of Emotion," *Speech Monographs* 6 (1939):87–104.

18. D. Lewis and J. Tiffin, "A Psychophysical Study of Individual Differences in Speaking Ability," *Archives of Speech* 1 (1934):43–60.

19. C. H. Ernest, "Listening Comprehension as a Function of Type of Material and Rate of Presentation," *Speech Monographs* 35 (1968):154–58.

20. D. W. Addington, "The Relationship of Selected Vocal Characteristics to Personality Perception," *Speech Monographs* 35 (1968):492–503.

21. J. Tiffin and M. D. Steer, "An Experimental Analysis of Emphasis," *Speech Monographs* 4 (1937):69–74.

22. P. B. Gove, ed., *Webster's Third New International Dictionary* (Springfield, Mass.: G. & C. Merriam Co., 1967), p. 40a.

23. Ibid., pp. 6–7a.

13

USING REASONING

O ne author defines reasoning, or critical thinking, as *"a process that emphasizes a rational basis for beliefs and provides procedures for analyzing, testing, and evaluating them."*[1] That statement precisely identifies the objective of this chapter. Understanding reasoning will aid you in comprehending others' positions and in explaining clearly your own.

Proving statements involves two processes: citing evidence and reasoning from it. To be meaningful to listeners, evidence must be explained or interpreted. Reasoning establishes a relationship between the evidence you have and the conclusions you draw as a result of that evidence. Thus, looking at the latest FBI crime report, you find that the crime rate was up last year. From that one piece of evidence, you may draw a number of conclusions: (1) penalties for crime should be increased; (2) salaries for law enforcement officials should be increased; (3) penal institutions should be improved; (4) more law enforcement officials should be employed; (5) more judges need to be appointed; (6) the permissive attitudes of judges need to be changed; (7) a better distribution of wealth in the United States must be devised; plus sundry other statements. The movement from evidence to a conclusion is called reasoning. For many listeners the reasoning that produced these conclusions would be clear and acceptable. For others, it would not. In instances when the reasoning is unclear and unacceptable, you have no recourse but to explain your reasoning until you have done your best to eliminate confusion.

Listeners must perceive as credible the reasoning that supports your statements. This is not to imply that listeners universally have the knowledge and ability to apply logical tests to determine an argument's validity. Listeners do arrive at a judgment of the speaker's statements, however, and one basis of that judgment is the reasoning involved. We have all heard listeners say of a speaker, "His ideas are too radical" or "His ideas are impractical" or "I couldn't accept his conclusion." These judgments may result from the listeners' inability to identify the specific error in reasoning committed by the speaker, or they may reflect the listeners' attitudes rather than the speaker's reasoning.

Audience analysis and an understanding of the listeners' attitudes will help you to identify those statements that will be perceived as unbelievable. Regardless of the listeners' attitudes, you must be concerned about the validity of the reasoning underlying your statements. Although sound and valid reasoning will not necessarily make a statement credible to a particular listener, it can help generally to develop credibility for your ideas. And for some listeners valid reasoning may be the most important factor in making a statement credible.

Invalid reasoning may have a more far-reaching effect than the immediate speech. Those who recognize fallacious reasoning may conclude, rightly or wrongly, that you are generally guilty of faulty reasoning and refuse to accept the credibility of your statements in future speeches.

Since the validity of your conclusions is dependent on the quality of your reasoning, an effort to establish the soundness of your reasoning will aid in generating credibility for your ideas. Structural models of reasoning are available to help you analyze your reasoning processes.

Although for many years Aristotle's was the popular model, in recent years many rhetoricians have preferred the one developed by Stephen Toulmin.[2] Although there are strengths as well as weaknesses in each of these models, the Toulmin scheme offers a more helpful guideline to a speaker. The Aristotelian model is primarily a *logical* model, and demands a degree of *certainty* that is rarely present in the rhetorical situation; moreover, it does not reveal all components of the reasoning process. On the other hand, Toulmin's is a rhetorical-logical model which offers three advantages: (1) it permits conclusions that are only probably or possibly true, and allows identification of the *degree* of certainty or probability; (2) it places all components of the reasoning process in the open and shows clearly their relationship to one another; (3) it places the basic premise of the argument, the warrant, in a position where support for it can be developed as a part of the reasoning process.

The Toulmin model is a method for analyzing arguments. It is *not* a plan for organizing a speech or even for organizing an argument in a speech.

The Toulmin Model

The Toulmin model may consist of as many as six parts: *claim, evidence, warrant, qualifier, reservation,* and a *backing for the warrant.* Figure 13.1 is an example of how one of the conclusions based on the FBI crime report fits into this structure.

Claim

The *claim* is the assertion, or conclusion, made on the basis of the evidence and the warrant. Claims may be classified under four headings: *designative, definitive, evaluative,* and *actuative.*

A *designative* claim deals with questions of fact—is a thing true? Did John Doe commit burglary? Is the economy declining? Will pornography have an adverse influence on the young? A *definitive* claim deals with questions of definition—what is it? Is a quota system democratic? Is the prevention of a protest an infringement of freedom of speech? Does Richard Roe's statement constitute slander? An *evaluative* claim deals with questions of value—what is the merit of a thing? Is the present tax policy beneficial to our economic system? Is a college education desirable for every person? Do intercollegiate athletics serve a useful purpose? An *actuative* claim deals with questions of policy—should a certain thing be done? Should the United States switch to a greater use of coal? Should more nuclear power plants be built in the United States?

Tracing one example through the different claims may help to clarify the difference among them: The United States has 8 million people unemployed (designative). This unemployment rate constitutes a recession (definitive). This unemployment rate is too high (evaluative). The federal government should adopt a program of public work to lower the unemployment rate (actuative).

Figure 13.1
A sample Toulmin model.

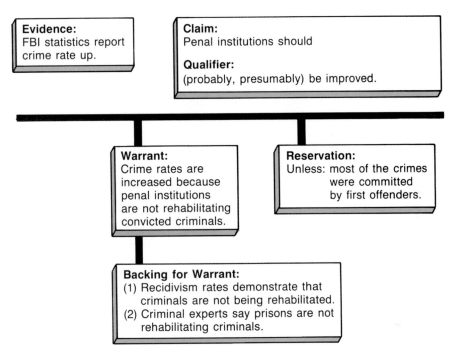

No matter what kind of claim is being made, be sure your argument is sound. "A sound argument, a well-grounded or firmly backed claim," says Toulmin, "is one which will stand up to the standard required if it is to deserve a favorable verdict."[3] Whenever you make a claim, be prepared to demonstrate you have made a justifiable one.

Types of *evidence* that can be used are described in the next chapter. Evidence is extremely important because it is what determines the soundness of a claim. All the available evidence must be examined, not just that which you can conveniently locate or find favorable to a claim. Where the evidence is acceptable to the listener, you simply have to establish the link between the evidence and the claim. In some instances, however, the listeners will not immediately accept the evidence. On those occasions, you will have to use a preliminary argument to eliminate the listeners' objections to the evidence. **Evidence**

The *warrant* is the link between the evidence and the claim, the basic premise upon which the claim rests. The warrant is the reason we consider the claim credible. In order to establish credibility, therefore, you must rely on warrants that are acceptable. If you use evidence that crime rates are increasing to develop a claim that permissive attitudes of judges need to be changed, the listener might well ask how you got from the evidence to that claim. The link is the warrant, in this instance the generalization that crime rates increase **Warrant** when judges are permissive. The listener must accept your warrant if it is to be effective in justifying your claim. If the listener finds the warrant unacceptable, you will have to support and develop it before the claim will be accepted as a sound one.

Some warrants, given the appropriate evidence, justify the claim unequivocally: *Evidence:* Icicles are hanging from the roof. *Claim:* The temperature is 32° or below. *Warrant:* Ice forms when the temperature is 32° or below. Other warrants justify only a tentative claim: *Evidence:* Ducks are flying south. *Claim:* Winter is coming. *Warrant:* Ducks flying south sometimes indicate that winter is coming.

Qualifier

The *qualifier* expresses the degree of certitude that is attached to the claim. On most issues with which speakers are concerned there is very little certainty. In the majority of instances the most that you can hope for is the development of a high degree of probability, a high degree of trustworthiness or reliability that your claims are accurate or true. Thus, most claims will include the word "most," "presumably," "probably," or some similar qualifier. The claim *must* be qualified if either the evidence or the warrant is qualified. If the claim is developed with sufficient rigor that the listeners will accept it as unqualified, however, you do not have to qualify it.

Reservation

The *reservation* identifies those contingencies that reduce or nullify the accuracy or correctness of the claim. Each type of reasoning has a unique set of reservations that must be dealt with before the reasoning can produce a proper claim. When the various types of reasoning are discussed, these reservations will be covered specifically. Whether or not these reservations are mentioned in the speech depends on whether or not the audience considers any of them significant. If so, you must deal with them. In some instances you may decide to discuss opposing arguments as a means of removing objections to a position or as a means of immunizing listeners against future counterpersuasive efforts.

Backing for the Warrant

Backing for the warrant consists of evidence and reasoning to make the warrant credible and acceptable to listeners. If the warrant is based on an assumption that is unacceptable to the hearers, the claim will be rejected as soon as that warrant becomes known. Be prepared to defend the warrant and show that it is supported by a sufficient amount of acceptable evidence.

Now that we understand the Toulmin model for analyzing arguments, let's take an actual example of argumentation from a speech and see how it looks in the Toulmin model. The speaker presented his argument in the following manner:

The achievements of the Cistercian monks serve to illustrate another aspect of modern ecologic philosophy. As I mentioned before, the swamps in which they established their monasteries were unfit for human life because of insects and

Figure 13.2
Toulmin model: analyzing an argument.

Evidence:	Claim:
(1) The Cistercian monks changed swamps, unfit for human life, into productive agricultural areas.	These instances demonstrate that transforming of the land,
(2) The Pennsylvania Dutch changed forests into a productive area for human life.	**Qualifier:** [when intelligently carried out,] is not destructive but, instead, can be a creative art.

Warrant:
These instances are typical of what can be done when land is transformed intelligently, in other words, made suitable for both human life and for the health of nature.

malaria. But monastic labor, skill, and intelligence converted these dismal swamps into productive agricultural areas, many of which have become centers for civilization. They demonstrate that transforming of the land, when intelligently carried out, is not destructive but, instead, can be a creative art.

My speaking of medieval times in Europe was not meant to convey the impression that only then have there been great achievements in the management of the land. One need only look at the Pennsylvania Dutch country to see a striking demonstration of land that has been created out of the forest, that became highly productive, and that has been well preserved. One could cite many similar feats all over the world. But the tendency at present is to determine the use of lands and waters, mountains and valleys, only on the basis of short-range economic benefits. And yet one can safely assert that sacrificing ecological principles on the altar of financial advantage is the road to social disaster, let alone esthetic degradation of the countryside. I shall now present a few remarks about how we can create land. By this I mean taking nature as it is presented to us and trying to do with it something which is both suitable for human life and for the health of nature.[4]

This argument is diagrammed in the Toulmin analysis in figure 13.2.

Notice that in the finished rhetorical effort one piece of evidence is presented, then the claim is stated, and that is followed by another piece of evidence. A strictly logical development of an argument offers all the evidence before the claim, but a rhetorical communication allows you to vary the development of the various parts of your arguments.

Figure 13.3
Toulmin model: argument with a particular claim.

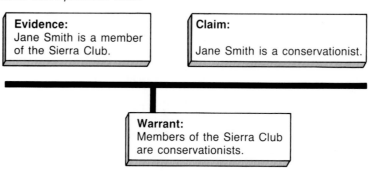

Figure 13.4
Toulmin model: argument with a general claim.

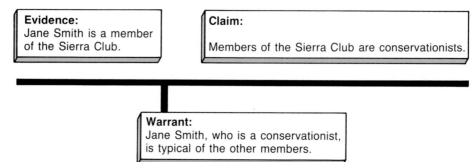

Types of Reasoning

Argumentation may be from a particular instance to a general principle, or from a general principle to a particular instance, or from a particular instance to a particular instance. The claim may be a particular conclusion (a statement that applies to only one instance) or a general conclusion (a statement that applies to a number of instances or a class of objects). Two such arguments are diagrammed in figures 13.3 and 13.4.

Four types of reasoning will now be discussed: reasoning by generalization, reasoning by analogy, reasoning by causal relationships, and reasoning by sign relationships.

By Generalization

When you look at a number of different members of a class of objects and make a statement about the whole class on the basis of those observed, you are engaged in reasoning by generalization. If you examine the records of 20 percent of the students at State University and find that all have total college board scores above 1,000, you may conclude that "Students at State University have total college board scores above 1,000." The soundness of that claim will depend upon how well you have met the tests that must be applied to any reasoning by generalization. In order to determine whether reasoning by generalization has produced a proper and credible claim, three basic questions must be answered affirmatively: (1) Are the instances representative of all the members of the class? (2) Has a sufficient number of instances been examined? (3) Can negative instances be accounted for? These are potential reservations to the claim. Let's consider each of these tests.

Are the instances representative of all members of the class? Efforts must be made to avoid bias in selecting the examples. Unfortunately, it is often difficult—especially in the field of public affairs—to select in a scientific way examples of the subjects with which a speaker is normally concerned. You have to take the evidence where you can find it. Where feasible, however, the samples must be selected as randomly as possible. In the ideal situation, a *random sample* should be used—that is, *a sample so selected that each member of the class has a theoretical chance of being chosen.* If we stood in front of Memorial Hall on the campus of State University and selected every fifth student who came out of the hall between the hours of 8 A.M. and 12 noon on Thursday, we would have a random sample of students who took classes in the building between the hours of 8 A.M. and 12 noon on Thursday, but we would not have a random sample of students at the university. Nor would we have a random sample of students who took classes there on other days of the week, and we probably wouldn't even have a random sample of students who took classes there on Thursday afternoon. But if we went to the student directory of the university and selected every fifth name, we would then have a random sample of the student body. If the method of selection prevents some members of the class from being chosen, it is not a random sample. If the sample is not random, then a significant reservation has been raised, and the propriety of the claim is in serious doubt. Logically, the claim can no longer be maintained. It may in fact be true; nevertheless, it is invalid logically.

Has a sufficient number of samples been used? Unless all members of a class of objects have been examined, you can never know for sure that you have included enough examples. If statistical procedures are applied to the data, the number of samples will determine the margin of error. But if statistical procedures are not applicable, you must make a subjective judgment about whether the number of examples is sufficient. One thing you know: if you have observed 100 percent of the examples, you have enough. On the other hand, you can be fairly sure you have an insufficient number if you have investigated only 5 to 10 percent of the cases. The difficulty is in determining what number between 10 and 100 percent constitutes a sufficiency when statistical procedures are not employed. This is why you need to engage in extensive research. As you find more and more consistent evidence, you can develop confidence in the validity of your examples as well as reduce the chance of using any exceptional instances. Because if the listener decides that your statements are based on atypical examples, your credibility will be diminished.

Figure 13.5
Toulmin model: reasoning by generalization.

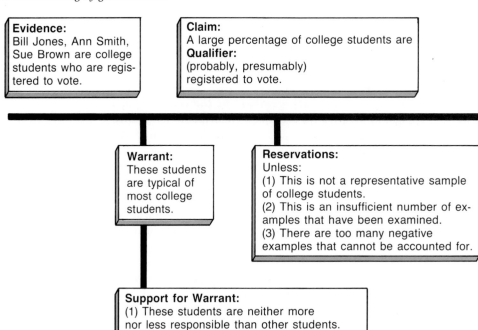

Evidence:
Bill Jones, Ann Smith, Sue Brown are college students who are registered to vote.

Claim:
A large percentage of college students are
Qualifier:
(probably, presumably)
registered to vote.

Warrant:
These students are typical of most college students.

Reservations:
Unless:
(1) This is not a representative sample of college students.
(2) This is an insufficient number of examples that have been examined.
(3) There are too many negative examples that cannot be accounted for.

Support for Warrant:
(1) These students are neither more nor less responsible than other students.
(2) These students are neither more nor less irresponsible than other students.

Can negative instances be accounted for? In other words, can the existence of examples that do not support the generalization be explained? Let's go back to the generalization that "Students at State University have total college board scores above 1,000." Suppose someone says, "Wait a minute, I know two people in one of my classes who have total college board scores under 1,000." If investigation discloses that those two persons are special students who are being allowed to take some courses but are not eligible for graduation, then the negative instances have been accounted for, and the original generalization still stands. If, however, investigation reveals that those two people are bona fide students, then there are deficiencies in the claim and it must be modified in order to be consistent with the evidence. The validity of this reservation may necessitate the inclusion of a qualifier such as "most."

Now that reasoning by generalization has been explained, you can see what it looks like in the Toulmin model in figure 13.5.

By Analogy

Rather than reasoning from a number of particulars to a general conclusion as in reasoning by generalization, reasoning by analogy reasons from one particular to another particular. For example, a salesman is about to buy a new car, and one of his concerns is how many miles the car will travel per gallon of gasoline. Until he drives several hundred miles he cannot know for certain, and since it is a new car, the dealer will not let him drive it the necessary miles. Moreover, there is no previous owner to consult. So he will be forced to use reasoning by analogy to arrive at a reasonable judgment about the number of miles the car will travel per gallon of gas. He may compare it with the car he now owns, and find the following characteristics shared by the two cars: (1) They are the same make. (2) Each is a four-door sedan. (3) Each has a 400 horsepower, V-8 engine. (4) Each has an automatic transmission. (5) Each has air conditioning. (6) Each has power steering. (7) Each has power brakes. (8) Each is blue. (9) Each has a plush interior. (10) Each has steel-belted tires. (11) Each has hidden front headlights. (12) Each has a stereo radio and tape deck. There is, however, one additional piece of known information about his present car: it gives approximately 12 miles per gallon of gas. Our driver now reasons that since the two cars are alike in a number of known respects, he can reasonably expect them to be alike in another unknown respect. So he concludes that the new car will give approximately 12 miles per gallon of gas. Thus his reasoning started with only one particular example and extended to only one particular example.

The preceding is a *literal* analogy, which compares two members of the same class. A literal analogy is the only kind that can produce an appropriate and legitimate claim. A second type is the *figurative* analogy, which compares members of two different classes. A figurative analogy was used by prosecutor Vincent Bugliosi in the murder trial described in his book *Till Death Us Do Part:*

I think that counsels' problem is that they misconceive what circumstantial evidence is all about. Circumstantial evidence is not, as they claim, like a chain. You could have a chain extending the span of the Atlantic Ocean from Nova Scotia to Bordeaux, France, consisting of millions of links, and with one weak link that chain is broken.

Circumstantial evidence, to the contrary, is like a rope. And each fact is a strand of that rope, and as the prosecution piles one fact upon another we add strands and we add strength to that rope. If one strand breaks—and I am not conceding for a moment that any strand has broken in this case—but if one strand does break, the rope is not broken. The strength of the rope is barely diminished. Why? Because there are so many other strands of almost steel-like strength that the rope is still more than strong enough to bind these two defendants to justice. That's what circumstantial evidence is all about.[5]

Although the figurative analogy does not result in a sound claim on its merits, it can be highly effective in getting listeners to understand or accept a point if the analogy is carefully chosen.

In order to determine whether reasoning by analogy permits you to defend the propriety of a claim, two specific questions must be answered affirmatively: (1) Are the compared examples alike in all essential respects? (2) Are differences between the compared examples accounted for? These are potential reservations for the claim. Let's consider these questions.

Are the compared examples alike in all essential respects? Essential respects are those that are related to the unknown attribute. In other words, some characteristics of a car affect how many miles it goes per gallon of gas; these are the essential respects. Other characteristics do not affect how many miles a car travels per gallon of gasoline; these are the unessential respects. Of the similar characteristics of the two cars cited previously, you will notice that only the first seven have any influence on gasoline economy. Now the question is: Are there any other essential respects in which the two cars differ? If we discover that the new car has dual four-barrel carburetors whereas the old one has a single two-barrel carburetor, we know this is an essential respect in which the two cars are dissimilar. Therefore, our conclusion that the two cars will give essentially the same number of miles per gallon is an improper claim. The two examples used in reasoning by analogy must be similar in all *essential* respects.

Are differences between the compared instances accounted for? Differences can be accounted for by showing that the differences are in unessential factors. If the two cars are different in color, that is an unessential difference with respect to fuel consumption. If one has hidden front headlights and the other one doesn't, that is an unessential difference. You must be prepared, therefore, to show that any cited differences between two examples are unessential differences. If you cannot, the reservation to the claim will stand, and the reasoning by analogy has serious and significant deficiencies in the claim.

Notice how reasoning by analogy looks in the Toulmin model in figure 13.6.

By Causal Relationships

Causal reasoning attempts to show why something happened or is going to happen. If something has happened and we are trying to determine why, this is called effect-to-cause reasoning. If we are trying to maintain that something is going to happen as a result of some specific factors, that is called cause-to-effect reasoning. If, going out to my car one hot July day to leave on a trip that will necessitate my driving 55 miles per hour for six hours on an interstate highway, I notice that my front tires are worn thin, I may reason—from cause-to-effect—that thin tires, a hot day, and fast, steady driving are likely to produce a blowout. Consequently, I may have two new tires installed to avoid my predicted effect. On the other hand, if I fail to see the tires before I leave and four hours later have a blowout, I may reason—from effect-to-cause—that the blowout was caused by the thin tire, hot day, and fast, steady driving.

In order to determine whether causal reasoning has resulted in a correct claim, four specific questions must be answered negatively: (1) Has the fact that two events are related in time been misinterpreted as a causal relationship? (2) Has an immediate cause been misinterpreted as a sufficient cause? (3) Have other factors intervened, or will they intervene, to prevent a normal effect from occurring? (4) Are there other causes that contributed to the effect? These are potential reservations to the claim. Let's consider each of them.

Figure 13.6
Toulmin model: reasoning by analogy.

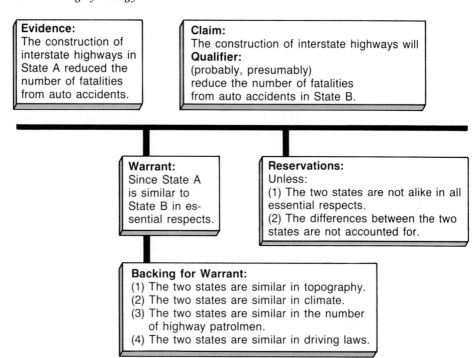

Has the fact that two events are related in time been misinterpreted as a causal relationship? This is what the Romans called the fallacy of *post hoc, ergo propter hoc;* in other words, when one event precedes another, we conclude that the first event actually produced the second one. Superstitions thrive on this kind of reasoning. A person whose path is crossed by a black cat has an accident later in the day and reasons that the cat caused the accident. One of the most entertaining of Ann Landers columns appeared several years ago. In it a reader lamented that "her life was ruined because of an offensive odor she couldn't get rid of. She made the rounds of nose specialists, endocrinologists, dermatologists, gynecologists—and no one could explain it. She said no friend or relative had ever mentioned the odor, but it was driving her crazy." The following letters were among the 500 received in response by Ann Landers.

FROM WHEELING: The woman with the "odor" is not sick—she is gifted. I, too, have the ability to smell things that no one else can smell. I can smell animals in the woods and birds flying overhead. I can also smell friends and acquaintances before they enter a room. I first realized I had this gift when I was four years old. I said to my mother, "Grandpa will be here soon." She asked, "How do you know?" I answered, "I can smell him." Sure enough, in five minutes Grandpa arrived. Please tell the woman who wrote not to worry. She's exceptional.

FROM MARSHALLTOWN, IOWA: Tell the lady with the strange odor to cheer up and she will smell better. Scientists have proved that happy people give off a fragrant scent. Negative brain waves (worry, anger, fear, anxiety) give off unpleasant odors. Animals can smell emotions but most people can't.

FROM LA PORTE, IND.: The woman who "Nose It All" should stop drinking coffee. The odor that is bothering her is the result of caffeine poisoning.

FROM JACKSON, MICH.: Tell "Stinky" to put a cup of salt in her bath water.

FROM JUNEAU, ALASKA: Tell the lady with the odor to sleep with a raw oyster over each eye at night. It's a sure cure.

FROM LONDON, ONTARIO: Her trouble is not in her mind, Ann, it's in her nose. She should line her nostrils with vaseline every night when she goes to sleep.

FROM FLINT, MICH.: The lady with the odor problem should change toothpaste and soap. She has an allergy that is throwing her chemistry out of balance.

FROM DES MOINES: If the woman will stop wearing synthetic fabrics (nylon, acetate, etc.) her odor will disappear. Synthetics stimulate glandular secretions which create odors.[6]

Obviously, the suggested remedies cannot be causative factors. These people have confused a prior event with a causal factor. You must avoid this kind of reasoning, for it creates deficiencies in the claim.

Has an immediate cause been misinterpreted as a sufficient cause? An event may serve as a trigger to produce a result, but not be sufficient to cause the effect by itself. A notable example of this kind of mistake is the claim that the assassination of Archduke Francis Ferdinand of Austria at Sarajevo caused World War I. Undoubtedly this event triggered the beginning of the war, but it would not have been sufficient to produce a world war if conditions had not been what they were at that time in Europe. Had conditions been different, the assassination of Archduke Ferdinand would probably have been little more than a minor ripple among all the world events of the day. You must ask whether the factor you are labeling a cause is one that is sufficient to produce the effect by itself. If not, the propriety of the claim must be questioned.

Have other factors intervened, or will they intervene, to prevent a normal effect from occurring? Whenever you argue that a given effect has occurred, or will occur, because of a given cause, you must be sure that no other factor has been introduced that will alter the relationship of the alleged cause and effect. If a building erected on former marshland collapses, for example, some may offer the claim that the collapse resulted from building it on an unsafe foundation. However, if someone points out that the contractor sank foundation supports fifty feet to solid rock, then the chances are that the fact the land was previously marshland had nothing to do with the collapse of the building.

Are there other causes that have contributed to the effect? Single factors are rarely the cause of an effect. In most instances there are multiple factors. Even when you have cited a number of factors as causes, you must be sure that there are no additional factors that could have contributed to the result. Let's look again at the example of the blowout. It could have resulted

Figure 13.7
Toulmin model: reasoning by causal relationships.

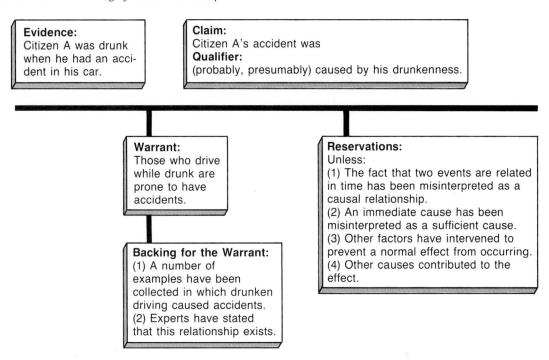

from the thin tire, hot day, and fast, steady driving; but it also could have resulted from striking a sharp stone on the highway. All such similar factors would have to be ruled out before the blowout could reasonably be blamed on the other three factors.

Figure 13.7 shows how causal reasoning looks in the Toulmin model.

Sign reasoning occurs when we take one event as an indication that a thing is true even though the reason for its being true is not explained. Thus, if we look out the window and see the leaves moving on a tree, we take that as a sign that the wind is blowing. If we hear the sound of water running in the downspout from the gutters on the roof, we infer that it is raining. If we hear the sound of squealing tires on the street, we assume that someone has either had an accident or narrowly averted one. If we see a long line of people standing outside a theater, we deduce that the movie being shown is a popular one. You will note that in none of these cases is there an explanation of why the occurrence is true. There is no explanation as to why it is raining, only the claim that it is.

In order to determine whether sign reasoning permits a claim that is sound on its merits, four specific questions must be answered: (1) Is the sign relationship accidental or coincidental? (2) Is the sign relationship reciprocal? (3) Have special factors intervened that alter normal relationships?

By Sign Relationships

(4) Is the sign reliable without the collaboration or concurrence of other signs? These are potential reservations to the claim. Let's consider each of these questions.

Is the sign relationship accidental or coincidental? In other words, is the sign only infrequently associated with the event. Enrollment in a university is taken as a sign that the individual can read and write with reasonable proficiency. Is it only coincidental that the college students we know have these competencies? If it is, the reasoning by sign will not have a high degree of probability, and the claim will not be a correct one.

Is the sign relationship reciprocal? In other words, can either be taken as a sign of the other? If we take enrollment at a university as a sign that the person can read and write with reasonable proficiency, can we also take reading and writing proficiencies as signs that the person is a university student?

Have special factors intervened that alter normal relationships? When we learn that a university student is an athlete, we must ask if some special factor has intervened—athletic ability—that has caused relationships to be altered. If some special factor can be shown to have intervened, the sign relationship to the event is highly improbable, and the propriety of the claim is questionable.

Is the sign reliable without the collaboration or concurrence of other signs? When you look out the window and see the leaves on a tree moving, do you also see a flag waving? If the leaves are moving, but a flag is hanging limp, it may, though not necessarily, mean that the wind is not moving the leaves. Instead someone may be shaking the tree or squirrels may be running on the limbs causing the leaves to move. Of course, it could be that the wind is blowing where the tree is, but not where the flag is. But the presence of a flag hanging limp increases the probability that the moving leaves are not a sign the wind is blowing. The more collaborative or concurrent signs that can be discovered, the more reliable is the claim based on the sign reasoning.

Figure 13.8 is an example of sign reasoning as it appears in the Toulmin model.

Special Fallacies

The term *fallacy* refers to "any trick of logic or language which allows a statement or a claim to be passed off as something it is not."[7] In the previous section, certain tests were suggested for each form of reasoning. If the reasoning is sound, the conclusion reached is sound. But if the reasoning fails to measure up to the tests, a fallacy has crept into the reasoning. A claim based on a fallacy cannot be accepted.

In this section we will be concerned with *special fallacies*. These special fallacies do not result from invalid use of the methods of reasoning. Instead they are tricky or specious devices that are too frequently used in human communication. Special fallacies involve such things as fallacies in the use of language, source materials, and audience attitudes and values. The special fallacy

Figure 13.8
Toulmin model: reasoning by sign relationships.

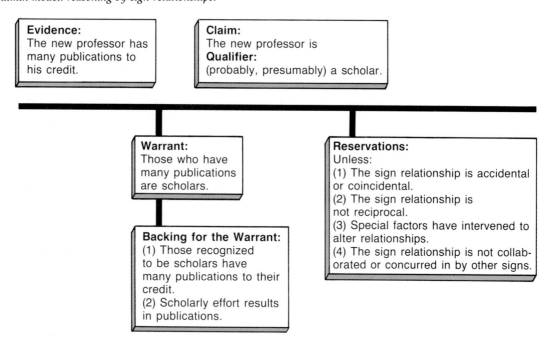

is a diversionary tactic to draw the audience's attention away from the non-logical basis of the conclusion, like a magician's showy movements used to mask the way he performs illusions. Some of the more common special fallacies are discussed in the following material.

Appeal to Tradition

In this special fallacy, the speaker argues that a position should be maintained because that is the way our people have always done it, or that a position should not be adopted because we have never done it that way before. For a long time, for example, some people in the South contended that Southerners should vote for the Democratic party because their parents and grandparents had voted for it. In other sections of the country, the same appeal was made for the Republican party. Ideally, the voter should examine the case for each party and for each candidate in every election.

Supporting a traditional course of action is not fallacious when supporting arguments are developed that show it is the best way. When we are asked to accept traditional ways simply because they are traditional, however, that is a fallacy.

Appeal to Ignorance (Argumentum ad ignorantiam)

In this instance, a person argues that because you cannot prove what she is saying is false, then it must be true. For example, some will say of a person accused of a crime: "Well, I think he is guilty, and he can't prove he is innocent, so he must be guilty." Or a speaker will say: "This is a good proposal I am presenting. Unless someone can prove it is not good, it should be adopted." In both of these cases, however, the burden of proving the case has been assigned to the wrong side. Those who are arguing for a change in policy have the burden to prove there is justification for that change. Thus, a person is innocent until proved guilty, and a proposal is not adopted until its advocate proves it should be.

Use of Question-Begging

A first type of question-begging is the use of a word that assumes the validity of a charge or point that should be proved. Consider the following examples: "We must get rid of the *bloated* federal bureaucracy." "The *unfair* income tax should be revised." "That *immoral* book should be banned." "Let's defeat this *corrupt* politician." *Bloated, unfair, immoral,* and *corrupt* are all question-begging words. The speaker must prove these implicit and unsupported charges before we can accept the statements.

A second form of question-begging is arguing in a circle. For example, a person might argue: "Education is good because it helps people." When asked why education helps people, the advocate replies, "Because it is good." Then, when asked why it is good, he answers, "Because it helps people." Arguing in a circle is fallacious because it uses two unproven assertions to support each other.

Appeal to Authority (Argumentum ad verecundiam)

Appeal to authority occurs when we are asked to support a position or adopt a policy simply because an authority says we should. For example: "We should cut the appropriations to higher education because our governor says the universities are wasting state funds." The error is compounded when the authority used is not even knowledgeable in the area in which we are asked to accept her opinion.

The fallacy of appeal to authority is not to be confused with the legitimate use of authority in developing evidence and reasoning to support a position. When a speaker cites the director of the Highway Patrol as saying that a speed limit above 55 miles per hour increases the number of accidents and then gives the statistics the director has collected, that is not a fallacious appeal to authority.

Attack on a Person (Argumentum ad hominem)

The *ad hominem* fallacy is an attack on the person or the source. A few years ago, for example, when the intercollegiate debate topic called for the cessation of nuclear testing, affirmative teams cited one particular scientist who had discussed the level of radiation resulting from nuclear fallout. In a number of instances, the negative team would ask the question: "Did he give that testimony before or after his stay in a mental hospital?" Notice that the attack is not germane to the testimony given. If one could show that this scientist had erred in using the wrong equipment, that would be a legitimate attack upon him. If one could show that he lacked the proper training or knowledge to use the equipment, that would be a legitimate attack upon him. If one could show that he was actually mentally ill during the collection of that data and that illness had adversely affected his ability to interpret the data, that would be

a legitimate attack upon him. But to ask the general question, "Did he give that testimony before or after his stay in a mental hospital?" suggests a connection that must be proved.

Frequently, we hear arguments of speakers answered by such statements as, "Oh, she's a born-again Christian," or "Oh, he's a member of the NAACP," or "She's one of those rabid conservationists," or "He's a Legionnaire." In each case, no effort is made to deal with the specific statement or argument of the individual. It is just assumed that no member of the particular group involved can present a valid argument.

An appeal to emotions asks the listener to accept a position solely for emotional reasons, because of feelings he experiences. A defense attorney uses this fallacy when she defends a client accused of embezzling funds: "Members of the jury, this man is your neighbor. He has lived in this community all his life and has never done physical harm to anyone. All of you know his mother. Think of the anguish she will endure if her only son is sent to prison." When we are asked to oppose a space program because there are people in this country who are starving, we are asked to behave in a certain way for an emotional reason.

Appeal to emotions can also involve an appeal to the listener's prejudice. When listeners are asked to oppose an action because it was "conceived by the Jewish bankers," an appeal to prejudice has been made. When listeners are told that "we must get the control of our government away from the

Appeal to Emotions

WASPs," an appeal to prejudice has occurred. In each of these instances, the listeners who respond to the appeal do so because of their distrust or dislike of a particular group of people.

Appeal to Popular Approval (Argumentum ad populum)

In this fallacy, the argument is made that a policy should be adopted or an argument accepted because the majority of people approve it. In some cases, the speaker doesn't even claim the majority of people approve, but merely says, "The people support this position." "The people" are not identified. "The people" may be Democrats, Republicans, Communists, or anybody else; we are never told. In other instances, the indeterminate "they" is used, as in, "They support our policy in the Middle East." The appeal is to get on the bandwagon and join the crowd, whoever the crowd is.

But the important fallacy in this kind of argument is that even if all the people in the United States favor a position, that does not make it valid. When native Japanese-Americans were placed in detention camps at the beginning of World War II, that action was approved by the great majority of Americans. That overwhelming public approval, however, did not make the policy right.

Summary

One of the ways in which you can develop the credibility necessary to have your ideas accepted is to prove what you say. Proof involves two processes—the use of evidence and the use of reasoning. This chapter has discussed the process of reasoning. The Toulmin model for analyzing reasoning has been used because (1) it does not require the certainty that the Aristotelian model does; (2) it places all the components of the reasoning process in the open and shows clearly their relationship to one another; (3) it places the basic premise of the argument, the warrant, in a position where support for it can be developed as a part of the reasoning model.

The Toulmin model consists of six parts: (1) evidence, (2) claim, (3) warrant, (4) backing for the warrant, (5) qualifier, and (6) reservations.

Four types of reasoning were discussed: (1) reasoning by generalization, (2) reasoning by analogy, (3) reasoning by causal relationships, and (4) reasoning by sign relationships.

To draw a proper claim from reasoning by generalization, three questions must be answered affirmatively: (1) Are the instances representative of all members of the class? (2) Have a sufficient number of instances been examined? (3) Can negative instances be accounted for?

Reasoning by analogy produces a sound claim if two questions can be answered affirmatively: (1) Are the compared examples alike in all essential respects? (2) Are differences between the compared examples accounted for?

A correct claim can be arrived at by reasoning from causal relationships if four questions are answered negatively: (1) Has the relationship of two events in time been misinterpreted as a causal relationship? (2) Has an immediate cause been misinterpreted as a sufficient cause? (3) Have other factors intervened to prevent a normal effect from occurring? (4) Are there other causes that contributed to the effect?

If the claim is to be free of deficiences when reasoning by sign relationships, four questions must be answered: (1) Is the sign relationship accidental or coincidental? (2) Is the sign relationship reciprocal? (3) Have special factors intervened that altered normal relationships? (4) Is the sign reliable without the collaboration or concurrence of other signs?

Special fallacies, tricky or specious devices, are used frequently to divert the audience's attention from the logical basis of a conclusion. Some common special fallacies are appeal to tradition, appeal to ignorance, use of question-begging words, appeal to authority, attack on a person, appeal to emotions, and appeal to popular approval.

Exercises

1. In a speech by one of your classmates, find an example of reasoning by generalization. Did you find the generalization credible? Why or why not?
2. Attend a lecture on campus. Analyze the speaker's reasoning. What aspects of this speaker's reasoning caused you to accept his or her ideas as credible? What about this reasoning caused you to doubt the credibility of his or her ideas?
3. Prepare a short speech analyzing a claim, which you did not consider credible, presented earlier by another member of the class. Explain why the claim did not seem credible to you.
4. Diagram in the Toulmin model one of your major arguments in your next speech. What parts will you omit in your speech? Why?
5. From letters to the editor of your school or community newspaper, select examples of reasoning that exemplify special fallacies.

Notes

1. Vincent E. Barry, *Invitation to Critical Thinking* (New York: Holt, Rinehart, and Winston, 1984), p. 9. Used by permission.
2. S. Toulmin, *The Uses of Argument* (Cambridge: Cambridge University Press, 1958).
3. Ibid.
4. Rene Dubos, "A Theology of the Earth," in *Representative American Speeches: 1969–1970,* ed. Lester Thonssen (New York: H. W. Wilson Co., 1970), pp. 90–91.
5. V. Bugliosi, *Till Death Us Do Part* (New York: Bantam Books, 1978), pp. 340–41.
6. Ann Landers, "Sleeping with Raw Oyster Over Each Eye Will Cure 'Odor'!" Los Angeles Time Syndicate, *Durham* (N.C.) *Morning Herald,* November 4, 1971, p. 3B. Used by permission.
7. Madsen Pirie, *The Book of the Fallacy* (London: Routledge & Kegan Paul, 1985), p. vii. See also Alex C. Michalos, *Improving your Reasoning* (Englewood Cliffs, New Jersey: Prentice-Hall, 1986), p. 26. Used by permission of the author, title and Routledge & Kegan Paul Publishers.

14

DEVELOPING CONTENT

Content is all the information used in developing the speaker's statement of purpose. Acceptance or rejection of the content ultimately determines whether or not listeners respond in the manner desired by the speaker. Listeners are more likely to find the content credible, and therefore acceptable, if it possesses one or more of the following four attributes: (1) it is consistent with or coincides with their own knowledge or attitudes, (2) it is consistent with their experiences, (3) it emanates from a speaker who is a highly credible source, or (4) it includes specific and credible content.

What is credible content? Credibility of content occurs on two levels. The first level is concerned with whether the content is *worthy* of belief on the basis of evidence and reasoning, regardless of whether it *is* believed. For example, the idea that was beginning to develop in the fifteenth century that the world was round was *worthy* of belief, even though many at that time did not believe it.

The second level of credibility is whether or not the content is *persuasive* to, or *believable* by, the listener. In early 1987, for example, despite President Reagan's denials, public opinion polls revealed that a majority of Americans believed that he had authorized secret shipments of military equipment to Iran to gain release of American hostages in Lebanon and had known of the diversion of funds from those arms sales to the Nicaraguan rebels.

The responsible and effective speaker tries to select content that is credible on two levels: it is not only *worthy* of belief, it is also *believable* or *persuasive* to the particular audience.

Ideas Consistent with Listeners' Knowledge and Attitudes

Statements or ideas that are consistent with knowledge and attitudes are accepted as credible. For example, the idea that work is an ennobling and necessary activity of humankind, has long been held by most people in this country as an inviolable principle. Any speaker making statements consistent with the "work ethic" would find many believing the statements merely because they consider the "ethic" itself valid. Without getting involved in the rightness or wrongness of the beliefs, we can think of a number that have long been held in this country: patriotism is good; democracy is the best form of government; freedom of speech is vital; freedom of religion is a right of all people; private enterprise is preferable to government ownership.

Anyone praising these or other such attitudes, or making statements consistent with them, is likely to strengthen her credibility. The speaker who stands in front of a labor union convention and says, "The product of American labor is what has made this country great," does not have to prove that claim. The listeners believe it in the marrow of their bones. The speaker who says to a business convention, "The ingenuity of American businessmen is responsible for the development and strength of the free enterprise system in this country," will not have this claim questioned. The speaker who comments to a group of college students that "Young people of today are better informed and more mature than any previous generation of young people," does not have to support that claim. In each of these instances the listeners believe these statements deep down inside. Audiences require no proof when a speaker is making statements wholly consistent with their beliefs or attitudes. The ethical speaker, however, must share these beliefs and have evidence to support their validity.

Do not make a statement unless you believe it yourself and can provide supporting evidence for it if needed.

In these instances, the speaker's claim is acceptable because of the audience's implicit belief, which serves as both evidence and warrant. In other cases, the evidence or warrant may be stated explicitly. Thus a belief or attitude of the listener is used as the basis for other statements. If you are talking to a group that believes federal public works programs should be used to combat unemployment, you may cite as evidence the unemployment rate and then present the claim that a federal public works program should be enacted immediately. You do not have to state explicitly your warrant that a federal works program is an effective method to reduce unemployment, nor do you have to prove it, because the listeners already believe it.

On the other hand, you can also use the knowledge of the listeners as evidence. If the audience knows that Richard Smith was drunk when he had an automobile accident last week, you can omit the evidence and go directly to the claim that "Richard Smith's drunkenness caused him to have the accident." You probably won't even have to state or develop the warrant that "Drunken drivers are prone to have accidents."

Constantly be alert for audience knowledge and attitudes you can use as evidence and warrants for the claims you are going to make in your speeches.

Use the methods explained in chapter 7 for analyzing the audience to which you are going to speak. With the materials that these audience analyses provide, you should become highly knowledgeable about the listeners' beliefs and attitudes, enabling you to know which statements you must prove, which need no proof, and which can serve as the basis for other statements.

Ideas Consistent with Listeners' Experience

We accept as real those things we actually experience. We believe our senses cannot betray us—a concept that one psychologist has called "primitive credulity." Each witness on the stand in a courtroom is convinced his account of events is the accurate one, after all; he perceived them through his own senses. If we hear an idea consistent with our experiences, we find it credible. On the other hand, we find unbelievable an idea that is inconsistent with our experiences. The fact that most academic theorists have never had actual experience in their field causes many practitioners to disbelieve their advice when it runs counter to experience. That is why businesspersons have said of certain economic theorists: "She can say that because she has never met a payroll."

Or a journalist may say of a journalism professor: "If he had ever put a newspaper to bed, he wouldn't say that." Farmers frequently express contempt for agricultural officials when they come out from Washington to give advice. One of the reasons for this attitude is that some of the advice runs counter to their own experiences. Credible ideas or statements are those that are consistent with our own experiences.

Show how your ideas are consistent with your listeners' experiences.

Ideas from a Respected or Authoritative Source

Because we consider our close friends trustworthy, we tend to believe what they tell us. We believe those things told us by authorities we respect because we believe that their qualifications lend validity to their statements. We give special credence to authoritative statements or ideas when there is general agreement among the experts. The difficulty comes when there is a division among respectable and qualified authorities. One of the problems the public has had in deciding on a number of issues in recent years is that there have been eminent and qualified authorities on both sides of these issues. Thus we have had outstanding experts testify for and against the building of nuclear reactor plants, the establishment of space colonies, the development of the Strategic Defense Initiative (the so-called Star Wars defense), the necessity to interrogate accused criminals without the presence of counsel. Despite these problems, authoritative testimony remains our most important and frequent source of information. We cannot know by experience, reasoning, or intuition what is going on today in Moscow, Berlin, or Tokyo, so we accept the account in the afternoon newspaper as accurate, unless or until we have reason to question it. Since we cannot know by any other method that Queen Elizabeth I of England lived, we accept the word of historians that she did. To make your ideas and statements credible, seek confirmation from sources held in high esteem by members of your audience.

Specific and Credible Evidence

The significant issues confronting our communities, our nation, and our world should be decided, not on the basis of people's beliefs and attitudes or on the basis of an individual's ethos, but on the basis of a careful scrutiny of the available evidence coupled with rational thought processes. Evidence thus serves an important function: it is the means by which reasonable persons establish and verify their ideas. Consequently, as a speaker who is committed to an intellectual or logical development of your ideas, seek to include sufficient valid evidence to demonstrate their veracity. Be certain that any evidence cited is credible on both levels—it is *worthy* of belief by careful thinkers, and it is believable by the particular audience to which you are speaking.

A number of experimental studies on the use of evidence in speaking have been conducted. Some indicated that evidence made a significant difference in changing attitudes;[1] some found that evidence made a difference in changing attitudes, although not a significant one;[2] others found that evidence made no difference.[3]

The conflicting results were a puzzle until recently when McCroskey and Dunham suggested that ethos might be a confounding element in some of these studies.[4] Specifically, they speculated that when the classroom instructor is the sponsor of research with students, the instructor's ethos is transferred to the message. Thus, a message that lacks evidence is still effective in changing attitudes because of the effect of the instructor's ethos. Holtzman subjected the theory to experimental scrutiny, preparing two forms of a speech, one with and one without evidence. Each speech was then presented to a different class by a sponsor who was unfamiliar to the students. Each speech was also presented to two classes with their own instructor as the sponsor. The results supported the theory. When the sponsor was unfamiliar, the speech with evidence shifted the attitudes of the students significantly more than the speech without evidence. But when the instructor was the sponsor, there was no significant difference in the effect of the two speeches. In other words, the high ethos of the instructor caused the speech with no evidence to be just as effective as the speech with evidence.[5]

Two descriptive studies of the use of evidence by high-ethos speakers have confirmed that these speakers use little evidence. In four major foreign policy speeches given in 1950–51 by Dean Acheson and Senator Robert A. Taft, the investigator found only five pieces of authoritative or statistical evidence.[6] Brandes investigated the use of evidence by "high-ranking" and "low-ranking" senators and found no differences between them, mainly because neither group used much evidence.[7] If this seems a contradiction, remember that even a "low-ranking" senator has high ethos compared with most speakers.

High ethos is so important in creating credibility for content that you must make whatever attempts are appropriate to develop high ethos for yourself. Chapter 6 presented five sources of ethos; use the appropriate ones whenever possible.

Although some early experimental studies indicated that the inclusion of evidence did not increase the persuasiveness of a speech, recent investigations suggest that the issue is complex, and that there are situations in which evidence is necessary if the speaker is to be effective in changing attitudes.

The remainder of this chapter will be concerned with (1) instances in which evidence is helpful, (2) ways in which evidence should be used, (3) types of evidence that can be used, and (4) sources of evidence.

First, evidence helps to change attitudes when the speaker has low ethos with the audience, *if* the speech is well delivered. When speeches with and without evidence were prepared and presented to subjects by low- and high-ethos speakers using good and poor delivery, it was discovered that the addition of evidence made a significant difference in changing attitudes "only in the low-ethos—good delivery treatment."[8]

Instances in which Evidence Is Helpful

Second, evidence is helpful if the ethos of the speaker needs to be improved. Using written messages on both questions of fact and policy with different levels of support—specific factual evidence, nonspecific factual evidence, and no evidence—Kline compared the effects on both low and high levels of intelligence. The results showed that all subjects exposed to the messages with specific factual evidence rated the authors of the messages as significantly higher on competence and trustworthiness than did the subjects exposed to the messages with nonspecific factual evidence or no evidence.[9]

Third, attitude change by a speech is sustained over a period of time more effectively if the speech includes evidence to support the claims.[10] Apparently, attitude change resulting from the impact of the speaker's ethos or the use of audience knowledge and beliefs lacks the foundation to withstand the influence of opposing evidence and speakers. The lack of substance leaves the listener vulnerable to opposing messages. It may be that evidence serves as a bulwark for the speaker's ideas when the listeners begin to have second thoughts about the speech or are confronted by opposing messages from other sources or other speakers with equally high ethos.

Fourth, evidence appears to operate as an effective immunizing agent against subsequent counterpersuasion. Two versions of both a pro and con speech on the same topic were prepared by McCroskey. One version of each included evidence and the other included no evidence. With the ethos of the speaker manipulated as high or low, the various versions of the speech were presented to subjects in alternating sequences. Invariably, the listeners who heard the speech with evidence first changed their attitudes more in the direction advocated by the speech than did those listeners who heard the speech with no evidence first. The high-ethos speaker lost ethos in the eyes of listeners when presenting a speech with no evidence following one in which evidence was used.[11]

How Evidence Should Be Used	To be effective in changing the attitudes of listeners, evidence should be used in the following ways: (1) qualifications of the source of the evidence should be cited, (2) evidence should be specific, and (3) evidence should be substantially unfamiliar to the listeners.
Cite Qualifications of Evidence Source	If the source of the evidence is to be cited, it will be more effective if you also present the qualifications of that source. Simply adding the source gives evidence no more effectiveness in changing attitudes than merely giving the evidence. One study even discovered that adding the source without its qualifications made the speech less effective than when the evidence alone was used to support the arguments.[12] Some studies have found that supporting assertions with evidence alone was just as effective as giving the evidence with the source and its qualifications.[13]
	Although it may appear from these studies that it is unnecessary to cite sources of evidence, there are other reasons for doing so. Give proper credit to sources to avoid accusations of plagiarism, and give the qualifications of sources to avoid lessening the impact of the message.
Use Specific Evidence	Evidence should be presented specifically; it should not be converted into general terms. If you have figures showing that 80 percent of the families in the United States have an adequate diet, don't say, "Most families in the United States have an adequate diet." Instead say, "Eighty percent of the families in the United States have an adequate diet." Specific evidence is important because it gives an impression of more precise or definite support for your claims than general evidence does. Moreover, the more specific the data, the more concrete your ideas will be. Something is concrete when it can be perceived by one or more of the senses. Although you cannot cause an actual perception as a result of your statements, you can evoke a mental image of a sensory perception. Thus, if you say something is soft as velvet, the listener has a mental perception of the feel of velvet, *if* he has ever touched velvet. Of course if he has never touched velvet, your words mean nothing to him. It is for this reason that you must be sure to present material that will evoke *familiar* sensory perceptions. Concrete data are important because we understand better those objects that we have sensorily perceived. Abstract statements and ideas are hard to comprehend because an abstraction is incapable of being perceived by the senses. Thus, we can talk about such things as loyalty, liberalism, or love, but nobody can see, feel, hear, taste, or smell any of these things.
	After studying the comparative impact of messages using specific, nonspecific, or no evidence, Kline concluded that for most topics, the effectiveness of nonspecific evidence "appears to be about midway between that of specific and that of no evidence. For other topics, nonspecific evidence appears little if any more effective than no evidence and for other topics it seems just as effective as specific evidence."[14]
	Experimental research has not yet identified the precise nature of those infrequent topics on which nonspecific evidence is as effective as specific evidence. Use specific evidence, therefore, to be assured of achieving maximum effectiveness of a message.

Evidence used to support statements in a speech should be fresh and unfamiliar to the particular listeners. Audience analysis will enable you to determine which specific materials are familiar and which are unfamiliar. Experimental studies have not clearly confirmed the advantage of unfamiliar evidence, but McCroskey concluded that currently it is more justifiable to assume unfamiliar evidence has an advantage over familiar evidence than to assume that unfamiliar evidence is not more effective.[15] A moment's reflection should convince us of the importance of unfamiliar evidence. Most of us have had the experience of being exasperated at a speaker who has told us nothing we did not already know. The usual feeling after such a speech is that we have wasted our time. But the most important reason for presenting unfamiliar information is that most people have already adjusted their attitudes to accommodate the information they possess; therefore, if you are to effect attitude change, you should provide either new information or a new analysis of old information.

Use Unfamiliar Evidence

"Evidence," according to one authority, "consists of those data that are intended to induce a sense of belief in the proposition which the data purportedly support."[16] Three general types of evidence are available: (1) opinion of others, (2) statistics, and (3) factual data.

Types of Evidence

Three types of opinion of others can be identified: (1) public opinion, (2) expert testimony, and (3) lay testimony.

Opinion of Others

Public opinion Public opinion is what the majority of people in a given geographical location believe on a given issue at a given time. Thus, there can be public opinion on permitting abortion on demand in the United States, on selling wheat to Russia in the midwest, on toxic waste dump sites in North Carolina, on teacher education programs in California, on the building of a horse racing track in Birmingham, Alabama. You must identify the geographical source of the public opinion you are citing.

How can you determine what public, or majority, opinion is? Many times you will know what it is just by listening to people in your community; opinion can be so strong there can be no mistaking it. Editorials in the newspapers, letters to the editor, and general conversations reveal the prevailing attitudes at the given moment on a specific issue. In other instances, public opinion is less obvious and you must rely on some objective measuring technique, such as polls, to determine its precise nature.

If the results of polls are used, you must be sure that such polls were properly conducted. Polls can be ingeniously biased to produce whatever result is desired. The wording of a question can influence the way a respondent will answer it. Burns W. Roper reported that when the SALT II treaty was being debated, a poll by his firm found 33 percent of the respondents favored the treaty. Roper, watching the "NBC News" that night, heard them report that "a just-completed poll showed 68 percent in favor of the SALT treaty—a 35 point difference." The reason for the difference, Roper discovered, was that the NBC poll never mentioned SALT II. It simply asked "whether people

would like to see an agreement between the United States and Russia that would reduce the likelihood of a nuclear conflict." Roper called for the press to increase its credibility by telling exactly what questions are asked.[17] There are a few pollsters, like Gallup and Roper, who have established a reputation for objectivity and accuracy by following carefully designed methods and by refusing to associate themselves with either a political candidate or party. These are the type of pollsters you should turn to for evidence to support your claims.

Even after you have uncovered public opinion polls that apparently provide an accurate representation of majority opinion, you are still faced with three problems in using public opinion to support your ideas. First, public opinion may be in error. Frequently, public opinion is based on myths or erroneous information. In 1964, for example, "the Survey Research Center discovered that 64 percent of adults polled remembered voting for John F. Kennedy in 1960."[18] In fact, Kennedy received only 49.7 percent of the votes cast in 1960.

Second, popularity is no indication of the merits of anything. Before you can responsibly use public opinion, you must ascertain that the opinion is consistent with other available evidence and whatever reasoning can be brought to bear on the topic. Public opinion is used because of its psychological or rhetorical value, but it must also meet logical requirements. Third, you are confronted with the fact that majority opinion is not always effective in persuading others. Hadley Cantril notes that the persuasiveness of majority opinion has frequently been demonstrated in experiments, and is frequently exhibited in everyday life. But, he observes,

This suggestibility to majority opinion is always highly relative, dependent upon the particular circumstances of the situation, cut across by numerous other influences that may be operative at the moment, and circumscribed by what the individual regards in *his* world. If people are suggestible to majority opinion, why, for example, did they not vote for Landon in 1936, when the widely publicized *Literary Digest* poll showed Landon the choice of the majority? Why do we still have two major political parties in the United States? Why do members of minority groups continue fervently to preach their causes when they know public opinion is ranged against them? Why do new values ever arise at all? Majority opinion is probably effective as a suggestion only when an individual has no clearly structured mental context adequate to interpret a situation and when the majority opinion does not conflict with other frames of reference or ego values.[19]

You cannot rely on citation of public opinion alone to get listeners to accept your point of view. Majority opinion can be used only as part of a mixture of evidence.

Expert opinion A second type of testimony is expert opinion. To qualify as expert opinion, two criteria must be met. First, the individual must be expert in the field on which she is speaking. It is not enough for a person to be an expert in some field. Thus a businessman speaking on religious matters is not giving expert opinion; a politician speaking on business matters is not giving expert opinion; a minister speaking on economic matters is not giving expert opinion. Of course, in some instances an individual may be expert in more than one field. Second, the expert testimony must come from one who is unbiased. When economists employed by the AFL-CIO testify, you may expect them to represent labor's point of view. If they present opinions detrimental to labor, they probably will not draw next month's pay from the AFL-CIO. On the other hand, economists employed by the National Association of Manufacturers can be expected to testify favorably to management. If not, they too will probably not receive next month's pay. You must look for experts who at least have the *opportunity* to be objective. University professors are often consulted because their position is not dependent upon their point of view and their scholarly bent generally inclines them toward objectivity. Even here, however, you must be cautious, for professors' conclusions can be prejudiced by their own philosophical view, their political affiliation, or their consulting fees!

There is a tendency for some to believe that expert testimony constitutes proof. Nothing could be further from the truth. In the final analysis, expert testimony constitutes an opinion, nothing more. An educated opinion, to be sure, but an opinion nonetheless. Testimony, therefore, is weak logical proof, even though it may be strong psychological proof because the listeners respect and accept the opinion of the expert cited. As Copi has pointed out,

If laymen are disputing over some question of physical evidence and one appeals to the testimony of Einstein on the matter, that testimony is very relevant. Although it does not prove the point, it certainly tends to confirm it. This is a relative matter, however, for if experts rather than laymen are disputing over a question in the field in which they are experts, their appeal would be only to the facts and to reason, and any appeal to the authority of another expert would be completely without value as evidence.[20]

Even more important, expert testimony can be partially or totally wrong. One writer on mental hygiene has pointed out that the "mere citation of expert opinion" cannot "be taken as an invariably dependable way of disposing" of controversial questions in that field.

The history of medicine is replete with instances of experts who backed what we now know to have been the wrong opinion. In the seventeenth century there were experts who opposed what Harvey had to teach regarding the circulation of the blood. And Pasteur's troubles with the medical experts of his day are common knowledge. That Charcot, France's leading authority on diseases of the nervous system in the late nineteenth century, refused to endorse the then novel teaching of syphilis as the cause of paresis is also common knowledge among those familiar with the history of paresis.

. . . In other words, we are not saying that experts should be ignored but their opinion on *controversial* issues should not be confused with tested knowledge. What they have to say should be taken as presumptive evidence rather than as coercive proof. As applied to our immediate concern—unsettled questions in the field of mental hygiene—this means that such questions cannot be disposed of by appeals to what "Freud taught" or "Adler advocated" or "MacDougall maintained." Appeal to authority is different from a direct and critical scrutiny of the available evidence. What a "doctor" says is probably more often right than what the "layman" says; but when another "doctor" contradicts the first one, then the poor "layman" may begin to appreciate the difference between fact and opinion, between data and their interpretation, or between symptomatology and diagnosis.[21]

Recently, two journalistic commentators called attention to a number of modern scientific experts who have given incorrect testimony. The following are some of the examples they listed. (1) In 1933, Dr. Ernest Rutherford, English Nobel Prize winning scientist, declared that atomic energy could never be controlled in a useful manner. (2) In 1949, the General Advisory Committee of the U.S. Atomic Energy Commission claimed that it was unfeasible to produce an H-bomb. (3) In 1950, Dr. Vannevar Bush said it was impossible to make accurate intercontinental rockets or ballistic missiles. (4) In 1953, the Lincoln Summer Study, whose membership included Dr. James Killian, Dr. Carl Kaysen, and Dr. Jerome Wiesner, stated without equivocation that Russia could not possibly develop ICBMs "for at least another 10–15 years." (5) In 1962, Dr. Jerome Wiesner declared that Lunar Orbital Rendezvous was unworkable and "too risky for astronauts to attempt."[22] Every one of these predictions, we now know, was inaccurate. Yet there were those at the time the statements were made who wanted to adopt policies based on the predictions.

The point is clear: Use expert testimony as evidence for psychological reasons, but seek out more substantial evidence to use as logical proof.

Lay testimony Lay testimony, the opinion of one who is not an expert in the field on which he is testifying, doesn't even have the virtue of being a more educated opinion. Nevertheless, there is no denying that some lay testimony is highly persuasive to some groups and, on occasion, may be more correct than expert opinion. Historian Daniel J. Boorstin points out that it was Cotton Mather and his fellow members of the clergy who led the fight to adopt inoculation to eliminate smallpox. Ironically, the doctors of the period were the outstanding opponents of inoculation.[23] A highly respected member of a community may give lay opinions on a number of topics and be listened to with great care.

One feature of testimony, whether it be lay or expert, that has long been recommended by rhetoricians is that the testimony be *reluctant,* which is testimony running counter to the best interests of the one giving the opinion. If the president of the AFL-CIO said that labor unions have too much power in controlling wages, that would be reluctant testimony. If the president of U.S. Steel were to say that steel companies were making too much profit, that would be reluctant testimony. Recent studies indicate that *unbiased* testimony is preferable to reluctant testimony, even though both are more effective than biased opinions.[24]

Whether testimony emanates from an expert or a lay person, the crucial question is: Will the listeners accept this person as a credible source? If they will not, it doesn't matter how competent the source is.

"Statistics are lenses through which we form images of our society. . . . Even **Statistics** when they misrepresent reality, they standardize our perceptions of it."[25]

Some refer to any quantitative data as statistics, but quantitative data consist of two types: numbers and statistics. Numbers are unorganized, unanalyzed data. They will be discussed under the next unit, factual data.

Statistics are those quantitative data produced "when the data have been organized and analyzed and relationships among them have been stated in summary or relative terms."[26]

Be aware of the varying attitudes that exist toward statistics. At one extreme are those who regard statistics as holy writ. Their attitude is that if data can be reduced to quantitative form, they must be true. After all, the data couldn't be counted if they weren't true. At the other extreme are those who refuse to accept the validity of any statistics. In their view, figures don't lie, but liars figure; as some phrase it, "There are liars, damned liars, and statisticians." There is ample justification for this skepticism.

Even though there are known invalid statistics, it is also true that some statistics are valid. To know which are valid and which are not, you must be familiar with their source and know where, when, and under what conditions the statistics were compiled.

One feature of statistics which many do not adequately understand is that there is no real referent for a statistic. For example, consider a basketball team whose five starters have the following heights: 6' 10", 6' 8", 6' 7", 6' 0", and 6' 0". The mean height of the team would be 6' 5". Yet there would be no member of the team who would be exactly 6' 5". If uniforms were purchased on the basis of the mean height of the team, no uniform would fit. It is like the man who said, "On the average I am comfortable," while standing with one foot on a cake of ice and the other on a hot stove; and like the statistician who drowned in a river with a mean depth of three feet. Unless you recognize that a given statistic may not have a real referent, you may unwittingly draw unwarranted inferences from it. This is the reason statistics cannot be classified under factual data: since there is frequently no real referent, statistics cannot be considered invariably as fact.

Quantitative data are probably the most effective type of evidence in causing a change in attitudes. Costley used a speech with three different types of content (quantitative data with comparisons, quantitative data without comparisons, no quantitative data). The speech using quantitative data with comparisons to audience experience caused the greatest shift of attitude, but the difference was not significant.[27] Gardiner prepared five different versions of the same persuasive speech, each using a different type of evidence: (1) statistics, (2) testimony, (3) examples, (4) generalizations, and (5) a combination of the other four types. Only two—statistics and generalizations—produced significant shifts, and the most significant shift was caused by the speech using statistics.[28]

If statistics are to be used properly and effectively, there are certain principles you must observe.

Use statistical measures correctly Use the proper label for any measure of central tendency. Although most of us were taught at some point in school that an average was arrived at by summing all the items and dividing that total by the number of items, this is not the meaning of the term "average" in statistics. Average, in statistics, is a general term meaning measure of central tendency. There are a number of averages, or measures of central tendency, of which the most commonly used are the mean, the median, and the mode. The mean is an arithmetic computation, the formula for which is $\Sigma X/N$; in other words, what is commonly referred to as the average. The median is the item or class of items occurring at the midpoint between the highest and lowest data, after the data have been placed in rank order. The mode is that datum or class of data that occurs most frequently. In a normal distribution the mean, median, and mode are the same. Correctly identify any measure of central tendency you use. To use the term *average* leaves some confusion about which precise measure you are referring to.

Make no comparison of percentages unless you know that the base used in the computation of each percentage was the same; otherwise any comparison is totally invalid. If a student makes 90 on one exam and 99 on the next, she has made a 10 percent improvement. But if another student makes a 60 on the first exam and a 78 on the second, she has made a 30 percent improvement. It is quite clear that any comparison of these two percentages in no way reflects the differences between the two students.

Cite specific sources of statistics In order for the listener to evaluate accurately the statistics presented, provide the specific source. Vague references such as "statistics show," "studies prove," or "statisticians say" will not give needed information. If a speaker goes into an agricultural section of North Carolina and convinces the farmers to use a particular type of seed corn because a study by the U.S. Department of Agriculture showed it improved production, without telling his listeners that the study was conducted in Iowa in 1939, he could cause the farmers to make a serious mistake. Tell your listeners where the statistics were obtained, when they were compiled, and by whom.

Round off statistics where possible It is rarely necessary or practicable to present precise statistics. Remember that listening is a difficult task, much more so than reading. Since it is difficult to comprehend a series of figures in written material, think how much more difficult it is to comprehend them in listening. You generally communicate more with rounded-off statistics than with precise figures. If you use the figure 72.39 percent, you may find that many listeners actually hear the figure as 39 percent, or in hearing the .39 they may miss the first two digits and have no idea what the important number is. To round that number off to "slightly over 72 percent" would make it far easier to comprehend, and it would be even easier to understand if presented as "just under three-fourths."

Convert statistics to concrete data where possible The value of concrete data has already been discussed. Since quantitative data are abstract and difficult to comprehend, they should be made concrete if at all possible. If you are addressing an audience in a wheat-growing area, you may refer to the number of bushels of wheat produced last year. A bushel of wheat is not abstract to those listeners; it is a very concrete object. But if you are talking to an audience in an area where wheat is not grown, you may want to convert the bushels of wheat to loaves of bread, a concrete object for your listeners. Or you might want to connect the bushels of wheat with some concrete object familiar to the listeners by saying something such as, "The wheat produced last year in this country would fill Shea Stadium level with the top row of seats ten times." In this way some of the abstractness of the statistics would be removed.

David Stockman, former director of the Office of Management and Budget, attempted to make budget cuts more concrete to a group of Republicans when he said, "There's plenty of room for more and deeper cuts. . . It isn't necessary . . . for the government to spend as much to teach someone a job as it costs a parent to send a son to Harvard—with his own limousine. It isn't necessary to employ one federal bureaucrat for every 26 Indians."[29]

Use statistics sparingly It is easy to use too many statistics. The result will be information overload, and listeners will be unable to cope with all the data. At a minimum, one of two results will occur. Either the listener will get the statistical information confused and assign the statistics to a wrong referent, or the confusion will cause the listener to give up and quit listening to the speaker.

Choose only those statistics that are important to the comprehension of your ideas. Omit all others even though they may be vivid and interesting.

Factual Data

Factual information, a third form of evidence, must be verifiable by objective measurements (The temperature is 75° today. The left offensive guard for Auburn University weighs 245 pounds.) or by sensory perception (There are three cars in the driveway. Her eyes are blue. The finish on the table is smooth.) or by historical investigation (The stock market crashed on October 29, 1929. The Japanese attacked Pearl Harbor on December 7, 1941. The New York Jets defeated the Baltimore Colts in the Super Bowl in 1970.).

Factual data must be investigated carefully; it may not be as factual as it seems. The objective measuring instruments may be out of order. If a thermometer is broken, it will not give an accurate reading. Weights will not be correct if the scales are out of balance. Or sensory perception may be erroneous. Personal characteristics frequently affect sensory perceptions. Some persons may claim that a pitcher of iced tea is bitter, while others say it isn't. Teenagers listen to music at a level they deem enjoyable, while their parents complain that the music is so loud it hurts their ears. Historical data may be erroneous. Abraham Lincoln is alleged to have written a letter to a Mrs. Bixby whose five sons were killed in the Civil War. Yet one investigator reported that not all of Mrs. Bixby's sons served in the army, nor did all those who served get killed.[30] It would appear, then, that either Lincoln wrote no such letter or, if he did, made a horrendous mistake.

Factual data may be presented in the speech as quantitative data, as simply statements of fact, or as examples.

Quantitative data Quantitative data in the form of numbers are factual data because they have real referents. Thus you use numbers to represent factual data when you say "The population of the United States is 240,468,000." "The president's salary is $200,000." A word of warning is in order, however; numbers can be just as invalid as statistics. One writer reported: "Recently it was authoritatively reported that more than half the money spent on birth control worldwide goes for abortions. That's the kind of number likely to stick in people's minds and influence important decisions, which would be a shame. Given the widespread taboos about birth control and abortion, and the very different economies of socialist and third-world societies, the figure can have been no more than the wildest guess. It should have been presented as a guess."[31] *Time* recently reported that the federal government's Center for Disease Control had "announced that a certain drug company may have infected 5,000 hospital patients with contaminated intravenous solutions, contributing to the deaths of 500 people. When asked how this figure had been determined, a government spokesman said that one estimate of 2,000 was 'unrealistic' and another estimate of 8,000 was 'unfair.' So the authorities split the difference."[32] On its morning news program of April 23, 1982, ABC radio news reported that the severe winter had created 200 million potholes in the United States. Who do you suppose counted those potholes?

Statements of facts Statements of fact are used by the speaker who says "Even numbered interstate highways run east and west, while odd numbered ones run north and south." "The president made a speech on national TV last night." "OPEC has raised the price of oil two dollars a barrel."

An example is the use of a particular case to support another statement by amplifying or extending it. The speaker who made the statement about the numbering of interstate highways might also say "An example is I-95, which runs from Miami, Florida, to Maine." The example, then, supports a more general statement. Examples may be used as specific instances or as illustrations.

A specific instance is an undetailed example. Notice how one speaker used four specific instances to support a generalization: "We know from past experience that it is when the public and private sectors are united in some grand national undertaking that we have been at our best—the Manhattan project, development of synthetic rubber, the railroads in an earlier day, and more recently, NASA. The mix has varied in each of these projects and there is no formula for the future. But certainly, we can achieve energy self-sufficiency only with a program that calls for the best that all of us in the private sector have to offer."[33]

The virtue of specific instances is that several can be presented in a short period of time. Thus if you are making a claim about which the listeners will have strong reservations, you can supply a number of specific instances rather quickly to weaken those reservations. After hearing several instances it will be more difficult for the hearers to convince themselves that you have based your claim on too few or unrepresentative examples.

An illustration is a detailed example. The late Hubert H. Humphrey, when vice-president, used an effective illustration in a speech in Tampa, Florida, in 1965 concerning the war on poverty.

I came to Washington seventeen years ago as a freshman senator. During that first year a scene took place in a Senate hearing room that symbolized just what we mean by the Great Society.

A woman from Tennessee, a garment worker, was testifying before seven U.S. senators on behalf of raising the minimum wage to seventy-five cents an hour. At one point, this is what she said:

"My youngest girl she's nine now, goes straight to the piano when we go to a house where they have one. She does want to play the piano so bad. I've thought that maybe I could save fifty cents or a dollar a week to buy a second-hand piano for her, but I haven't found a way to do it yet. Maybe I've been foolish to talk to you people about music for one of my children when the main question is getting enough to eat and wear, or blankets for the bed, or a chair to sit on. But down in Tennessee we love music, and factory workers don't live by bread alone any more than anyone else does."

Piano lessons for a little Tennessee girl; full, productive lives for our citizens and the places where they live—these are what the war on poverty is all about, what the Great Society is all about. This is what we work for.[34]

Obviously, an illustration is much more time-consuming than a specific instance, so if you are developing a controversial claim in a limited amount of time, you will probably have to forgo the use of illustrations in order to include a number of specific instances. But it is obvious that the illustration is much more interesting to listen to and gets the listener much more involved in the example. Therefore you should, if at all possible, work some illustrations into your speech.

Audio-Visual Aids

Now that we have seen what evidence you should present to develop credibility, we need to recognize that evidence often requires audio-visual assistance. For this reason audio-visual aids are sometimes necessary.

An audio-visual aid is anything, other than the speaker, that is used to assist in communication. An audio-visual aid may be a recording, an object, a line or bar graph, a picture or drawing, or simply written words reinforcing what you are saying. Audio-visual aids help to make content more comprehensible, more interesting, and more vivid. In the following pages, we will consider the means of presenting audio-visual aids to listeners and the principles that should be observed in using them.

Means of Presenting Audio-Visual Aids

A number of media are available to aid in presenting your audio-visual aids to the listeners. This unit will discuss these media and suggest ways in which they can be used.

The first group of media to be considered is called *demonstration boards*. A *chalkboard,* the same as that on which your teacher writes with chalk, may be used to write on during your speech. If you are giving a classroom speech, you may write on the board in the room. For speeches in other situations, however, you will have to buy or make a chalkboard that you can carry to the site of your speech. Letters and numbers on a chalkboard should be at least 2 1/2 to 3 inches high in order to be easily seen from the back row in a normal size classroom.[35] A significant disadvantage of chalkboards is that many people have poor handwriting, which creates legibility problems.

A *feltboard* or *flannelboard,* as the name implies, is made by attaching felt or flannel cloth to a hardbacking of wood, Celotex, or metal. The object to be displayed should be given a backing of felt, flannel, sandpaper, cotton, pipe cleaners, or any substance that will adhere to the surface of the board. Objects shown on the feltboard must be relatively light in weight to keep from falling off.

A *hook 'n loop* board is one that is covered with Velcro. It comes in two forms: a loop type material and a hook type material. When the two are pressed together, they form a tight union and will support rather heavy objects. The loop material is used on the board and the hook material is attached to the back of the objects to be displayed.

A *magnetic board* must obviously be made of metal. Objects to be displayed on this board must have small bar or strip magnets attached to them. Strip magnets are strips of rubber saturated with magnetized steel filings. They can be sewn, glued, or pinned to objects displayed.

A *flip chart* is a pad of large sheets of paper. This visual aid is excellent for showing a sequence of steps or activities, with a different step or activity on each sheet.[36]

Poster board can also be used to present visual material. One of the disadvantages you must guard against is the tendency for listeners to direct their attention to aspects of the visual aid that you are not discussing. One way to prevent that is to prepare the material in such a way that you can leave covered that which is currently not being discussed. You can cover each unit with a strip of paper that can be removed as you are ready to discuss that section. This *strip tease* technique allows you to control what the listeners can attend to, and thus prevent them from moving on from the topic you are discussing to the next one that you plan to discuss. Only your ingenuity limits what you can do with a poster board. You can prepare add-on materials by simply using a loop of fresh masking tape that can be pressed on the back of the object to be displayed and then pressed on the poster board.

Graphs are especially helpful if you are going to use numerical data and make comparisons. These data can be prepared in different ways to serve different purposes. Pie graphs, bar graphs, and line graphs can be used to help listeners clearly see unusual relationships and varying proportions.

The second group of media consists of electrical equipment that can be used to present information to an audience. The *overhead projector* flashes information from a transparency onto a screen. The ease of operation—the speaker only has to lay the transparency on top of the overhead projector—makes this an ideal visual aid for a speaker if his information can be put on a transparency. You can increase the effectiveness of a transparency by constructing the basic idea and then using overlay units to add other features that you want to discuss.[37] Many transparencies are developed by commercial firms. In addition, the Learning Resources Center in your institution can easily produce them, generally for only a small fee. Research has indicated that letters on transparencies must be at least 3/16, and preferably 1/4, inch high in order to be readable at a distance of twenty to forty feet.[38]

A *slide projector* is one of the easiest electrical media to use and is also one of the most popular. A revolving tray sitting on top of the projector holds the slides. An important and advantageous feature is that, with the projector in the rear, the speaker can stand in front of the audience with a remote control unit and operate the projector. The slides are made when the film is developed. Certain guidelines should be observed in the use of slide projectors: (1) A day or two before the speech, check to make sure there is an electrical outlet for the projector and that the cord is long enough to reach it. If the slides constitute a significant part of the speech, it will be prudent to have a backup projector. (2) Be certain the screen on which the slides will be shown is large enough to be seen easily by all members of the audience.

A *filmstrip projector* pulls a strip of 35mm film past the lens by a series of sprocket holes. There is no feed or take-up reel. A large number of commercial and free filmstrips are available. Since most filmstrips are very short, they are ideal for demonstrating brief segments in a speech.

All of these projectors require a screen large enough for the images to be seen easily. For most rooms, the screen should be 60″ × 60″. It should be 70″ × 70″ for a large room. The square shape is required for vertical slides and transparencies.[39]

There are three other pieces of audio electrical equipment that can be used in the public speaking situation. These are the *audio tape recorder,* the *motion picture projector,* and the *video tape recorder*. This equipment is less appropriate for most public speaking situations; nevertheless, there are times when one of these pieces of equipment will be helpful and you will want to use it. You may want to let your listeners hear some sound or some speaker on the audio tape recorder, show a short segment of a movie, or show some action scenes on a television screen.

Some general principles should be applied to all visual aids. First, plain letters work better than fancy ones. Plain ones project a simplicity that is appealing, while fancy ones can be difficult to read quickly. Second, the spacing of letters is important. Each letter should not be given the same amount of space, but it should appear that the letters are evenly spaced. For example, if the letter A is given the same amount of space as other letters, it will appear that the A has been given more space than the others. When the A is given a little less space than the others, however, the impression is given that the letters are evenly spaced. Third, visual aids should appear uncluttered. Put only the necessary information on your visual aids. Fourth, colors should be used wisely. A few harmonious colors are better than a large number. Experts recommend that you create a strong contrast among the colors. On a dark background, yellow, orange, red, green, blue, and violet have the greatest carrying power. On a light background, black, red, orange, green, blue, violet, and yellow have the greatest carrying power.[40] Attention to these principles will ensure that your visual aids are attractive and will be easily interpreted.

Preparation of Visual Aids

Prepare visual aids in advance There are several reasons for preparing a visual aid before the speech. If you wait to prepare it until the moment in the speech when it is to be used, you generally find yourself unable to create the visual aid and continue talking. Periods of silence thus occur, permitting and encouraging the listeners to focus their attention on other stimuli. You then have a difficult task of regaining their attention; that of some of the listeners will never be regained. Moreover, a visual aid prepared in advance can be attractively constructed: lines straight, circles round, angles precise, colors added to give emphasis and variety to the various parts.

Principles for Using Audio-Visual Aids

Keep the visual aid covered when not in use If a visual aid is placed uncovered in front of an audience, the listeners begin to scrutinize it and attempt to decipher it. Whatever you say during this time generally goes unheard because few people can attend to two different stimuli simultaneously. Objects themselves should be placed out of sight: in a recess in the lectern, in a box on a nearby table. If the visual aid is on something like poster board, it can be placed on an easel with its blank side to the audience or another blank poster board in front of it. Once you are finished with the visual aid, you should recover it or remove it from the listeners' view. If left in view, it can be just as distracting during subsequent parts of the message as during prior parts. A word of warning: Do not expose the visual aid too briefly. That only frustrates the listeners. Show it and explain it sufficiently for it to be understood.

Avoid talking to the visual aid Remember that you are there to communicate with human beings, not with a visual aid. Talking to the visual aid has a bad psychological impact on listeners; it conveys a lack of interest in talking to them. Furthermore, it prevents you from receiving feedback from the listeners. If some of them indicate a lack of understanding while you are looking at the visual aid, you will probably miss that feedback and go blithely on to other ideas, leaving bewildered and confused listeners whose attention you will probably lose permanently.

Use hand nearer the visual aid for pointing Using the hand that is away from the visual aid causes you to turn your body toward it, leaving your back toward the listeners. This eliminates direct communication between you and the listeners and discourages close attention by the listeners. It also encourages you to look at the visual aid instead of the listeners. The human body likes to follow the path of least resistance—for the head that means looking straight forward. When the body is turned toward the visual aid, it is only natural for the head to turn that way. Even if you make a special effort to maintain eye contact, your natural impulse is to resume looking toward the visual aid. If you use the hand nearer the visual aid, however, your body remains turned toward the listeners; communication is direct and, following the path of least resistance, eye contact is easily and naturally maintained with the listeners. When you look at the visual aid to find the spot to which you want to point, you naturally look back to the listeners.

Keep visual aids out of hands of listeners A visual aid handed to listeners to be passed around creates a constantly distracting ripple through the audience. At least three persons are more involved with the aid than with what you are saying: the person who just had it, the one who has it, and the one who is expecting to receive it. And this does not mention the ones who are never able to understand your ideas once they resume attending to you. Many of these give up in frustration. Even if you have a visual aid for every member of the audience, do not put it in their hands during the speech. It becomes too easy for listeners to attend to different parts of the visual aid. If you want each person to have a copy to examine, you can announce that ushers will have copies at each exit or that they will be available at the conclusion of the speech.

Make the visual aid large enough A visual aid should be seen by all members of the audience. There is nothing more irritating than to sit in an audience and be unable to see a visual aid the speaker is using. The size of the aid is determined by the size of the audience, not by the size of the room. If the speech will be given in a room that is thirty feet long, the visual aid can be made large enough to be seen at the rear of the room and it doesn't matter how many people will be present. If the speech is to be given in a room a

Figure 14.1

The sample visual aid: the Laffer curve. From Jude Wanniski, The Way the World Works: How Economics Fail—and Succeed. (New York: Basic Books, Inc., 1978), p. 97. © Basic Books, Inc. Used by permission.

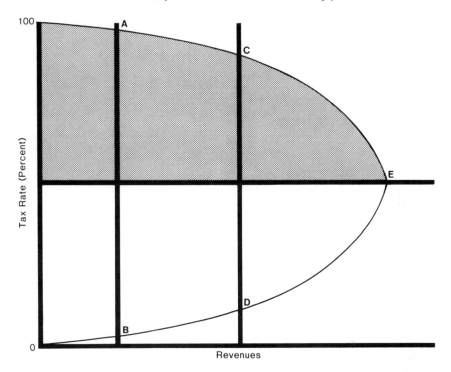

hundred feet long, but there will be no more than fifty people present, the visual aid needs to be large enough to be seen far enough back to accommodate fifty people. They can be asked to seat themselves close to the speaker. In some large auditoriums, it is simply not practicable to make a visual aid large enough to be seen by all members of the audience. In such situations, it is better to avoid using a visual aid than to irritate and frustrate some because they are unable to see it.

Keep the visual aid simple and attractive Remember that a visual aid should be exactly that—an *aid,* not the complete source of information. A visual aid is used because you need some assistance in communicating your ideas. If the visual aid tells the whole story, you don't need to discuss it. Moreover, the less complex the visual aid is, the less the listeners will be distracted by it. The simpler the aid, the easier it will be for you to focus the listeners' attention on the important details. Examine the visual aid in figure 14.1. Note its attractive simplicity, and yet it cannot be understood without an oral or written explanation.

Figure 14.2
A sample visual aid: table of ten major military powers and social indicators, 1975.

TEN MAJOR MILITARY POWERS AND SOCIAL INDICATORS, 1975

	USA	USSR	West Germany	China	France	UK	Iran	Italy	Japan	Israel
Military Expenditures Billion US $	90.9	94.0	15.3	18.0	13.1	11.5	7.7	4.7	4.6	3.5
Rank among 140 countries in:										
GNP per capita	6	27	9	103	11	23	44	28	21	25
Literacy	1	1	1	26	1	16	85	30	1	37
Population per physician	18	1	9	93	23	26	69	11	33	2
Infant mortality per 1,000 live births	13	34	21	51	8	13	106	26	2	25
Life expectancy at birth	7	29	18	56	10	10	77	10	3	10

Source: World Military and Social Expenditures 1978

Now examine the table in figure 14.2. In this visual aid, the mass of data would be distracting to listeners. They would be shifting attention from one idea to another and from one number to another. In addition, the information is understandable without any explanation. So a listener could stop listening to you and focus full attention on the visual aid.

Sources of Content

Once you have committed yourself to giving a speech, you must begin to assemble the ideas and evidence you are going to use in that particular speech. Four general sources may be consulted in the search for ideas and evidence: (1) personal experience, (2) interviews, (3) documents, and (4) library resources.

Personal Experience

Begin with your own knowledge and experiences. The use of personal experience has a number of virtues. First, it is easier to talk about. You don't have to remember what someone else has said or written; you are talking about things you have done. You can rely on your own vocabulary to describe the experiences. If you are relating what someone else has said or written, you are restricted to repeating the exact words of that person or to finding synonyms for those words. You cannot go beyond the words of that other person, which makes it more difficult for you to use your own vocabulary.

A second advantage of personal experience is that the information has to be new to listeners unless you have talked to the group previously or have published the material someplace where the listeners could have read it. Thus, you can use personal experience without any concern about whether or not the listeners are familiar with the content. Even if you are talking about experiences that others have talked about to this same group, it is still fresh information because no two people perceive the same things in a given situation, and no two people react in the same way to the stimuli they perceive.

But the most important advantage of using personal experience is that it contributes to your credibility, thus causing greater attitude change on the part of the listeners. Ostermeier presented to subjects persuasive messages in which he varied the number of self-reference materials (defined as firsthand personal experiences) and the number of prestige reference materials (defined as the firsthand experience of others). The results of the study showed that increasing the number of self-references caused the subjects to perceive the source as being more competent and more trustworthy, and it caused the subjects to change their attitudes more. Ostermeier concludes that an audience considers personal experience "direct information" about the speaker, while firsthand experiences of others is considered "indirect information."[41]

A particularly effective reference to personal experience to develop his point was used by the Canadian statesman Lester Pearson in his speech accepting the Nobel Peace Prize in 1957:

I have, therefore, had compelling reason, and some opportunity, to think about peace; to ponder over our failures since 1914 to establish it, and to shudder at the possible consequences if we continue to fail.

I remember particularly one poignant illustration of the futility and tragedy of war. It was concerned, not with the blood and sacrifice of battles from 1914–1918, but with civilian destruction in London in 1941 during its ordeal by bombing.

It was a quiet Sunday morning after a shattering night of fire and death. I was walking past the smoking ruins of houses that had been bombed and burned during the night. The day before they had been a neat row of humble, red brick, workmen's dwellings. They were now rubble except for the front wall of one building, which may have been some kind of community club, and on which there was a plaque that read "Sacred to the memory of the men of Alice Street who died for peace during the Great War, 1914–1918." The children and grandchildren of those men of Alice Street had now in their turn been sacrificed in the Greater War, 1939–45. For peace? There are times when it does not seem so.[42]

Interviews

Interviews with knowledgeable and experienced persons in the surrounding community should not be overlooked as valuable sources of information. As a college student, you have an unparalleled opportunity to consult experts and near experts. And most professors will be happy to talk to you if the interview is conducted in the proper way. Adhering to the following four principles should make for a happier and more productive interview.

First, make a prior appointment for the interview. This will save you time and effort. Anyone knowledgeable or important enough to be interviewed will generally have many other obligations. Without a definite appointment, you may find yourself making several trips before the person is free to see you. Making an appointment also indicates respect for the person you want to

interview. The appointment indicates that you put some thought into the decision to conduct the interview; you did not just drop by because you had a spur-of-the-moment inspiration.

Second, conduct interviews only after most of the other research has been completed. There is no need to take up someone's valuable time with questions whose answers you can get by reading a book or periodical article. Moreover, in your reading you may find information that you do not understand. In the interview you can then get help with that material. You may also find that you have difficulty in locating information about certain facets of your topic. You can start your interview by asking the person being interviewed for information on those areas. If she can't or doesn't want to, then you can ask her to suggest some sources. If the interview is held too early in the research effort, however, you lack the knowledge to ask some important questions.

Third, take specific questions to the interview. I shall never forget the student who was doing a term paper on debate who came to my office for an interview and began with the statement, "Tell me what you know about debate." Have your questions written out so that you will not forget an important one. This does not mean that you cannot ask questions that are suggested by the interviewee's replies to your prepared questions, or other remarks. It simply means that you go to the interview knowing the important questions you need to ask.

Fourth, conduct the interview with sensitivity. Show respect for the respondent's feelings and privacy. After the Alaskan earthquake of 1964, some of the survivors were immediately flown back to Seattle. The memory of one insensitive television reporter still lingers. Thrusting a microphone into the face of one woman as she disembarked from the plane, he asked: "How did you feel when you saw your husband and sons disappear into the hole in the ground?" Remember that most people do not like to give out personal information. Many citizens resented the 1970 census because the questionnaire included so many questions seeking personal and family data. If you need or desire such information, present the first personal question gingerly and be prepared to move to another line of questioning at the first hint of displeasure by the respondent.

Actual documents themselves constitute another important source of information. Pictures (especially the negatives, because prints may have been falsified), deeds, or contracts are documents that can furnish significant evidence. Howard Porter, a Villanova basketball player, denied reports during the 1970–71 season that he had already signed a contract with the Pittsburgh Condors. At the end of the season when Porter signed with another basketball team, the Pittsburgh management produced in court a signed contract, on the basis of which the NCAA voided the record of the Villanova team and reclaimed from the school the financial share of the NCAA tournament which it had received. **Documents**

Documents are generally too small to be perceived by listeners in a speaking situation. Nevertheless, the fact that you have them in your possession can be persuasive. If desirable, you can hold them up during the speech and offer to let any listener examine them after the speech. If some documents happen to be large enough to be readable by the entire audience in the course of the speaking situation, they can be used as visual aids.

Even the most knowledgeable person will frequently want to do some research to check some point on which his memory is fuzzy or to check the latest data on a specific topic. The less knowledgeable speaker will have to do considerable research. A number of library materials provide valuable information. Some of these sources provide the actual factual data themselves; others recommend sources of information. **Library Resources**

Statistical Abstract of the United States is an annual publication of the Bureau of Census of the Department of Commerce. It is the most reliable source of statistics available, containing statistical information on practically every phase of life in the United States. More than thirty chapters on such topics **Sources of Data** as education, labor force, employment and earnings, prices, communication, and population include statistical information gathered from a wide variety of sources, identified in footnotes which frequently suggest additional sources for consultation.

Statesman's Year Book is an annual publication providing specific and significant data on every nation in the world (as well as on major international organizations). Discussed are such things as type of government, governmental expenditures, educational programs, type and quantity of industrial goods produced, type and quantity of agricultural goods. Where a nation consists of governmental subunits, such as states in the United States and provinces in Canada, the information is given, not only for the country as a whole, but also for each individual subunit.

Facts on File is a weekly summary of world news. In addition to its *News Digest* published weekly, a cumulative index published twice each month provides a complete reference to all *News Digests* of the current year.

The vertical file is a collection of various pamphlets and clippings filed under specific and general topics. The folders holding the materials are generally kept in filing cabinets. The clippings are from newspapers, magazines, and other published sources that you would generally not see because it would require examination of such a wide range of materials. The H. W. Wilson Company publishes a *Vertical File Index* each month except August.

What They Said is an annual volume of quotations spoken by persons of "fame and influence" on a wide variety of topics. The statements are organized by specific topics under three major headings: national affairs, international affairs, and general. An index of speakers is included.

The Encyclopaedia Britannica, Encyclopedia Americana, Colliers Encyclopedia, and the *New International Encyclopedia* offer, on a wide variety of topics, essays that supply valuable background information. Most of these essays are written by outstanding experts in the particular field.

American Men and Women of Science, Biography Index, Current Biography, Directory of American Scholars, Dictionary of American Biography, Dictionary of National Biography (British), *International Who's Who, Who's Who, Who's Who in America, Who's Who in the East, Who's Who in the South and Southwest, Who's Who in the West, Who's Who in the Midwest, Who's Who Among Black Americans, Who's Who of American Women*—all offer valuable sources of biographical information needed by a speaker.

Indexes to Sources of Data

Any library's card catalog provides an index by subject, author, and title to all books possessed by that library.

Readers' Guide to Periodical Literature indexes approximately 130 current, popular periodicals such as *Time, The Atlantic, Harper's Magazine,* and *Fortune.* Articles are listed under both subject headings and author.

Humanities Index indexes approximately 260 periodicals of a scholarly bent in various fields classified as the humanities. Articles may be found under the author's name and the subject heading.

Social Sciences Index is an index to articles in approximately 150 periodicals in various social sciences. Articles are listed under author's name and subject heading. Prior to 1974, *Humanities Index* and *Social Science Index* formed the *Social Sciences and Humanities Index,* which was known as *The International Index to Periodicals* until 1965.

The Education Index indexes (by author and subject) selected books, government documents, yearbooks, and periodical articles on the subject of education that were published in the English language during the period covered by the specific volume.

The Art Index indexes (by author and title) all books, government documents, and periodical articles on the broad subject field of art that were published in the English language during the period covered by the specific volume.

Public Affairs Information Service Bulletin is an index to pamphlets, books, government documents, "and other useful library material [in the English language] in the field of economics and public affairs."

The New York Times Index is an index to all the stories, listed by alphabetical headings, which have appeared in the *New York Times.* Not only is it an important guide to information in the *New York Times,* it is extremely valuable in helping to locate information in other newspapers that are not indexed! By finding the date a story appeared in the *New York Times,* you can then work around that date in any local newspaper in which you are interested.

The Monthly Catalog of the United States Government Publications indexes all government documents. Although it is a little confusing to use, it is often worth the effort, since some of the government documents frequently contain information found in no other source.

The *Index to Journals in Communication Studies* catalogs the fourteen major periodicals in the various fields of communication.

Summary

The content of a speech will aid in developing credibility for your ideas. Content will be acceptable to the listeners if it is consistent with or coincides with their knowledge or attitudes, if it is consistent with their experiences, if it emanates from a highly credible source, or if it is supported by specific and credible evidence.

Evidence is helpful in changing attitudes, both immediately and over a period of time; it is helpful in increasing your ethos; and it is helpful in operating as an immunizing agent against subsequent counterpersuasion.

If evidence is to be maximally effective in changing attitudes, it should have the qualifications of the source cited; it should be specific; and it should be unfamiliar to the listeners.

You can use the following general types of evidence to support your claims: (1) opinions of others, (2) statistics, and (3) factual data.

Important sources of information are your own personal experiences, interviews with knowledgeable and experienced people, documents, and library resources.

Exercises

1. Prepare a two-minute speech supporting one main point with three specific instances and one interesting illustration.
2. Attend a public lecture on campus. What did the speaker say that was consistent with the listeners' knowledge or attitudes? Did these statements increase or decrease the speaker's credibility? In what ways?
3. Find three pieces of testimony for one of the ideas in your next speech. Evaluate the expertise and objectivity of each source. Will they add to the credibility of your ideas? Why?
4. Find three pieces of factual data for one of the ideas in your next speech. Explain why you can place confidence in the validity of this information. How will this information contribute to the credibility of your claims?
5. Find three pieces of statistical information for one of the ideas in your next speech. Explain how you will conform to the principles for using statistics. Convert one of the statistics into the most concrete form you can. Explain how that concreteness will enhance the credibility of the statistic itself and the claim which it supports.
6. Prepare the questions for some person whom you plan to interview on your next speech topic.

Notes

1. R. S. Cathcart, "An Experimental Study of the Relative Effectiveness of Four Methods of Presenting Evidence," *Speech Monographs* 22 (1955):227–33; E. P. Bettinghaus, Jr., "The Relative Effect of the Use of Testimony in a Persuasive Speech upon the Attitudes of the Listeners," M.A. thesis, Bradley University, 1953. The following study found certain types of evidence to be significantly more effective in changing attitudes: J. C. Gardiner, "An Experimental Study of the Use of Selected Forms of Evidence in Effecting Attitude Change," M.A. thesis, University of Nebraska, 1966.
2. H. Gilkinson, S. F. Paulson, and D. E. Sikkink, "Effects of Order and Authority in an Argumentative Speech," *Quarterly Journal of Speech* 40 (1954):183–92; T. H. Ostermeier, "An Experimental Study on the Type and Frequency of Reference as Used by an Unfamiliar Source in a Message and Its Effect upon Perceived Credibility and Attitude Change," Ph.D. diss., Michigan State University, 1966; D. L. Costley, "An Experimental Study of the Effectiveness of Quantitative Evidence in Speeches of Advocacy," M.A. thesis, University of Oklahoma, 1958.
3. D. C. Anderson, "The Effect of Various Uses of Authoritative Testimony in Persuasive Speaking," M.A. thesis, Ohio State University, 1958; G. A. Wagner, "An Experimental Study of the Relative Effectiveness of Varying Amounts of Evidence in a Persuasive Communication," M.A. thesis, University of Southern Mississippi, 1958; W. R. Dresser, "Studies of the Effects of Satisfactory and Unsatisfactory Evidence in a Speech of Advocacy," Ph.D diss., Northwestern University, 1962.

4. J. C. McCroskey and R. E. Dunham, "Ethos: A Confounding Element in Communication Research," *Speech Monographs* 33 (1966):456–63.

5. P. D. Holtzman, "Confirmation of Ethos as a Confounding Element in Communication Research," *Speech Monographs* 33 (1966):464–66.

6. C. S. Goetsinger, Jr., "An Analysis of the 'Validity' of Reasoning and Evidence in Four Major Foreign Policy Speeches, 1950–51," M.S. thesis, Purdue University, 1952.

7. P. D. Brandes, "Evidence and Its Use by Selected United States Senators," Ph.D. diss., University of Wisconsin, 1953.

8. J. C. McCroskey, *Studies of the Effects of Evidence in Persuasive Communication,* Speech Communications Research Laboratory, Department of Speech, Report SCRL 4–67 (E. Lansing, Mich.: Michigan State University, 1967), p. 42.

9. J. A. Kline, "Interaction of Evidence and Readers' Intelligence on the Effects of Short Messages," *Quarterly Journal of Speech* 55 (1969):407–13.

10. McCroskey, *Studies of the Effects of Evidence,* pp. 39–45. See also T. B. Harte, "The Effects of Evidence in Persuasive Communication," *Central States Speech Journal* 27 (1976):45–46.

11. J. C. McCroskey, "The Effects of Evidence as an Inhibitor of Counterpersuasion," *Speech Monographs* 37 (1970):188–94.

12. R. N. Bostrom and R. K. Tucker, "Evidence, Personality, and Attitude Change," *Speech Monographs* 36 (1969):22–27.

13. H. Gilikson, S. L. Paulson, and D. E. Sikking. "The Facts on Order and Authority in an Argumentative Speech," *Quarterly Journal of Speech* 40 (1954):183–92; Cathcart, "An Experimental Study"; Bostrom and Tucker, "Evidence, Personality, and Attitude Change."

14. Kline, "Interaction of Evidence," pp. 407–13.

15. McCroskey, *Studies of the Effects of Evidence,* p. 54.

16. G. R. Miller, "Evidence and Argument," in *Perspectives on Argumentation,* eds. G. R. Miller and T. R. Nilsen (Chicago: Scott, Foresman & Co., 1966), p. 25.

17. J. Greenfield, "An Acerbic View," *Birmingham News,* April 25, 1982. Used by permission.

18. D. Gergen and W. Schambra, "Pollsters and Polling," *The Wilson Quarterly* 3 (Spring 1979):70.

19. H. Cantril, *The Psychology of Social Movements* (New York: John Wiley & Sons, 1941), pp. 74–75.

20. I. M. Copi, *Introduction to Logic* (New York: Macmillan Publishing Co., 1953), pp. 60–61.

21. D. B. Klein, *Mental Hygiene* (New York: Henry Holt & Co., 1956), p. 201.

22. Robert S. Allen and John A. Goldsmith, "ABM Debate—Scientists Can Be Wrong," September 1, 1969. Syndicated column. By permission.

23. D. J. Boorstin, *The Americans: The Colonial Experience* (New York: Random House, 1958), pp. 224–25.

24. W. E. Arnold and J. C. McCroskey, "The Credibility of Reluctant Testimony," *Central States Speech Journal* 18(1967):97–103.

25. William Alonso and Paul Starr, "A Nation of Numbers Watchers," *The Wilson Quarterly* IX (Summer, 1985), 93–96.

26. M. M. Blair, *Elementary Statistics* (New York: Henry Holt & Co., 1944), p. 1.

27. Costley, "An Experimental Study of the Effectiveness of Quantitative Evidence."

28. Gardiner, "An Experimental Study of the Use of Selected Forms."

29. J. M. Perry, "Stockman Dials the Right Number, Soothes GOP Loyalists at Fund-Raiser," *Wall Street Journal,* November 25, 1981. Reprinted by permission of *The Wall Street Journal,* © Dow Jones & Company, Inc. 1981. All rights reserved.

30. C. D. MacDougall, *Hoaxes* (New York: Macmillan Publishing Co., 1940), pp. 161–62.

31. P. Weddle, *Argument: A Guide to Critical Thinking* (New York: McGraw-Hill, 1978), p. 90.

32. "Of Imaginary Numbers," *Time,* August 2, 1971, p. 37. Reprinted by permission from *TIME*, The Weekly Newsmagazine; Copyright Time, Inc.

33. J. F. McGillicuddy, "The Economy, Energy and the President's Proposals," *Vital Speeches of the Day* 45 (1979):708.

34. H. H. Humphrey, "Anniversary of War on Poverty," from *Congressional Digest* 45, no. 3 (March 1966), "The Controversy over the Federal Anti-Poverty Program, Pro & Con": pp. 76, 78, 80. Used by permission.

35. Walter A. Wittich and C. F. Schuller, *Instructional Technology* (New York: Harper and Row, 1979), p. 127.

36. Les Satterthwaite, *Audiovisual: Utilization, Production, and Design* (Dubuque, Iowa: Kendall/Hunt Publishing Co., 1983), pp. 140–55, 180–83.

37. Jerrold E. Kemp and Deane K. Keaton, *Planning and Producing Instructional Media* (New York: Harper & Row, Publishers, 1985), p. 37.

38. Sarah Adams, R. Rosemier, and P. Sleemer, "Readability, Letter Size, and Visibility for Overhead Projection Transparency," *AV Communication Review* (Winter, 1965), pp. 412–17.

39. Wittich and Schuller, p. 207.

40. James W. Brown, R. B. Lewis, and F. F. Harcleroad, *A-V Instruction: Materials and Methods* (New York: McGraw-Hill Book Company, Inc., 1959), pp. 240–41, 246–47.

41. T. H. Ostermeier, "Effects of Type and Frequency of Reference upon Perceived Source Credibility and Attitude Change," *Speech Monographs* 34 (1967):137–44.

42. L. B. Pearson, *The Four Faces of Peace* (New York: Sidney Hillman Foundation, n.d.), p. 4. Used by permission.

15

USING LANGUAGE TO COMMUNICATE MEANING

*M*eaning is what communication is all about. You have a certain meaning you want others to understand, appreciate, or accept, so you attempt to communicate that meaning to them. Unfortunately, the accurate communication of meaning is extremely difficult. It is probably never achieved perfectly, frequently not even approximately. Credibility of ideas is difficult to achieve if your meaning is unclear.

Three primary factors work to prevent even a reasonable communication of meaning: (1) The meaning as known and interpreted by the speaker does not accurately reflect the realities of the situation. For example, your roommate may be extremely sick one night before you go to bed. The next morning when you get up to go to class, you find that your roommate is still sleeping, so you leave him undisturbed. After class, you stop by and tell the professor the reason your roommate was absent is that he is sick. When you return to your room, you find your roommate awake, well, and angry because you did not wake him so he could go to class. Your meaning in that message to the professor simply did not reflect the reality of the situation. (2) The language used does not clearly symbolize the meaning that exists in the mind of the communicator. A number of factors can cause this problem. The communicator may lack the necessary vocabulary. The communicator may deliberately attempt to conceal the meaning, and may use language that is offensive or embarrassing to the receivers. The speaker's ambiguous language may result from imprecise thought processes. (3) The verbal symbols used by the speaker to represent meaning do not evoke identical meanings in the mind of the receiver. This was vividly illustrated when a teenage girl, who had decided she needed to go on a diet even though she was definitely not fat, was trying on pants in a clothing store. When she came out in one pair, her father and mother both said, "Those are too tight." To their puzzlement, she stalked back into the dressing room, changed into her own clothes, and refused to try on more pants. Later she confided to her grandmother that it was embarrassing to have her parents say in front of the salesperson that she was too fat. When her parents said the pants were too tight, they meant *the pants were too small.* But to the daughter the words meant *she was too fat.* Verbal symbols do not necessarily evoke the same meaning in your listener's mind that they do in yours.

Definition of Meaning

Meaning refers to the understanding a specific person has of anything in his environment; meaning exists within the person. From the day we are born we begin to attach meanings to things around us. For one baby, "mother" comes to mean the thing that cheerfully feeds it when it's hungry, replaces a wet diaper with a dry one, rocks and coos to it when it's sleepy. For another baby, "mother" comes to mean the thing that unhappily gives it a bottle of cold milk when it's hungry, ignores it when it cries with a wet diaper, and makes loud noises when it wants to go to sleep. Obviously, the meaning attached to the female in its environment will be vastly different for each of these babies. And when each learns that the verbal symbol used to refer to that object is "mother," there will be a drastic difference in the meaning that verbal symbol has for each of them.

Not only do we develop meaning as a result of sensory experiences, we also develop meanings about things that cannot be experienced in a sensory way. These meanings we learn through information given by verbal symbols. For example, one father, in answer to his child's query about ghosts, says, "A ghost is the spirit of a dead person. Its presence is sometimes signified by the flickering shadow on the wall, and sometimes by the rustling of the leaves on the trees." Another father, in answer to the same query, says, "There is no such thing as a ghost. It's just the figment of someone's fertile imagination." Neither of these children has sensorily experienced a ghost, but each has a definite meaning for "ghost" that is vastly different from the other's. Because of that meaning, one child goes through life fearful of shadows and rustling leaves while the other perceives shadows and rustling leaves more neutrally.

Not only are meanings *developed* in us, but they are not the same for everybody; meaning varies from person to person and from situation to situation.

Relationship of Words and Thought

We use language to communicate values, ideas, and feelings. Communication is dependent upon the ability of the language used to evoke in the mind of the listener the meaning that exists in the mind of the speaker. Meaning has been clearly communicated when the meaning you intended agrees with the meaning your hearer receives.[1] If you are to be effective, the listener must understand your meaning. As Quintilian advised, it is not enough to strive to make statements understandable; you must strive to make them so clear that it will be impossible for a hearer to misunderstand them. Two political journalists report that this is one of the strengths of President Reagan. They quote a "Democratic state chairman from blue-collar Toledo" who said before the 1984 presidential election: "If we can get the blue collars to think about issues, we can win. But they like Reagan. He makes them feel good about the country. There's the macho thing, and *I've never heard him use a word I didn't understand* (italics added), and working people like that."[2]

Thought and language are intertwined; it is difficult to determine which comes first. Do we have a thought because we have a word that makes it possible, or do we create a word because we have a thought? An oft-cited fact is that the Eskimos have a number of words for snow, whereas we have only one. Because snow is such an all-pervasive and important part of their lives, Eskimos need to distinguish among the various kinds of snow, and their language must communicate unmistakably the difference that exists.

The Speech

To ask whether thought or word comes first is like asking which comes first, the chicken or the egg? There are times when our thoughts and actions cause us to seek language in order to express them. There was no need for the word "sputnik" until the Russians blasted one into space. Sometimes we are limited in our thoughts by the paucity of our language. On other occasions our language causes us to think in a certain way.

To use language precisely, you must have precise thoughts; to think clearly, you must possess a language that will permit you to do so.

Relationship of Words and Referents

In order clearly to discern the difficulties of communicating meaning to others, we must first understand the relationship between words and their objects. Words are symbols that stand for our conception of or response to some real thing or concept. An individual has a toothache, an experience that is real and painful. But no one else can see it, feel it, hear it, smell it, or taste it. There can be no sensory perception of that toothache by any other person. Even the

Figure 15.1
The triangle of meaning.
Adapted by permission from C. K. Ogden and I. A. Richards, The Meaning of Meaning *(New York: Harcourt, Brace, & World, 1923), p. 11.*

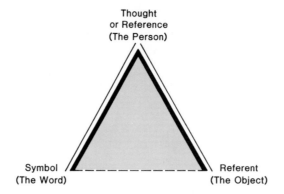

dentist with all her equipment cannot perceive the toothache. In some instances she may find certain signs that lead her to believe that a particular tooth could be causing pain, but the dentist cannot actually perceive the pain. The individual then uses words, symbols, that stand for the response to the pain. In this way he communicates the existence of the pain to others. He presents these symbols to the dentist, who then probes, takes X-rays, and locates the problem inside the tooth that is causing the pain. Without language, the victim of the toothache would have a difficult, maybe impossible, task in letting the dentist know that the pain exists. There is no direct relationship between an object and the symbol used to represent it. That relationship is created in the mind of the speaker. Ogden and Richards demonstrated this fact graphically with their triangle of meaning, shown in figure 15.1.

The dotted line between the referent, or object, and the symbol, or word, indicates that there is no direct connection between the two. The connection is made in the mind of the perceiver. If I see a certain four-legged animal and say "cat," and you speak English and agree with my perception, you nod in agreement. But if I have applied the wrong symbol, you would shake your head and say, "No, dog." The fact that I had applied the wrong symbol would in no way change the nature of the animal. Nor would its nature be in any way affected, if the two of us decided that we would no longer refer to it as "dog" or "cat," but would hereafter use as its symbol the word "glip." The symbol has no relationship to the object, except that created in the mind of the user.

You are probably thinking by now, "So what? I already knew that. What difference does it make?" True, so long as we are talking about concrete objects, it really makes little difference. Because whether we use "cat" or "glip" or some other symbol to stand for the animal, we can observe the concrete object itself and know what the symbol represents.

When we begin to talk about abstractions, however, we find no concrete referent to which we can go. The referent exists in the mind of the speaker. When the psychologist talks about the id, there is no referent to which she can point. When the politician talks about liberalism, there is no referent to which he can point. When the minister talks about heaven, there is no referent to which he can point.

When we make evaluative statements, the referent exists only in our mind. In other words, symbols that communicate abstractions and value judgments are really telling us about the person speaking, not the objects to which the symbols are applied. If two of us stand looking at a picture and I say, "That is a beautiful picture," I am telling you more about myself than about the picture. What that sentence communicates is my reaction to that picture. You may have just been thinking to yourself, "That is a horrible painting." If so, it is obvious that neither of us is talking about the painting, but instead we are describing our reactions to the painting. Yet, how often do we get into an argument with someone over whether a movie "is" funny, or a book "is" boring, or a certain person "is" interesting. If we remember that there is no relationship between the object and the words we use, except the connection we make in our minds, we can avoid such arguments.

Although words are not the things they symbolize, we frequently respond to them as though they were. Some people wince when called a "conservative"; others get upset when called a "liberal." The old saying "sticks and stones may break my bones, but names will never hurt me" should be true, but it isn't. To identify a person as a "ditchdigger" is to place a certain stigma on him in our society; to identify one as a "doctor" infuses him with an aura of prestige. S. I. Hayakawa, an authority on meaning and semantics, has called attention to the efficacy of words in influencing our behavior:

The word *black* has evil connotations in our culture. For a long, long time we avoided saying "black people." We said "Negroes," because the word black had connotations of dark, black, evil, satanic, sinister, and so on. White had connotations of purity, loveliness, elegance, truth, brightness, clarity, and so on. When people call themselves Black Nationalists, Black Panthers, they, like everybody else, are victims of the English language. So they wear black berets, black sweaters, black trousers, black shoes, and black sunglasses, and they role-play being black, suggesting dark, evil, sinister, satanic.

The policemen of Oakland, California also speak the English language, and they have a semantic reaction to all this Black Panther business. They act as if there were evil, satanic, ferocious, predatory black forces at loose in the world. The Oakland Police Department arms itself, and prepares for all kinds of trouble. So the black people and the white policemen are all role-playing around the words *black-white, black-white*—both of them trapped by the English language.

What would happen if the Black Panthers had called themselves, instead, the Soul Brothers Mutual Assistance Society? It's a beautiful name. Soul Brothers. That's fine. Mutual Assistance. That's fine. And the cops wouldn't have to organize themselves in this ferocious way against the Panthers.[3]

When you use words, constantly be aware that there is no relationship between the symbols you use and the objects they represent except that which exists in your own mind. You should further recognize that evaluative language reveals more about the person using the language than about the object the language represents. Despite the validity of these statements, realize that people do, in fact, frequently respond to language as though it were the object itself.

Relating Meaning to Reality

If you are to communicate precisely with language, if you are to develop credibility for your ideas, you must free your thoughts of error. If your thoughts are unclear or imprecise, there is no way your language can be clear and precise. The application of the following principles will help you clarify your thinking and, consequently, your use of language.

It Is Impossible to Know Everything

With the explosion of knowledge that has occurred in the last few decades, it is now impossible for anyone to know everything about anything. Even experts who spend a lifetime studying one small facet of a subject never reach the point where they know everything about it.

But we who are not experts must remember that we can possess only a fraction of the available knowledge pertaining to even those events which we ourselves witness firsthand. No one is able to perceive all facets of a situation, and what one does perceive may be influenced by one or more of many factors.

Interest may determine perceptions: one person standing on a street corner may focus her attention on the people passing by, to the exclusion of all else, because she is interested in psychology and is an observer of human behavior. *Attitudes* may determine perceptions: if one has an unfavorable attitude toward those who are on welfare, he may be very sensitive to the line of people waiting at the welfare office for their weekly check; another person who does not have an unfavorable attitude toward welfare recipients may be oblivious to the welfare office line. *Experience* may determine perceptions: if a person has just been bitten by a dog, probably he will be extremely wary when dogs come into his presence; another person who has had no unpleasant experience with dogs may be unaware of their presence. We perceive only a small amount of what occurs about us.

Moreover, what we do perceive we may perceive inaccurately. In a football game on TV a few years ago, a friend and I saw an offensive player go downfield for a pass. Just before the ball arrived, a defensive back ran over and jumped with his arm directly in front of the offensive player's face. The offensive player dropped the ball, but the referee did not call a face-guarding penalty. My friend and I were bemoaning the fact that the official had blown the play when suddenly the play was shown again on instant replay. But the instant replay camera, from a different angle, showed quite clearly that the defensive back was a full five yards in front of the pass receiver. Many of us have a distorted angle when we perceive the events about us. Unfortunately, we have no instant replay to reveal our distorted perceptions.

Figure 15.2
Continuum of the concepts intelligent *and* unintelligent.

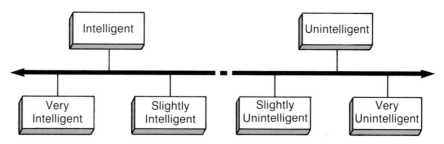

Most of us have a tendency to think in "either-or" terms, and in some ways our language encourages this kind of thinking, because it has a tendency to make us think in terms of opposites. We talk about someone's being beautiful or ugly, good or bad, intelligent or unintelligent, efficient or inefficient, fast or slow, patient or impatient, sane or insane. Rarely, however, is anyone ever 100 percent any of these things. All sane people have some moments of at least mild insanity, and most insane persons have at least some moments of sanity. A good person is occasionally bad, and a bad person has some moments of goodness. We tend to forget this fact, however, and use language that encourages dichotomous thought.

Things Are Seldom as Clear-cut as They Seem

If we remember that most evaluations can be put on a continuum, then it will encourage more precise thinking, which will result in more precise language. In figure 15.2, the concepts *intelligent* and *unintelligent* are on a continuum. There are varying degrees of intelligence, and even the labels we have applied, such as "slightly intelligent," are labels that apply to several points on the continuum. Although most of us know that concepts come in varying degrees, we still have a tendency to use words that communicate finality and certainty.

If pressed, most of us admit that our language reflects only our own view of the world. Yet in actual practice most of us blithely use language with little or no awareness of this fact. Someone says: "Did you see the movie at the Varsity?" The answer comes back: "Yes, that's a good movie." The statement seems to invest the movie with the attribute of goodness, but what the respondent is really saying is "I enjoyed that movie." Had he said it in this precise fashion, the "goodness" would have resided within the person talking rather than the movie. The first person could next say, "I didn't enjoy that movie." Each could then explain why he did or did not enjoy the movie, and the chances are good that they would now be talking about the movie rather than about themselves. They might discuss the plot, the characterizations, the acting, or the photography; and the language would begin to resemble reality, so long as they didn't merely indulge in value judgments about those items.

Your Language Reflects Your View of the World

Identify value judgments with such labels as, "it seems to me," "I believe," "in my opinion," "I think." A few years ago, a controversy developed in Pittsburgh about what to do with Forbes Field, former baseball home of the Pittsburgh Pirates. Notice the difference in the following statements made by opposing forces in the controversy. A citizen's group opposing demolition of the field issued this statement:

Forbes Field, in addition to being a beautiful work of architecture, comparable in quality to other monumental turn-of-the-century steel and glass buildings such as Les Halles and the Eiffel Tower in Paris and the Crystal Palace in London, can readily accommodate a variety of uses.

That statement sounds as though the characteristics attributed to Forbes Field inhere within the structure itself, doesn't it? There is no intimation that the beauty is in the eyes of the beholder. Consider, however, the statement of the chancellor of the University of Pittsburgh: "Forbes Field, in my own personal opinion, is ugly, obsolete and unsafe. . . ."[4] The chancellor's statement makes it quite clear that the attributes he attached to Forbes Field exist within him rather than in the structure itself. It should also be noted that the word *unsafe* is one for which factual data could be amassed, thus removing it from the category of a personal evaluation.

Judge Each Instance on Its Own Merits

Most of us tend to generalize (on the basis of one or several instances) about our various experiences. Seeing a car fail to stop at a stop sign and go crashing into another car, we conclude that it is dangerous to fail to stop at stop signs. Learning that a couple of friends have had accidents while driving their cars under the influence of alcohol, we generalize that people who have been drinking should not drive. There are many other instances where valid generalizations are drawn daily from a small number of specific instances. But there are also many instances where generalizing causes one of two problems: (1) either an overgeneralization occurs or (2) a previously drawn generalization prevents a valid response to the immediate instance.

In his book *Body Language,* Julius Fast overgeneralizes when he writes "the southern white sees the black as a nonperson, an object not worth concerning himself about."[5] That overgeneralization lumps Ralph McGill and Terry Sanford, and thousands of southern whites like them, with the Grand Dragon of the Ku Klux Klan and the presidents of the various White Citizens Councils, and thousands like them. In Fast's eyes, apparently, *all* southern whites are alike. On the other hand, some southerners overgeneralize when they say, "Northerners have a double standard on the race issue," failing to recognize that many northerners are fully aware of and reject the double standard used by some northerners in discussing racial problems of the two sections. And the list of cases in which overgeneralizing occurs is endless.

On other occasions, we permit a previously drawn generalization to obscure the actual features of the immediate instance. Mark Twain gives a wonderful example:

People who claim to know say that I smoke the worst cigars in the world. They bring their own cigars when they come to my house. They betray an unmanly terror

when I offer them a cigar; they tell lies and hurry away to meet engagements which they have not made when they are threatened with the hospitalities of my box. Now then, observe what superstition, assisted by a man's reputation, can do.

I was to have twelve personal friends to supper one night. One of them was as notorious for costly and elegant cigars as I was for cheap and devilish ones. I called at his house and when no one was looking borrowed a double handful of his very choicest; cigars which cost him forty cents apiece and bore red-and-gold labels in sign of their nobility. I removed the labels and put the cigars into a box with my favorite brand on it—a brand which those people all knew, and which cowed them as men are cowed by an epidemic.

They took these cigars when offered at the end of the supper, and lit them and sternly struggled with them—in dreary silence, for hilarity died when the fell brand came into view and started around—but their fortitude held for a short time only; then they made excuses and filed out, treading on one another's heels with indecent eagerness; and in the morning when I went out to observe results the cigars lay all between the front door and the gate. All except one—that one lay in the plate of the man from whom I had cabbaged the lot. One or two whiffs was all he could stand. He told me afterward that some day I would get shot for giving people that kind of cigars to smoke.[6]

In other words, these friends of Mark Twain were unable to respond to the realities of the situation because they allowed a generalization to control their reactions—even to the point of denying a sensory experience.

Remember that each member of a class is a separate entity, even though it possesses many characteristics in common with other members of that class. There has been a tendency for some of the news media to talk about "college students" as though all college students possess the same characteristics. But college students and professors know that almost every campus has students who can be classified as reactionaries, conservatives, moderates, liberals, and radicals, with all the shadings and nuances found within each of those labels.

To avoid the error of overgeneralizing or of failing to respond validly to the immediate instance, general semanticists suggest that we index members of any class of objects. Remember that New Yorker$_1$ is not New Yorker$_2$ is not New Yorker$_3$ . . . is not New Yorker$_{99}$. Remember that each individual has particular attributes. We must await specific information about the individual before we can draw any conclusions.

Of course, there are times when one reacts legitimately to the specific situation on the basis of a generalization. If you live in an area where poisonous snakes abound and you see a snake in your yard, you must behave as though it is a poisonous one until you have definite evidence it is not.

Things Change with Time

Some people talk and act as though we live in a static, unchanging world. They expect events and objects to remain constant, and people to behave consistently. There are in this country nearly 1 million women who have had mastectomies. One surgeon who performed some of them recently told columnist Ellen Goodman "I don't do mastectomies anymore." After surveying research that questioned radical mastectomies, he quit doing them. Then he examined research that challenged simple mastectomies and quit doing them. He said to Goodman "I don't . . . believe in mastectomies anymore."[7] Some, especially former patients, will criticize the doctor for behaving inconsistently. But he was undoubtedly doing what the current research suggested when he performed mastectomies, and he is doing today what the current research suggests. To expect a doctor or any person to behave the same way over a period of years is to imply a desire for a foolish consistency that Emerson called "the hobgoblin of little minds."

During the late 1960s and early 1970s, Joan Baez was an ardent foe of the Vietnam War. She made many negative statements about the U.S. government and positive statements about the North Vietnamese government. In

1979, however, she made negative statements about the Vietnamese government's treatment of the Cambodians. In fact, she traveled to Southeast Asia to help the Cambodians and to call attention to the atrocities being committed by the Vietnamese. Some of her antiwar cohorts were critical of her statements and her actions. But Joan Baez recognized what her former allies did not: Things had changed; 1979 was not 1969.

There are those who picture the South as a region of economic deprivation, but they are thinking of the South that in the 1930s Franklin D. Roosevelt called the "nation's number one economic problem." Even as late as 1965, the South ranked last among the four major regions in the country in the number of families with incomes of fifteen thousand dollars and above. In 1978, however, the South ranked second among the regions in this important economic indicator.

If you are to communicate meaning that coincides with the reality that the language signifies, you must consider the phenomena you are discussing in the context in which they occurred.

A person who exhibited the same personality in response to every situation would win an award for being an oddity. The happy, carefree, witty conversationalist would be totally out of place at a funeral. Yet because an individual behaves in a certain way in one place, we attach a label to him as though that describes him in all places.

Things Change with the Situation

Students are frequently amazed when they meet one of their professors in a social situation and find her different from what she is in the classroom. Some think it is hypocritical for a person to behave differently in one situation than she does in another; but it is simply an adaptation to changing conditions. A black robe on a minister in the pulpit on Sunday morning is appropriate; that same robe worn to the grocery store would be ludicrous. To argue that adaptations of this sort are hypocritical is to demand a simplicity of behavior that ignores the complexities of one's environment.

In arriving at any meaning, therefore, you will be able to establish a more realistic relationship between your meaning and the event itself if you first ascertain the situation in which the phenomenon occurred.

Your language can communicate precise meaning only if your thoughts have developed valid meanings. If you are unwilling to apply the necessary principles to produce clear and precise thinking, there is no way your language can be clear and precise. And if listeners recognize that your language is unclear and imprecise, you will have a difficult time establishing credibility.

Style

Once you have assured yourself that your meanings are closely related to reality, you may next turn your attention to the rhetorical process of selecting and arranging the precise language you will use to communicate that meaning to listeners. The result of this process will be the *style* of your speech. Style results from language freely chosen and freely arranged. Grammar involves language chosen and arranged because of prescribed rules.

The style of a speech is important because, as Carbone has confirmed, it can contribute significantly to a speaker's credibility.[8] Five factors affect the style of a speech: clarity, appropriateness, economy, originality, and vitality.

Clarity

Clarity is the use of words that evoke your intended meaning in the mind of your listeners. If you are to be effective in communicating, each listener must understand your meaning.

Exactness in word choice is one way of achieving clarity of meaning. If the words chosen do not mean what you intend, it is difficult for the intended meaning to be evoked in the mind of the listener. During the telecast of a football game recently, the commentator, a former football coach, said "Anytime you have a big receiver—6'4", 200 pounds—it's *apropos* to throw to him." The commentator could have used the word *appropriate* (which he undoubtedly meant), or *correct, proper, legitimate,* but not *apropos.* On the other hand, a minister invited people in his radio audience to come to his church for the morning service, promising them they would not be *impersonated.* He probably meant *intimidated,* but listeners could only guess!

Extensional and Intensional Levels

One of the difficulties in selecting the right word stems from the fact that words generate two levels of meaning: extensional and intensional. *Extensional* meaning, according to Hayakawa, "is something that *cannot be expressed in words,* because it is that which words stand for. An easy way to remember this is to put your hand over your mouth and point whenever you are asked to give an extensional meaning." On the other hand, the *intensional* meaning of a word is that meaning which exists in a person's head.[9] A word must have intensional meaning or it is just meaningless noise signifying nothing. But a word may not have extensional meaning. The word "ghosts," for example, has no extensional meaning because we cannot put our hand over our mouth and point to one.

The intensional meaning of a word will vary from person to person, then, depending upon the experiences the individual has had. This is why, as Church has pointed out, communication is most precarious in those situations in which the people trying to communicate are most different from one another. And, he says, "it is partly a matter of vocabulary." The reason is that "each of us, out of his own linguistic history, has built up a very special vocabulary, and the further apart we are in education, social class, occupational specialty, and the rest, the less in common our stocks of words will have."[10]

To help overcome this problem, you should seek similarities between yourself and your listeners and try to select words that occur commonly in those areas. In a recent study the experimenters selected pairs of subjects who were most alike and pairs of subjects who were least alike. The subjects then participated in a modified form of the game "password." Only semantic clues were accepted; no nonsemantic clues such as rhyming, proper names, and other forms of the password were permitted. The results revealed that the communication of meaning between the two subjects was positively related to the similarity of their past experiences.[11]

The Speech

Ambiguous words are an obstacle to clarity. Some words are ambiguous because they are too technical for the particular listener. A student who goes home for vacation and begins to talk to younger brothers or sisters about pragmatism will not communicate clearly because of the technical nature of the language involved. Some words are ambiguous because they are too abstract. Terms like "Protestant ethic" and "middle-class values" have too many different meanings to communicate precisely. Some words are ambiguous because they are euphemisms—a substitution of a mild, indirect, or vague expression for a harsh or blunt one. An "exceptional" child may be either retarded or gifted, since educators apply the term to both ends of the continuum. As *Time* said in an essay on euphemisms, "In everyday conversation the euphemism is, at worst, a necessary evil; at its best, it is a handy verbal tool to avoid making enemies needlessly, or shocking friends."[12]

Some euphemisms are harmless. To say "members of the vertical transportation corps" for elevator operators, or "members of a career offender cartel" for Mafia, or "negative patient care outcome" instead of die harms no one.[13] But some euphemisms so distort reality that they cause unrealistic responses on the part of the recipient. To say "protest" instead of riot, "payola" instead of bribery or cheating, "police action" instead of war, "anticipatory communism" instead of stealing, or "liberate" instead of capture and occupy, so distorts reality that invalid reactions are elicited from hearers. As *Time* observes, "If 'substandard housing' makes rotting slums appear more liveable or inevitable to some people, then their view of American cities has been distorted and their ability to assess the significance of poverty has been reduced."[14]

Gobbledygook interferes with clarity. For example, an exit is defined by the Occupational Safety and Health Administration rulebook as "that portion of a means of egress which is separated from all other spaces of the building or structure by construction or equipment as required in this subpart to provide a protected way of travel to the exit discharge." To avoid confusion, the rulebook defines "means of egress" as "a continuous and unobstructed way of exit travel from any point in a building or structure to a public way and consists of three separate and distinct parts: the way of exit access, the exit, and the way of exit discharge."[15] Gibberish such as this does nothing to aid communication.

If you present your meaning in an ambiguous form, hearers tend to distort the meaning to accord with their own attitudes. Zimbardo presented to college students sentences in which ambiguity was varied. Some received them in written form, and others received them aurally via tape recording. One encouraging finding was that there was little distortion of meaning when the communication was well structured. Despite the imprecision of language, it does a remarkable job of communicating when used correctly. On the other hand, Zimbardo discovered that when the message was ambiguous, there was a consistent, systematic correlation between the assigned meaning and the person's attitude.[16] Undoubtedly, some take advantage of this tendency, but for those who are interested in accurate communication of meaning, ambiguity must be avoided.

One of the ways to avoid ambiguity is to define unclear words or concepts. Definition offers listeners a precise meaning for whatever you are talking about. In discussing types of workers, one speaker used definition to make his meaning clearer:

So we have the emergence of what have been called *autonomous individuals*. I first came across this very descriptive expression in a speech by John Panabaker, chairman of Mutual Life Assurance Company of Canada.

Autonomous individuals are confident that personal disaster will not befall them, that they will live a long life and that financial hardship is not a major risk. So they look at the workplace in a much different way. They do not fear their company or fear for the jobs. They are mobile and aggressive. Their social and work relationships are not viewed as permanent or even long-lived. They do want to contribute and to achieve, but the driving force is not economic survival. That doesn't mean that they're less moral or ethical. In fact, they may be more honest and straightforward than the pre-1960 generation.[17]

Any effort exerted to create unambiguous messages will be worthwhile. Carbone found that messages attributed to high-credibility sources had fewer ambiguous sentences than those messages attributed to low-credibility sources.[18]

Appropriateness

The language used must be appropriate—to yourself, to your listeners, to the subject, and to the occasion.

If the speaker is an educated person, then his language must be that of an educated person. This does not mean that it can't be informal, but it does mean that it must be informal *educated* language. If the president of a university said, "The fuzz are looking for him because he is a fairy hawk," it would not only be unclear in meaning to many but would also seem inappropriate, coming from a university president.

Language must also be appropriate to the listeners. The vocabulary used in talking to a group of high school students must necessarily be different from the vocabulary used in talking to a group of Ph.D.s. The technical language appropriate to a speech professor discussing ethos with a group of speech professors would not be appropriate if the same professor were discussing ethos with a group of high school or college students. The statement above, "The fuzz are looking for him because he is a fairy hawk," would be unclear to most people. But the scholar of inner city language and the ghetto dweller would immediately recognize this sentence as saying, "The police are looking for him because he is one who robs homosexuals." If accurate meaning is to be communicated, you must use language that is appropriate to the listeners you are addressing.

The intensity of the language must also be appropriate to the listeners. Defining intensity as *"the quality of language which indicates the degree to which the speaker's attitude toward a concept deviates from neutrality,"* Bowers found that, in a speech against concepts, language of low intensity was significantly more effective in changing attitudes than language of high intensity.[19]

The occasion will also determine what kind of language is appropriate. If you were talking to a small group in a very informal situation, you would certainly have difficulty in creating credibility with any semblance of formality in your language. To a large group in a less informal situation, you could be more formal in the use of language. In a very formal situation, you might use no informal language; you would certainly use very little. Long ago, classical rhetoricians identified three levels of style—low, middle, and sublime—as being appropriate for different occasions. Today we encourage speakers to use, in most situations, the conversational mode, an informal style that is oral rather than written.

Analysis of extemporaneous speeches and essays prepared by the same students on the same topic showed that (1) oral language was significantly more readable than the written language; (2) average sentence length was significantly shorter in oral language than in written language; (3) the vocabulary of oral language was less varied; (4) oral language used significantly more personal words than written language; (5) oral language used significantly fewer syllables per one hundred words than written language.[20] Expanding on this study, Carbone found that messages attributed to high-credibility sources used a vocabulary that was more diverse and included more unfamiliar words and a style that was more oral than written.[21]

DeVito compared random samples of the writings of ten university professors with random samples of their oral comments given in response to questions made up by the experimenter from the professors' writings. The results indicated that (1) there were significantly more self-reference words (I, me, our, we, us) in oral than in written style; (2) written style had more quantifying terms, but not significantly so; (3) oral style had significantly more pseudoquantifying terms (much, many, a lot) than written style; (4) there were significantly more allness terms (none, all, every, always, never) in oral than in written style; (5) oral style had significantly more qualification terms (if, however, but) than written style; and (6) terms indicative of consciousness of projection (apparently, seems, appears, to me) occurred significantly more in oral than in written style.[22]

At first glance it would appear that DeVito's finding of a greater use of pseudoquantifying terms and allness terms in oral language would indicate that imprecise communication is taking place. Happily, evidence exists that there may be more precision in these terms than appears. Simpson first presented twenty such terms *(always, never, often, generally, occasionally, frequently)* to students in 1942 and asked them to assign a numerical percentage to each.[23] Some twenty years later he again presented the same twenty terms, plus five additional ones, to "students drawn from all sections of the United States but predominantly from the Midwest." The results for the two groups of students, twenty years apart, were "strikingly" similar. "For only one word, *sometimes,* was the difference greater than five percentage points (20 vs. 27), and in over one-third of the terms the percentages are identical."[24]

In summary, informal oral style is distinguished from written style by the following characteristics:

1. The average sentence length is shorter.
2. The vocabulary consists of fewer different words.
3. The vocabulary includes a larger number of short words.
4. More self-reference words are used.
5. More pseudoquantifying terms are used.
6. More allness terms are used.
7. More terms indicative of consciousness of projection occur.
8. Fewer quantifying terms (precise numerical terms) are used.
9. More informal language, such as contractions and colloquial words, is used.
10. More qualifying terms are used.

For your informal speeches, use language that is described by these ten characteristics. This is the language that most people speak and hear on a daily basis. It is familiar language to them. When you use this type of language, you will be relatively sure that your listeners will understand what you are saying.

Economy should not be confused with brevity or conciseness. Economy in language means to express one's meaning in the most effective way—regardless of the number of words used. Just as an individual buys an expensive pair of shoes because it is more economical than purchasing a cheap pair that wears out much quicker, so the speaker is more concerned with the effectiveness of the words used than with the number of words.

Striving to attain economy in language does not mean elimination of all redundancy, for some redundancy is vital to effective oral communication. But it does mean elimination of excess words, which not only fail to add helpful redundancy but even to obscure meaning in a forest of words.

Sometimes economy is achieved through the use of fewer words. An excellent example of both wordiness and conciseness was reported by the Washington Post–Los Angeles Times News Service. Robert H. Finch, then HEW Secretary, asked his executive secretary, L. Patrick Gray III, to circulate a message urging his staff to send him shorter briefing memoranda. Unfortunately, Mr. Gray's message itself lacked conciseness, so some unknown recipient revised it to show that the meaning could be communicated more effectively in significantly fewer words.

For example, Gray's opener was:
"As a general rule, and certainly not applicable in all situations, the briefing memoranda forwarded to the secretary have been loaded with an excessive amount of verbiage."
The translation read: "Most of the briefing memoranda forwarded to the secretary have been too wordy."
Gray's memorandum continued:
"In the future, the briefing memoranda should highlight the issue, set forth alternative courses of action or approaches to resolve the issue, and finally, a recommendation regarding the action to be taken by the secretary should be made with reasons therefor."
Translation: "Briefing memoranda should highlight the issue, state alternatives to resolve the issue, and suggest the action to be taken by the secretary."
Gray said: "It is envisioned that this sort of writing will not require more than a page and half to two pages at the most."
Translation: "No more than two pages should be required."
An equally terse translation— "supporting data may be appended" was offered for Gray's statement that "additional supporting data, information, comments and supporting documentation may be included beneath the writing referred to above, as deemed necessary."
Gray concluded with:
"The secretary does not, in any way, intend that the free flow of information to him be restricted or limited; however, he does desire that the central issue be highlighted and acted upon in the manner set forth in this memorandum."
Translation: "The secretary does not want the flow of information to him restricted. He does insist that the central issue be highlighted and presented as described above."[25]

On other occasions, economy is attained by using a larger number of words. A paragraph from Martin Luther King's "I Have a Dream" illustrates this:

It is obvious today that America has defaulted on this promissory note insofar as her citizens of color are concerned. Instead of honoring this sacred obligation, America has given the Negro people a bad check; a check which has come back marked "insufficient funds." But we refuse to believe that the bank of justice is bankrupt. We refuse to believe that there are insufficient funds in the great vaults of opportunity of this nation. So we have come to cash this check—a check that will give us upon demand the riches of freedom and the security of justice. We have also come to this hallowed spot to remind America of the fierce urgency of now. This is no time to engage in the luxury of cooling off or to take the tranquilizing drug of gradualism. Now is the time to make real the promises of Democracy. Now is the time to rise from the dark and desolate valley of segregation to the sunlit path of racial justice. Now is the time to open the doors of opportunity to all of God's children. Now is the time to lift our nation from the quicksands of racial injustice to the solid rock of brotherhood.[26]

If King had been concerned only with brevity, he could have expressed those ideas, though not as effectively, in a statement similar to the following:

It is obvious today that America has failed to give blacks the freedom and justice they deserve. We have come to this hallowed spot to remind America of the need for immediate action. There can be no delay. Now is the time to eliminate segregation and racial injustice, and to extend democracy and justice to all citizens.

If you are to be effective, you must search for fresh ways to express ideas. Of course, there are times when a trite expression may communicate meaning more effectively than an original phrasing, but in most instances the original statement will be more attention-getting and more effective.

As you try for originality in language, however, you will be quickly reminded of the relationship between thought and language. Unless you can have an original thought, it will be extremely difficult to achieve originality in language. Until he had the thought, there was no way that late Governor Frank Clement of Tennessee could make the following statement in his keynote address at the 1956 Democratic National Convention: "But [Roosevelt] sat there in his wheelchair taller than his critics could stand." Nor could he have given his description of John Foster Dulles as "the greatest unguided missile in the history of American diplomacy," unless the thought had preceded it.[27]

An important way in which originality can be brought to the language of a speech is to use figurative language, which expresses the thought indirectly rather than directly as it would be if literal language were used. There are both advantages and disadvantages to using figurative language. Brandes has pointed out that it is advantageous because it (1) helps us to understand a new concept either by comparing it with the old concept or by going from the known to the unknown, (2) saves time by "pictorialization," (3) avoids saying something directly which the audience may accept if it is said indirectly, (4) injects a vivid and new sensation because of the establishment of a new relationship. On the other hand, Brandes also concedes that figurative language can sometimes be disadvantageous because (1) the technique may show, and therefore the intent of the speaker becomes suspect, (2) circumlocution may waste time, (3) it may lead to faulty thinking, causing a breakdown in communication if the audience does not understand the allusions.[28]

Concentrate on achieving correctness, clarity, appropriateness, and economy in the use of language. Leave the use of figurative language to a later period when you have mastered these more important elements of language. There is one form of figurative language that seems to come naturally, however, and that is the metaphorical use of language. One student of language has observed that "Some of our literary professors have misled us about metaphor. It is not an extra beauty stuck on to language—it is language."[29] People in all walks of life use such statements as "The car ate up the miles." "The quarter-miler roared around the track."

Reinsch compared the effectiveness of figurative language with literal language by preparing three forms of a speech: one with only literal language, one in which four metaphors replaced the literal language, one in which four similes replaced the metaphors. All three forms of the speech caused subjects hearing them to change their attitudes in the desired direction significantly more than subjects who heard no speech. But the speech using metaphors caused the subjects to shift their attitudes significantly more than those who heard the literal speech. Although the speech using similes shifted attitudes more than the literal speech, the change was not significantly greater.[30] You should feel free, then, to use language metaphorically. But metaphors should be developed carefully. One writer says they "ought to be short—almost epigrammatic—and they have to be kept internally consistent. Metaphors are the mint in our juleps, the brandy in the sauce, the pimiento in the olive."[31]

Another important way of achieving originality in language is to use certain stylistic devices. But you do not want to become so involved with stylistic devices that you seem to be more concerned with them than with communicating. There are, however, a few such devices which, if used sparingly, can add impact to a message. *Alliteration,* the repetition of a sound in two or more adjacent words, can be used effectively. Notice the impact of these phrases from Clement's keynote address: "candidates of competence and conscience," "party of privilege and pillage," "cunningly conceived to convince," "fantastic, frantic, and fatal policy."[32] *Asyndeton,* the omission of conjunctions between a series of related clauses, may occasionally be used effectively. An example of asyndeton occurs in John F. Kennedy's inaugural address: "we shall pay any price, bear any burden, meet any hardship, support any friend, oppose any foe to assure the survival and the success of liberty."[33] *Parallel structure,* a similar phrasing of parts of a sentence or paragraph of equal importance, is probably the easiest stylistic device for the beginning student to use. In his speech, "I Have a Dream," Martin Luther King, Jr., used parallel structure effectively. Following is one example:

But *one hundred years later,* we must face the tragic fact that the Negro is still not free. *One hundred years later,* the life of the Negro is still sadly crippled by the manacles of segregation and the chains of discrimination. *One hundred years later,* the Negro lives on a lonely island of poverty in the midst of a vast ocean of material prosperity. *One hundred years later,* the Negro is still languished in the corners of American society and finds himself an exile in his own land. So we have come here today to dramatize an appalling condition.[34]

Vitality

Vitality, or forcefulness, of style is achieved largely through the characteristics of the sentences employed. Sentences are the grammatical units by which we most commonly express our ideas. They may be active or passive, simple or complex, short or long, loose or periodic. Rhetoricians have traditionally advised the use of active sentences—the boy drove the car—rather than passive sentences—the car was driven by the boy. They believed that active sentences were more forceful and easier to comprehend. J. A. DeVito has produced evidence that this may be an oversimplification. Active sentences were easier for the subjects to recall when an initial noun phrase was used as a prompt. When active and passive versions of the same passage were analyzed by three readability formulas, however, no significant difference in the readability level was found.[35]

Although you do not want to be reduced to the use of short, simple sentences of the "Ned sees the dog" variety, there is evidence that you should be wary of using many long sentences. J. W. Black, using expert advice, produced ten sentences each of the following lengths: 3, 5, 7, 9, 11, 13, 15, and 17 words. The sentences were recorded and played back to four groups of subjects. Half of each group heard the recording in a quiet condition; the other half heard them with varying degrees of masking noise. Subjects were asked to write the last three words of each sentence. The results revealed that louder noise or increased length of a sentence made it less likely "that a listener would identify the final three words of the sentence, and the longer the sentence the more disastrous was the effect of noise."[36] In addition, too many long sentences bleed vitality from your style.

At times you may introduce variety and suspense into your style by changing a sentence from the loose to the periodic form. A *periodic* sentence is one in which the thought is not complete until the end of the sentence. For example, a periodic sentence would be constructed in this manner: If inflation is to be curbed, wages and prices must be controlled. A *loose* sentence would express that same idea as follows: Wages and prices must be controlled if inflation is to be curbed. It is obvious that the periodic sentence prompts the listener to keep listening to find out what must be done, whereas the loose sentence tells the listener quickly what the main thought of the sentence is so that he may quit listening to the last part. Too many periodic sentences, however, may impart an artificial flavor to an oral speech style, so they must be used sparingly.

Another type of sentence that may be used sparingly is that known as a *chiasmus,* a sentence with two parts in which the second "is syntactically balanced against the first but with the parts reversed. . . ."[37] Someone recently used a chiasmus to express the changed attitudes toward policemen: "Kids used to look up to the cop on the beat; now kids look to beat up on the cop." A chiasmus has also been used to point up the results of inflation: "We used to go to the stores with money in our pockets and come back with food in our baskets—now we go with money in baskets and come back with food in our pockets." Probably the most widely publicized chiasmus, however, is one used by John F. Kennedy in his inaugural address: "Ask not what your country can do for you—ask what you can do for your country." Obviously, too many of this kind of sentence would destroy the oral quality of a speaker's style. But one or two—rarely more than two—well placed in the speech can do much to enliven the style and invigorate the attention of the listener.

A final type of sentence to be considered is the *rhetorical question,* one asked by the speaker to which a reply is neither required nor expected. The answer may either be implied in the question itself or provided shortly thereafter by the speaker. Norman Lear, creator of the television series "All in the Family," used two rhetorical questions without answering either one:

But average American viewers are currently watching 7 hours and 34 minutes of television every day of their lives. Children between the ages of 6 and 11 are watching an average of 27 hours a week, 1400 hours a year. By the time a youngster graduates from high school, he or she will spend more time in front of the tube than in the classroom—and I ask you, how much of what is available for them to view do you believe can materially raise the level of their taste? How much of it do you believe serves to teach, illuminate, and inspire?[38]

You will have a difficult time developing credibility if you give the impression you are playing with style, to the exclusion of ideas; but you should, through use of different kinds of sentences, infuse variety and vitality into your speech.

Summary

Meaning—the understanding a specific person has of anything in his environment—exists only in the individual's mind and must be communicated to others by means of language, an imprecise instrument at best. You must always be aware that there is no direct connection between the words you use and the objects they represent. The only connection is that made in your own mind.

Thought and language are interdependent. Unless your thoughts, or meaning, accurately reflect reality, language must of necessity distort reality for the listener. Six suggestions are offered to help in relating meaning to reality: (1) recognize that it is impossible to know everything; (2) remember that things are seldom as clear-cut as they sound; (3) remember that language reflects your view of the world; (4) judge each instance on its own merits; (5) understand that things change with time; (6) understand that things change with the situation.

Once you have ascertained that your meaning is related to reality, you can turn your attention to the rhetorical process of choosing the style of your message. Style is defined as the "selection and arrangement of those linguistic features which are open to choice." Five factors that help to determine style are discussed: (1) clarity, (2) appropriateness, (3) economy, (4) originality, and (5) vitality.

Exercises

1. Prepare a two-minute speech in which you define some abstract word or phrase that is in common use, such as *women's lib, the whole man, New Federalism, affirmative action, flat tax, secular humanism, scientific creationism.*
2. You have been invited to speak to a high school assembly in your hometown. What qualities of style would you be concerned with in order to create credibility for your ideas? How would this affect your use of language?
3. Analyze the language used by a classmate in a speech. What does the language do to establish credibility? In what ways could the speaker have used language differently to improve his or her credibility?
4. Phrase the main points of your next speech in parallel form.
5. Prepare three periodic sentences to use in your next speech.
6. Select an essay and rewrite it in an oral style.
7. Prepare two chiasmi for use in your next speech.

Notes

1. R. E. Nebergall, "An Experimental Investigation of Rhetorical Clarity," *Speech Monographs* 25 (1958):243.
2. Jack W. Germond and Jules Witcover, "Politics Today," *The Birmingham News,* September 19, 1984, p. 11A. Used by permission.

3. S. I. Hayakawa, "A Search for Relevance," in *Communication: General Semantics Perspectives,* ed. L. Thayer (New York: Spartan Books, 1970), pp. 87–88.

4. AP Dispatch, *Durham Sun,* July 15, 1971.

5. J. Fast, *Body Language* (New York: M. Evans and Co., 1970), p. 70.

6. Mark Twain, "Concerning Tobacco," in *What Is Man* (New York: Harper and Brothers, 1917), pp. 275–76.

7. E. Goodman, "Can You Trust Doctor Who Changes Mind?," *Birmingham Post-Herald,* January 25, 1980. © 1980, The Boston Globe Newspaper Company/ Washington Post Writers Group, reprinted with permission.

8. T. Carbone, "Stylistic Variables as Related to Source Credibility: A Content Analysis Approach," *Speech Monographs* 42 (1975):99–106.

9. S. I. Hayakawa, *Language in Action* (New York: Harcourt, Brace and Co., 1949), p. 47.

10. J. Church, "Cognitive Differences as Impediments to Communication with Some Uneasy Hindthoughts on the Questions What? and Whether?," in *Communication: Theory and Research,* ed. L. Thayer (Springfield, Ill.: Charles C Thomas, Publisher, 1967), pp. 175–76.

11. C. F. Vick and R. V. Wood, "Similarity of Past Experience and the Communication of Meaning," *Speech Monographs* 36 (1969):159–62.

12. "The Euphemism: Telling It Like It Isn't," *Time,* September 19, 1969, p. 26. Reprinted by permission from *TIME, The Weekly Newsmagazine;* Copyright Time, Inc.

13. Diane Hubbard Burns, "A Rose by Another Name Might Smell Better," Reprinted from the *Orlando Sentinel* in *The Birmingham News,* June 15, 1985, p. 4A.

14. *Time,* September 19, 1969, p. 26.

15. U.S. Department of Labor, Occupational Safety and Health Administration, *General Industry: OSHA Safety and Health Standards* (29 CFR 1910), OSHA 2206, Revised, November 7, 1978, p. 52.

16. P. G. Zimbardo, "Verbal Ambiguity and Judgmental Distortion," *Psychological Reports* 6 (1960):57–58. Examples of the indeterminate type of ambiguity are "Anyone who has known a scientist personally will know why science is where it is today." "If you have followed recent developments in science, you will know that there can be one solution to the problem."

17. James M. Hay, "The Public Face of the Chemical Industry," *Vital Speeches of the Day* 53 (1987):180. © City News Publishing Company. Used by permission.

18. Carbone, "Stylistic Variables as Related to Source Credibility."

19. J. W. Bowers, "Language Intensity, Social Introversion, and Attitude Change," *Speech Monographs* 30 (1963):345–52.

20. J. W. Gibson et al., "A Quantitative Examination of Differences and Similarities in Written and Spoken Messages," *Speech Monographs* 33 (1966):444–51.

21. Carbone, "Stylistic Variables as Related to Source Credibility."

22. J. A. DeVito, "Psychogrammatical Factors in Oral and Written Discourse by Skilled Communicators," *Speech Monographs* 33 (1966):73–76.

23. R. H. Simpson, "The Specific Meanings of Certain Terms Indicating Different Degrees of Frequency," *Quarterly Journal of Speech* 30 (1944):328–30.

24. R. H. Simpson, "Stability in Meanings for Quantitative Terms: A Comparison over 20 Years," *Quarterly Journal of Speech* 49 (1963):146–51.

25. *Durham* (N.C.) *Morning Herald,* March 17, 1969. Copyright, The *Washington Post*. Reprinted with permission Los Angeles Times–Washington Post News Service.

26. D. E. Saunders, ed., *The Day They Marched* (Chicago: Johnson Publishing Co., 1963), pp. 81–82. Copyright 1963 by Martin Luther King, Jr. Permission by Joan Daves.

27. Frank G. Clement, "Keynote Address," *Vital Speeches of the Day* 22 (1956):674–79. Used by permission.

28. P. D. Brandes, "Coding the Communication," unpublished mimeographed manuscript, 1969.

29. H. R. Walpole, *Semantics* (New York: W. W. Norton & Co., 1941), p. 154.

30. N. L. Reinsch, Jr., "An Investigation of the Effects of the Metaphor and Simile in Persuasive Discourse," *Speech Monographs* 38 (1971):142–45.

31. J. J. Kilpatrick, "The Writer's Art," *Birmingham News,* July 4, 1982. Used by permission.

32. Clement, "Keynote Address." For a fuller discussion of Clement's use of style, see B. E. Bradley, "Back to the Red Clay Hills," *Southern Speech Communication Journal* 25 (1960):199–204.

33. *Inaugural Addresses of the Presidents of the United States,* 87th Cong., 1st sess., House Document no. 218 (Washington, D.C.: U.S. Government Printing Office, 1961), pp. 267–70.

34. Saunders, *The Day They Marched,* p. 81. Italics added.

35. J. A. DeVito, "Some Psycholinguistic Aspects of Active and Passive Sentences," *Quarterly Journal of Speech* 55 (1969):401–6.

36. J. W. Black, "Aural Reception of Sentences of Different Lengths," *Quarterly Journal of Speech* 47 (1961):51–53.

37. W. F. Thrall, A. Hibbard, and C. H. Holman, *A Handbook to Literature* (New York: Odyssey Press, 1960), p. 82.

38. Norman Lear, "Does TV Have the Courage to Pioneer a New Commercial Ethic?" in *Representative American Speeches, 1984–1985,* ed. Owen Peterson (New York: H. W. Wilson Company, 1985), pp. 194–95. Used by permission.

PART 4

FORMS OF COMMUNICATION

16

SPEAKING TO INFORM

*R*ecalling his operation for an appendectomy, one author reported that he awoke shortly after the last stitch had been tied off and experienced intense pain. He immediately assumed that something had gone wrong. Nothing was wrong. He had awakened two hours earlier than he should have because it was Sunday and the recovery room was not in operation. When he failed to recover as soon as he thought he should, he began to worry about his progress. Later he was told that his recovery had been normal, but he lamented that the hospital should have given him information about what was going to happen. The writer concludes: "There ought to be simple mimeographed sheets for people, outlining what will definitely happen, what usually happens, what may go wrong and whether it is anything to worry about, and what you should tell your physician—as simple as that."[1]

This case reflects the intense desire among members of our society to be given information about the world around them. Today's citizens want to know why the doctor prescribes a particular medicine, why the city council voted as it did on a significant issue, what the ingredients and safety levels of consumer products are. Most people are no longer willing to be relegated to second-class citizenship. And that is what participation without knowledge is. This current desire for knowledge is healthy for any society; it is vital for a democratic one where citizens play a key role in shaping governmental policies.

Despite the occurrence of many instances in which people are given insufficient information, speaking to inform is a frequent and important type of communication. Lectures designed to impart information are presented daily in schools and colleges and to the general public. After installing a new television set, the technician instructs the owner about proper operating procedures. When a car is taken to the repair shop, the owner explains to the service manager what has been happening, when the problem started, under what conditions it recurs, and all other seemingly relevant data that will help the service manager more easily diagnose what is wrong. The president's press secretary informs the media about the president's itinerary on a planned tour of Europe and what the president hopes to accomplish.

Innumerable times each day, all of us either request or give information. Not infrequently, we are led astray or lead others astray by information that is poorly presented or misunderstood. Some attention to the principles of informative speaking may improve our communication with others.

In a speech to inform, you want the listener to understand the ideas presented, not for the purpose of persuasion, but simply to have the hearer comprehend. The knowledge of the listener must be expanded; if not, the informative speech cannot be considered an effective one. The informative speech is focused more on adding new cognitive elements than on influencing the listener's belief or behavior. A more knowledgeable listener is the goal of the informative speaker.

The following pages will discuss the objectives of informative speeches, informative methods that you can use, and the organization of informative speeches.

Objectives of Informative Speeches

There are several obvious similarities between informative and persuasive speeches. Informative speeches, no less than persuasive speeches, need to gain the attention and hold the interest of the listeners. No one can be informed if stimuli other than the speaker are distracting the hearer's attention. Informative speeches are also similar to persuasive speeches in the types of evidence that are appropriate for them. Testimony, statistics, and factual data may be used to develop the content of either type of speech. The same sources of evidence should be consulted, subject to the same tests of credibility; and visual aids can be used to make the content more interesting and more understandable.

Nevertheless, there are three objectives that distinguish informative from persuasive speaking: clarity, balanced development, and retention of material.

Clarity

First, *clarity* is indispensable to the informative speaker. The speaker's meaning must be singularly clear. Audience comprehension is hindered if there is vagueness of meaning. Some persuasive speakers, on the other hand, may use ambiguity as a stratagem, even though it frequently backfires. Using such imprecise words as *patriotism, free speech,* and *welfare cheaters,* politicians allow their listeners to attach whatever meaning they desire to these terms.

Clarity begins in the mind of the speaker. Comprehension must necessarily precede clarity of thought. Until you understand the subject thoroughly, you cannot possibly explain it clearly to someone else. The more you study your subject and understand it, therefore, the easier it will be to achieve clarity of expression.

Clarity can be achieved and vagueness avoided more easily if you use precise and familiar language, construct sentences in easy-to-follow syntax, select supporting materials that obviously support the reasoning, organize the ideas into a coherent and unified whole, avoid nonverbal forms of communication that contradict the verbal message, and adapt all these elements or factors to the particular listeners.

Balanced Development

Second, the informative speech seeks to provide a *balanced* or *impartial development* of the topic. As a persuasive speaker you can present arguments and evidence supporting your position and ignore opposing positions or information. But biased or overly selective treatment of material is inappropriate for informative speaking. Using materials in informative speaking that deliberately distort or present a misleading perspective is indefensible. As an informative speaker you must present all facets of the topic and strive to develop a full understanding of the subject. Without a thorough analysis of the topic and a thorough development of the available evidence, you cannot achieve an unbiased, impartial treatment of a topic. Don't be misled into thinking, however, that a thorough treatment must include every detail about a subject; that would only confuse and bore the listeners. Thorough treatment means including an in-depth discussion of important aspects of the subject.

A seeming lack of objectivity can stem from several sources. The audience may suspect bias when pertinent data are ignored. For example, you might discuss the merits of two alternative routes for a highway by considering three topics: (1) cost, (2) engineering problems, and (3) traffic flow. If, however, one route would have a greater impact on residential areas than the other, listeners who live in those areas may assume you are unobjective unless you also discuss that consideration.

You may also appear unobjective if you inject your own value judgments into the presentation. If, after discussing two proposed routes for a highway, you conclude, "So you can see the northern route is bad because it diverts traffic away from our downtown motel district," that is a value judgment and indicates a desire to influence the listeners. In an informative speech, you should present the information and allow the listeners to draw their own conclusions. In this case, the audience may not share the value judgment that it would be bad to divert traffic away from downtown, especially if there is a congestion problem.

On some occasions, the sources of information cited may make the speech appear to be unobjective. Factual information from a source listeners regard as neutral seems more objective than the same factual information from a source they perceive as biased. To be an effective informative speaker, you must choose the particular sources of information with great care.

Retention of Material

A third objective of an informative speech is to present material in a way that facilitates *retention of the material*. Most psychologists now agree that there are three types of memory—immediate, short-term, and long-term. Immediate memory lasts for only a second or so and then is lost. Information in the short-term memory is available for recall for about thirty seconds and then either goes into the long-term memory or is lost. To get information beyond the listener's short-term memory and into the long-term memory, you must make it possible for memory traces to be strengthened. A memory trace is "a fragile, highly perishable neural response" resulting from a sensory experience. If this memory trace is strengthened, however, "it becomes an actual *change* in the nervous system" instead of a fleeting response.[2] This process is analogous to strolling across a plot of grass between two sidewalks; the slight trace left there is quickly obliterated by rain, wind, snow, or mowing. If you walk that way every day, however, a clear path emerges. As an informative speaker, therefore, you must create paths or "mental sets" for your information in the minds of your listeners.

A number of methods can be used to improve retention of your material.

Use repetition State your purpose, preview the main points, develop each point separately, and then focus on the purpose and summarize the main points at the end. This repetition should begin to create some pathways. Baird found, for example, that the use of a preview or a summary "significantly increased comprehension."[3] Two types of restatement can be used: reiteration and paraphrase. Testimony from other sources to support your ideas can also utilize either method of repetition to reinforce your ideas in the listeners' minds.

Establish an association between your ideas and knowledge familiar to the listener "It is easier to learn and remember something if you understand its overall meaning and can relate it to material you already know."[4] When you use an interesting example that the listener recalls later, you have established an association. For example, I remember only one point made in a speech by a leading educator some twenty years ago: that an educational institution must tailor its programs to the needs of its students and its region. I remember that point because of a story the speaker used to emphasize the importance of considering needs. According to the story, a southern evangelist went on a speaking tour of New England during the Reconstruction period. Near the end of the tour, he spoke in Boston. After the speech, during a question and answer period, one member of the audience stood and said, "Sir, I'd like to know what you southerners are most interested in." Without hesitation, the evangelist replied, "Money." Seeing that the questioner was disturbed by his answer, the evangelist said to the Bostonian, "Now let me ask you what is it you Bostonians are most interested in?" Drawing himself a little more erect and speaking with pride in his voice, the Bostonian answered, "Education, culture, and religion." Looking him directly in the eye, the evangelist said, "That's good. Each of us is interested in the things we need the most!"

Motivate the listeners to understand Fewer repetitions are necessary for the listeners to learn the material when they are motivated. Emphasize the relevance and importance of your information to the listeners; that will motivate them to listen more carefully. One way to motivate your hearers to attend to your information is to present your ideas as interestingly as possible.

Organize your material into a clear and meaningful whole Numerous studies have demonstrated that organized information is more easily learned than unorganized material.

Emphasize important information One of the major reasons we do not remember information is a failure to concentrate when it is being presented. You can increase listeners' recall by providing aural cues that cause them to attend to important information. Examples of cues that draw attention to information are "Now listen," "This is an important point," "Let me emphasize this point." Other means of emphasis are to pause before a statement and to use gestures. Some have suggested that vocal variety, such as using a slower

rate of speaking or increasing the loudness level, is an effective means of emphasizing important information and increasing listener recall. The empirical evidence is contradictory, however, about the effectiveness of these last two methods.[5] Nevertheless, some "ugly American" tourists in foreign countries have tried to make the natives understand them simply by speaking slowly and loudly—in English!

Methods of Informative Speaking

When speaking to inform, you may use any of the following methods: narrate, report, instruct, demonstrate, define, analyze, describe, exemplify, compare, and contrast. Understand that any of these methods may be used to develop a main point or a subpoint. In fact, each may be used as the method of developing an entire speech.

These methods of exposition are complementary, not mutually exclusive. You may use only one of the methods or you may use several. Furthermore, these methods are not restricted to informative speeches. They are simply methods of informing, and since persuasive speeches also provide information, these methods are appropriate for persuasive speeches. They are also used in various forms of interpersonal communication, such as conversations, interviews, and group discussions. Whether these methods are used in a persuasive or informative speech or in some interpersonal form of communication, their identifying characteristic and basic objective is to inform.

Narration involves relating a sequence of events or telling a story. You may tell about the assassination of President John F. Kennedy, the Watergate break-in, the U.S. bombing of Libya in 1986, the explosion of the Challenger spacecraft. In the courtroom, a lawyer narrates the sequence of events involved in

Narrate

a crime. Questions you will want to ask in preparing the narration are the following: *What* happened? *How* did it happen? *When* did it happen? *Where* did it happen? *Who* did it? *Why* did it happen?

Effective narration should have four attributes. First, it should include or involve movement. Thus, narration will frequently be organized in a time sequence. Second, it must have a focus easily recognizable by listeners. Events and details must be chosen that are particularly relevant to the central purpose. Third, the events and details must be internally consistent. Any inconsistency in the account will decrease the credibility of the narration. Fourth, the events and details used to develop the narration must be sufficiently thorough and complete to create the desired conclusions and impressions. Failure to include all pertinent information may cause listeners to comprehend incorrectly.[6]

Report

A report and a narrative are very similar. The major distinction is that a report is generally a firsthand account, whereas a narration is not. Thus, an individual reports on his trip to a national political convention, a committee chairperson reports on the deliberation and decision of her committee, a labor mediator reports on the negotiations and agreements of a union-management controversy, or the treasurer of an organization gives a financial report for the last fiscal period.

The same questions you consider in preparing a narrative are appropriate in preparing a report. You will want to ask similar questions: What happened? How did it happen? Who will be affected? When did it happen? Where did it happen? Who did it?

Instruct

Instruction makes a concept or a process understandable by explaining what it is, how it is done, or how it operates. Concepts, such as the Keynesian theory of economics, progressive education, or academic freedom, may be explained in a speech to instruct. Or you may explain a process—how to fingerprint a person, compute a chi square, or forecast the weather.

Demonstrate

Demonstration exhibits the operation of some activity or procedure. You may show how to grip a golf club, provide heart resuscitation, or cope with a snake bite. Obviously, the speech using demonstration will also include instructions to help the listener understand fully what is being demonstrated. But the speech using demonstration goes beyond instruction and shows visually how something is done. Visual aids are thus especially appropriate for demonstration. Charts, maps, slides, diagrams, photographs, replicas, the actual object itself are some visual aids that can be used. In addition, nonverbal methods of communication are frequently used. You may act out the motions of swinging a tennis racquet so that the audience can more readily understand the separate phases of that action.

Forms of Communication

Definition gives the listener a precise meaning of what you are talking about. **Define**
Effective communication is frequently dependent upon clear definitions of such
terms as "terrorism," "country and western music," "discrimination," or "male
chauvinism" to enable the listener to understand clearly what is meant by the
particular term being used.

Keep in mind that not all people define things in the same way. Thus,
your definition doesn't have to be the same as another person's definition of

the same term or concept. Unless the audience understands your definition clearly, however, you will not successfully communicate with them.

If the definition is to be credible, it must be a reasonable one. Credible definitions can be constructed with the aid of dictionaries, books and articles by knowledgeable people, and observation of current practices.

The definition should identify the primary characteristics of the object or concept, be expressed in language easily understandable to the hearers, and be precise.

Six types of definition are available.

1. Classify, by likenesses or differences, with other members possessing similar characteristics. Note how one speaker defined a *concentration ratio:* "It's a figure, a percentage, that shows what fraction of an entire industry's production and sales is attained by a limited number of companies."[7] In this definition, a concentration ratio is classified as a percentage and then differentiated from other percentages.
2. Trace the etymology of the term. This method was used in the following application: "Intelligence is derived from two words—'inter' and 'legere' meaning 'to choose' and 'between.' An intelligent person is one who has learned to choose between good and evil, who knows that trust is better than fear, love than hate, gentleness than cruelty, forbearance than intolerance, humility than arrogance, truth than falsehood."[8]
3. Tell what a thing is not, that is, define by negation. In explaining "pursuit of happiness," one speaker used this method:

   . . . we have come to believe that the pursuit of happiness is reducible to the pursuit of pleasure. . . .

   Our age has developed the ultimate defense of pleasure as a guide to the moral life. Four years ago, a young Californian explained to an audience how she knew that certain of her actions had been right. She said, "I knew it was right because it felt good when I was doing it." She was not explaining her justification for taking some new drug or for performing a new sexual act. Her name was Susan Atkins, a member of the Manson family, and she was describing her horrible justification for the savage murder of seven people. The criterion of pleasure does not differentiate between higher and lower pleasures or between good and bad pleasures. Once it is agreed that the criterion is pleasure, pleasure becomes its own justification.[9]

4. Give an operational definition—tell what it does. For example, one can use an operational definition to identify a voltmeter as a device used to measure the voltage between two points of an electrical current.
5. Present examples of the item. Listeners may not know the meaning of "pachyderm," for example, but if they are told that it is a large animal with a thick skin such as the rhinoceros, hippopotamus, and elephant, they will probably understand the term.

6. Compare and contrast the item with others that are familiar to the listeners. For example, propaganda may be defined in this way: "Propaganda, like persuasion, attempts to change the attitudes and behavior of others. Unlike persuasion, propaganda places no restrictions on the use of invalid reasoning, untrue evidence, or unethical procedures."

Therefore, you can define by classification, etymology, negation, operational definition, example, or comparison and contrast.

Although definition may be used in all types of speaking, there is frequently insufficient time to develop a definition in detail. It is sometimes advantageous, therefore, to devote an entire speech to defining a term or concept in order to be able to examine that definition in depth.

Analyze

Analysis identifies the major divisions or constituent parts of a topic, such as the causes and effects of an event or the essential characteristics of an object. You may analyze the causes and effects of inflation, the essential characteristics of a successful writer, or the qualities of a good stock to purchase. The most important question for you to ask is: What are the logical divisions of the subject?

Valid analysis must be logical. It must use a consistent principle to divide a topic into its parts, the parts must be mutually exclusive, and the division of the parts must be exhaustive. For example, one way to analyze highways is to examine the basis of access to them. Thus, we have two types: those with limited access, and those with unlimited access. This analysis conforms with the three requirements above: It uses the same principle, the parts are mutually exclusive, and the division is exhaustive. On the other hand, if highways were analyzed on the basis of three divisions—limited access roads, unlimited access roads, and farm roads—then the three divisions would not be mutually exclusive.

Describe

Description explains how something appears—its spatial appearance, shape, or dimensions. The speaker may describe Bourbon Street in New Orleans, an automobile assembly line, the painting of Andrew Wyeth, the Rocky Mountains, the outer banks of North Carolina, or the Alamo.

Some suggested questions to ask in preparing an effective description are: How long is it? What shape is it? How deep is it? How wide is it? What color is it? What is its texture? What is its temperature? As these questions clearly indicate, description relies heavily upon sensory data. The purpose of description is to stimulate sensory images in the minds of listeners. Consequently, concreteness and specificity are obviously important characteristics of description.

Focus on the items relevant to the purpose of the speech. A description of highways, for example, may focus on safety features, construction materials, scenic aspects, or topographical adaptations. Unless you have determined the purpose of the speech, there will be no principle or criterion for selecting descriptive information. But the use of unfocused descriptive data will only confuse listeners.

One of the pitfalls of description is "information overload," or crowding too many bits of data together so that the listener has little opportunity to digest them. One way to avoid this is to present data that create sensory images for only one of the senses at a time. Additionally, you should supplement description with other methods of conveying information that make fewer cognitive demands on listeners.

Exemplify

This method of informing attempts to create understanding by presenting one or more examples of the ideas, thus making clear the meaning. In discussing our criminal justice system, one speaker stated a generalization and then used an example to develop it.

Some prisons are almost like acting schools that teach convicts jargon the Parole Board wants to hear.

There was one sad case of a convict in one of our maximum security institutions who willingly applied himself to rehabilitation. But he just couldn't find a way to please the Parole Board.

One year they told him he needed to learn a trade—so he became a shoemaker. The next year they told him he needed an education—so he got his high school diploma.

The next year they said group therapy was the key to release—so he joined a therapy group. The next year they said he needed to do more time.

This man is only one of thousands of offenders who resent our system. And they have every reason to resent it.[10]

Two methods of informing by example may be used: (1) a specific instance, which is an undetailed example, or (2) an illustration, which is a detailed example. Specific instances are useful to demonstrate typicality, but illustrations may be more "powerful" because they involve the listener more. Examples, whether detailed or undetailed, may be either factual or hypothetical.

Keep examples relevant to your point. If the point of the story has to be labored, the relationship of the example is probably not clear enough for it to be included. Let the introduction of the example establish the connection between it and the point you want to make.

Use interesting examples. Listeners generally find interesting those examples that include a delicate balance of familiar and unfamiliar information; they get bored if a speaker presents only familiar information. Specific and concrete data make examples interesting. Listeners get involved with examples that evoke a sensory response. Examples are more interesting if they concern people, especially if the listener knows them personally or recognizes the names. Examples from your own personal experiences are particularly interesting because they provide information about you as well as the topic.

Adapt examples to the particular audience. Adapt them to the listeners' age, sex, occupation, region of residence, political affiliation. If you are talking to a group of southern farmers about ways to conserve energy, you should not cite examples from urban residents or even from midwestern farmers. The best examples would involve southern farmers.

Compare

A comparison or analogy examines the points of similarity between two things. Unfamiliar objects or concepts can be made more comprehensible if you cause the listeners to perceive a relationship between them and something they already understand. A comparison may be literal or figurative. It is literal if the comparison involves two members of the same class. For example, if Ronald Reagan were compared to Thomas Jefferson as a president, that would be a literal comparison. A comparison is figurative if it involves members of different classes. For example, if the tactics of a football team were compared to the tactics of the U.S. Army under General Grant in the Civil War, that would be a figurative comparison.

Contrast

The speaker uses contrast in exploring points of dissimilarity between two objects or concepts. The use of opposites can clarify meaning for listeners by delineating more clearly and more vividly the characteristics of an unfamiliar object or concept. You might make more understandable the nature of a community college by contrasting it with a university in these ways: (1) The community college does not have students in residence as a university does. (2) Unlike the university, which does not admit everyone who applies, the community college has an open-door admissions policy. Like a comparison, a contrast may be either literal or figurative.

Comparison and contrast can be used together. To pay tribute to a running back who had missed most of his senior year because of a pulled hamstring muscle, one football coach used a figurative comparison and contrast: "Plow horses don't have pulled hamstrings; thoroughbreds do."

Organization of an Informative Speech

Most informative speeches are organized in the traditional pattern of introduction, thesis, body, and conclusion. Because of the positive effect organization has on comprehension, clear and obvious organization is imperative in informative speaking.

Introduction

Most of the types of introductions discussed in chapter 11 are appropriate for an informative speech. Probably the most useful and effective introduction, however, is one that establishes the importance and relevance of the subject for the particular group of listeners involved.

In chapter 11, three purposes of an introduction are identified: (1) to attract the attention of the hearers, (2) to safeguard or improve the ethos of the speaker, and (3) to assist the listeners in beginning to think about the topic to be developed in this particular speech. All three purposes apply to an informative speech, but perhaps the least important is creating goodwill for the speaker. It is more important in an informative speech to gain the attention of the listeners and to lead them into the topic of the speech.

Thesis Sentence

The nature of the informative speech makes appropriate a straightforward and explicit statement of the thesis, such as, "This morning I want to discuss with you . . ." "Tonight I want to explain to you . . ." "In the next few minutes, let's examine the characteristics of. . . ." A preview of main points is especially important in an informative speech because the repetition helps in achieving the main goal: comprehension and retention of the ideas by the listener. The thesis sentence should be carefully worded to reflect an informative rather than a persuasive tone or purpose.

Once you have selected the main ideas to be used in developing the thesis **Body of the Speech**
sentence, decide the order in which those ideas will be presented. Most of the
patterns of organization discussed in chapter 10 can be used, but some are
particularly appropriate to the purpose of informing. The chronological pattern, spatial pattern, topical pattern, and causal pattern are most commonly
used in organizing an informative speech.

Because of the importance of clear organization in informative speaking,
make the main points unmistakably clear. "Headline" your main points clearly
and vividly by providing definite signposts to alert the listeners to your main
points. Use internal summaries and clear transitions to aid in movement from
one thought to another.

Most psychologists accept the theory that our short-term memory can
retain no more than seven items, plus or minus two. But many more items can
be held in the memory if they are grouped ("chunked," according to psychologists) into categories. Help the listener remember ideas by grouping them
into categories. Keep in mind that organization is created by the speaker; it
does not spring full-blown from a topic. Search for the categories that will
most effectively group the information and translate those categories into main
points. The number of categories should be limited to three or four, however;
only rarely should an informative speech have as many as five main points.

Consideration of a specific example may clarify the task of grouping.
For instance, the process of refinishing old furniture involves some twenty activities:

1. Apply paint remover.
2. Remove old finish with putty knife or scraper.
3. Use steel brush to remove paint not eliminated with paint remover.
4. Wipe with fine steel wool covered with paint remover.
5. Clean furniture with cloth soaked with neutralizer.
6. Tighten screws and nails.
7. Replace missing screws and nails.
8. Fill exposed nail or screw holes with wood putty.
9. Repair cracks with wood putty.
10. Sand lightly for a smooth finish.
11. Apply stain if desired.
12. Apply a coat of filler.
13. Apply a coat of sealer.
14. Apply first coat of varnish.
15. Sand the dried varnish with very fine sandpaper.
16. Apply second coat of varnish.
17. Sand dried varnish with very fine sandpaper.
18. Apply third coat of varnish.
19. Rub surface down with powdered pumice.
20. Rub surface down with rottenstone.

I have heard speeches about refinishing old furniture in which the speaker presented each of these activities as a separate entity. You can see how difficult it would be to recall all those items. Now, let's group those activities under three categories, and see how much easier it is to follow and to recall the activities.

A. Remove the old finish.
   1. Apply paint remover.
   2. Remove old finish with putty knife or scraper.
   3. Use steel brush to remove paint not eliminated with paint remover.
   4. Wipe with fine steel wool covered with paint remover.
B. Prepare furniture for new finish.
   1. Clean furniture with cloth soaked with neutralizer.
   2. Tighten screws and nails.
   3. Replace missing screws and nails.
   4. Fill exposed nail or screw holes with wood putty.
   5. Repair cracks with wood putty.
   6. Sand lightly for a smooth surface.
C. Apply the new finish.
   1. Apply stain if desired.
   2. Apply a coat of filler.
   3. Apply a coat of sealer.
   4. Apply the varnish.
      a. Apply first coat of varnish.
      b. Sand the dried varnish with very fine sandpaper.
      c. Apply second coat of varnish.
      d. Sand dried varnish with very fine sandpaper.
      e. Apply third coat of varnish.
      f. Rub surface down with powdered pumice.
      g. Rub surface down with rottenstone.

When the information in the body of an informative speech is grouped in this manner, you will more readily get listeners to retain the material in their long-term memory.

Conclusion

Almost any type of conclusion discussed in chapter 11 is appropriate for an informative speech. The least appropriate conclusions are the appeal for action or the challenge. Unless done with great care, these conclusions force you to cross the line from informing to persuading, thus causing listeners to doubt your objectivity and destroying any credibility that has been created.

The most effective conclusion to further your aims as an informative speaker is the summary or recapitulation. A summary focuses the minds of the listeners on the main ideas of the speech, thus reinforcing the central purpose and enhancing the ability of the listeners to comprehend and remember the material.

Summary

Although persuasive speeches generally involve information and utilize one or more of the methods of informing, there are some speeches whose sole purpose is to have the listeners comprehend the material presented. Because there are many similarities between informative and persuasive speeches, the distinction between them is not always clear-cut.

Nevertheless, there are three objectives that in many instances set informative speaking apart from persuasive speaking: (1) clarity; (2) a balanced or impartial development of the topic; (3) a presentation that facilitates the listeners' retention of the material.

Informative methods, although not mutually exclusive or restricted to informative speeches, include the following: (1) narration, (2) reporting, (3) instruction, (4) demonstration, (5) definition, (6) analysis, (7) description, (8) exemplifying, (9) comparison, (10) contrast.

Most informative speeches are organized in the traditional pattern of introduction, thesis, body, and conclusion. Because of the importance of organization to comprehension, it is imperative that the informative speech be clearly organized. You must make every possible effort to make your organizational plan clear to listeners early in the speech through an easily identifiable thesis and comprehensive preview of main points. You may continue to keep your organizational pattern apparent to receivers and provide a sense of movement or progress by employing internal summaries and transitions.

Exercises

1. Prepare a six-minute speech explaining how to do or how to make something.
2. Choose a term or concept with which your classmates are unfamiliar. Prepare a definition, using information from at least three sources to aid in developing it.
3. Read a speech in the current issue of *Vital Speeches*. Identify and discuss the speaker's use of at least three methods of exposition. What was the general purpose of the speech?
4. Attend a lecture in which the general purpose is to inform. Discuss the speaker's success in achieving the three objectives of informative speaking. If the speaker failed to achieve any of them, explain why. Then explain how the speaker could have succeeded.

Notes

1. E. Krupat, *Psychology Is Social* (Glenview, Ill.: Scott, Foresman & Co., 1975), pp. 179–80.
2. C. G. Morris, *Psychology: An Introduction* (Englewood Cliffs, N.J.: Prentice-Hall, 1976), p. 191.
3. J. E. Baird, "The Effects of Speech Summaries upon Audience Comprehension of Expository Speeches of Varying Quality and Complexity," *Central States Speech Journal* 25 (1974):124–25.
4. Morris, *Psychology*, p. 195.
5. R. Ehrensberger, "An Experimental Study of the Relative Effectiveness of Certain Forms of Emphasis in Public Speaking," *Speech Monographs* 12 (1945):94–111; A. T. Jersild, "Modes of Emphasis in Public Speaking," *Journal of Applied Psychology* 12 (1928):611–20.
6. W. L. Bennett, "Storytelling in Criminal Trials: A Model of Social Judgment," *Quarterly Journal of Speech* 64 (1978):5.

7. W. E. LaMothe, "A Case of Mistrust," *Vital Speeches of the Day* 42 (1976):698. Used by permission.

8. J. M. Kletsche, "For What Do We Educate?" *Vital Speeches of the Day* 42 (1976):684. Used by permission.

9. John R. Silber, "Democracy: Its Counterfeits and Its Promise," *Vital Speeches of the Day* 42 (1976):676. Used by permission.

10. D. Walker, "Making Our Criminal Justice System Work," *Vital Speeches of the Day* 42 (1976):732. Used by permission.

17

SPEAKING TO PERSUADE

Coercion is frequently used to influence the attitudes and behavior of others. In South Africa coercion is used to maintain separation of the black and white races. Sometime during the term you are taking this course, an airplane may be hijacked. Then will come the news that the passengers are being held as hostages until some demand of the hijackers has been met. Or the evening television news will show crowds of demonstrators in a place like Seabrook, Maine, trying to develop support for a nuclear freeze. In the Soviet Union, citizens with "wrong" attitudes will be dispatched to Siberia until they are "rehabilitated." In differing degrees, all these are coercive means of affecting behavior and attitudes of others.

Most of us, at some time, have wished we had the means of coercing someone to our point of view, but we generally recognize that coercion has its disadvantages. First, if we can coerce someone, then someone else can coerce us. So we protect others from ourselves in order ultimately to protect ourselves. Second, someone who is coerced to a position may not be committed to it. That person may revert to the original, preferred behavior at the first opportunity. It is true that there are examples of approved coercion, such as a parent coercing a child to study. It is also true that coercion can create behavior to which the coerced person does become committed. In most cases, however, the coercion of adults is a method that is both resented and ethically questionable.

Persuasion, on the other hand, offers a legitimate, effective way to affect others' attitudes and behavior. First, it permits the intended receiver to decide personally the position he or she will adopt. Second, it results in stronger commitment to the new position. Although the commitment is made in varying degrees and is subject to reversal by another persuader, the important feature is that the individual makes the decision voluntarily. Third, it is a nonviolent method for settling controversies and making changes in our society.

What exactly is persuasion? It is the process whereby an attempt is made to induce changes in attitudes and behavior through involvement of a person's cognitive and affective processes. As pointed out earlier, it is possible to alter attitudes without affecting behavior. And some may change behavior without modifying their attitudes. You should be reluctant, therefore, to infer a relationship between attitudes and behavior. Nevertheless, the objective of the persuasive speech is to cause a change in both attitudes and behavior.

Obstacles to Changing Attitudes

No matter how skilled or clever the persuader, forming and changing attitudes are not easy tasks. In some instances, the task is so enormous as to be hopeless. A Moslem trying to persuade a group of Methodist bishops to give up their Christian faith and become Moslems is confronted by firmly held attitudes and deep-seated convictions. On the other hand, it is not very difficult to persuade someone to do what she desires to do. In fact, some observers of human behavior have concluded that this is the only time persuasion is truly effective. Aldous Huxley has observed: "Social and political [persuasion] . . . is effective as a rule, only upon those whom circumstances have partly or completely convinced of its truth."[1] Yet surveys of voters in the presidential political campaigns of 1940, 1948, 1960, and 1964 revealed that 8 to 20 percent changed parties during the campaign.[2] Furthermore, behavioral scientists and communication scholars have accumulated a large number of experimental studies showing that attitudes can be changed if the appropriate methods are used. Nevertheless, a number of factors operate to hinder or prevent attitude formation or change.

Selective Perception   Our various senses are bombarded constantly with innumerable stimuli. These sensations are carried to the brain, whose function is to give some order to them so that a meaningful pattern can be detected. Perception is the process of creating that meaningful pattern. Some discuss selective perception and selective attention as separate processes, but there is no difference in them. All perception is selective, and there can be no perception without attention.

We selectively perceive stimuli because of our interests, training, prejudices, assumptions, values, cultural differences, personality differences, and physical limitations. A hard-of-hearing person, for example, does not perceive all sounds in the environment. If an automobile accident were witnessed by a doctor, a lawyer, a minister, and an auto mechanic, each would perceive different aspects of the event. The doctor would perceive the physical injuries of the people involved. The lawyer would tend to perceive where the vehicles were as they collided and who had violated the traffic laws. The minister would most likely perceive the mental and physical suffering of the victims. The auto mechanic would probably perceive the damage to the two vehicles and estimate the cost of their repair.

The situation can affect our perceptions. Two researchers did a study in which one subject was the buyer and the other subject the seller. In one situation there was a broad overlapping of the range in which each could make a good bargain; in the second situation, the good bargain range for each was very limited. After the subjects had completed their bargaining efforts in each situation, the experimenters asked the subjects for their reactions. In the wide bargaining range, the subjects were pleased with the results and observed that real businesspeople ought to conduct their business in similar fashion. In the narrow bargaining range, however, the subjects were unhappy with the results and disliked one another, and each observed that the other was a skinflint.[3]

Our assumptions affect our perceptions. For years we assumed that women were physically weaker than men, more gentle, less ambitious, and the like. Consequently, our society decreed that they could not perform many of the jobs men could. In recent years, however, the women's movement has attacked and destroyed these assumptions. Now women are perceived as possessing all the different qualities of men, and in as many varying degrees as men.

Since selective perception can cause listeners to ignore threatening information, attempt to relate important information to the interests, assumptions, cultural differences, and experiences of the listeners. In this way, they may perceive and respond to data that might otherwise go unnoticed.

Although many of the stimuli that impinge upon us daily never make it past our short-term memory, a lot of data become a part of the long-term memory. Most psychologists now believe that data that make it into the long-term memory are there relatively permanently. This does not mean that we can actively recall all these data; the ability to store information is apparently much greater than the ability to retrieve it. Some can apparently be remembered only when certain parts of the brain are stimulated electronically. Some of the data are repressed or suppressed as a defense mechanism. Humans have a strong tendency to drop from their conscious memory their unpleasant experiences, while remembering the pleasant ones. Most of us look back on our childhood and think what a wonderful time that was. Only rarely do we recall an unpleasant experience from that period of our lives. The nostalgic mood of the 1970s was based on selective recall, retaining in the conscious memory only the pleasant features of previous years. Movies such as *American Graffiti* and television shows such as *Happy Days* and *The Waltons* gained their popularity by focusing on the pleasant aspects of earlier times. This selective remembering reflects a desire, caused by the harsh and bitter struggles of the late sixties and seventies, to return to what is remembered as a simpler and happier way of life. Many recall the "happy" days of the Great Depression. Not a few even remember the exciting and adventurous days of World War II as happy ones, not consciously remembering the loneliness and grief that accompanied the separation of families and the death of friends and kin.

Do not assume that listeners will recall information to which they have been exposed. If the material is important to your purpose, present it afresh in the speech.

Selective Exposure

Further complicating the persuader's task is the selective exposure of many individuals to communications. In other words some tend to listen only to those that reinforce or support their current attitudes. McGinnies and Rosenbaum found that those females who favored "a firm stand in Vietnam were more likely to expose themselves to a communication in which it was evident that such a policy would be defended. Those female subjects who were only luke-warm in their support of such a policy were less inclined to attend either directly or indirectly to the president's talk."[4]

Recent experimentation has indicated, however, that not all persons avoid communications that oppose their beliefs. The evidence implies that those who have confidence in their ability to refute opposing messages are willing to expose themselves to differing communications. Walster asked women to discuss articles about religion with an unknown partner. They were told that the partner agreed with them on the issue, but the amount of knowledge on religion the partner was alleged to have varied from much to medium to little. A control group had no partner. The subjects were then given the choice of discussing an article which favored or opposed their beliefs. The more knowledgeable the woman thought her partner was, the more likely she was to choose material opposing her religious beliefs.[5]

Lowin tested the same hypothesis by preparing four brochures containing political statements that were extremely difficult or extremely easy to refute. The brochures indicated that they were circulated by organizations supporting one of the two candidates in the 1964 presidential campaign. Half identified the candidate as Barry Goldwater, half as Lyndon Johnson. The brochure offered to send additional free materials upon request. The booklets were then sent to Democratic clubs, Republican clubs, and supporters of both Johnson and Goldwater. Results supported the hypothesis. Those receiving a pamphlet with strong arguments agreeing with their position were more likely to request additional information than either those who received a pamphlet with weak arguments agreeing with their position or one with strong arguments disagreeing with their position. On the other hand, those receiving a pamphlet with weak arguments disagreeing with their position were more likely to request additional information than either those receiving a pamphlet with strong arguments disagreeing with their position or one with weak arguments agreeing with their position.[6]

We can conclude, therefore, that selective exposure to communications is a more complicated process than has been recognized. How it operates depends upon the confidence we have in the validity of our own opinions or our ability to cope with opposing communications. We are apparently willing to expose ourselves to arguments either strongly in favor of our position or weakly opposed to it, and we avoid arguments either weakly in favor of our position or strongly opposed to it.

The strongest possible arguments must always be developed and presented, even when those listening already favor the position being advocated.

Degree of Commitment

The degree of commitment to a position is another barrier to changing a person's attitudes. Sherif and Sherif refer to an issue which is relevant, significant, or meaningful to an individual as an ego-involving issue. The person's stand or commitment on the issue reveals the extent of ego-involvement. Sherif and Sherif believe that the greater the ego-involvement of the individual, the more difficult it will be to effect a change in the individual's position.[7]

After varying source and communication in a number of ways in an experiment, Tannenbaum concluded that "susceptibility to change is . . . [related] to the intensity of initial attitude": the more intense the attitude initially, the more difficult it is to change; the less intense the attitude initially, the easier it is to change.[8] Strong commitment to a group has the same effect. Kelley and Volkart obtained questionnaires from members of twelve Boy Scout troops revealing their attitudes toward such activities as woodcraft skills, forest lore, and camping activities. A week later an outside speaker criticized these activities and suggested that Scouts would profit more from learning about their cities and engaging in activities available in town. An attitude scale completed after the speech revealed that those boys who placed a low valuation on membership in the Boy Scouts tended to change in the direction suggested by that communication. Among those who placed a high valuation on membership in the Scouts, however, the communication had a negative, or boomerang, effect.[9]

To change an individual's attitudes from those of the group to which he is committed, you must first weaken that person's allegiance to the group.

Public Commitment

Not only is the degree of commitment of an individual to a concept or thing important, but the type of commitment is important. A commitment may be privately or publicly held.

If a person has publicly committed herself to a proposal, it is more difficult to change her attitude. So long as an individual's commitment is known only to her, she is apparently more willing to change if presented with reasons for doing so. Once she has revealed that commitment to others, however, there is apparently an ego-involvement which makes her reluctant to change her mind. Hovland, Campbell, and Brock presented to subjects messages either favoring or opposing lowering the voting age to eighteen. Following the message, subjects in each group were asked to write a paragraph stating their attitude. To determine the impact of public commitment on the flexibility of attitudes, half of the subjects were told that their written opinions would be published; they were asked to sign their names. All subjects then received the message presenting the opposite side, and a final opinion was obtained from

each subject. The results showed that those subjects who signed their names to the original opinion were more reluctant to change than those whose original opinion had been given anonymously.[10]

To be effective you must eliminate the effect of public commitments that oppose your intent. Acknowledge these commitments, but show that conditions have changed since the commitments were made, and present your interpretation of the changed conditions. Since most people agree that changed conditions demand new decisions, this will permit most to change their attitude without feeling that it reflects a weakness of character.

Discrepancy between Listeners' Attitudes and Speaker's Position

The amount of discrepancy between your position and that of your listeners may vary within an audience and from audience to audience. Some audiences will be extremely homogeneous in attitude; others will be extremely heterogeneous. Even the homogeneous audiences may vary in their degree of variance from your position. If we use a continuum to show different degrees of audience attitude, we may locate at least seven different positions, as shown in figure 17.1.

Obviously, the smaller the discrepancy between your position and that of your listeners, the smaller will be the change effected by the message. If you are mildly in favor of a position and are talking to an audience that is neutral on the issue, you have little chance of moving listeners very far along the continuum. On the other hand, if you advocate a position of strong commitment to an audience occupying the position of strong opposition, you have the opportunity to move listeners four points on the continuum. Two investigators found that a large discrepancy between the communicator and the receiver caused a greater shift in attitude than a small discrepancy.[11]

322   *Forms of Communication*

Figure 17.1
Continuum of audience attitude.

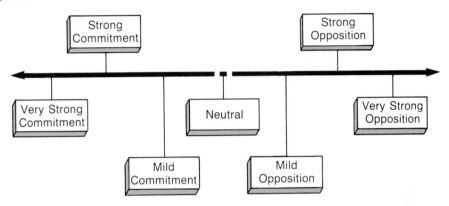

This may not mean, however, that you should attempt to create the greatest discrepancy possible between your position and the attitudes of your listeners. Sherif and colleagues maintain that the important factor is the *latitude of acceptance* on the part of the hearer; in other words, how many positions on the continuum the hearer will find acceptable. They argue that an important element in determining the effect upon attitude change of a persuasive communication is the amount of discrepancy between the position advocated in the message and the hearer's attitude. Their reasoning is that if there is little discrepancy between the message and the hearer's attitude, the hearer will perceive the discrepancy as actually being less than it is and will respond favorably. But if there is much discrepancy, the listener will perceive it as being greater than it is and react unfavorably to the message by making a minimal favorable response, no response, or a negative response. The factor that will determine whether the discrepancy is too great to assimilate is the latitude of acceptance, which "is the position on an issue (or toward an object) that is most acceptable, plus other acceptable positions."[12] As shown in figure 17.2, a person whose most acceptable position was at the mild opposition point, but whose latitude of acceptance did not include the strong commitment point, might assimilate any position from mild opposition to mild commitment. That listener would respond unfavorably, however, to any message calling for a position of strong or very strong commitment. In support of this, Freedman[13] and Whittaker[14] found that subjects who were highly involved in the issues changed attitudes more following more moderate requests for change, whereas subjects having low involvement in the issues changed attitudes more with increasing discrepancy.

Further complicating the problem of message and receiver attitude discrepancy is evidence that the initial prestige of the source affects the impact of discrepancy. A high-prestige source can effect attitude change with a greater discrepancy between her position and her listener's than a low- or moderate-prestige source. Aronson, Turner, and Carlsmith presented to subjects opinions about poetry that were slightly, moderately, or greatly at variance with

Speaking to Persuade 323

Figure 17.2
Continuum of audience position on an issue.

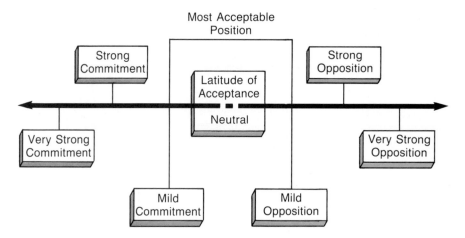

the subjects' opinions. When T. S. Eliot was given as the source of the discrepant opinion, maximum attitude change occurred with the highest discrepancy. When another student was given as the author of the discrepant statement, maximum change took place with the moderately discrepant opinion.[15]

After reviewing a number of studies concerned with message discrepancy, Insko concluded that for most uninvolving topics the influence of a moderately credible communicator increases as the amount of disagreement between the speaker and listeners increases.[16]

Until further research proves otherwise, emphasize your similarities to your audience. Attempt to minimize discrepancy between yourself and those listeners who are *involved* in the issues.

Group Pressure

The effect of group pressure as an obstacle to persuasion has been felt by almost everyone. Who has not felt reluctant to adopt a new clothes style or a new hairstyle because none of their peer group has accepted it? A generation ago, few students would have dared to wear blue jeans to a college classroom for fear of being considered underdressed. In the last several years, few college students would dare not to wear blue jeans to a college classroom for fear of being considered overdressed.

Experiments have even shown that group pressure will cause people to perceive a stationary light as moving and to judge some lines to be longer than others when in fact they are rather obviously shorter or the same length. An important explanation of these results, undoubtedly, is that we doubt our own abilities when confronted with group perceptions that differ.[17]

On the other hand, we succumb to group pressure because we value membership in the group. One of the reasons country club members rake the sand traps and repair ball marks on the golf greens more than people playing on a public course is that the members of a country club constitute a group with a relatively fixed membership who meet in many situations. For fear of being ostracized, no member wants to be known as one who doesn't behave properly on the golf course. On a public course, however, a golfer may rarely, if ever, see again the people playing there. Consequently, there is no group from which to be excluded because of aberrant behavior.

When advocating a position counter to that held by a peer group of the listeners, you may show that new information has changed the situation, that some members of the group have begun to doubt the group's position, or that your position is more consistent with a larger purpose of the group.

In summary, there are at least eight potential obstacles to changing attitudes: (1) a forewarning of the persuasive intent of the message, (2) selective perception of the communication, (3) selective recall of the message, (4) selective exposure to the communication on the part of at least some listeners, (5) the degree of commitment of the individual to a position, (6) any public commitment to a position, (7) the amount of discrepancy between the listener's and the speaker's positions when the listener is involved in the issue under consideration, and (8) group pressure on the listener not to change.

These obstacles to changing attitudes make the persuader's task difficult, but they do not make it impossible. Behavioral science literature is full of experimental studies in which subjects' attitudes have been changed significantly. Admittedly, many of the experimental situations are artificial and the subjects are more sophisticated in some ways and less sophisticated in others than the general population. But these experimental studies coupled with the many instances of attitude change in various phases of national life indicate that attitudes can be changed.

Speakers should avoid the error of thinking that attitudes can always be changed with one persuasive message. An understanding of the role of attitudes in a person's life and an acquaintance with history convince us that persuasion is a slow process that must be continued over a period of time if meaningful attitude changes are to occur and persist. The campaign to abolish slavery in this country went on for almost thirty years before a president could be elected who would say that slavery was evil. Moreover, he was elected as a minority president, and even then he promised not to interfere with slavery where it currently existed. The movement to eliminate child labor from our industrial society took over fifty years. Labor union leaders and advocates had been working for approximately seventy-five years before federal legislation gave full recognition to unions.

This is why the incumbent politician who has not incurred the wrath of constituents generally has an advantage over an opponent: he has had longer to change the voters' attitudes. And this is why most politicians who have defeated an incumbent did so by attacking him. For a challenging politician to run solely on a positive program leaves the long-term persuasion of the incumbent unharmed. To have a chance, the out-candidate must indict the incumbent's programs or credibility, or that of the incumbent's associates.

In order to be optimally successful in changing attitudes, you must commit yourself to a long-term persuasive effort.

Methods of Forming and Changing Attitudes

Following their review of "the literature on attitude persistence," Petty and Cacioppo concluded that the multiple research results and theories could justifiably be considered as supporting "just two relatively distinct routes to persuasion." They identified these as the *central* route and the *peripheral* route. The *central* involves "careful and thoughtful consideration of the true merits of the information presented in support of an advocacy." The *peripheral* involves "some simple cue in the persuasion context (e.g., an attractive source) that induced change without necessitating scrutiny of the true merits of the information presented." Their Elaboration Likelihood Model of persuasion is predicated on these two routes. They define *elaboration* as "the extent to which a person thinks about the issue-relevant arguments contained in a message."[18]

In the following pages, we will look at the various issue-relevant and nonissue-relevant ways in which attitudes are formed and changed.

Build a Case with Evidence and Reasoning

To meet your responsibility as an ethical speaker, develop a position based on a set of arguments supported by valid evidence and logical reasoning. You should not attempt persuasion without first accomplishing this objective. As a realistic persuasive communicator, however, realize that you must do something with the evidence and reasoning you present: interpret it, present it so the listener will perceive it, make it acceptable and credible to the listener, and make it meaningful to the listener. This section will attempt to explain how attitudes can be formed and changed.

Attitude changes may result from rational deliberation about issue-relevant data and the unification of "that information into an overall position," or they may result from peripheral (nonissue-relevant) cues, such as source expertise, attractiveness, mere number of arguments, pleasant music, source likability, etc. Sometimes, however, a source feature, such as expertise, "may itself serve as a persuasive argument" providing source information (biased or unbiased) that helps the listener evaluate "the true merits of any given argument."[19]

Attitudes changed by issue-relevant information, say Petty and Cacioppo, are "more internally consistent, accessible, enduring, and resistant than" when they are based on the peripheral cues listed above.[20]

Research also indicates that attitude changes caused by issue-relevant arguments are better predictors of behavior than changes initiated by cues that are not issue-relevant.[21]

The strength and number of your arguments are important. When a message had high relevance, three strong arguments were more persuasive than three weak ones and were just as persuasive as a combination of the three strong and three weak arguments. When a message had low relevance for listeners, however, three strong arguments were no more persuasive than three weak arguments. But a combination of the three strong and three weak arguments were more persuasive than either of the three argument messages.[22]

There is an interaction between the number and strength of the arguments and the likability of the speaker. When a message with low relevance was presented by a likable source using one strong argument, it was significantly more persuasive than a message using five strong arguments presented by a dislikable source. When the message had high relevance, however, the dislikable source using five strong arguments was significantly more persuasive than the likable source using one strong argument.[23]

The personal relevance of an issue affects listeners' reactions to arguments. When the personal relevance of an issue was ambiguous for listeners, an increase in the number of sources presenting strong arguments strengthened persuasion, but an increase in the number of sources presenting weak arguments lessened the persuasive impact.[24]

The repetition of strong arguments has a positive effect on their acceptance. When a persuasive message using strong arguments was repeated to listeners three times, hearers developed more favorable thoughts and revealed more attitude change, while those hearing the message using weak arguments conceived more unfavorable thoughts and showed less attitude change.[25]

To maximize the impact of your case, therefore, do the following: (1) Make clear the importance and personal relevance of your message in order to increase its persuasiveness. (2) When your topic has high relevance for your hearers, use the strongest possible arguments to support your position. When your topic has low relevance for your listeners, use all the arguments you can find. Remember, one person's weak argument is another person's strong argument. (3) Repeat your arguments at least three times.

Use the Foot-in-the-Door Technique

This peripheral route procedure involves asking someone to do you a favor, and then later requesting that person to do you a larger favor. Freedman and Fraser first confirmed that this process worked.[26] Seligman, Bush, and Kirsch demonstrated that the first request should not be too small, however. They varied the size of the first request and discovered that "the greatest compliance" with the second request resulted from "the largest sized first requests."[27] The reasoning is that once a person has done you a small favor, he has made a commitment which induces him to feel obligated to respond favorably to the second request, provided it is not too small or too large. Suppose, for example, you want to ask a neighbor to contribute to The United Way, for which you are soliciting. You might ask the neighbor to do a small sixty-minute typing job as a contribution to The United Way. After the typing job has been completed, you go back and explain that The United Way still has unmet needs because of a lack of money. Then you ask her to give a $100 contribution to The United Way. The chances are very good that because of the small commitment of sixty minutes to do the typing job, the person will feel obligated to comply with the larger request and give the hundred dollars.

How can you use this in a speech? Let's say you are going to ask the members of the PTA at your local school to contribute funds to pay for off-duty police to direct traffic at key intersections for an hour before school starts in the morning and an hour after school ends in the afternoon. Very early in your speech, you ask for a show of hands of those who feel that there are not sufficient safeguards for school children at key traffic intersections and would be willing to sign a petition expressing that concern. Then at the end of your speech, you tell the people that you have petitions for them to sign, but you think more needs to be done. You then ask them to contribute $100 each to help pay for the off-duty police who must be hired to serve as traffic guards. There should be a tendency for those raising their hands at the beginning to comply with this larger request for funds.

Burgoon and Bettinghaus suggest the following message strategies when using the foot-in-the-door method of obtaining compliance:

1. The initial request must obtain compliance and must be clearly smaller than later requests.
2. The initial request must be "of sufficient magnitude to trigger self-perceptions that commit the person to future compliance."
3. Another person can make the second request and sometimes be more successful in obtaining compliance than the person making the first request.[28]

This technique must be used with great care. Your credibility can be destroyed if listeners get the impression that you are trying to manipulate them.

<table>
<tr><td>Use the Door-in-the-Face Technique</td><td>This peripheral method of gaining compliance works in the opposite way from the foot-in-the-door procedure. Cialdini, et al., conceived the idea of making the first request so extreme that the recipient would reject it. Following rejection, a more moderate request is presented. It is imperative, however, that the person making the first request also make the second request because the recipient must perceive concession by the requester. This is crucial "in producing compliance with the smaller request." If the receiver does perceive concession on the part of the requester, however, then compliance by the receiver will occur.[29]</td></tr>
</table>

Using the example of the traffic guards for school children, we can see that the door-in-the-face procedure works in the opposite way. Instead of asking the parents to a sign a petition at the beginning, the speaker would ask them to give $1,000 each to pay for the intersection guards. After she had discussed the advantages of having the guards and explained how they would operate, she would say: "It is not fair of me to ask you to give $1,000 each. I think $100 per family would be fairer. We will just have to get the rest of the money to pay for this project from other sources." This concession should provoke reciprocal concessions from the listeners.

Burgoon and Bettinghaus suggest the following strategies for the door-in-the-face procedure:

1. The initial request must be sufficiently large that the receivers do not perceive its rejection "as a reflection of their attitudes." Moreover, "the request must not be so large as to make rejection reasonable."
2. The first request must be rejected and the second request must be "unambiguously smaller" than the first one.
3. The first request "must not be so large and absurd as to evoke hostility," or there will be no compliance.

4. The speaker must be perceived as offering concessions or there will be no compliance. Because concessions are required, the same speaker must make both requests.
5. "The second requests do not have to be small or trivial, but must be perceived as smaller than the first request."[30]

Using the door-in-the-face technique can destroy your credibility if your listeners perceive that you are trying to manipulate them.

Show that Desired Behavior Is Approved by Esteemed Person or Group

Adopting behavior derived from another person or group because the behavior is associated with a satisfying self-defining relationship to the person or group has been labeled "identification."[31] Use of this peripheral cue begins at an early age. Children adopt the behavior and attitudes of their parents because of their affection for them. But the practice doesn't end with childhood; it continues throughout our lives. Freshmen on a college campus learn very quickly what behavior and attitudes are in vogue at the moment and quickly acquire them for their own. The peer group can be even more influential for college students than an expert in a given field. One study found, for example, that "college students' judgments of language usage were not affected as much by standards attributed to an expert in language as by those attributed to other students."[32]

Kelley and Woodruff presented a recorded speech challenging the validity of modern teaching methods to different groups of students at a teachers' college. The recording included applause at seven important places in the speech. One group of students was informed that the speech had been recorded earlier at their school, thus implying that the applause, indicating a favorable response, had come from members of their own college faculty and community. The other group of students were led to believe that the hearers applauding were not members of their own college community. The speech caused attitude change in the desired direction for both groups, but the change was greater where students thought the applause came from "prestigeful" members of their own college community.[33]

Show that Your Proposal Is Consistent or Inconsistent with a Value Premise

If you can demonstrate that your proposal is consistent with a value premise held by your listeners, that will act as a peripheral cue and enhance the possibility of their accepting that proposal. Thus, because most Americans value efficiency, you may claim a new governmental program is efficient. On the other hand, because most Americans dislike inefficiency, opponents may argue that the proposed program is inefficient.

DiVesta and Merwin indicated the importance of a value premise to an attitude when they attempted to change the attitudes of a group of students toward teaching as a career. Choosing as the value premise the students' need for achievement, they presented to one group a communication arguing that teaching would facilitate satisfaction of the need for achievement, to a second group a communication arguing that teaching would not facilitate satisfaction of the need for achievement, and to a third group a communication on the topic "Going to College." The positive and negative messages on the ability of teaching to satisfy the need for achievement caused corresponding changes in the students' appraisal of teaching as a means of facilitating achievement. Although the support was not sufficient "to be considered conclusive," a questionnaire indicated parallel changes of attitude toward a teaching career.[34]

Observe how George A. Stinson, chairman of the board of National Steel Corporation, stressed value premises held by his listeners at the Mountain State Forest Festival, Elkins, West Virginia:

I said earlier that I wanted to call this talk, "Take me Home, Country Road," because I believe that in the sixties and seventies the nation sometimes strayed away from some fundamental concepts that have made our country strong from its beginnings. There is no doubt in my mind that the most fundamental factor which has made America great has been its commitment to high moral and ethical principles and values. Democracy has worked because we believe in our Bill of Rights which strikes one central theme and that is individual freedom.

But individual freedom doesn't work unless it is supported by economic freedom—freedom to hold a job, to start a business, to save our money, and generally to participate in a sound economic system. This lies at the heart of our superb standard of living, our strength as a nation to be the leader of the worldwide family of nations, and the general sense of well-being which our citizens have always enjoyed.[35]

Whatever value premise you choose to use, you will want to be sure it is one held by your particular group of listeners. One of the causes of communication difficulties between older and younger generations is that each bases its proposals on values they cherish rather than on values the other group cherishes.

Appeal to an Alternative Value Premise

This may serve as an issue-relevant argument or as a peripheral cue. It is an issue-relevant argument if you attempt to show that a currently held value premise is not adequate to cope with contemporary conditions, that new times demand new values. Ecologists in recent years have argued that the esteem of a community for industrial growth is not a realistic value premise for the future. Consequently, they suggest that we replace that value premise with an alternative one that has respect and concern for conserving the environment. Many educators have long held the opinion that knowledge for its own sake was an adequate value premise on which to base our educational system. Today young people reject that value premise and argue that a more meaningful value premise on which to base educational processes is preparation for a career.

In the following excerpt, the speaker, A. E. Jones, immediate past president of the International Federation of Purchasing and Materials Management, attempts to create support for international trade by linking it with peace and civilization:

If I had to limit myself to one single issue, one single cause to which we in purchasing are most ideally positioned to contribute, there is no doubt in my mind that the cause would be that of peace. The one common goal of ours, of business and industry in general, of all mankind, is world peace.

Peace and trade are preconditions of one another. The nations of the world are all in the same business of buying and selling. Since World War II the volume of world exports has increased by about 800 percent. It is a common fact that international trade increases the standard of living for all countries and that all industries are stimulated by trade. There is no country in the world today that is entirely self-sufficient. Nor is there any nation lacking in resources, goods, or services needed by other nations.

Trade, my friends, is a mutually beneficial enterprise and one of the oldest forms of international communication. It has been said that trade "is the great civilizer. We exchange ideas when we exchange fabrics." Trade is certainly one of the most persuasive reasons for nations to find political accommodation.[36]

It is a peripheral cue if you simply claim that an alternative value premise should be adopted.

Every individual has had fear used on him as a peripheral cue at sometime in his life. What child hasn't been told: "If you're not good, Santa Claus won't come to see you." Fear is an issue-relevant argument, however, when we buy traveler's checks because we fear the consequences of carrying a large sum of money and losing it.

Arouse Fear in Listeners

John C. Lawn, Drug Enforcement Administrator, alerted his listeners to the fearful consequences of drug use:

"Another drug phenomenon we see is what the media has termed, 'designer drugs.' I don't like that name because in our society the term 'designer' has a positive connotation, and these drugs are so potent, so dangerous, the last thing we need to do is make them sound more glamorous.

These synthetic analogs of controlled substances kill and cripple for life. To help you understand how potent they can be, imagine that a heroin dose would be about the size of an aspirin tablet. To get the equivalent dosage of the heroin analog, fentanyl, one would need much less than one grain of salt. Fentanyl can be between 150 to 1,000 times stronger than heroin. These controlled substance analogs have killed several hundred people, mostly in California, and have left countless others permanently disabled with symptoms that resemble Parkinson's disease.

The continuing bad news is cocaine. We have an epidemic enveloping our country today. Last year, consumption rose 11 percent. Cocaine-related hospital emergencies increased 51 percent in one year. Deaths caused by cocaine abuse have increased by 325 percent since 1980.

. . . And there is also the correlation between cocaine abuse, chronic depression and, ultimately, suicide. Overall, 37 percent of those calling into the hotline believed that their only salvation to their cocaine addiction was suicide, and 9 percent had actually tried to kill themselves. In our country life expectancy has increased substantially for all age groups. That is, except for one—teenagers. Illicit drugs and alcohol are, in great part, responsible."[37]

There is no doubt that fear influences our attitudes and behavior. On the basis of the experimental work done so far, the primary question seems to be: How much fear can a persuader safely induce in listeners? The first study in this area, conducted by Janis and Feshbach, unpredictably showed strong fear arousal to be less effective than moderate or low fear arousal. They presented messages stressing the importance of brushing one's teeth three times a day, after each meal. Subjects were assigned to four groups: a strong fear group, a moderate fear group, a minimal fear group, and a control group that heard a lecture on another topic. Questionnaires administered a week later clearly showed that the greatest effect had been produced by the minimal fear arousal.[38]

Because of this study, persuaders were for many years advised to avoid strong fear arousal. In recent years, however, a number of studies have produced contradictory results. One of the weaknesses with the Janis and Feshbach study was that it did not depend upon observation of actual behavior, but instead relied upon an expression of verbal behavior. Using observed behavior, Dabbs and Leventhal found different results. They presented persuasive messages—with strong, moderate, and weak fear appeals—to college students asking them to get tetanus shots. University records were used to discover how many actually got inoculated in the next month. Almost twice as many of those hearing the strong fear message got the shot as did those hearing the moderate fear communication. And nearly four times as many of the strong fear recipients got the shot as did those in the control group.[39]

A study of adults by Leventhal and Niles produced essentially the same results. A message presented the relationship between smoking and lung cancer to a low fear group, a moderate fear group, and a high fear group. A message with a different level of fear appeal presented the relationship between smoking and lung cancer to each group. All subjects were recommended to have an X-ray taken in adjacent facilities and to initiate a program to stop smoking. There was no difference in the number of people in the high and moderate fear groups who had the X-ray examination made. Fewer of the low fear subjects, however, had X-rays made. Moreover, questionnaires given to all subjects after the communication provided data that indicated a positive relationship between the strength of the induced fear and expressed intention to adopt one or both of the proposed measures.[40]

In a similar experiment Leventhal and Watts got slightly contradictory results. A majority of subjects receiving a strong fear arousal message did not have X-rays taken, although they reported more success in stopping smoking than those subjects receiving the mild fear arousal communication.[41] Leventhal speculates that the subjects behaved in this way because in the strong fear arousal condition the X-ray became an unattractive behavioral alternative, since it might reveal the need for surgery. Giving up smoking, however, though still unpleasant, was less threatening than surgery.[42]

Haefner replicated the original Janis and Feshbach experiment exactly and obtained opposite results: the high fear arousal message was more effective in changing attitudes than the mild fear message.[43]

Hewgill and Miller speculated that there would be an interaction between credibility of the source and level of fear arousal in the message. They hypothesized that a high-credibility source using a high fear message would cause more attitude change than a high-credibility source using a low fear message. On the other hand, they theorized that a low-credibility source using a low fear message would cause more attitude change than a low-credibility source using a high fear message. The results revealed that "the high fear message was clearly more effective than the low fear message for the high-credibility source, but there was no difference for the low-credibility source."[44]

A number of other recent experiments have found the high fear arousal message to be more effective than a low fear message.[45] Leventhal, who has done more work with persuasion and fear than anyone else, has concluded that when attitude change does not result from a high fear message, it is frequently because the subject feels incapable of coping with the danger.[46]

The most recent evidence indicates that you need have no concern about the amount of fear you arouse in listeners, provided you offer a practical means of removing the cause of fear.

Offer a Reward or Incentive

This peripheral cue is frequently used as a motivating stimulus. In an attempt to find out whether eating food while reading persuasive communications would facilitate the changing of attitudes, Janis, Kaye, and Kirschner set up three experimental conditions: one in which subjects were given food while they read four persuasive messages; one in which there was no food; and one in which there was no food and the messages were on extraneous matters. The experimenter, who supplied the food, specifically said he did not endorse the communications. Without identifying them, however, he did acknowledge that he agreed with certain sections and disagreed with others. A second experiment added a fourth condition to the three above: a fourth group of students read the messages in a room in which a hidden bottle of butyric acid gave off an unpleasant odor. The experimenter denied any responsibility for the odor. When the two sets of data were combined, the authors found that three of the messages had shifted subjects' attitudes significantly more in the food condition than in the nonfood condition. The fourth message shifted the attitudes more in the food condition, but not significantly. The unpleasant odor in the second experiment had no effect on attitude change.[47]

There is disagreement on how much reward is most effective for changing attitudes. Those who favor the reinforcement theory for attitude change predict that attitude change will be positively correlated with the magnitude of the reinforcement.[48] On the other hand, Festinger and his followers claim (on the basis of their experimentation with the theory of cognitive dissonance) that the more reward a person is given for performing an undesirable act, the less he will change his attitudes. Festinger and Carlsmith demonstrated this when they had undergraduates perform repetitive, unpleasant laboratory tasks. Some of the students were then hired as assistants and paid $1 to tell a fellow student that the tasks were enjoyable and interesting. Other students were paid $20 to do the same thing. The authors postulated that the subjects receiving $1 would experience a great deal of dissonance because they had lied for such a small reward. To remove the dissonance, the subject would change his attitude toward the tasks. On the other hand, the subjects receiving $20 would experience little dissonance because they would feel amply repaid for lying. The results confirmed these predictions.[49]

On the other hand, Rosenberg devised an experiment in which subjects were paid either 50 cents, $1, or $5 to write counterattitudinal essays. The results showed that the subjects receiving $5 shifted their opinion significantly more than those receiving 50 cents.[50]

You can offer rewards to your listeners in various ways: show that the proposal will benefit the community; point out that it will positively affect loved ones of the listeners; explain that it will give an economic advantage to the listener.

William R. Miller, Vice Chairman, Bristol-Myers Company, pointed out to his audience the rewards coming to the elderly as a result of developments in pharmaceuticals:

Very soon now—long before we reach the twenty-first century—this tide of progress will spread beyond the scientific and medical communities where it began, to engage and affect the rest of us. For no one will this be more important . . . more rewarding . . . than the elderly. In fact, the medical and technological breakthroughs that lie ahead offer the only hope of materially alleviating the disabilities of arthritis, senility, cancer and mental disorder that, for so many, make living longer not a blessing but a bane—and an ever-heavier burden for their families and our society.

Along with enabling elderly people to *live*—in some full meaning of that word—rather than just exist, the new therapeutics should in the next century succeed in making a significant dent in the cost of their health care.[51]

Appeal to Motivating Factors

As both issue-relevant arguments and as peripheral cues, motives are to humans what spurs are to horses. They arouse and urge us to increasing levels of activity. They energize us to respond more readily and to adopt motive-related attitudes and behavior. In chapter 7 we considered Maslow's hierarchy of needs as factors to be considered in selecting a subject. Although Maslow's organization of needs is not wholly defensible, it is a helpful way of considering our motives. It is indisputable that those same needs serve as affective agents motivating people to adopt specific attitudes and behavior. To encourage support for your proposal, establish an affective relationship between it and as many of your listeners' needs as possible. Keep in mind, however, that all people are not motivated alike. Fortunately, you don't have to identify the many motivations. Remember that motives are internal; consequently, they have to be inferred by others. Identify unifying agents and use those. For example, people belong to organizations for varying reasons. Look at the different reasons people join a conservation group: some because of an altruistic desire to see conservation principles applied; some because it provides them an opportunity for leadership; some because it provides an opportunity for fellowship, an opportunity to associate with other people; some because they see the movement as providing protection and security for their family; some because it will advance their political aspirations; some for other reasons. You do not need to identify each of these motives in order to relate your proposal to a specific one, however. That would probably present an impossible task. You can relate to all these motivations by establishing a relationship between your proposal and conservation.

There may be times, nevertheless, when a single motivating factor must be identified and used. Following is a list of motivating factors. As you will notice if you try to organize them into Maslow's hierarchy of needs, most of them can be assigned to as many as four of the levels. One person may want wealth to satisfy safety needs, another to provide for the family he loves, another for the esteem it yields, and another because being wealthy is a self-actualizing need.

Persuasive Motives

Success	Strength	Competition	Love of family
Wisdom	Idealism	Cooperation	Social approval
Security	Curiosity	Conformity	Self-realization
Health	Pleasure	Adventure	Respect for diety
Status	Wealth	Recognition	Achievement
Fear	Pride	Acquisition	Superiority
Economy	Affection	Fellowship	Protection

This list is not intended to be exhaustive, but you can start with it to find motives that will move your particular group of hearers.

Provide Explicit Instructions on the Action Advocated

Frequently people are persuaded that a particular action is desirable or necessary, but they fail to perform the act. Evidence indicates that the peripheral cue of giving specific instructions on when, where, or how the action can be completed increases the likelihood that it will be done. Leventhal, Singer, and Jones attempted to induce fear of tetanus in subjects in order to get them to obtain shots. One group heard a high fear message, the other heard a moderate fear message. Half of each group was given specific instructions on when, where, and how they could obtain tetanus shots. The other half of each group was simply asked to get the shots. The experimenters found that significantly more of those receiving specific instructions obtained the shots, regardless of the fear level of the message.[52]

If you want a receiver or group of receivers to perform an action, therefore, explain specifically how it can be done.

One-Sidedness versus Two-Sidedness

After you have decided on the position you are going to advocate in a particular speech and have selected the main ideas to develop that position, decide whether you want to use a one-sided or a two-sided speech. A two-sided persuasive speech is not one in which you are neutral. It is not an objective presentation of arguments on both sides of an issue, with the listeners permitted to make up their minds which side to choose. In a two-sided speech, you present a series of arguments (pro) supporting the position you advocate. In addition, however, you present some major opposing arguments (con) and offer refutation of their validity. The one-sided speech discusses only those arguments supporting your position. Evidence indicates that on some occasions the one-sided approach is more advantageous, and on other occasions the two-sided approach is preferable.

One-Sided Approach

Experimental studies have indicated that there are four conditions under which the one-sided approach is more effective.

1. When members of the audience are already favorably disposed toward the communicator's position. Toward the end of World War II, Hovland, Lumsdaine, and Sheffield prepared two speeches; each of them argued that the war with Japan would be a long one, but one also included consideration of opposing arguments. Each was presented to a different group, with a third group serving as a control. Analysis revealed that of those who initially believed that the war with Japan would be long, the one-sided speech was far more effective in changing their position.[53]
2. When members of the audience are poorly educated. Hovland and colleagues discovered that the poorly educated members of the two experimental groups were more prone to shift opinion in the direction advocated by the speaker after hearing the one-sided speech than after hearing the two-sided speech.[54] One author cautions that we probably should not conclude that the one-sided presentation would be more

effective with an uneducated audience. He points out that listeners "were not allowed to talk to one another after" receiving the message "and before giving their own opinions nor did they get to hear someone argue that the message was wrong." In a normal situation the members of an audience have a chance to talk to other members and to hear the opinions of the educated and opposed.[55]

3. When members of the audience are required to commit themselves publicly after being exposed to a persuasive communication. Hovland, Campbell, and Brock developed two speeches (one favoring and one opposing) on giving eighteen-year-olds the right to vote. Each speech was given in the first sequence to one audience and in the reversed sequence to another audience. In each case before the hearers heard the second speech they were asked to write an essay "presenting their frank opinions on the issue after the first communication." The subjects were told that these essays were going to be bound and circulated among their teachers and classmates. They were asked to sign their name exactly as they wished it to appear in the pamphlet. Each speech was also given in the first and second situation to two other audiences. Again the subjects were asked to write an essay, but this time they were told that the papers would be anonymous, and they were explicitly told not to sign their names. Examination of the results revealed that the subjects who thought they were publicly committing themselves responded less to the second communication than those who thought their commitment remained anonymous.[56]

4. When comprehension of the speaker's conclusion is important. One group of investigators obtained comprehension scores from subjects after they had heard either a one-sided or two-sided speech. The results showed that the "one-sided presentations tended to produce greater comprehension of the speaker's conclusion."[57]

Two-Sided Approach

The two-sided presentation is sometimes more effective than the one-sided in changing attitudes. Insko presented to groups of students a summary of the prosecution and defense arguments from a fictitious trial. Each position was presented as a one-sided case and as part of a two-sided case. In the two-sided version each position was presented in both the first and second sequence. The results showed that those students hearing the two-sided presentation, regardless of which side was presented first, changed their attitudes more than those hearing the one-sided presentation.[58] Specifically, the two-sided presentation has been found to be more effective in three situations.

1. When the audience is well educated. The more highly educated person, when coupled with the two-sided speech, overrides the disadvantage of the listener's initial position. The two-sided communication is "more effective among the better educated regardless of initial position."[59]

2. When the audience initially disagrees with the speaker's position. In this situation, the two-sided presentation is more effective in changing the listeners' opinions.[60]

3. When the audience will be exposed later to counterpersuasion. Lumsdaine and Janis presented to groups of college students one-sided and two-sided versions of an alleged radio program to the effect that the Soviet Union would not soon be able to produce atomic arms in quantity. Both versions produced a net change of opinion in the desired direction in excess of 60 percent. When all subjects were then exposed to a communication expressing the opposite point of view, an interesting thing happened. The net change dropped to 2 percent among those originally hearing the one-sided speech, whereas the net change remained above 60 percent for those who originally heard the two-sided speech.[61]

The two-sided speech has an immunizing effect; it inoculates the listener against subsequent counterpersuasion.

Organization of a Persuasive Speech

Persuasive speeches, like informative speeches, generally have an introduction, thesis, body, and conclusion. Nevertheless, there are some important differences in organizing a persuasive speech.

Introduction

Any of the types of introductions discussed in chapter 11 are appropriate for a persuasive speech. Probably the most important purpose of the introduction, however, is to ensure that the speaker has maximum ethos with the listeners. Too many studies have demonstrated that persuasion is dependent upon the speaker's ethos for this vital purpose to be slighted. This is not to imply, however, that the other purposes of the introduction—to get the listeners' attention and to lead them into the subject—are unimportant or should be ignored. And in cases where the speaker's ethos is no problem, one of the other purposes may assume the greatest importance.

Thesis

In most cases you should state your purpose explicitly in the speech: "This morning I want to persuade you that . . ." "My purpose tonight is to get you to agree with me that. . . ."

On other occasions, because of strong hostility of the listeners, you may use what is called the *implicative* method. The thesis is never stated. In some cases even the main points are left unstated. The theory is that the evidence and supporting materials will lead the listener to infer your purpose. Unfortunately, research has indicated that without clear statement of the thesis, the listener frequently fails to draw the conclusion desired.

If hostility from the listeners is indeed a severe problem, a *deferred thesis* method may be used. In this case, the explicit statement of the thesis is not made until after all the arguments and supporting materials have been presented. Then the speaker says explicitly, "My purpose tonight has been to persuade you that . . ." "After hearing these arguments, I hope you will agree with me that. . . ."

The *deferred thesis* method is preferable to the *implicative* method on both practical and ethical bases. It ensures both that the listeners will not draw a "wrong" conclusion from the speech and that there will be no doubt about where you stand.

The body of a persuasive speech may be organized in almost any of the ways discussed in chapter 10. Some patterns of organization, however, are more appropriate for persuasive speeches, including the motivated sequence, the problem-solution, and the causal patterns. Two other methods especially suited to persuasive speaking also need to be considered at this point. **Body**

Organizing a one-sided speech In many persuasive speeches, you have a series of arguments for or against a particular proposal. The stock patterns—such as time, space, or cause-effect—are then inappropriate. You must decide which is preferable: to put the strongest argument first (use an anticlimax order); to put the strongest argument last (use a climax order); or to put the strongest argument in the middle (use a pyramidal order). In communication theory, if the anticlimax order is more effective, we call it a primacy effect; if the climax order is more effective, we call it a recency effect. Unfortunately, the issue of primacy-recency is a complex one that is dependent upon a number of factors. The relevancy of primacy-recency also is affected by whether you are concerned with attitude change or with the listener's retention of ideas. These effects must be considered separately, in light of the conclusion by Berlo and Gulley that change of attitude is not related to recall of assertions or evidence.[62]

Relatively few of the studies concerned with the primacy-recency issue have used only one-sided speeches. Most of the studies that have used only a one-sided speech have been concerned with measuring the impact of argument position on retention rather than on attitude change. More studies have found that recency significantly improves retention than have found that primacy has this effect.[63]

None of the studies has found any one order of presentation of one-sided speeches more effective than any other in changing listeners' attitudes.[64]

Organizing a two-sided speech Once you have decided to use the two-sided approach, you must decide on the order of the pro and con arguments. Janis and Feieraband first turned experimental attention to this problem, presenting to high school students a speech that developed pro and con arguments urging them to volunteer for their local Civil Defense Organization. Some heard the speech with the pro arguments first, others heard it with con arguments first. The results revealed that those exposed to the pro arguments first accepted the conclusions of the message significantly more than those exposed to the con arguments first.[65]

Recent evidence suggests that your credibility also becomes an important consideration. Rea established the credibility level for a number of speakers. He then presented a speech attributed to a speaker of high credibility to one group using a pro-con sequence and to another group using a con-pro sequence. He next had the same speech attributed to a speaker of low credibility presented to one group in the pro-con sequence and to another group in the con-pro sequence. He discovered that for the speech attributed to the high-credibility source, the pro-con sequence was more effective in shifting opinion. For the speech attributed to the low-credibility source, the con-pro sequence was more effective in shifting opinion. Another interesting finding was that the pro-con sequence, when attributed to the low-credibility source, tended to produce a boomerang effect, increasing the number of subjects moving away from the position advocated by the communicator.[66]

Apparently, when you have high credibility, the audience is ready to believe anything you say that seems credible, so they are affected more by your first arguments. But when you have low credibility, the listeners are less prone to believe you until you have done something to give them a reason to believe you. The fact that you present con arguments before pro arguments probably convinces the listener that you have sufficient objectivity and devotion to "truth" to make your pro arguments more credible when they come last in the body of the speech. You must determine your level of credibility with a particular audience, then, in order to decide which sequence to use in developing a two-sided presentation.

Conclusion

Although any of the types of conclusions discussed in chapter 11 are appropriate for a persuasive speech, some are used more frequently than others. Especially apt are conclusions that summarize, make an appeal for action, or present a challenge that stimulates the listeners. Obviously, you must focus on the main purpose of your speech in the conclusion, but it is equally important to leave your ethos high with the listeners.

Summary _____

Coercion is an undesirable alternative to persuasion because, first, its success is dependent upon force or power, and, second, the person may not be committed to the position to which he is coerced.

Persuasion, on the other hand, permits an individual voluntarily to adopt a position, results in a stronger commitment to that position, and provides a nonviolent method for influencing others.

Persuasion may be defined as the process whereby an attempt is made to induce changes in attitudes and behavior through involvement of a person's cognitive and affective processes.

Changing the attitudes of listeners is not easy; it is made more difficult by a number of potential obstacles that may deter or weaken attitude change. Accumulated evidence indicates that (1) forewarning of persuasive intent can sometimes prevent change, (2) selective perception can sometimes operate to the detriment of attitude change, (3) selective recall of the message can interfere with change, (4) selective exposure to the communication on the part of at least some can deter change, (5) the degree to which a person is committed to an attitude determines resistance to change,

(6) public commitment increases the likelihood of resistance to change, (7) the amount of discrepancy between the speaker and listener affects resistance to change, and (8) group pressure on the listener may prevent change.

Despite the obstacles known to exist, much evidence has been accumulated from observation and empirical studies to show that attitude change does occur. At least six methods are available: (1) build a case with evidence and reasoning; (2) show that the desired behavior is approved by an esteemed person or by the reference group; (3) show that the proposal is consistent or inconsistent with a value premise of the hearer; (4) appeal to an alternative value premise; (5) arouse fear in the listeners; (6) offer reward or incentive to the hearers; (7) appeal to motivating factors; (8) provide explicit instructions on action advocated.

You will have to decide whether to present a one-sided or two-sided development of your arguments. Research has indicated that the one-sided approach is more effective in four instances: when members of the audience are already favorably disposed toward your position; when members of the audience are poorly educated; when listeners are required to commit themselves publicly following the speech; when comprehension of your conclusion is important. The two-sided development is more effective when the audience is well educated, when it initially disagrees with your position, or when it will be exposed later to counterpersuasion.

Persuasive speeches, like informative ones, generally have an introduction, thesis, body, and conclusion. Sometimes you should either leave the thesis unstated or defer it to the end of the speech.

Exercises

1. Prepare a six-minute persuasive speech in which you use fear arousal as your primary method of attempting to change the attitudes of your listeners. Explain in a brief paragraph specifically how you plan to remove the cause of the fear.
2. Read a persuasive speech in the current issue of *Vital Speeches*. Identify the methods the speaker uses to attempt to change the listeners' attitudes. Evaluate the speaker's use of those methods. How would you have handled them differently?
3. Attend a persuasive speech in the community. Identify the obstacles to changing attitudes with which the speaker had to cope. Describe the method by which he or she successfully dealt with them. If the speakers were unsuccessful in coping with any, explain why. Explain how you would have done it differently.
4. Think of a value held by the people in your community. Explain how you could use that value to attempt to change their attitude toward a social problem on which you have a different attitude.
5. Select one method of changing attitudes that you will use in your next speech. Explain in detail, including specific supporting material, how you will use that method.

1. A. Huxley, "Notes on Propaganda," *Harper's,* December 1936, p. 36.
2. P. F. Lazarsfeld, B. Berelson, and H. Gaudet, *The People's Choice* (New York: Columbia University Press, 1968), pp. xxiii, 65–66; B. Berelson, P. F. Lazarsfeld, and W. N. McPhee, *Voting: A Study of Opinion Formation in a Presidential Election* (Chicago: University of Chicago Press, 1954), p. 23; T. W. Benham, "Polling for a Presidential Candidate: Some Observations of the 1964 Campaign," *Public Opinion Quarterly* 29 (1965):185–99.
3. H. H. Kelley, "Attribution Theory in Social Psychology," in *Nebraska Symposium on Motivation,* ed. D. Levine (Lincoln, Neb.: University of Nebraska Press, 1967).
4. E. McGinnies and L. Rosenbaum, "A Test of the Selective-Exposure Hypothesis in Persuasion," *Journal of Psychology* 61 (1965):237–40.
5. J. Mills, *Experimental Social Psychology* (London: Macmillan & Co., 1969), p. 138.
6. A. Lowin, "Approach and Avoidance: Alternative Modes of Selective Exposure to Information," *Journal of Personality and Social Psychology* 6 (1967):1–9.
7. C. W. Sherif and M. Sherif, *Attitude, Ego-Involvement and Change* (New York: John Wiley & Sons, 1967), pp. 134–35; C. W. Sherif, M. Sherif, and R. E. Nebergall, *Attitude and Attitude Change* (Philadelphia: W. B. Saunders Co., 1965), pp. 168–97.
8. P. Tannenbaum, "Initial Attitude toward Source and Concept as Factors in Attitude Change through Communication," *Public Opinion Quarterly* 20 (1956):425.
9. H. H. Kelley and E. H. Volkart, "The Resistance to Change of Group-Anchored Attitude Change through Communication," *Public Opinion Quarterly* 20 (1956):425.
10. C. I. Hovland, E. H. Campbell, and T. Brock, "The Effects of 'Commitment' on Opinion Change Following Communication," in *Order of Presentation in Persuasion,* ed. C. I. Hovland (New Haven: Yale University Press, 1957), pp. 23–32.
11. C. I. Hovland and H. Pritzker, "Extent of Opinion Change as a Function of Amount of Change Advocated," *Journal of Abnormal and Social Psychology* 54 (1957):257–61.
12. Sherif et al., *Attitude and Attitude Change,* p. 24.
13. J. Freedman, "Involvement, Discrepancy, and Change," *Journal of Abnormal and Social Psychology* 69 (1964):290–95.
14. J. Whittaker, "Attitude Change and Communication-Attitude Discrepancy," *Journal of Social Psychology* 65 (1965):141–47.
15. E. Aronson, J. Turner, and J. M. Carlsmith, "Communicator Credibility and Communication Discrepancy as Determinants of Opinion Change," *Journal of Abnormal and Social Psychology* 67 (1963):31–36.
16. C. A. Insko, *Theories of Attitude Change* (New York: Appleton-Century-Crofts, 1967), p. 348.
17. S. E. Asch, *Social Psychology* (New York: Prentice-Hall, 1952), pp. 450–501.
18. Richard E. Petty and John T. Cacioppo, "The Elaboration Likelihood Model of Persuasion," *Advances in Experimental Social Psychology,"* Vol. 19 (New York: Academic Press, 1986), p. 128. Used by permission. Hereafter referred to as Petty and Cacioppo, 1986.

19. Petty and Cacioppo, 1986, pp. 175, 186–87. See also J. Crocker, S. T. Fiske, and S. E. Taylor, "Schematic Bases of Belief Change," in *Attitudinal Judgment,* ed. R. Eiser (New York: Springer-Verlag, 1984). W. J. McGuire, "The Probabilogical Model of Cognitive Structure and Attitude Change," in *Cognitive Responses in Persuasion,* eds. R. E. Petty, T. M. Ostrom, and T. C. Brock (Hillsdale, New Jersey: Erlbaum, 1981).

20. Petty and Cacioppo, 1986, p. 176.

21. Ibid, p. 179.

22. R. E. Petty and J. T. Cacioppo, "The Effects of Involvement on Responses to Argument Quantity and Quality: Central and Peripheral Routes to Persuasion," *Journal of Personality and Social Psychology* 46 (1984): 69–81. See also, William L. Benoit, "Argumentation and Credibility Appeals in Persuasion," *The Southern Speech Communication Journal* 52 (1987):181–97.

23. S. Chaiken, "Heuristic Versus Systematic Information Processing and the Use of Source Versus Message Cues in Persuasion," *Journal of Personality and Social Psychology* 39 (1980):752–56. See also R. Rhine and L. Severance, "Ego-Involvement, Discrepancy, Source Credibility, and Attitude Change," *Journal of Personality and Social Psychology,* 16 (1970):175–90.

24. S. G. Harkins and R. E. Petty, "The Effects of Source Magnification of Cognitive Effort on Attitudes: An Information Processing View," *Journal of Personality and Social Psychology* 40 (1981):401–13. See also Petty and Cacioppo, 1986, p. 189.

25. J. T. Cacioppo and R. E. Petty, "Central and Peripheral Routes to Persuasion: The Role of Message Repetition," in *Psychological Processes and Advertising Effects,* eds., A. Mitchell and L. Alwitt (Hillsdale, N.J.: Erlbaum, 1985). See also Petty and Cacioppo, 1986, pp. 143–44.

26. J. L. Freedman and S. C. Fraser, "Compliance Without Pressure: The Foot-in-the-Door Technique," *Journal of Personality and Social Psychology* 33 (1976):520.

27. C. Seligman, M. Bush, and K. Kirsch, "Relationship between Compliance in the Foot-in-the-Door Paradigm and Size of First Request," *Journal of Personality and Social Psychology* 33 (1976):517–20. Used by permission.

28. M. Burgoon and E. P. Bettinghaus, "Persuasive Message Strategies," pp. 155–59 in *Persuasion: New Directions in Theory and Research,* edited by M. E. Roloff and G. R. Miller (Beverly Hills, Calif.: Sage Publications Inc., 1980). Copyright © 1980. Reprinted by permission of Sage Publications, Inc.

29. R. B. Cialdini, J. E. Vincent, S. K. Lewis, J. Catalan, D. Wheeler, and B. L. Darby, "Reciprocal Concessions Procedure for Inducing Compliance: The Door-in-the-Face Technique," *Journal of Personality and Social Psychology* 31 (1975):206–15. Used by permission.

30. Burgoon and Bettinghaus, op. cit., pp. 157–59.

31. H. C. Kelman, "Compliance, Identification, and Internalization: Three Processes of Attitude Change," *Journal of Conflict Resolution* 2 (1958):51–60.

32. M. Sherif and C. I. Hovland, *Social Judgment* (New Haven: Yale University Press, 1961), pp. 89–90.

33. H. H. Kelley and C. Woodruff, "Members' Reactions to Apparent Group Approval of a Counter-Norm Communication," *Journal of Abnormal and Social Psychology* 52 (1956):67–74.

34. F. J. DiVesta and J. C. Merwin, "The Effects of Need-Oriented Communications on Attitude Change," *Journal of Abnormal and Social Psychology* 60 (1960):80–85.

35. G. A. Stinson, "What's Right with America," *Vital Speeches of the Day* 46 (1979):88.

36. A. E. Jones, "World Peace through World Purchasing," *Vital Speeches of the Day* 46 (1979):91.

37. J. C. Lawn, "Drugs in America," *Vital Speeches of the Day* 52 (1986):323. Used by permission.

38. I. L. Janis and S. Feshbach, "Effects of Fear-Arousing Communications," *Journal of Abnormal and Social Psychology* 48 (1953):78–92.

39. J. M. Dabbs, Jr., and H. Leventhal, "Effects of Varying the Recommendations in a Fear-Arousing Communication," *Journal of Personality and Social Psychology* 4 (1966):525–31.

40. H. Leventhal and P. Niles, "A Field Experiment on Fear Arousal with Data on the Validity of Questionnaire Measures," *Journal of Personality* 32 (1964):459–79.

41. H. Leventhal and J. C. Watts, "Sources of Resistance to Fear-Arousing Communications on Smoking and Lung Cancer," *Journal of Personality* 34 (1966):155–75.

42. H. Leventhal, "Fear Communications in the Acceptance of Preventive Health Practices," *Bulletin of the New York Academy of Medicine* 41 (1965):1144–68.

43. D. P. Haefner, "Arousing Fear in Dental Health Education," *Journal of Public Health Dentistry* 25 (1965–66):140–46.

44. M. A. Hewgill and G. R. Miller, "Source Credibility and Response to Fear-Arousing Communications," *Speech Monographs* 32 (1965):95–101.

45. F. A. Powell, "The Effect of Anxiety-Arousing Messages When Related to Personal, Familial, and Impersonal Referents," *Speech Monographs* 32 (1965):102–6; P. Niles, "The Relationship of Susceptibility and Anxiety to Acceptance of Fear-Arousing Communications," Ph.D. diss., Yale University, 1964, as cited in Mills, *Experimental Social Psychology,* p. 189; H. Leventhal and R. Singer, "Affect Arousal and Positioning of Recommendations in Persuasive Communication," *Journal of Personality and Social Psychology* 4 (1966):137–46; H. Leventhal, R. Singer, and S. Jones, "Effects of Fear and Specificity of Recommendation upon Attitudes and Behavior," *Journal of Personality and Social Psychology* 2 (1965):20–29. H. Leventhal, S. Jones, and G. Trembley, "Sex Differences in Attitude and Behavior Change under Conditions of Fear and Specific Instructions," *Journal of Experimental Social Psychology* 2 (1966):387–99; H. Leventhal, J. C. Watts, and F. Pagano, "Effects of Fear and Instructions on How to Cope with Danger," *Journal of Personality and Social Psychology* 6 (1967):313–21.

46. H. Leventhal, "Findings and Theory in the Study of Fear Communications," in *Advances in Experimental Social Psychology,* ed. L. Berkowitz, vol. 5. (New York: Academic Press, 1970), p. 120.

47. I. L. Janis, D. Kaye, and P. Kirschner, "Facilitating Effects of 'Eating-While-Reading' on Responsiveness to Persuasive Communications," *Journal of Personality and Social Psychology* 1 (1965):181–86.

48. Mills, *Experimental Social Psychology,* p. 213.

49. L. Festinger and J. M. Carlsmith, "Cognitive Consequences of Forced Compliance," *Journal of Abnormal and Social Psychology* 58 (1959):203–10.

50. M. Rosenberg, "When Dissonance Fails: On Eliminating Evaluation Apprehension from Attitude Measurement," *Journal of Personality and Social Psychology* 1 (1965):28–42.

51. W. R. Miller, "Pharmaceuticals for the Elderly," *Vital Speeches of the Day* 52 (1986):397–98. Used by permission.

52. H. Leventhal, R. Singer, and S. Jones, "Effects of Fear and Specificity of Recommendation upon Attitudes and Behavior," *Journal of Personality and Social Psychology* 2 (1965):20–29.

53. C. I. Hovland, A. A. Lumsdaine, and F. D. Sheffield, *Experiments on Mass Communication* (Princeton, N.J.: Princeton University Press, 1949), pp. 201–27. See also C. I. Hovland, I. L. Janis, and H. H. Kelley, *Communication and Persuasion* (New Haven: Yale University Press, 1968), pp. 105–8.

54. Hovland et al., *Communication and Persuasion,* pp. 105–8; Hovland et al., *Experiments on Mass Communication.*

55. Mills, *Experimental Social Psychology,* pp. 166–67.

56. Hovland et al., *The Order of Presentation in Persuasion,* pp. 23–32.

57. D. L. Thistlethwaite, J. Kemenetzky, and H. Schmidt, "Factors Influencing Attitude Change through Refutative Communications," *Speech Monographs* 23 (1956):20.

58. C. A. Insko, "One-Sided versus Two-Sided Communications and Counter Communications," *Journal of Abnormal and Social Psychology* 65 (1962):203–6.

59. Hovland et al., *Communication and Persuasion,* p. 108.

60. Ibid.

61. A. A. Lumsdaine and I. L. Janis, "Resistance to 'Counter-propaganda' Produced by One-Sided and Two-Sided 'Propaganda' Presentations," *Public Opinion Quarterly* 17 (1953):311–18.

62. D. K. Berlo and H. E. Gulley, "Some Determinants of the Effect of Oral Communication in Producing Attitude Change and Learning," *Speech Monographs* 24 (1957):18.

63. A. Jersild, "Modes of Emphasis in Public Speaking," *Journal of Applied Psychology* 12 (1928):611–20; R. Ehrensberger, "An Experimental Study of the Relative Effectiveness of Certain Forms of Emphasis in Public Speaking," *Speech Monographs* 12 (1945):94–111; H. Sponberg, "The Relative Effectiveness of Climax and Anti-Climax Order in an Argumentative Speech," *Speech Monographs* 13 (1946):35–44; H. Gilkinson, S. F. Paulsen, and D. E. Sikkink, "Effects of Order and Authority in an Argumentative Speech," *Quarterly Journal of Speech* 40 (1954):183–92; P. H. Tannenbaum, "Effect of Serial Position on Recall of Radio News Stories," *Journalism Quarterly* 31 (1954):319–23; Berlo and Gulley, "Some Determinants of the Effect of Oral Communication"; G. L. Culton, "The Effects of Speech Structure and Argument Strength on Audience Attitudes and Retention," M.A. thesis, Kansas State University, 1962.

64. Sponberg, "Relative Effectiveness of Climax"; Gilkinson et al., "Effects of Order and Authority"; Berlo and Gulley, "Some Determinants of the Effect of Oral Communication"; Culton, "Effects of Speech Structure."

65. I. L. Janis and R. L. Feieraband, "Effects of Alternative Ways of Ordering Pro and Con Arguments in Persuasive Communications," in *Order of Presentation in Persuasion,* pp. 115–28.

66. R. G. Rea, "An Experimental Study of Source Credibility and Order of Presentation in Persuasion," M.A. thesis, University of Arkansas, 1961.

18

SPEECHES FOR SPECIAL OCCASIONS

Speech of Introduction
Speech of Presentation
Speech to Commemorate
Speech to Entertain
Speech of Nomination

O ccasional speeches are given for special events and specific audiences. They are generally rather brief, only rarely more than five to ten minutes in length. They have many of the characteristics of other speeches, and they should possess the following specific attributes:

1. Clear, effective organization should make evident the unity of the ideas.
2. Careful preparation should be revealed in the development of the ideas, with various types of appropriate supporting material.
3. Brevity should be the hallmark of these speeches. Words should be used as though there were a limited supply available. Cut excess words ruthlessly.
4. Clarity of language must be foremost. In the short time available, every word must count and be clearly understood.
5. Interesting and attention-getting supporting materials must be used to develop the ideas.
6. Effective and attention-holding delivery is required.

Speech of Introduction

Objective The most common use of the speech of introduction is to present a person who is going to make a speech. But it is also used to present a newcomer to a community, a church, a social group, or any other organization. Specifically, your purpose is to create acceptance of the person being introduced and to give her name and identity. Your most important objective is to establish the credibility of the person you are presenting. If you do your job properly, the listeners will want to know the speaker's name and to hear what she has to say.

Main ideas The speech should discuss relevant personal characteristics of the person being introduced, such as education, experience, objectivity, goodwill, intelligence, and knowledge of subject. If you are introducing a speaker, you should point out the importance or significance of the subject of the speech.

You should make clear the purpose of the meeting if that is relevant or important. If the subject or the occasion of the speech is significant, you may want to acknowledge that fact and discuss briefly their special significance. If the choice of the speaker was determined by the specific subject or occasion, you will probably want to note that fact and explain why to the audience. If the speaker has specific qualifications—position, special capabilities—to talk on the subject, you may call that to the attention of the listeners.

If the size of the audience is unexpectedly or unusually large, you may call attention to that fact by congratulating the planners of the event or the members of the audience themselves. But you should never apologize for or criticize the smallness of the group.

You will want to call attention to the fact that this is a special occasion, if that is the case. This may be the first time the speaker has been back to this community since she graduated from high school twenty-five years ago. Or she may have just been selected as president of her company two weeks ago. Or perhaps this is the last time your group will meet at this location.

Do not apologize that the speaker is a substitute for a previously announced one. You may, however, announce that the expected speaker was unable to come and that this speaker was gracious enough to substitute. Avoid any comparisons of the two.

Supporting materials Supporting material should consist primarily of factual data, including such information as educational background, work experience, accomplishments, honors and awards, and personal achievements.

Various sources can be used to obtain information about the person you are introducing: newspaper articles, friends, and associates. In cases where the person has achieved a level of renown, you may consult biographical works, such as *Directory of American Scholars, Who's Who in America, Current Biography, Who's Who in Education, Who's Who Among Black Americans, Who's Who of American Women.* In some notable cases you may be able to consult a biography or an autobiography. If none of these sources is available, ask the speaker to provide information. You should also ask the speaker if there is anything special he wants mentioned.

Be sure the information you collect is accurate. Nothing is more embarrassing to both of you than for the speaker to have to correct something you have said. Give all the important information, but don't exaggerate or build the speaker up too much. That only creates an embarrassing situation for both of you. Don't say anything you don't mean sincerely.

Style Your language should be suited to the status of the speaker. In most cases, a plain style will be appropriate. This is language that is suitable for most daily communication. In some instances, the person you are introducing may be a dignitary or some accomplished individual. Then you will want to use a more formal and dignified style. In any case, use language that is clear and understandable to the listeners. Most importantly, when talking about the person being introduced, avoid superlatives; generally they only embarrass both the person and the listeners. Avoid any semblance of insincerity.

Organization One of two methods of organizing a speech is appropriate for a speech of introduction. You may organize the information in a chronological pattern (the high school years, the college years, the family years) or a topical pattern (accomplishments as a mother, contributions as a private citizen, services as a politician). Because it is such important information, put the name of the person and the subject of the speech at the end of the introduction. Then stop!

Delivery The delivery of the speech should be appropriate to the mood of the occasion. For an informal situation, the speech may be delivered more casually. For a formal event, the speech may be delivered from a manuscript or from memory, although it is preferable for you to deliver it extemporaneously. If you do use a manuscript, be sure you are sufficiently familiar with the material to be able to maintain much eye contact with the listeners. If your speech is memorized, be careful to maintain a conversational tone as you deliver your speech. It is imperative that the information in your speech be provided, so get it to the listeners in whatever way is appropriate. Don't forget to announce the title of the speech and the name of the speaker at the end of your introduction. Be especially careful to pronounce the speaker's name correctly!

Speech of Presentation

Objective The purpose of the speech of presentation is to give an award or a gift to people who are retiring, have completed a project of merit, are moving away, have earned an athletic letter, have performed some distinguished service, or for some other reason deserve recognition. The award tells the recipient that she has earned the esteem of the givers, and that those giving the award or gift want to express their appreciation for the recipient's efforts.

Main ideas Your speech should focus on the good qualities of the person receiving the gift or recognition, or explain the reasons for the person's recognition. Describe the award that is being given, and identify any symbolic values it might have. If it has certain intrinsic or extrinsic values, explain what they are. If a retiring colleague is being given a golf bag and a set of clubs, you might note that the gift has the extrinsic values of preventing boredom, providing enjoyment, enhancing physical well-being, and gently reminding the recipient of the genuine esteem his colleagues have for him.

If the award is from an organization, then mention it and explain why it is appropriate for that organization to give an award or recognition to this particular person. Tell why the presentation is being made. Try to summarize the sentiments of the organization or group that is giving the award. Make the recipient aware of the esteem that the group or organization has for him.

Praise for the person receiving the gift or recognition should be genuine, without becoming overly emotional. Some light humor can help to prevent the occasion from becoming maudlin. Overpraise, especially that which sounds insincere, can embarrass the recipient and the listeners.

If the award is one that has been given to others, you will probably want to remind your listeners of that fact. If the quality of former recipients will magnify the value of the award, you will probably want to recall their names and cite some of their deeds, especially if the listeners' silent comparison of the deeds will be favorable to the current recipient.

If the award has been won in competition with others and a few finalists were named, you should recognize them and congratulate them on their quality efforts.

Keep the focus, however, on the person and the occasion. Don't overstress the award or its value. The award is a symbol and its true value lies in the reason for bestowing it.

Supporting materials Specific examples demonstrating worthy qualities of the person receiving the award or gift should be highlighted. This information can be obtained from friends, competitors, neighbors, newspapers, and in some cases from books, periodical articles, and speeches.

Style Your language should be suited to the mood of the occasion, informal for a casual situation, formal for a ceremonial event. Your language should reflect the esteem and appreciation the organization has for the recipient's achievements and contributions. Figures of speech are appropriate for a formal occasion. Your words should be put together in a more rhythmical arrangement. You might read Lincoln's three formal occasional speeches—the First and Second Inaugurals and the Gettysburg Address—to understand the definite rhythm he develops. Understand, however, you are not doing this to emulate Lincoln's style, but to understand better the importance of rhythm in language. Your speech can be delivered extemporaneously, written and read from a manuscript, or presented from memory. If you deliver it other than extemporaneously, however, be sure you maintain adequate eye contact with the listeners.

Dignity, simplicity, and sincerity should be the characteristics of your language.

Organization The most appropriate pattern of organization will usually be a topical one, identifying as the main topics the qualities of the person or persons being recognized. In some instances, a causal pattern might be used, with the individual points identifying the causes that produced the effect, the award or recognition being presented.

Delivery Except for very unusual situations in which the ceremony is formal, the presentation will be delivered extemporaneously in a relaxed, informal manner. For a formal occasion, the speech may either be read from a manuscript or given from memory. If it is read, be sure that you know it well enough to give fairly long segments without looking at the manuscript. Be sure you maintain a conversational tone whether reading or giving from memory. The presentation should be easily heard by all listeners.

When the recipient comes forward for the gift or award, shake his hand first, then hand him the gift or award. Do not continue to clutch it after he has taken hold.

Speech to Commemorate

Objective The purpose of this type of speech is to observe anniversaries, dedicate new buildings or new projects, to eulogize the memory of a noted or beloved person, to inaugurate new programs or new administrations, or to celebrate a date in history (the end of the Civil War, the end of World War II, the passage of the Civil Rights Act).

Main ideas A commemorative speech should deal mainly with factual data. That factual data should be brought to life, however, by recalling specific achievements made possible by particular human efforts, major obstacles that were successfully overcome, and instrumental virtues demonstrated by key participants.

If you are commemorating an individual, avoid exaggerating his qualities and achievements. A more effective ploy might be to recall ways in which the person overcame his foibles, weaknesses, or deficiencies to achieve a constructive or noble objective. By all means, avoid controversial events, facts, or persons.

Supporting materials Sources of information to develop the ideas may be newspapers of the period involved, books, articles in periodicals, speeches of the period, and old-timers who lived in the area at the time the event occurred.

Style Facts should be presented as vividly as possible to aid in creating an inspirational mood. Language should be considered important and you should strive to achieve an eloquent style. Appropriate figures of speech should be used wherever possible.

Organization A topical or chronological pattern of organization to develop your main divisions will probably be best to let you focus on whatever main topics you desire. A straightforward chronological account may not be generally desirable, but one that focuses on the past, present, and future may be desirable and appropriate. The introduction should probably be a brief reference to the event being commemorated. The conclusion should focus on some challenging or inspirational feature of the object, person, or event you are remembering.

Delivery The physical presentation of the speech should be in keeping with the formality of the occasion. Physical action should be subdued, and the solemnity of the occasion should be reflected in the voice.

Speech to Entertain

Objective The primary objective of this speech is to make people enjoy themselves. It frequently occurs after a meal, which explains why it is sometimes called an after-dinner speech. This is a time when people are relaxed and content and not in the mood for a long discussion of serious issues or problems.

Main ideas This speech can draw its main ideas from almost any topic. Especially appropriate are the following topics: describing unusual experiences, telling a dramatic narrative, giving a travelogue (with or without color slides), recounting startling facts, or depicting a fantasy. Only very serious subjects have to be avoided.

Supporting materials The speech to entertain should utilize interest and attention by presenting novel, vivid, concrete, surprising, or suspenseful information. Examples can highlight ideas and serve as excellent supporting proofs. The speech rarely draws a moral or states a judgment, although it may

imply either. Humor is a frequently used type of supporting material, although it doesn't necessarily have to be, nor is it necessarily the best. If humor is used, however, it should be in good taste, tactful, and appropriate to the listeners and the occasion. It should not be barbed or malicious. The primary characteristics of humor should be exaggeration and the unexpected ending. You can also use understatement and satire for humorous effect. Humor doesn't even have to be funny in the sense that it is laugh-provoking. It can be the quiet kind of humor that causes a person to smile inside.

A series of unrelated jokes strung together do not constitute an entertaining speech. A comedian may be able to get away with that, but an entertaining speaker must have a theme and main points which at times can be developed in humorous or interesting ways.

Style Language should be the kind that highlights comparisons and contrasts. It should be colorful and specifically descriptive, using words that exaggerate comparisons and contrasts.

Organization Any pattern of organization can be used in an entertaining speech.

Delivery The entertaining speech should be delivered extemporaneously. Nothing spoils its effect more than seeing the speaker reading from a manuscript. Notes should not be used. If it is a humorous speech, it can be delivered with a deadpan expression or in a way that reveals the speaker's enjoyment with the material. If you are going to react to the humorous material, you must follow, not precede laughter of the listeners. Then be ready to resume your speech as soon as the listeners are ready. The speech should be brief.

Speech of Nomination

Objective This is a speech of praise that provides the reasons and justification for naming and supporting a particular candidate for a specific position. It is in reality a persuasive speech, because it attempts to convince the listeners that the object of the speech has the requisite qualities to perform ably the duties required of the position to be filled.

Main ideas The first thing you should do is discover and define the needs of the office. This may help you to ascertain, for example, that the holder of the position must deal with various types of people, must make a number of economic decisions, and must speak regularly to different groups. Then you can match the nominee's qualifications with those needs. You should make no comparisons, however, with other nominees.

Supporting materials The qualifications, experience, and achievements of the nominee will supply the supporting materials for your speech.

Sources of information will be newspapers, friends, teachers, employers, and family members of the nominee, and various biographical sources: *Directory of American Scholars, Who's Who in America, Current Biography, Who's Who in Education, Who's Who Among Black Americans, Who's Who of American Women.* You will probably also want to consult with the nominee.

Style The language of the speech should be energetic, colorful, descriptive, positive, and familiar.

Organization The topical pattern of organization allows you to focus on the demands of the position and the qualifications and the attributes of your nominee. You can also use a problem-solution pattern of organization, identifying the problems that have been unsolved in the past, then arguing that the solution is to elect your candidate whose qualifications would ensure that those problems would be solved successfully.

Delivery To be most effective, your speech should be delivered extemporaneously. Obviously, however, you would have to be sufficiently familiar with the nominee's background and qualifications to be able to speak with few notes. In this situation, a speech read from manuscript would be far less effective.

Exercises

1. Develop a 3–5 minute entertaining speech on one of the following topics: (a) the funniest professor I have had, (b) the most humorous date I have experienced, (c) the most exciting movie I have seen, (d) the most interesting book I have read.
2. Prepare a 3–5 minute speech introducing a classmate to the rest of the class. Using factual information, describe the background and achievements of the person.
3. Develop a 3–5 minute speech nominating a friend for an elective office in some campus organization, such as a fraternity or sorority, student government, or honor society.
4. Prepare a 3–5 minute speech presenting an award to a member of your class or to someone outside the class. Describe the good qualities of the person and explain the symbolic value of the award.

APPENDIX A
THE CRITICISM OF SPEECHES

*T*he statement "Speech finely framed delighteth the ears"[1] certainly epitomizes the result of a good speech and indicates that all hearers of a speech engage in speech criticism, whether they realize it or not.

The primary focus in this book is on the principles of oral communication to help you become a more effective oral communicator; throughout the speech course you are taking you will have a number of opportunities to use those principles in communicating with your classmates. Since the nature of the academic situation demands that you receive at the end of the term a grade that reflects the quality of your efforts, your professor will evaluate most of your speeches—generally in both written and oral forms. In many instances he will supplement those evaluations with those of student comments offered during oral critique sessions at the end of a group of speeches. Not uncommonly students will also be asked to furnish written criticisms. In other instances the professor will not evaluate the speeches himself, but will instead substitute ratings by the class members. These are known as "peer group" ratings and are increasingly being used on speech assignments in more and more classrooms. Because you will be involved in some form of speech criticism during the course, it is imperative that you learn how to criticize speeches in a meaningful way.

This section has five objectives: (1) to consider the reasons for learning to criticize speeches, (2) to examine the bases for criticizing a speech, (3) to establish the criteria by which we judge a speech, (4) to present a model speech for consideration, and (5) to compare the model speech with the criteria.

Reasons for Learning to Criticize

A first reason for learning to criticize oral communication is to develop an appreciation of and respect for speechmaking. Many people do not understand the work, the skills, and the art that are involved. Their attitude is like that of the educator who asked, "Why do we need speech courses in schools? People have been talking since they were small children." After you have listened critically to speeches, identified the communicative principles being used, and recognized some of the problems resulting from failure to use certain precepts, you should have an understanding of the vast difference between "just talking" and "talking with a purpose." Aristotle maintained that truth, skillfully presented, would win against falsehood; but falsehood would win if it were skillfully presented while truth was not. As a speech critic you will quickly perceive the accuracy of Aristotle's analysis.

Second, learning to criticize speeches helps you improve as a speaker. The critical comments of professor and classmates help you identify your strengths and weaknesses. You then know what things to continue doing and what areas you need to work on. Self-analysis is an important and practical means of improving speaking; but it is also true that you frequently fail to perceive yourself the way others do. And speaking requires such a concentrated commitment to the purpose of communication that it is often impossible to describe what you did at a particular moment. Not only does criticism help you identify strengths and weaknesses, it also provides suggestions of specific methods for improvement. When a critic says, "I didn't know when you moved into your second main point," you have a specific task to work on for the next speech. You know you need to work on transitions from one point to the next and to use attention-getting signposts to identify main points. When a critic says, "I was bothered because you never looked at me," you know you need to work specifically on eye contact in the next speech. For this reason many who speak regularly have someone—an assistant, spouse, adviser, close personal friend—attend their speeches and offer criticism. Experienced speakers know that no matter how effective they are, they have to be constantly on guard against the unconscious development of habits and idiosyncracies that interfere with precise communication. And even if no bad habits have been acquired, there is always room for improvement. Finally, criticism motivates you to want to improve. Unless you are totally indifferent to your peers, which is highly unusual, you do not like to know that something you are doing falls below their standards. So you are motivated to correct it. Or when you hear their favorable comments and realize that with just a little more effort you can obtain an even more favorable response, you are motivated to work a little harder.

A third reason for learning to criticize speeches is that such criticism establishes standards for evaluating speeches in nonacademic situations. You cannot listen critically to speeches in the classroom without carrying that behavior into other situations. Students frequently report, "I never paid any attention to the speeches I heard until I had a speech course. Now I hear all the things they are doing wrong." Of course, critics should hear the good points as well as the bad, but the point here is that the individual is now listening to speeches from a critical point of view. Unfortunately, too many people listen to the speakers in their community in an uncritical way. That is one reason irresponsible, demagogic speakers can achieve influential positions on significant issues confronting the people. As your ability to criticize speeches improves, you will become a more enlightened "consumer" of persuasive speaking efforts. Your defense against illogical and unethical methods should be strengthened. Hence, you can make decisions on more valid bases.

The fourth reason for learning to criticize speeches is closely related to the third: speech criticism helps to ensure the existence of high-quality speaking in the general community. When standards are consciously applied to any activity, practitioners begin to measure their efforts by those criteria. In effect, each of you in this course becomes a teacher of communication principles when you go back into your community and apply them in criticizing the speeches you hear there. It is no accident that ancient Greece had more than its share of effective speakers. Rhetoric stood at the core of the academic curriculum and high standards were abroad in the land. Prospective speakers knew they were going to be measured against those criteria and so prepared their communicative efforts with those standards in mind.

Bases for Criticizing Speeches

There are five different bases from which speeches may be criticized: (1) whether or not the speech achieves its desired results; (2) whether or not it attains certain artistic standards; (3) whether or not the ideas are sound; (4) whether or not the speaker is responsible or ethical; (5) whether or not it measures up eclectically to these four criteria. There are advantages and disadvantages to applying any of these standards.

In basing criticism on the results of the speech, ask: What was the speaker **Results** attempting to accomplish? Until this question can be answered with some certainty, there is no way to evaluate the speech on the basis of this criterion. Even if you can prove beyond doubt that specific events definitely occurred because of the speech, you cannot praise the speech for causing them until you have established that the speaker's objective was to initiate those events.

Examine the speech to discover whether the speaker stated explicitly the purpose of the speech. If not, ascertain whether the speaker implied clearly what the purpose was. Realize that there is a large amount of guesswork and speculation in your answer.

Once you have arrived at your analysis of what the speaker was trying to accomplish, ask a second question: Did the speaker accomplish the purpose? If the speaker asked the audience to make a total contribution of $100 to give to the Red Cross, you need only find out how much money was actually given. If a student speaker tries to persuade your class that the legislature should reduce tuition to the university and then asks you to sign a petition to the legislature, you will only need to observe how many listeners actually sign the petition. Even here, however, you may be forced to make a value judgment. Suppose twelve out of twenty-five students sign the petition. Has the speech accomplished its purpose? Suppose fifteen out of twenty-five sign it? It is clear that you have problems even when the speaker is seeking a behavioral response, but those problems are compounded when something other than a behavioral response is sought. If the speaker was trying to change an attitude held by listeners, there may be no measurable way of determining whether a change occurred. You may look for behavioral responses that reflect attitude change. Since we know, however, that attitude change does not necessarily produce behavioral change, you still cannot conclude that there is no attitude change simply because there is no behavioral change.

Then ask another question: Can a direct causal relationship be established between the speech and the audience response? Suppose you see on the evening TV news the report of devastating damage by a flood to a large area in an adjacent state, and the announcer says the Red Cross is sending in supplies but needs additional funds badly. On the spot you pledge to yourself to contribute on the following day. But before you can get to the Red Cross office which is several miles from campus, you arrive at your speech class to hear another student give a speech asking for donations to the Red Cross. He has made arrangements to take the contributions to the Red Cross office immediately after class; to save yourself that long trip, you give him your money even though you thought the speech was a poor one. But an observer would see only that you gave as the speaker requested. This could lead the observer to the erroneous conclusion that the speech was effective because it achieved its purpose. As a critic, be extremely cautious about assuming a causal relationship between a communicative effort and a later occurrence.

As a perceptive critic, ask the question: Which is more important, the immediate or the long-range response? The audience at Gettysburg, Pennsylvania, on November 19, 1863, is reported to have reacted negatively or neutrally to Lincoln's speech. Apparently it was not until later that people decided it was a classic, and today it is one of the most heralded rhetorical efforts ever made. Why did that immediate audience react in the way that it did? Were they right or wrong? Are we wrong today in our evaluation of that speech? These are questions you must ask. Of course, in the classroom you have no opportunity to await long-range results in evaluating speeches, but you still have to be aware of overweighing the immediate result.

Finally, there is a question vital to your task: Do the effects of a speech determine its quality? If a speech does not achieve its purpose, is it a poor speech? Lincoln made a conscious effort in his first inaugural to placate the South and avert the impending military struggle. Yet the war came. Can we say that the speech was a poor one? Throughout the 1930s Winston Churchill warned England of what would happen if Hitler were appeased as Chamberlain was proposing to do. Yet the people persistently rejected Churchill's ideas for those of Chamberlain. Can we say that Churchill's speeches were poor ones? On the other hand, if a speech does achieve its purpose, is it a good speech? Adolf Hitler's speaking stands as a monumental example of speeches that accomplished their purpose. With their admitted reliance on the "big lie," can we say those speeches were good ones? Recognize that there are times when people's attitudes are too crystallized to heed opposing messages, no matter how valid those messages may be. Whether the end results of a speech determine its quality is a particularly pertinent problem for the student critic, because classroom criticism frequently reveals that the reason students like a speech is that they agree with what the speaker has said.

Obviously, evaluating a speech on the basis of its effects is fraught with problems. It is much like trying to cross an open field by moonlight on a cloudy night: just when you come to a difficult spot, the moon goes behind a cloud and you are left in the dark. You will often be in the dark when you evaluate a speech solely on the basis of its effects.

Artistic Standards

In evaluating a speech on the basis of artistic standards, be unconcerned with what happened as a result of the speech. Ask, instead, whether the speaker utilized appropriate principles of communication.

Examine the topic of the speech to determine whether it is suited (a) to the speaker's interest, knowledge, and experiences, (b) to the audience, and (c) to the occasion. Determine whether the topic was sufficiently narrow to be adequately developed in the time available for the speech.

Evaluate the content of the speech. Investigate unsupported generalizations to determine whether the speaker left them unsupported because of obvious audience acceptance or through failure or inability to obtain corroborating evidence. Scrutinize the evidence for accuracy, relevancy, freshness, specificity, and concreteness. Determine whether needed qualifications of sources have been supplied. Examine the reasoning to detect any weaknesses in the development of claims from evidence and the warrants that establish the relationship between them.

Consider the organization of the speech. Does it have all the parts it should? If a part is missing, is there a rational explanation for its absence? Does the speaker state the purpose clearly and explicitly? If not, why not? Is there a sense of movement in the ideas? Can the main ideas be identified easily, or must the listener labor to uncover them? Is there a sense of unity and coherence to the speech as a result of transitions and summaries that bind the smaller and larger parts together?

Appraise the language used by the speaker. Consider its appropriateness to the speaker, the audience, and the occasion. Examine the language to determine whether it clearly communicated the speaker's meaning in an original and economical way. Understanding that a speech is "not an essay on its hind legs," analyze the language to see if there is an oral quality to it. Investigate the sentence structure to ascertain whether it is clear, correct, and varied.

Study the delivery of the speech. Does the speaker impart a sense of sincerity? Does the speaker have a communicative attitude? Does he seem to be interested in talking to this particular audience? Is there an awareness of the audience? Does he adapt specifically to their reactions? Does he use effective and purposeful bodily action? Are gestures dynamic and varied? Does he maintain eye contact with listeners? Does he permit notes to become a barrier to communication? Does he speak loud enough to be heard by all present? Is the rate of speaking varied and neither too fast to be understood nor too slow to hold your attention? Is there variety in the pitch of the voice? Does the speaker use stress and emphasis to make important words stand out from unimportant ones? Are his pronunciations sufficiently standard that attention is not called to them because of their strangeness? Does the speaker use pauses for emphasis and to ease the listener's task?

Finally, remember that even though you can analyze and evaluate the speaker's use of all of these principles, it is the overall interaction of them that produces the total impact of the speech. Probably more than in any other enterprise, the gestalt approach is important in evaluating a speech. The impact of a speech is not merely a sum of the individual parts; sometimes it is more than the sum, sometimes less.

The major difficulty in judging a speech exclusively on the basis of esthetic standards is that it tends to divorce speechmaking from its very rationale for being. After all, the purpose of speaking to a specific group is to achieve a purpose, and if that purpose is not accomplished, then it is difficult to see the point of saying, "But the speech was good on the basis of esthetic standards."

Ideas

When you judge on this basis, you are unconcerned about the results achieved or about the esthetic standards employed. What mainly concerns you is whether or not the speaker was presenting valid ideas, what some critics would refer to as *the truth*. Those who use this criterion argue that, after all, that is what speaking is all about—an effort to discern what is the truth in a given instance. If that truth can be discovered through the speaking of an unskilled advocate, then the objective has been attained even if the people to whom he was talking failed to recognize that truth or to be affected by it.

There is no denying the argument that the ultimate end of speaking is the determination of truth, or the determination of which ideas are the most valid at a particular moment. Unfortunately, there is a major problem which confronts the critic: How do you ascertain which speaker has the truth? Most speaking occurs in the area of public affairs; in that area it is most difficult to determine which speaker's ideas are most valid. Unless that determination can be made, you must either make assumptions or turn to other criteria as a basis for judging a speech.

Speaker's Motives and Ethics

Quintilian, the great Roman speech teacher, said an orator is a *good* man speaking well. In using this basis for criticism, determine the speaker's purpose for communicating. Is the speaker interested in the general welfare, or is he trying to help a select group of friends or to advance his own cause? Unfortunately, unless you are a mind reader, there may be some difficulty in uncovering the speaker's motivation. Unless there is clear evidence to indicate the speaker's intentions, you may be influenced by the same tendency that influences most people: to attribute good intentions to those who agree with our ideas and bad intentions to those who disagree. If that is the case, very little merit can be afforded such criticism.

Even after validly concluding that the speaker desires the acceptance of her proposal for the general welfare, you are still confronted with the task of deciding whether or not the speaker has used ethical means of attaining objectives. Has the speaker built a rational case for her position, or has she merely appealed to listeners' emotions? Has she used evidence that can be verified or fabricated it?

In the final analysis, you may be left with a *good* person, speaking responsibly, whose speaking does not meet minimum esthetic standards and fails to achieve the desired results.

Eclectic Principles

When using the eclectic principles basis, do not rely on one of the four previously mentioned bases. Instead, apply all of them in reaching a decision about the merits of a speech. Discover what happened as a result of the speech. If the desired response was not obtained because of something beyond the control of the speaker, then she cannot be blamed. Include that information in your judgment. Determine how well the speaker used the esthetic standards available and appropriate to that effort. If you discover that principles of communication were not used, or were badly used, conclude that the speech really had very little to do with what happened. If a protest mob is ready to enter a building forcefully, and someone cries, "Charge the police line," just before the mob surges forward, you can attach little significance to those words. As a critic, be interested in the validity of the ideas presented by the speaker, but also determine how skillfully they were presented and what response they brought from the listeners. The speaker's character and ethics are important in your evaluation, but not to the exclusion of the other three criteria. In sum, when basing your evaluation on eclectic principles, attempt to determine the effects of a speech, analyze the esthetic standards employed, try to ascertain the validity of the ideas advanced, describe the ethics involved, and then arrive at a critical estimate of the total communicative effort.

Now that we have examined the reasons for engaging in speech criticism and have discussed the bases on which our judgments may be founded, let's consider the standard for judging a speech.

Artistic Standards for Judging a Speech

The following are the attributes we can expect a good speech to possess.

1. We can expect a good speech to have structure. It should have an introduction, a thesis sentence, a body, and a conclusion. It should also have transitions that help listeners move from one part to another.
2. We can expect a good speech to have substance. It should present main ideas developed by different types of supporting materials: testimony, statistics, and facts.
3. We can expect a good speech to employ sound reasoning.
4. We can expect a good speech to use language that is clear, appropriate, original, vital, and economical.
5. We can also expect a good speech to be well delivered, both verbally and nonverbally. We can make no judgment on this criterion, however, if we only read the text of the speech.

A Model Speech

Next, we are going to consider a model speech. As you read the following speech, look for the first four characteristics described in the previous section.

Who Is Wise?

Ronald W. Roskens   President, University of Nebraska[2]

1 Speaking as "Poor Richard," Benjamin Franklin once asked "Who is
2 wise?" His answer, as usual, was both definitive and provocative:
3   Who is wise?
4   He that learns from everyone.
5   He that governs his passions.
6   He that is content.
7   Nobody.
8   Are we to conclude that in the absence of perfection there is no
9 wisdom? Is wisdom something divine, beyond the reach of mere mortals?
10 Of course not! Wisdom, like integrity, may be elusive and difficult to define.
11 Yet wisdom is present in human affairs when the abstract and the practical
12 merge, impelling us to act, and coloring those actions which we take.
13 Although some wag has said, "some are wise and some are otherwise," the
14 capacity for wisdom resides within all of us.
15   Most of us regard our universities as seats of wisdom. We at the
16 University of Nebraska cannot, of course, lay sole claim to wisdom. Even
17 so, the rigors of our environment are intended to cultivate this latent trait.
18 As John Masefield said a generation ago, "Wherever a University stands, it
19 stands and shines; wherever it exists, the free minds of men, urged on to full
20 fair inquiry, may still bring wisdom into human affairs."

The crucial question is, how well have we at the University of   21
Nebraska discharged our responsibility to nurture your wisdom? It is time   22
to conduct *the* final examination. In this instance, however, the tables are   23
turned. Now it is we, the faculty and staff of the University who must   24
render an accounting. And it is you, our distinguished graduates, who will   25
rate us; not only today but as your lives unfold.   26

For the purposes of this examination we will assume that you give us   27
reasonably high marks in those areas we traditionally associate with a   28
university education. So, let us concentrate on wisdom. I invite you to   29
ponder four questions which are extensions of Poor Richard's definition.   30
And bear in mind that your responses—or, more precisely, your future   31
actions—will be the litmus test which determines the extent to which we   32
are entitled to regard ourselves as a "great" university.   33

Question one: if, as Poor Richard says, he is wise who learns from   34
everyone, do *you* sense the need to form your own opinions and draw your   35
own conclusions?   36

The ability to make wise choices—which is the ultimate aim of   37
education—cannot be taken for granted. We are bombarded with   38
information, much of which is speculative rather than factual. Public   39
opinion polls often seem to dictate rather than measure the national pulse.   40
Quick fixes are, however, no substitute for sober contemplation. The   41
individual who refuses to think independently runs the risk of becoming a   42
clone of someone else.   43

Wisdom pervades the character of those who recognize that the rigors   44
of sifting and weighing facts are and must be lifelong habits. And so we   45
ask: even as you listen to others, are you prepared to chart your own   46
course?   47

If not, we have failed you.   48

Question two: if, as Poor Richard says, he is wise that governs his   49
passions, do *you* sense the need to avoid contributing to the "grossness of   50
our national product"?   51

This deliberate play on words acknowledges some disturbing trends   52
which seem to permeate our public conduct. The media bear witness to the   53
childish tantrums and crude behavior of so-called celebrities. Our television   54
screens are filled with images focused upon the "heartbreak of psoriasis"   55
and the fatal impact of "ring around the collar." Crude messages   56
emblazoned on T-shirts and bumper stickers belie any claim that primitive   57
impulses are no longer in vogue.   58

We often act as though the responsibility for these trends lies   59
elsewhere. Acquiescence to them is perhaps the easier route. But vulgarity,   60
incivility, and discourtesy are not the hallmarks of wisdom. As Ovid wrote,   61
"studies culminate in manners."   62

This is a good time for good taste. And so we ask: have our   63
interactions with you helped you fashion a code of conduct characterized by   64
restraint and good taste, particularly when your behavior impacts upon the   65
sensibilities of others?   66

If not, we have failed you.   67

68	Question three: if, as Poor Richard says, he is wise who is content, do
69	*you* sense the need to pursue the outer limits of your capabilities?
70	Thoreau tells us that "dreams are the touchstones of our characters."
71	As educated individuals we should understand that the impediments to
72	realizing our aspirations often lie within ourselves. If we are content merely
73	to accept what comes to us and to fashion a life which brooks no challenges,
74	mediocrity—or even failure—will be our lot. We will have killed our own
75	dreams, and no matter how much we might have succeeded in the eyes of
76	others our accomplishments will not have approached the potential which
77	lies within us.
78	The wise individual understands that the best steel is forged under the
79	most extreme conditions. And so we ask: do you understand that dreams
80	and fulfillment will go hand in hand only if your talents are fully invested?
81	If not, we have failed you.
82	Question four: if, as Poor Richard says, nobody is truly wise, do *you*
83	sense the need to keep faith with your fellow human beings and with the
84	social institutions we have created?
85	Each of us is human, and the essence of that humanity is that we
86	have, and will inexorably exercise, the capacity to make mistakes, to be less
87	than perfect. Human weaknesses are inevitably magnified when subjected to
88	the harsh glare of public scrutiny. The shortcomings of one public official
89	trigger a disregard for all elements of government. One practitioner fails,
90	and an entire profession falls into disrepute.
91	Wisdom and skepticism must go hand in hand. The wise individual
92	understands, however, that social institutions are the instruments of our will
93	and reflect the strengths or weaknesses of those who create them. And so
94	we ask: will you balance your skepticism with compassion and avoid the
95	dangers of self-fulfilling prophecies?
96	If not, we have failed you.
97	We return to Mr. Franklin's question: who is wise? The Hebrew
98	prayerbook *Ethics of the Father* tells us:

99	There are seven marks of an uncultured, and seven of a wise man. The wise man
100	does not speak before him who is greater than he in wisdom; and does not break in
101	upon the speech of his fellow; he is not hasty to answer; he questions according to
102	the subject matter, and answers to the point; he speaks upon the first thing first, and
103	upon the last last; regarding that which he has not understood he says, I do not
104	understand it, and he acknowledges the truth. The reverse of all this is to be found
105	in an uncultured man.

106	Do you sense the seeds of such wisdom in yourself? If you do, the
107	University has passed this final examination. If you do not, hopefully you
108	will have found at this University the bases for such wisdom, and may take
109	comfort in the fact that "learning never ends."
110	Whatever your answer, you will find that your time at the University
111	has profoundly influenced you. You will for the rest of your lives play out
112	your experiences here, even as we continue to reach out to you through your
113	memories and in your skills.

Appendix A

Who is wise? All of us—if we continue to care about learning and to   114
learn about caring. For that is the essence of wisdom.   115

Before we begin a critical analysis of Roskens's speech, see if you can complete the following assignments.

1. What is the function of the introduction?
2. Identify the thesis sentence.
3. How many main points are there? What are they?
4. Where does the conclusion begin?
5. What type of reasoning is used most frequently?
6. Find the following types of supporting material: (a) explanation, (b) testimony, (c) definition, (d) example.
7. Find two examples of repetition.
8. Find an example of each of the following: (a) parallelism, (b) rhetorical question, (c) alliteration, (d) metaphor.

Evaluation of Model Speech with Artistic Standards

Before we examine together the speech that you have just read and analyzed, we need to identify the type of speech we are considering. Obviously Roskens wants his listeners to be entertained, in the sense of being interested and not bored. But that is not his main purpose. Clearly, Roskens wants his listeners to receive information, but that is not the main purpose of his speech. Roskens wants his listeners to accept certain attitudes toward higher education and to reject particular behaviors of society, but his main purpose is not to persuade his listeners to take an action or to adopt a particular attitude. Roskens's speech is for a special occasion, a commencement, and he wants to create favorable attitudes toward and acceptance of his ideas. In criticizing the speech, therefore, we will not apply the standards appropriate to speeches to entertain, inform, or persuade.

Next, we need to consider the basis on which we are going to criticize Roskens's speech. We shall criticize the speech on the basis of eclectic principles, not on the basis of results. We do not have the data to make such an evaluation. We do not know how many times the audience responded—with laughter, applause, hissing, and so forth. We have no shift-of-opinion forms on which the listeners registered their attitudes toward any of Roskens's ideas. We cannot, then, evaluate the results of the speech. We can, however, criticize the speech on the basis of its ideas, Roskens's motives and attitudes, and artistic standards.

On the basis of its ideas, Roskens's speech rates high marks. His main idea, wisdom and its development, is an important and worthy one to consider with college graduates and their families. The four main points that Roskens uses to develop his main idea seem valid.

Roskens's motives and ethics seem praiseworthy. Except for the acclaim that he would receive for a notable speech, there appears to be no personal motive impelling him to make this particular speech. He builds a rational case for his ideas and uses no unethical means to get them accepted. The evidence he uses is verifiable and representative.

Our most searching analysis of Roskens's speech can be made by evaluating it on the basis of artistic standards. We shall do this by comparing his use of communication principles with the criteria for judging a speech that we established earlier.

We said we can expect a speech to have structure. There is an introduction (lines 1–26). Roskens opens his speech with a brief poem. Then he focuses on the main idea of the poem and begins to develop interest in it. By the end of the introduction, Roskens has made it especially relevant to his specific audience. The introduction ably achieves two of the three purposes of an introduction: it gets the attention of the listeners and leads them into the subject of the speech. Since Roskens's position and reputation give him high credibility, there is no need for him to be concerned with that issue. He then states clearly his thesis and gives a preview: "So, let us concentrate on wisdom. I invite you to ponder four questions which are extensions of Poor Richard's definition" (lines 29–30). The body develops the four questions, and these are identified as main points with numbers as signposts (lines 34–96). The conclusion completes the unity of the speech by returning to the question asked in the first line (line 3) of the poem in the introduction and answering it with a selection quoted from a Hebrew prayerbook (lines 99–105). Moving from that quotation to a restatement of the question posed by Poor Richard, Roskens gives his own answer (lines 114–115). Thus, Roskens establishes the unity of his speech by threading his main idea (wisdom) through the introduction, thesis, main points in the body, and conclusion. Effective transitions throughout the speech add to its unity (lines 8–9, 21–22, 45–47, 63–66, 79–81, 93–96, 97, 106–107).

We said we can expect a good speech to have substance. Mr. Roskens's speech does. It has main ideas (lines 34–36, 49–51, 68–69, 82–84). His ideas are supported by different types of supporting materials. Roskens uses explanation (lines 10–14, 37–43, 71–77, 85–90, 107, 111–113), humor (lines 13–14), testimony (lines 1–7, 18–20, 61–62, 70, 99–105, 109), definition (lines 37–38), and examples in the form of specific instances (lines 54–56). Note that the testimony used by Roskens is given by writers well known to educated persons. Thus their credibility is extremely high. The one instance of humor, in the form of a quotation, is simply attributed to "some wag," a clear indication that it is to be interpreted as humorous.

The reasoning of Roskens's speech is not its strength. Neither is it a weak point. Most of the reasoning is in the form of assertions, many of which are unsupported. But his assertions would probably not be challenged by the majority of people, for they are supported by experience and common sense. Some examples are "Public opinion often seems to dictate rather than measure the national pulse" (lines 39–40). "But vulgarity, incivility, and discourtesy are not the hallmarks of wisdom" (lines 60–61). "Wisdom pervades the character of those who recognize that the rigors of sifting and weighing facts are and must be lifelong habits" (lines 44–45). "The wise individual understands, however, that social institutions are the instruments of our will and reflect the strengths or weaknesses of those who create them" (lines 91–93).

Some assertions are supported by testimony, as when Roskens said, "But vulgarity, incivility, and discourtesy are not the hallmarks of wisdom. As Ovid wrote, 'studies culminate in manners' " (lines 60–62). At other times assertions are supported by other assertions: "Human weaknesses are inevitably magnified when subjected to the harsh glare of public scrutiny. The shortcomings of one public official trigger a disregard for all elements of government. One practitioner fails, and an entire profession falls in disrepute" (lines 87–90). By substituting assertions for examples, Roskens probably helped to establish greater dignity for his remarks. On one occasion, Roskens supported his assertion with specific instances: "This deliberate play on words acknowledges some disturbing trends which seem to permeate our public conduct. . . . Our television screens are filled with images focused upon the 'heartbreak of psoriasis' and the fatal impact of 'ring around the collar.' Crude messages emblazoned on T-shirts and bumper stickers belie any claim that primitive impulses are no longer in vogue" (lines 52–58). The strength of Roskens's assertions largely flows from their ready acceptance by the listener rather than from tight, closely reasoned argumentation.

The language of Roskens's speech possesses several virtues. It is exceptionally clear. Every sentence has been carefully crafted so that subject, verb, predicate, clauses, and modifiers are properly placed and can be easily identified. The language is also economical. There are no unnecessary words; every word contributes to the communication of his ideas. The language is appropriate. It is the language of an educated person, elegant without being pretentious. The language is original. Parallelism and restatement are used to strengthen the impact of the ideas and to emphasize the unity of the speech. To summarize each of his four main points, Roskens introduces a rhetorical question by the same phrase, "And so we ask," (lines 45–46, 63, 79, 93–94) and followed by the same sentence, "If not, we have failed you" (lines 48, 67, 81, 96). These repetitions add to the impact of each summary. Originality of language is also achieved by the use of alliteration—"intended to cultivate this latent trait" (line 17), "good time for good taste" (line 63), "inexorably exercise" (line 86), "bases for such wisdom" (line 108), "profoundly influence" (line 111)—and metaphor—"your responses . . . will be the litmus test which determines . . ." (lines 31–32), "The individual . . . runs the risk of becoming a clone . . ." (lines 41–43), ". . . dreams and fulfillment will go hand in hand only if your talents are fully invested" (lines 79–80).

Roskens achieves vitality of language through the use of effective sentences. He presents rhetorical questions that require the listeners to answer them in their own mind, and he uses some that he goes on to answer himself. The second paragraph of the introduction begins with two rhetorical questions: "Are we to conclude that in the absence of perfection there is no wisdom?

Is wisdom something divine, beyond the reach of mere mortals?" (Lines 8–9). After answering these questions, Roskens next uses a rhetorical question—"how well have we at the University of Nebraska discharged our responsibility to nurture your wisdom?" (lines 21–22)—as a transitional device to the statement of his thesis. A rhetorical question, "Do you sense the seeds of such wisdom in yourself?" (line 106), is used in the conclusion to focus the listeners' thoughts on the central idea of the speech. His final rhetorical question, "Who is wise?" is answered with a balanced sentence that takes a clause and repeats it syntactically with the parts reversed: "All of us—if we continue to care about learning and to learn about caring."

Clearly, Roskens understands and employs the principles of effective rhetorical communication. As students, you would do well to go and do likewise!

Summary

Students profit from learning how to criticize speeches because it helps to develop an appreciation of and respect for speechmaking, it aids the individual in becoming a better speaker, it establishes standards for evaluating speeches in nonacademic situations, and it helps to ensure the existence of high-quality speaking in the general community.

Speeches may be criticized on the basis of five different criteria: the results, the artistic standards employed, the validity of the ideas, the speaker's motives and ethics, and the eclectic basis of all the preceding four.

Notes

1. II Macc. 15:39, *The Holy Bible,* Authorized King James Version (New York: Hawthorne Books, Inc., 1956).
2. R. W. Roskens, "Who Is Wise?" *Vital Speeches of the Day* 47 (1981):529–30. Used by permission.

Appendix B
Model Speeches

The Resources War

Harry M. Conger   Chairman, President, and Chief Executive Officer,
Homestake Mining Company
Vital Speeches of the Day 52 (December 1, 1985): 107–109.
© City News Publishing Company. Used by permission.

I'm here today to talk on the subject of the Resources War. It is a "war" that cannot be won unless it is waged. It must be waged if our nation is to remain a first-rate economic and military power. Unfortunately, the stakes are high and yet most Americans are not tuned into the problem.

I would like to discuss the problems we face as well as some solutions.

Throughout our nation's two-hundred-year history, we Americans have optimistically viewed our spacious territory as the "land of plenty." Indeed, America possesses lands of awesome beauty and splendor. Generation after generation of Americans has come to believe that the land would give forth endless resources on a road of endless prosperity.

Only in the 1970s, however, did we suddenly come face to face with the realization that our natural bounty is finite. The Arab oil embargoes made this painfully clear. As a nation, we struggled to cope with the first days of our dependence on others for vital resources. Riding in a taxi yesterday, I heard a good 'ol country song that reminded me of this problem. The fellow sang, "Have we seen the best of the free life? Are the good times really over for good?"

Of course, I don't believe they are and neither do you. But the problem of our dependence on foreign imports of resources may be reaching a crisis point. Oil is only the surface of our increasing minerals dependence.

The economic handicaps of such dependence on foreign imports have had a telling impact on our daily lives. But what does it bode for our nation's security? Is our nation's destiny falling into hands other than our own? How safe is America as she enters the Eighties?

The silent truth is that she may not be safe for long. More and more we rely on foreign sources of supply for strategic raw materials vital to our defense industries. In response to this growing crisis, I wish to urge upon you the need for a "new realism." No American should ignore the importance of mining and minerals to our nation's security.

Since the end of World War II, we have been locked in fierce competition with the Soviet Union for sources of strategic minerals. This competition is often referred to as the "Resources War." It is waged by proxy in the jungles of South America, the deserts of Africa and the Middle East, and now in the cold of the Arctic poles. In the future it may even be waged on the moon.

In terms of minerals self-sufficiency, the U.S. and the Soviet Union are poles apart, no pun intended. Halfway through the Eighties, we find that we are more than 50 percent dependent on foreign sources for at least 19 strategic minerals. In contrast, the Soviet Union is only dependent on imports for two commodities: flourospar and barite.

This minerals imbalance gives the resources war a peculiar, and certainly dangerous twist: not only do the Soviets want to keep us at a disadvantage, but they also want to disrupt or even block our sources of raw materials. We hold no such leverage over them.

The resources war is a war that is joined everyday. It is waged even as we gather here. If, for instance, the central African nation of Zaire were to suddenly fall into the hands of a Soviet-backed communist government, what would come of our heavy dependence on her for supplies of cobalt and chromium, to name a few?

Our reliance on Zaire for these two minerals provides a vivid example of what is at stake in the resources war. Cobalt and chromium may not be the best-known minerals, but it may surprise you to learn that without them, we couldn't fly an F-16 or F-15. They are vital to the production of jet-fighter engines.

Given the strategic importance of cobalt and chromium, I doubt that many Americans would question the importance of a friendly Zaire to our nation's security. The Soviets have certainly understood this. That explains why they have attempted time and again, through the use of neighboring surrogates, to undermine the stability of Zaire. It is a dangerous ploy, for everybody involved.

This is but one example of how the resources war is waged. It amply reveals the stakes involved. In almost every case, the players and situations are similar. We find ourselves at the severe disadvantage of being dependent on unstable, lesser-developed nations for much of our supplies of vital resources.

The resources war is the "stuff" of survival in a world that is still not safe for democracy and freedom-loving peoples. With each loss of a valuable trading partner and ally to Soviet or unfriendly control, our nation's security and economic well-being is dealt a tremendous blow. That goes for the entire free world as well.

This is a struggle that simply cannot go ignored by opinion leaders such as you.

Perhaps by now you may be wondering what my purpose is for telling you about the resources war. Let me assure you that I am not a lobbyist blowing a siren because our industry profits are down. No, the resources war is something that concerns us all.

Admittedly, I am not a defense expert. I cannot pretend to know everything about how America can best secure her foreign supplies of strategic raw materials.

But as a miner, I can tell you that we have been fighting the resources war with one hand tied behind our back. Despite the stakes involved, we have seriously neglected our domestic mining industry over the years. The mining industry is on the edge of crisis and ruin. It's almost as if we have brought the resources war on ourselves.

The serious nature of this struggle requires that we take a more conscious, comprehensive look at the importance of mining. How much longer can we ignore the strategic and economic penalties in not having a healthy mining industry at home?

What are the problems facing mining? How and why did one of our hands get tied behind our back? How can we free that hand and bring mining back in this country? What can we do to ease our dependence on imports and thus lower the stakes of the resources war?

First, let me cover the problems we face:

Problem number one: overregulation. Over the years mining has acquired the image of being dirty, environmentally destructive and a nuisance. To correct the excesses of mining, conservationists sought more and more government regulation of the industry. This has led to a situation in which mining is now suffocated by excess regulation. We went from one extreme to the other. The regulatory regime is so burdensome that minerals extraction and production have become anything but cost-effective.

Problem number two: land use restrictions. Astounding as it may seem, two-thirds of our public lands are off limits to mining. Talk about handicaps! It's like the NFL telling the 49ers they can only use Joe Montana in four games a year. The U.S. mining industry is dying off because accessible ore deposits are running out and mines are closing down. Just a few weeks ago Kennecott closed its Utah copper mines. Few took notice of this event, despite the fact that it is the industry equivalent of GM shutting down its Chevrolet division!

Problem number three: production costs. When mineral-rich, near-the-surface ore deposits are used up, extractive mining companies must dig deeper. This requires technology-intensive extraction methods, which in turn requires huge capital outlays. Thus production costs have risen in conjunction with the steady depletion of our richest, known ore deposits.

Problem number four: foreign competition. Extraction and processing of resources is shifting to lesser-developed nations. In these countries, production costs are much lower. Ore deposits are "younger," closer to the surface and thus richer in mineral content. They are more easily extracted and processed. When these natural advantages are added to lower labor costs and government export subsidies, the cards become even more stacked against the U.S. mining industry. We also cannot overlook the negative effects of a strong dollar. How can we compete with cheap imports caused by an artificially high U.S. dollar? Despite the generally strong recovery, many mining companies are reeling from losses due to shrinking markets and depressed prices. Both conditions are aggravated by unfair foreign competition.

Obviously, I wasn't kidding when I said we are fighting the resources war with one hand tied behind our back. But there are solutions to the problems we now face. We must get down to the business of restoring proper strength to our mining industry, before it's too late. As part of a comprehensive effort toward revitalizing this all-important industry, we suggest the following four-point program:

First, we urge comprehensive and thoughtful implementation of the Mineral Policy Act of 1970 and the National Materials Minerals Policy, Research and Development Act of 1980. These administrative policies set forth the fundamental goals of mineral strength and reliability for America. They recognize the importance of mining to all other industrial production, particularly in defense.

Second, we seek more cost efficient tax policies. In the past couple of decades, fiscal policies have put a stranglehold on mining. The opposite should be happening. I, for one, could never understand why Uncle Sam would want to render American industries helpless in an increasingly competitive world market. We need to explore ways in which domestic tax policies could be used to help, not hurt, our industry compete more effectively with overseas producers. Depletion allowances should not be tampered with, so that domestic companies will have the extra capital needed for research and development of more cost-effective extraction methods. The goal should be the removal of all handicaps.

Third, we urge that more public lands be released for exploration. Mining is not what it was. Today, multiple use of land is appropriate and can be conducted with proper regard for the environment. Where long-term use of a site is required, land reclamation and restoration will follow. So, I say, "let's don't close off 66 percent of our land until we know what's beneath it." Who knows, there may be reserves of cobalt and chromium out there! In any case, what we need are policies that will bring about a proper balance between environmental concerns and minerals production.

Finally, more attention needs to be given to the national stockpile. The U.S. Congress recognized the importance of minerals to our national security when it authorized creation of a stockpile. That was in 1939. But since then, the effort to meet acceptable stockpile levels for certain strategic minerals has been halfhearted at best. Many people wrongly believe that minerals are like tap water. They think minerals can be turned on at random and in seemingly endless supplies. The reality is harsh. It takes years to find and get at most of our remaining ore deposits. In a crunch, our capacity for minerals production would not meet needs. The national stockpile, if correctly used, would alleviate the potential for shortages during a crisis period.

My friends, we simply cannot win the resources war unless we wage it. We cannot achieve realistic minerals self-sufficiency unless we untie the bonds that have handicapped mining in America for too long.

Our increasing dependence on foreign sources for strategic minerals imperils our national security and threatens our prosperity at home. The resources war pits our survival as a free nation against the insatiable appetite of the Soviet Union for world domination through elimination of the U.S. as economic and military leader of the free world.

We can overcome our minerals malnutrition and win this war. But first, we must understand what the stakes are. We must realize that America cannot remain a first rate economic and military power if we have a second rate mining industry. And most importantly of all, we must never forget one elemental truth: "Our horn of plenty begins with a hole in the ground."

The Most Pressing Issue for Our Times

William J. Byron   President, The Catholic University of America
Vital Speeches of the Day 51 (August 15, 1985): 653–55.
© City News Publishing Company. Used by permission.

You are gracious and generous to permit me to speak to you in my native language. I apologize for not being able to address you in your native tongue.

I would like to pay you the compliment of a relatively brief but serious commencement address. The thoughts I will share with you today began forming in my mind by way of response to a question proposed to me by a small group of honor students at the University of Seattle in the United States. I was visiting the university for a public lecture on another topic. The students wrote, in advance of my visit, to ask if I would meet with them in a small group to discuss this direct and very probing question, "What is the most pressing issue you see for us in our generation?" I have been giving that question a lot of thought. I would like to explore it today with you.

My reaction to the question began with an acknowledgement that "most pressing" could mean "most immediate" or "quite urgent," but that it should not be taken in so short-term a context as to lose sight of that which is truly significant. Immediacy, urgency and significance are not always the same thing. So I chose to take "most pressing" to mean simply "most important" in a time frame that would be coextensive with the average life expectancy of those college students. This time frame pushes the perspective out by at least fifty or sixty years, assuming that life on the planet can extend its lease that long. In a very real sense, the students were asking for an estimate of just how long their lease on life would be. They are concerned about survival.

I was being asked to identify an issue of deepest significance and greatest importance to be dealt with by this collegiate generation over its allotted span of life. The question is one that can and should be asked in Taipei, as well as Seattle. It can be asked anywhere in the world. Consider the candidates for inclusion on this list of most pressing issues.

Foremost in the minds of the young in most of the world is the question of war—nuclear war with no winners. We will trip over ourselves into war, many fear, if we continue the nuclear weapons buildup in a senseless arms race with other nuclear powers. No one doubts the importance of the issue of war and peace in our time. But is *it* the "most pressing"?

Another candidate for that title is poverty—around the world and around the corner. Poverty is sustained deprivation. We have to ask: Deprived of what? Sustained by what or by whom? We can measure deprivation of food, shelter, employment, education and health care over against the levels of these necessities which basic human dignity requires for every human person. We know poverty when we see it. We do not so readily recognize its causes. Do systems—economic, political, cultural, and social—sustain the poverty we see? Or, is it sustained by persons; persons other than the poor themselves? Or, is poverty sustained by a combination of systems and persons? How do we get at the problem? How do the poor gain necessary participation in the economic system? How do deprived persons get out from under the oppressive restraints on their human potential? Is this complex problem of poverty the "most pressing" one with which our graduating collegians around the world will have to deal in the decades allotted to them?

Perhaps hunger is the most important problem. Surely for millions it is at this moment the most urgent. Hunger is the most urgent form of poverty. Chronic malnutrition and severe deprivation of food spell ultimate physical deprivation and denial of life itself. Will hunger be the "most pressing" issue confronting our world in the next half century? By the very debilitating nature of the hunger problem, it is obvious that those who must rise to the challenge of eliminating hunger are not those who are afflicted by the scourge of hunger. The same can be said of poverty.

Maybe ecological deterioration is the issue most deserving of attention. If we continue to pollute our streams, abuse our soil, poison our air and lose our croplands to erosion on the one hand and urbanization on the other, we will be without the physical base we need to sustain life. Sustainability may be *the* issue for the next half century.

Is population the most pressing problem? How about the problem of economic development, without which problems like overpopulation and undernutrition will never be brought under control?

376   *Appendix B*

Should the memory of the Holocaust in Germany serve to remind us that an ever present problem is our capacity to hate, to murder, to disregard and destroy human life and dignity? The contemporary "life" issues offer additional nominations for the top spot on our list of "most pressing" issues.

There are other pressing problems of course. I think of family instability, the breakup of marriages, the loss of a sense of commitment in our lives and relationships. One of the most difficult words for American youth to utter today is "forever." I know this uncertainty about themselves and their future touches youth all over the world.

I see a widespread problem of purposelessness in America's young. The nation offers them no central project; the economy tells many of them they really aren't needed. The nuclear cloud and the survival syndrome contribute ambiguity rather than clarity of purpose to their lives. The young of other nations are also searching for a sense of purpose, for direction in their lives.

Other problems—all pressing, none open to simple solutions—deserve a place on our list. This final set of problems falls into what I like to call the "isms" category. In English, the suffix "ism" throws a noun into boldface or italics. It signifies a bias, an emphasis, and almost always a disproportion. Racism, sexism, militarism, capitalism and communism would be good contemporary examples. Are the problems they connote high or low on the "most pressing" list for our times?

Atheism is surely a pressing and significant problem for this or any age. If the problem of atheism were attended to, would solutions to the other problems more readily fall into place?

Other "isms" will occur to anyone interested in taking inventory of the really important problems in the world in which we live. The list, then, is long. It is not the point of this exercise to collect, but to choose. The original question put to me by serious and appropriately concerned students was: "What is the most pressing issue you see for us in our generation?" My answer to them was, "materialism." This is the "ism" most to be feared. And materialism, I believe, is an international problem. Poor nations are not exempt; the affluent countries are most vulnerable.

It seems to me that the common denominator underlying the candidates for inclusion in any inventory of urgent, pressing, important and significant problems to be dealt with by the generation now coming out of our educational systems into our world social, political, economic and cultural systems is materialism. The word reminds us of the present and constant danger of overemphasizing the material side of our existence to the exclusion of the spiritual. To have becomes more important than to be. To possess is better than to share. To do for self takes precedence over doing for others. Property takes on more importance than people—other people, that is. And things, rather than ideas, assume a controlling influence in the lives of the materialistic majority in a materialistic society.

As the problem becomes all-pervasive, it touches virtually everyone. This, of course, means that virtually anyone can make a direct contribution toward a solution. Anyone can assess the extent to which the material has displaced the spiritual in his or her life, and decide to take corrective action to restore the balance. Anyone can take a self-administered test to estimate the relative importance of things and ideas in his or her life. Anyone can notice neglect of the soul and obsession with the body. Soul and body belong together, but they belong in balance. We are for the most part quite unbalanced. An unbalanced materialism has produced an unbalanced commercialism in many parts of the world. This permeates our recreation— our music and films—and is now stifling our spirit.

We are a people drowning in a sea of materialism, and we are not really aware that something deadly serious is afflicting us. So we bemoan our fate, buy better locks, withdraw from the needy, and escape these suffocating realities by freely permitting ourselves to become addicted to dependency devices of one kind or another, some more harmful physically and psychologically than others, all, however, taking their toll at that pay station which is me—the individual, unique human person of whatever national origin. And it is precisely there, with the person—the unique, free individual who has the power to choose—that the solution must begin.

Materialism is not the answer. We seem to be incapable of recognizing that fact. Materialism is, in fact, the question—the most pressing, significant, urgent and important question with which the present generation has to deal.

I have a suggestion for today's graduate. I suggest that you write a letter to yourself. Write it in response to the question: "What is the most pressing issue you see for yourself in the years ahead—the span of years that will constitute your postgraduation lifetime?" Be honest, of course, in writing to yourself. And be wise in using what you write. Keep that letter in a place where it can be read once a year, on your birthday, say, or on another easy-to-remember date.

Your personal response—for your eyes only—to the "most pressing issue" question will, perhaps, give you the opportunity to ask yourself: do you believe that to live easily is to live happily? Surely, happiness will figure somewhere in that letter you write. You want happiness for yourself and others. Happiness for yourself and others will have something to do with your personal engagement in the most significant issue of your time. But if the issue you select is truly important, it will admit of no easy engagement, no simple solution, no passing commitment of your time and energy. You will not live happily, if you set out now to live easily.

In that letter you write to yourself, make an estimate of the extent to which materialism has a grip on your life. That is the exact extent of the gap between you and true happiness. It also measures the distance between you and the beginning of your personal contribution to a solution to the most pressing issue you see for your time. Materialism has each one of us in its grip to some extent. So no one of us can say, "I don't know where to begin." Begin right there. Get a better balance between matter and spirit in your life. If a sufficient number of others in your generation do the same all over the world, you will notice your world coming into balance too, and that's the balance that peace and justice are made of. This is possible. And it is possible in the future that begins for you today.

The Quest for Convenience

Charles T. Lukaszewski
Vital Speeches of the Day 51 (August 15, 1985): 649–50.
© City News Publishing Company. Used by permission.

*A*merica is on a quest for convenience. We spend thousands and thousands of hours looking for the fastest and easiest ways to get our work done. Every aspect of our society has been reshaped by technological progress. However, by putting every ounce of energy into convenience, we've left nothing to help our society grow. New conveniences intensify the relevance of values in society, but they demand those values be cast in modern terms. Our thirst for convenience is overpowering value growth in America and creating urgent problems that must be solved.

That Americans want convenience is no secret. In fact, we're made aware of it each and every day. Advertisements bombard us with the "user-friendly," the "high tech," "wash-and-wear," and the "new and improved." The self-cleaning oven saves mom scrubbing time, while "Dawn" takes the grease out of her way. The "24 hour drive-thru" and the Instant Cash Machine also make life that "little bit easier." Convenience, it seems, is everywhere.

Nor can we ever get enough of it. How many times a day does the thought, "There's got to be a better way to do this," cross your mind? Everybody thinks it, and you can often safely bet that someone's already found that better way, for American history is a history of invention. The United States Patent Office is flooded by an average 325 new applications each day. When the Office was first established, it took a few weeks to get a patent, but it is now so deluged that, even with the aid of large computers, the process takes 25 months or more. Inventors know America constantly wants a better way to do things. They know we're on a quest for convenience.

The technological changes wrought by this quest affect our values in important ways. A study on the subject conducted by Harvard University concluded, "technology has a direct impact on values by bringing about new opportunities." We can see the truth of this statement if we look around our country today. Convenience technologies have not only changed every aspect of the way we live, but also opened more avenues to more people than ever before. Unfortunately, we are finding it difficult, if not impossible to take advantage of them because our value system has not kept pace with technology.

I have already touched on the direct nature of the relationship between convenience and values. The fact that conveniences can't satisfy every human need is a simple way to demonstrate that they coexist. Technology takes us conveniently from New York to London in just three hours aboard a supersonic transport, but technology can't blend a good cup of coffee. It takes a human taste tester to find the perfect beans. And technology can whiz my SAT scores to the college of my choice, but it can't write the essay that will gain me admission. Values are just as necessary with convenience because people are just as necessary.

Given that convenience and values coexist, we should ask how they affect one another. It's obvious that the values we hold result in convenience. We cherish life, liberty and the pursuit of happiness, all three of which are enhanced by conveniences. For instance, American democracy has been immeasurably strengthened by computers and television. The joining of these two tools has made it possible for every American to participate in the political process. This is just one way in which an important value can be enhanced by conveniences.

However, those same conveniences can upset the value system. The television that brings us into politics brings other pictures from around the world: hunger and racism in Africa, the arms race between superpowers, and bad news in one's hometown. Children, who do not fully understand values, grow up to these pictures on TV every day. They are not prepared to interpret what they see, and psychologists believe this may harm their personal value systems later. Convenience and values are tied together because they affect one another in important ways.

Unfortunately, America's value system has not kept pace with convenience, and this has created urgent problems while strangling value growth. Two examples symbolize America's "social slip." First, we've found it almost impossible to answer moral questions raised by new conveniences, questions like: who should get expensive new medical treatments, is television too violent, what are we to do with our nuclear arsenal? Baby Jane Doe is a case in point. Modern technology could have sustained her life if her parents chose to, but in making that decision they had no precedents to guide them, no established right or wrong. Moral and ethical dilemmas like this are becoming commonplace, because we've gotten so far ahead of ourselves that convenience can't stimulate our values fast enough.

A second example lies in the failure of institutions in urban America. Professor Richard Rosenbloom conducted a study on the subject in the sixties. He found that traditional institutions and values were incapable of coming to grips with the new problems of America's cities. The things he saw persist today: cities unable to deal with education, crime control and public welfare problems; businesses unable to bring their know-how to bear on urban projects; and economic and political interests getting in the way of housing for the poor. We face problems today that twenty years ago were considered the fault of value decay. This says little of our social progress in that time.

I've explained that convenience and values are intimately related. But in America today these two forces are no longer working in tandem. The serious problems this is causing *must* move us to update our value system. For, if we do not, the danger of conveniences being used inappropriately, and potentially harmfully, becomes a certainty. Our exclusive focus on finding easier ways of living is responsible, because it's left basic social values neglected. The culprit, therefore, is not the quest for convenience itself, but rather the importance we have placed on it.

The point I'm making is best expressed by economist Robert Heilbroner: "Advances in technology must be compatible with an existing society." Conveniences are very important, but we've seen the problems and dangers of neglected value growth. We can solve our problem by putting a little less energy into easier lifestyles and a little more into updating our values. We know convenience and values stimulate one another. If we reorder our priorities to take advantage of this, we can have convenience and value growth at the same time. The quest for convenience can continue to better the lives of all Americans. We need only our values to temper it.

Scoliosis

Susan Jones   Auburn University
Used by permission.

Everyone sit up straight! How many of you have ever been told this, sit or stand up straight? Most of us think that this was just an annoying command our mother liked to give to criticize us about our poor posture. But have you ever thought about how lucky you are to be able to stand up straight? There is a spinal abnormality that develops during adolescence, and if not detected and treated early, can cause severe curvature of the spine. This abnormality is called scoliosis. I am very familiar with scoliosis because my sister has it and has just recently finished treatment.

Today, I would like to talk to you about the problem of scoliosis. First, I will explain what scoliosis is, its treatments, and its effects on a person's health. Second, I will tell you about school screening programs, one solution to this problem.

Scoliosis, as defined in a paper entitled *Scoliosis* published by The Scoliosis Association, Inc., is a lateral or sidewards curvature of the spine. Scoliosis is not a disease and does not result from anything that the parents or child did or did not do. A pamphlet entitled *Brace Yourself for Scoliosis* published by the University Youth Spine Center lists several causes of scoliosis. These include being born with improperly formed vertebrae, having muscle weakness or paralysis, or suffering a severe injury. In most cases, the cause of scoliosis is unknown and is referred to as idiopathic scoliosis. According to *Scoliosis—A Handbook for Patients* published by the Scoliosis Research Society, this type of scoliosis is responsible for approximately 75 to 90 percent of cases treated in most scoliosis centers.

Consider this fact: the Scoliosis Association states that 10 percent of the adolescent population has some degree of scoliosis. This means one million children in the United States alone have scoliosis, and approximately one-fourth of these will require medical attention.

The term "medical attention" brings me to my next point: the effects of scoliosis on a person's health. According to an article entitled "Diagnosing and Treating Curvature of the Spine," by Louise Fenner, a writer for the Food and Drug Administration, as a spine with scoliosis grows, it gradually rotates on its own axis. This rotation pulls the rib cage around so that, in the back, one side of the rib cage becomes higher. The ribs on the inward side of the curve are gathered together, while those on the outer edge are spread apart. This distortion of the rib cage can restrict the lungs and result in respiratory problems. Also, heart problems can possibly result. Research has shown that, on the average, adults with advanced forms of scoliosis die younger than those without scoliosis.

These effects, however, do not have to occur. There are three basic treatments for scoliosis which I would like to cover briefly. Discussed in *Brace Yourself for Scoliosis* are observation, bracing, and surgery. Observation is exactly what it says. The patient is watched to make sure the curve does not progress further. Braces are designed to stop the progression of mild or moderate curves. Finally, surgery is employed when no other treatment can prevent the curve from interfering with a healthy life-style. Surgery involves fusing a portion of the spinal column to prevent curve progression.

As is the case for most illnesses, in order for treatment to be successful, diagnosis must be made early. The solution I propose is school screening programs—a way of early detection. Because the onset of scoliosis is gradual and coincides with "growth spurt" years, a program designed to check children between the ages of ten and thirteen could provide detection before scoliosis has time to progress too far. Doris R. Cantrell, a graduate of Auburn University, wrote her master's thesis on the "Reliability of Health and Physical Education Teachers' Screening for Scoliosis After Instruction." Her study involved eight junior high schools and eight health or physical education instructors. These teachers underwent three two-hour training sessions to learn the testing procedure. The test involved two observations—a standing and a forward bending test. In the standing observation the child is observed from the back. The teachers look for obvious curvature and differences in hip or shoulder levels. These things are again looked for in the forward bending test. Four thousand and nineteen students were examined during the course of her research. During the examination period 85.7% adequate referrals were made. This statistical interpretation indicates that health and physical education teachers, after instruction, can adequately screen students and refer to specialists those thought to have scoliosis. These referrals are early detection and are what could keep scoliosis from progressing too far. Therefore, they are a possible solution to the scoliosis problem.

Today, I hope you have learned about a problem of our society that frequently goes unnoticed. I have explained what scoliosis is, its types of treatment, and its effects on a victim's health. The solution I have proposed is school screening programs. I hope, now, that you understand how the programs would work. Also, by learning of the successful early detections made in Doris Cantrell's study, I believe that you can see that screening programs are one solution to the problem of scoliosis.

1. Brower, Eleanor M. and Nancy H. Hinckley. *Brace Yourself for Scoliosis*. Ohio: The University Youth Spine Center, 1979.
2. Cantrell, Doris R. "Reliability of Health and Physical Education Teachers' Screening for Scoliosis After Instruction." diss. Auburn University, 1982.
3. Fenner, Louis. "Diagnosing and Treating Curvature of the Spine," *Consumers Research*, October, 1984: 24–25.
4. *Scoliosis*. The Scoliosis Association, Inc., 1979.
5. *Scoliosis: A Handbook for Patients*. Scoliosis Research Society.

Confidentiality of Personal Records: The Key to Privacy

John Byrne   Miami University, Ohio   Coached by Mark Hickman
Given at the Interstate Oratorical Association, Mankato, Minnesota,
Winning Orations, 1984.

*I*n New York City an applicant rejected for life insurance without explanation managed to find out that the turndown was based on a report that he had had cancer several years before. The false information, never verified by the company, had come from a neighbor. Eventually he was able to prove the report incorrect and obtain a policy. The applicant—New York City Mayor Ed Koch. Ford Johnson was dismissed from his $250,000-a-year job when it was discovered during a scientific survey that he had admitted to trying marijuana once or twice. The survey, he had been told, would be strictly confidential. These examples are significant because they serve as evidence of a growing problem in our society—the mishandling of personal and confidential information. What was strictly confidential last month could be almost anyone's knowledge this month. An essay by Trudy Hayden in *The Right to Privacy vs. The Right to Know* states that we all have "the right to control information about oneself—when and to whom it shall be given, and for what purposes it shall be used." Unfortunately, this right is being abused, and it's time we took steps to stop its abuse. But first we need to understand why this breach of confidentiality of our personal records is significant and calls for immediate action and exactly what the causes of this problem are. Only with such an understanding can viable solutions be considered.

Naturally we cannot have a total right of confidentiality of our personal records. This ends when our birth certificates are registered as public records. Certain other items, however, such as our medical, criminal, personnel and tax records should be kept confidential, perhaps more than others, but often times they are not. According to Trudy Hayden, "the collection, maintenance, and dissemination of arrest records are supposedly justified by the needs of law enforcement. However, the primary use of arrest records today is for making employment decisions, [essentially] we are saying that an accusation alone is a blot on one's innocence, whatever the eventual outcome, however unfounded the arrest." The collection of personal information has become a threat to privacy and freedom because information, once recorded, can be turned to new uses and new interpretations. Have you ever wondered how junk mail people get a hold of you, or why, when you go in for a job interview, the employer seems to know more about you than what you've put on the application you have submitted? It all comes from your personal records. "How Your Privacy Is Being Stripped Away," an article in the April 30, 1984, issue of *U.S. News and World Report,* states that on a typical day each of our names passes from one computer to another on the average of five times, "inexorably eating away at the last vestiges of that ever American concept of simply being left alone." This information becomes easy access to almost anyone. In most cases, it can be as simple as making a phone call. The problem has indeed become significant and steps must be taken to stop its rapid growth.

In order to successfully determine solutions to this problem, we need to know exactly what is causing it. Basically there are three identifiable causes: the development of a government of services in the United States, the expansion of modern informational technology, and an overwhelming amount of leaks by those in charge of our personal records.

The Right to Privacy vs. The Right to Know, published in 1977, states that "we have developed a government of services resting on the principle that society, collectively, through its government, has [certain] responsibility to its individual members. To carry out these responsibilities the government collects extensive personal information on the individuals who require its services." It is in this collection of information that the problem arises. It seems obvious that this data must change hands several times before the service is complete, thus turning confidential information into public knowledge. Another cause is the expansion of modern informational technology. Data processing has made it impossible to leave the past behind because computers are constantly picking up the tracks which people leave—their job, insurance, and credit ratings above all. According to the April, 1983, issue of *Changing Times* magazine, "the catalyst here is the computer and its magnificent ability to store and disseminate information. Once records are fed into computers it's possible not only to compile more information faster but also to provide almost instant access to it by people unknown to us and for reasons never stated to us." The final cause of this problem is that there has been an overwhelming amount of leaks by those in charge of our personal records. Rather than refer inquiries to the individual, many employers disclose what should be privileged information about their employees to creditors, insurance companies, banks, fellow colleagues and to other firms to which former employees have applied for jobs; and a good deal of this information turns out to be incomplete, inaccurate, or misleading. Perhaps the biggest perpetrator of leaks, however, is our government. According to *An Analysis of Privacy Issues* published by the United States Department of Justice in 1978, the criminal justice system cannot properly function without access to personal information and criminal justice agencies aren't very concerned whether or not the public has access to this same information. These leaks of information, which many times aren't even true, have caused a severe reduction in the accuracy of our personal records. Compound that inaccuracy with easy accessibility and we lose control over the knowledge accumulated and therefore perceptions formed of us by others.

As is obvious, there has been a relatively large-scale failure to protect the privacy of our personal records. As our society continues to grow, this almost becomes inevitable. However, steps can be taken to help stop this problem. "How to Protect Your Privacy," an article in the February, 1980, issue of *McCalls* outlines two ways we can act: screening and subsequently reducing what information is collected and attempting to limit investigations into our private lives. First, according to *McCalls,* "we must avoid collecting and manipulating personal information as a substitute for acting directly upon society's real and complex problems [and at the same time] minimize our collection of personal information altogether." If you are associated with any organization in any way, see what can be done about a reduction in the collection of personal information. When applying for credit, seeking a loan, or looking for a job, we spend half of our time filling out forms and divulging personal information. It's time we stopped to realize the possible side effects. Rather than risk a situation such as Ford Johnson's, ask why specific pieces of information are needed and who might see them. If you are not satisfied with the answer simply don't give the information out. You have that right. Another step would be to "take an active role in limiting or curtailing investigations into your personal life." "How to Protect Your Privacy" states that "a company must notify you if it wishes to conduct [such] an investigation and you yourself may be able to provide the information that they need. If an insurance company wants to see your entire medical file, ask your doctor to forward only the information which is genuinely applicable." He is bound to your request by federal law.

You could lose your job tomorrow because of a onetime arrest which later proved unfounded. Or perhaps you'll lose a major life insurance policy because one doctor diagnosed you as having a serious illness while a second opinion later proved the original diagnosis false. We need to use what rights we have to keep such misunderstandings from happening. Indeed, steps are already being taken. As is evidenced by Section 9 of *Senate Report No. 98-221* on The Freedom of Information Reform Act, Congress is considering legislation to help secure the confidentiality of our personal records; however, the problem must initially be dealt with by each of us as individuals. We can place all the restrictions we want on the individuals disclosing this information, but for a true solution to this problem we must take an active role in limiting the information we make available about ourselves. We need to shop around for the organizations that will encroach the least upon our right to privacy. Certain insurance companies say that they will ask only for the information that they need; major banks now promise in their literature that their customer's records will be kept strictly confidential. In fact, anything written in such literature is considered to be a contract, and any violation of that contract would be a violation of the law.

You and I have both the need and desire for a private life—a life we can cherish as our own and share with those whom we want to share it with. Personal records are a part of this private life. If we can control all information about ourselves—when and to whom it shall be given out and for what purposes it shall be used, and if we can keep from giving out too much meaningless information, then we can succeed in keeping this part of our lives private. Henry David Thoreau once said, "a private life is essential to each man's existence." Confidentially, he was right.

Smoking
Lori Kennedy   Auburn University
Used by permission.

"It's the puff of glamour, the smile of sin, the grit of pain all rolled into one." This is what William Weis and Bruce Miller think about smoking. More than 500,000 Americans a year die as a result of smoking. Smoking is a very real problem facing our society today. It affects all of us. I know it has directly affected me by causing the death of two members in my immediate family. As a result I became interested in the problem of smoking and did extensive research in the area. If it hasn't already it will probably affect you too in one way or another sometime during your lifetime.

Today, I would like to talk to you about smoking, a serious problem facing us today, and one possible solution to it: quitting. First, I will tell you why people smoke and the effects of it. Second, I will offer one solution to the problem, quitting, and how it can be achieved.

Dr. Dee Burton and Gary Wohl in their book, *The Joy of Quitting,* offer a couple of initial reasons people start to smoke. First is the influence of others: "all my friends do," "it's the cool thing to do," or "because my parents do." All of these are influences of others. A second reason people start to smoke is media hype. Burton and Wohl found that, in 1975 alone, 275 million dollars were spent on cigarette advertising in the United States. This advertising was done in magazines, newspapers, billboards and such. There were no television commercials because they have been outlawed. These ads suggest to women that it's the liberated thing to do. It's sexy, sophisticated, and glamorous. These ads also promote the idea that these cigarettes are safer because they're low in tar and nicotine, which is a chemical found in tobacco, but there's no evidence to support this. According to Morton Arkava, author of *Kick the Smoking Habit,* there are a few other reasons people smoke. They like the taste of tobacco, it helps them relax, or they think it prevents weight gain, which is false. You're smoking rather than eating, and chewing gum would work just as well as a cigarette.

All of these are reasons people begin smoking. Why do they continue to smoke? They become addicted: it's habit forming, or it's a way for them to relieve stress. I've discussed why people smoke: the influence of others, media hype, the taste of tobacco, helps them relax, and they think it prevents weight gain. They continue to smoke because it's addictive, habit forming, and a way to relieve stress.

Now let's look at the effects of smoking. There are several bad effects of cigarette smoking. According to the Surgeon General in a report entitled the *Health Consequences of Smoking,* smoking can cause several bad health effects. The first of these is lung disease. Approximately 70 percent of chronic obstructive lung disease deaths are attributed to cigarette smoking. Eighty-five percent of lung cancer is directly attributable to smoking.

Emphysema is another lung disease caused from cigarette smoking. Emphysema causes a shortness of breath, making it difficult to breathe. My grandfather had emphysema and he just ran out of breath and died.

Another effect of smoking is to pregnant women. It can harm the fetus. The average birthweight of a child born to a smoker is less than that of a child born to a nonsmoker. Smoking can cause spontaneous abortion. In addition, the children of smokers show a greater susceptibility to respiratory diseases.

Heart disease is another effect of smoking. Cigarette smoking is one of the major risk factors contributing to the development of chronic heart disease. Dr. Alton Ochsner in his book *Smoking and Your Life* states that cigarette smoking causes an increase in heart beat and blood pressure. This puts a strain on your heart and can be especially dangerous in people who are already suffering from a heart condition. Dr. Ochsner also says that according to the Surgeon General's report the death rate among smokers from coronary disease is 70 percent higher than among nonsmokers. Cigarette smoking causes a weakening of the heart and reduces your life.

So far I have discussed with you the problem of smoking: why people smoke and the effects, such as lung disease, harm to the fetus of a pregnant woman, and heart disease. I would now like to offer the only true safe solution to smoking: quitting. The book *Smoke-Free Workplace,* by William Weis and Bruce Miller, points out that no matter the length of time you've smoked it's always beneficial to stop. Within the first few days after you quit, your body starts to repair the damage caused to your heart and lungs.

But how do you quit? In his book, Dr. Alton Ochsner offers a program to stop smoking. First, stop: abruptly, completely, and permanently. Just go cold turkey. Second, build up your resolution. Say, "I'm going to stop. I'm going to break this habit." Next, burn the bridges to the habit. Throw away any cigarettes, cigarette holders, ashtrays—anything that might tempt you to pick up a cigarette. Time your break. Do it at a time when you're not in a totally smoking environment. Deny the withdrawal symptoms which consist of nervousness, irritability, and craving for a cigarette. This is half the battle. Adopt a substitute habit: chew gum, drink a glass of water, or something like this when you want a cigarette. Finally, think of the benefits. You're probably prolonging your life.

Remember, it's never too late to stop. Do it abruptly, completely, and permanently. Build up your resolution. Burn the bridges to the habit. Time your break. Deny the withdrawal symptoms. Adopt a substitute habit. Finally, think of the benefits.

I hope today I've given you some insight into the problem of smoking. First, we looked at why people smoke and the effects. Next, we looked at the one safe solution to the problem: quitting. I hope now you can see just how serious the problem of smoking is and now know how to beat this dangerous habit.

1. Arkava, Morton L. *Kick the Smoking Habit.* Saratoga, California: R & E Publishers, 1984.
2. Burton, Dee and Gary Wohl. *The Joy of Quitting.* New York: Macmillan Publishing Company, Inc., 1979.
3. *Health Consequences of Smoking: The Changing Cigarette.* Washington, D.C.: U.S. Department of Health and Human Services, 1981.
4. Ochsner, Alton. *Smoking and Your Life.* New York: Julian Messner, 1965.
5. Weis, William L. and Bruce W. Miller. *The Smoke-Free Workplace.* New York: Prometheus Books, 1985.

The Jungle Revisited

Kimberly Hyden   Ball State University, Indiana   Coached by Kenda Creasy Dean and Kevin W. Dean
Given at the Interstate Oratorical Association, Mankato, Minnesota, Winning Orations, 1985.

There was never the least attention paid to what was cut up for sausage. . . . Meat that had tumbled out on the floor in the dirt and (the) sawdust. The water would drip over it, and . . . the rats would race about . . . it. The rats were nuisances, (so) the packers would put poisoned bread out for them, they would die, and the rats, bread, and meat would go into the hoppers together. . . .

In 1906, when Upton Sinclair wrote *The Jungle,* conscience was the stockyard's only regulation. If they felt that rat dung would enhance the flavor of meat, then it was added. No questions asked. *The Jungle* led to pure food legislation and helped clean up and control the food processing industry. Unfortunately, today the jungle is a little closer to home, for when this *pure* food leaves the stockyards for use in *restaurants,* pure food *laws* no longer apply.

The Government estimates that we will spend some 300 billion dollars on food this year alone, and nearly half of that will be spent in restaurants. For some of us, restaurant-eating is a way of life, but as *World Health* of October, 1983, points out, restaurants are now "the main culprits" in food contamination. As a result of their carelessness, Dr. Howard Robert reports that in the last twenty-four trips you made to Noble Roman's, Wendy's, Long John Silver's, or the local pub, you have gotten food poisoning severe enough to warrant medical attention, and one in ten trips will get you a mild case of food poisoning that you may have mistaken for indigestion or a bad stomachache. But why is food poisoning so common? According to *Nation* magazine of March, 1984, it is because one in three of the restaurants that we assume to be safe—isn't.

Sometime over the course of this weekend we will all eat in a restaurant (most of us more than once), and we owe it to ourselves to reduce the risks we are taking for due to unsafe sanitation laws and inconsistent inspection policies, eating out has become risky business.

The healthfulness of restaurants urgently needs to be evaluated, but before we can correct the sanitation and inspection dilemma, we must be aware of the constituents of this dilemma.

The last time you took a break at McDonald's chances are it never crossed your mind that the Government had a hand in preparing your cheeseburger. Theoretically, this Governmental influence should guarantee you that your cheese isn't moldy and your pickles aren't limp, but it doesn't. Government regulations are hopelessly outdated and amazingly inaccurate. Ironically, even though food-related research is now costing more than 400 million dollars a year, food safety laws have not been revised since 1960, and those laws governing restaurant sanitation and inspection leave a lot to be desired.

The regulation governing restaurant sanitation, for example, allows "refrigerating facilities (to) be kept at fifty degrees Fahrenheit." But according to the July/August, 1983, *FDA Consumer,* food spoils at fifty degrees. This regulation also states that "food (should) be . . . free from . . . *gross spoilage*." A closer examination reveals that "gross spoilage" encompasses only "insect infestation" and "rodent contamination." There are at least two problems with this statement. First, how much constitutes gross? Researchers Hinich and Staelin report that regulations allow restaurants to serve prepared mushrooms that contain no more than twenty-one maggots and seventy-five mites per fifteen ounces, and that's not gross. And second, this regulation makes no attempt to ban the use of food that has spoiled due to heat, handling, or aging.

Of course, serving spoiled or contaminated food in restaurants is a well kept secret thanks to the second problem: inconsistent inspection policies. Restaurants *are* inspected for sanitary approval, but the frequency and accuracy of these inspections are questionable at best.

Legally, health officers are required to inspect each food establishment in his or her assigned area twice a year. As the daughter of a restaurant owner, I've seen inspection at its worst. In the thirty-six years since our restaurant opened, it has received only thirty of the seventy-two required inspections with the most recent inspection coming two years ago this month. In a conversation with a health officer I learned it is standard practice to conduct inspections only once a year, and admittedly, some years contain fifteen months or more.

But even frequent examinations do not guarantee a restaurant's healthfulness. According to *U.S. News and World Report* in December of last year, Food and Drug Administration sponsored health officers should "be the consumer's advocate. (They) have got to keep an arms length from industry and not in anyone's pocket." Unfortunately, *New York* magazine reported in June of 1983, that "inspectors have been charged (in recent years) with accepting bribes from (merchants) who wanted violations overlooked." With this in mind it should be no surprise that in a survey *Nation* found that "products from 32% of the businesses checked . . . didn't meet Federal standards, even though inspectors had given (them) 'satisfactory' ratings."

Under pressure from the FDA, New York health officers took a step in the right direction by conducting a series of unscheduled inspections. *The New York Times* reported that between April 1 and September 9 of last year, 646 area restaurants were cited for "violating (the) health code" and closed until the violations were corrected. These businesses included several Burger Kings and Kentucky Fried Chickens, Luigi's and Mayor Koch's favorite restaurant.

Unfortunately, New York City is not the only place where restaurants pose a health hazard. According to *The New York Times,* on June 3, 1984, at a sports banquet in Hoboken, New Jersey, 169 athletes, cheerleaders, and coaches were hospitalized for food poisoning. The cause? The banquet's main course was refrigerated at just under fifty degrees.

If you have never had a severe case of food poisoning, consider yourself lucky because author Elliot Dewberry points out that the instances of food-borne illnesses has increased more than twentyfold since 1946, and now, one in twenty cases of medically detected food poisoning results in death.

If you find these statistics a little hard to believe, call Hoboken, New Jersey, where seven of the athletes, cheerleaders, and coaches died.

The December 3, 1984, *U.S. News and World Report* stated that the FDA:

is viewed by industry and the American public (alike) as both a guardian angel and the devil incarnate. (It is) . . . an agency of 7,000 people (who) . . . have the responsibility for monitoring a 450 billion dollar industry that accounts for twenty-five cents of every dollar spent in the country.

This is a responsibility that they seem not to take seriously. According to *Nation,* the FDA sponsors "a total of 359 . . . Federal (food-related) programs." The first step toward establishing new legislation would be to give one of these 359 agencies the exclusive right to set the standards for restaurant sanitation and inspection. Once established, this agency should accept the *Burns Statutes* as law. The *Burns Statutes* are not laws but rather recommendations for restaurant sanitation and inspection that are based on the utmost common sense. The statutes recommend that refrigerating facilities be kept between thirty-two and thirty-six degrees Fahrenheit and nonperishable foods should be kept in airtight storage cases to protect them from "filth . . . insects, (and) vermin," as well as bacterial spoilage. The *Burns Statutes* also recommend that the inspection process be made a checks and balance system with inspectors as well as restaurant management being subject to legal prosecution if the articles are violated. This plan would be achieved by using some of the 400 million dollars in research funds to establish a state level committee whose only duty would be inspecting the inspectors.

The *Burns Statutes* contain many good ideas, and one simple piece of legislation can make them law and stop millions of *us* from being needlessly poisoned. Food poisoning is never pleasant, and it can be deadly. It can also be prevented by executing a simple three point plan every time you eat out. First, upon entering a restaurant, look for a current health permit. This permit is issued following a satisfactory inspection and should be visible to *all* customers. Although the possession of a health permit does not guarantee a restaurant's sanitation, its absence assures contamination. Second, avoid ordering spicy food or foods that have been prepared in advance. *Travel Holiday* of May, 1983, reports that spices are often used to mask food discoloration and odor, and according to *World Health,* the "preparation of food . . . in advance of eating . . . allow(s) (harmful bacteria) to multiply," and third, if something you've ordered tastes at all strange, *stop eating,* and demand an explanation. Consumer awareness— and involvement—will make all the difference.

In 1906, Upton Sinclair told us of "meat that was . . . found (to be) sour, and how they would rub it up with soda to take away the smell, and sell it at the . . . lunch counters." Seventy-nine years later not much has changed. For due to unsafe sanitation laws and inconsistent inspection policies, it's still a jungle out there.

GLOSSARY

A

active listening: Listening which involves all four aspects of the listening process: creating mental images, empathizing with the speaker's emotions, capitalizing on the difference between the speaking and thinking rate, and responding to the speaker's communication.

actuative claim: An assertion or conclusion that deals with questions of policy, whether or not a thing should be done.

affective component: One of three components of an attitude. It consists of the feelings that a person has about an object, concept, or person.

alliteration: The repetition of a sound in two or more words in the same sentence.

analogy: A method of reasoning concluding that when two particulars are alike in a number of known respects, they will be alike in an unknown respect.

> **analogy, figurative:** One in which the comparison involves members of two different classes.

> **analogy, literal:** One in which the comparison is of two members of the same class.

analyze: To identify the major divisions or constituent parts of a topic.

articulation: The creation of sounds by interfering with the outward flow of air through the mouth and nose to create the various sounds of a language.

assimilation: The acceptable running together of sounds in normal speech. Too little assimilation results in overly precise speech. Too much assimilation results in unintelligible speech. A proper amount creates speech that is intelligible and easy to listen to.

asyndeton: The omission of conjunctions between a series of related clauses.

attention: The focusing of perception on specific stimuli in the environment and the processing of those stimuli.

attentive listening: Involves maintaining eye contact with the speaker, avoiding distracting projects, avoiding daydreaming and distracting behavior.

attitude: A judgment, evaluation, or feeling about a person, object, or concept.

attraction: One of the five sources of ethos. It is created by developing a positive orientation with people.

audience analysis: The identification of listeners' characteristics that affect the way they will probably respond to a communication.

audio-visual aid: Anything, other than the speaker, that is used to assist in communication. The term includes such things as demonstration boards, felt or flannelboards, hook 'n' loop boards, magnetic boards, flip charts, poster boards, graphs, overhead projectors, slide projectors, filmstrip projectors, audio tape recorders, motion picture projectors, and video tape recorders.

B

backing for the warrant: Evidence and reasoning used to make the warrant credible and acceptable to listeners.

barriers: Anything that interferes with communication, causing an incorrect meaning or no meaning to be communicated.

behavioral component: One of three components of an attitude. It involves the actions that a person takes toward an object, concept, or person as a result of one or more attitudes.

boomerang   A change of attitude by listeners opposite from that desired by a speaker.

C

causal pattern: A method of organizing the main points in a speech according to their cause-effect relationship.

causal reasoning: An attempt to explain why something has happened or will happen.

centrality: A characteristic of an attitude. It refers to its importance or role in the whole attitude system.

channel: The means by which communicative stimuli are transmitted from a source to a receiver.

chiasmus: A sentence of two parts in which the second is syntactically balanced against the first but with the parts reversed.

chronological pattern: A method of organizing the main ideas in a speech according to their relationship in time.

claim: An assertion or conclusion made on the basis of evidence and a warrant.

cognitive component: One of three components of an attitude. It refers to the perceptions, thoughts, and beliefs a person has about an object, concept, or person.

cognitive consistency: Refers to the effort on the cognitive level to restore balance to our attitudinal system when two or more attitudes become imbalanced.

communication: The way in which human beings develop and share meaning.

competence: One of the five sources of ethos. It is established by expertise or an indication that the speaker is a source of valid information.

conclusion: The final part of a speech designed to focus the listeners' thoughts on the subject of the speech, leave a favorable image of the speaker in the listeners' minds, and give a sense of completeness to the speech.

constructive listening: Involves keeping an open mind, looking for points of agreement, identifying the central idea and organizational pattern of the speech, and deciding whether to listen for general ideas or specific details.

content: All information used in supporting the speaker's statement of purpose.

conversational mode: A manner of delivering a speech that gives an impression that the speaker is conversing with the listeners.

credibility-centered ethics: A form of ethics recognizing that a speaker's credibility will be dependent upon the ethics he embraces.

credulity, primitive: The belief that those things we experience are real, i.e., that our senses cannot mislead us.

D

definitive claim: Concerned with questions of definition, what a thing is.

demographic analysis: Identification of potential listeners' important and salient characteristics in order to make inferences about their attitudes.

designative claim: Concerned with questions of fact, whether a thing is true.

direction: A characteristic of an attitude. It identifies whether the attitude is positive or negative, favorable or unfavorable.

door-in-the-face technique: To make of another person an extreme request that will be refused, then to present a more moderate request that will generally be granted.

E

economy: The use of no more words than necessary to communicate a particular meaning.

empathy: The feeling by listeners or spectators that they are a part of whatever they are observing. It is what makes us recoil when we see someone else about to get hit.

ends and means ethics: A type of ethics claiming that desirable ends justify any means of attaining them.

enthusiastic listening: Desire to hear what the speaker has to say, and to focus on positive features of the communicative situation.

ethos: The impression the speaker makes with his communication. The credibility of a speaker stemming from competence, trustworthiness, similarity, attraction, and sincerity.

euphemism: The substitution of a word that is inoffensive for one that would offend listeners.

evaluative claim: Concerned with questions of value, what the merit of a thing is.

evidence: Something that gives reason for believing. It is something that shows or proves.

exemplify: To present examples to make meaning clear.

extemporaneous: A well prepared speech that has not been written or memorized. The exact choices of words and construction of sentences are made during delivery of the speech.

eye contact: To look directly into the eyes of the people with whom we communicate.

F

facial expression: To reflect in your face the emotions and feelings that you experience as you communicate with others.

factual information: Evidence that is verifiable by objective measurements, sensory perception, or historical investigation.

fallacy: A process of reasoning that is faulty or in error.

fallacy, special: Tricky or specious devices—use of language, source materials, and audience attitudes and values—used to prevent others from perceiving the nonlogical basis of a person's statement or conclusion.

    appeal to tradition: The argument that a current practice should be continued because that is the way it has always been done.

    appeal to ignorance: The argument that because others cannot prove that a proposal will not work, it should be adopted even though its advocate cannot prove that it will work.

    appeal to authority: The argument that a proposal should be adopted because some authority—a governor, a professor, a minister—says we should.

    attack on a person: The argument that a proposal should not be adopted because the person advocating that position is not a desirable person.

appeal to emotions: The argument that a person should take a certain action because it is something he would enjoy or it is something that would be detrimental to someone he dislikes.

appeal to popular approval: The argument that a proposal should be adopted because it is desired by a majority of the people.

feedback: The reactions and responses of listeners that are perceived by the communicative source.

foot-in-the-door technique: To request a small favor from a person, and when it is granted to request a larger favor.

frame of reference: A perspective from which to evaluate and respond to messages, people, and situations.

G

general purpose: An objective in a speech, the general response you want the listeners to make.

generalization: The making of a conclusion about a class of objects based on the examination of a representative sample.

gestures: Movements of the head, shoulders, hands, and arms used to assist in communicating ideas.

I

identification: To adopt the behavior of another person or group because it is associated with a satisfying, self-defining relationship to a person or a group.

illustration: A detailed example.

impromptu speech: To give a speech unexpectedly with no prior warning or preparation.

inform: To provide data in order that the listeners will become more knowledgeable.

intensity: A characteristic of an attitude. It refers to the strength—strong, mild, weak—of an attitude.

intrapersonal communication: Communication that takes place in one person. It involves no one else.

introduction: The opening part of a speech designed to get the attention of the listeners, establish the ethos of the speaker, and start the listeners thinking about the subject of the speech.

issue-relevant argument: An argument resulting from careful and thoughtful deliberation about the quality of the reasoning and evidence presented to support an argument.

K

kinesics: The study of body action and its function in communication.

L

latitude of acceptance: The number of attitude positions on a continuum that a person will find acceptable.

listening: A communication skill of great complexity that involves four distinct processes: receiving, perceiving, interpreting, and responding.

receiving: One of the four processes of listening that consists of seeing and hearing.

perceiving: One of the four processes of listening that enables a person to focus on specific stimuli in the environment.

interpreting: One of the four processes of listening that involves discerning the intended meaning of a communication.

responding: One of the four processes of listening that involves overt responses and requires active processing of the speaker's ideas.

loose sentence: A sentence in which the main idea is revealed in the first part of the sentence.

loudness: The psychological interpretation by a listener of the intensity or amplitude of a vibrating object.

M

manuscript speech: A speech that has been written and is delivered by reading from the manuscript.

meaning: The understanding that a specific person has of anything in her environment.

    intensional: Meaning that cannot be observed because it exists only in the mind of a person.

    extensional: Meaning that can be observed. The person using a word can point to the object. Thus, another person can observe the meaning of a symbol.

    triangle of meaning: A triangle that graphically shows the relationship between a symbol and an object.

measure of central tendency: A measure that identifies an average measurement of a group.

    mean: A measure of central tendency that is computed by summing the values of all items and dividing the sum by the number of items included.

    median: A measure of central tendency that is determined by ranking the items from lowest to highest and then identifying the item one-half the distance between the lowest and highest. That item is the median.

    mode: A measure of central tendency that identifies the datum or class of data that occurs most frequently.

memorized speech: A speech that is completely written out, memorized, and delivered from memory.

motivated sequence: A method of developing a persuasive speech originated by Alan H. Monroe. It utilizes five main divisions—*attention, need, satisfaction, visualization,* and *action*—to present a persuasive speech.

N

narration: To relate a sequence of events or to tell a story.

nonfluencies: Breaks in a speaker's fluency, usually filled by "uh," "and-uh," "you know," etc.

nonverbal: Communication that is achieved by bodily action, facial expression, vocal inflection, and other non-language sounds.

O

objective listening: To listen with an open mind, to avoid selective perception, and to guard against emotional reactions to anything a speaker says.

occasional speeches: Special types of speeches which are adapted to the specific occasion. See also Speech of Introduction, Speech of Nomination, Speech of Presentation, Speech to Commemorate, and Speech to Entertain.

one-sided speech: A persuasive speech that only presents arguments for the position advocated by the speaker.

opinion, expert: Testimony given by a person who is an expert in the field on which he is speaking.

organization: A method of developing not only the major parts of a speech, but also the subordinate divisions within each of those parts.

P

parallel structure: To phrase in a similar way parts of a sentence or paragraph that are of equal importance.

pause: A meaningful moment of silence during speaking.

perceiving: One of the four processes of listening that enables a person to focus on specific stimuli in the environment.

performance apprehension: The normal anxiety that occurs in a person confronted with a situation in which the performance is important and the outcome uncertain.

periodic sentence: A sentence in which the main idea is not presented until the end of the sentence.

peripheral cue: A cause of persuasion that does not involve deliberation about the quality of information presented in a persuasive message. Instead, persuasion results from some quality of the speaker, such as appearance or sincerity.

persuade: To create a new belief or attitude, to change the direction of an existing attitude, to increase the intensity of an existing attitude, or to obtain a behavioral response.

pitch: The psychological interpretation of the sound produced by the frequency of the vibrations of a vibrating object.

preparation outline: An outline used in preparing a speech. It helps to check the logical relationship of ideas and supporting materials. It is not used in giving the speech.

preview: Tells the listeners exactly what the main points of the speech will be. Is an extension of the thesis sentence.

problem-solution pattern: A method of organizing a speech so that there are two main parts of the body: explanation of a problem and description of a solution.

pronunciation: The way in which words are spoken.

public opinion polls: Scientific methods of identifying attitudes and beliefs of various groups of citizens.

purposeful listening: To have a specific objective in mind when one listens to any communication.

purpose-oriented analysis: A method of analyzing an audience which focuses on the potential interaction of a particular speech topic and relevant attitudes of a specific group of listeners.

Q

qualifier: Suggests the degree of certainty that a claim has.

quality: The characteristic of a sound that enables a listener to recognize its source.

R

range: The interval between the lowest and highest tones produced by a human voice.

rate: The number of words spoken in a given amount of time, usually a minute.

Readers Guide to Periodical Literature: A source that indexes approximately 130 current, popular periodicals.

reasoning: The drawing of inferences from a body of evidence or from systematic or logical thinking.

reasoning by analogy: The process of drawing inferences about an unknown characteristic of one member of a class as a result of comparing its characteristics with those of another member of that same class.

reasoning by generalization: The process of drawing a conclusion about a whole class of objects on the basis of an examination of only a representative number of the whole class.

receiving: One of the four processes of listening that consists of seeing and hearing.

reservation: Incidental factors that minimize or invalidate the accuracy or correctness of a conclusion.

S

salient: A characteristic of an attitude. It refers to the awareness or lack of awareness a person has of an attitude.

self-actualization: The desire of a person to do or be what he thinks he was created to do or be.

set: A predisposition to focus on specific stimuli in a situation and to respond in a particular way.

signposts: Various linguistic cues that help listeners to perceive movement in a speech and understand relationships among the ideas presented.

similarity: One of the sources of ethos. It is achieved by establishing common backgrounds, interests, goals, and attitudes with those to be persuaded.

sincerity: One of the five sources of ethos. It is established by revealing a true concern for listeners and by dealing honestly with them.

situation: The place or the area in which communication occurs.

situation ethics: A system of ethics claiming that each individual situation must be examined to determine what is the good thing to do, because there are no natural laws to be followed absolutely.

Social Science Index: A source that indexes approximately 150 current periodicals in the social sciences.

social utility ethics: A form of ethics claiming that programs and policies that do the greatest good for the group are the most ethical, even if they have bad effects on some members of the group.

source: The origin of a communicative act.

spatial pattern: A method of organizing ideas that arranges them according to their space relationships.

specific instance: An undetailed example.

specific purpose: The particular objective of a speech.

speech of introduction: A speech used to introduce a person scheduled to make a speech or to present a newcomer to a community, church, social group, or some other organization.

speech of nomination: A speech of praise to justify naming and supporting a specific candidate for a particular position.

speech of presentation: A speech whose purpose is to give an award or gift to a person deserving recognition for some reason.

speech to commemorate: A speech to observe some event that deserves recognition.

speech to entertain: A speech whose main purpose is to make people enjoy themselves.

stability: A characteristic of an attitude. It refers to the firmness with which an attitude is held.

stage fright: An imprecise term referring to the normal anxiety, or emotional tension, that occurs in anyone confronted with a situation in which the performance is important and the outcome uncertain. See also *performance apprehension.*

style: The result of language that is freely chosen and freely arranged.

supporting materials: Information used to develop and explain a speaker's main and subsidiary ideas.

T

testimony: The expression of an opinion on a topic by any person.

testimony, expert: The expression of an opinion by a person who is an expert in that field.

testimony, lay: The expression of an opinion by a person who is not an expert in that field.

testimony, reluctant: The expression of an opinion that opposes the best interests of the person expressing the opinion.

testimony, unbiased: The expression of an opinion that has been arrived at objectively.

thesis sentence: The sentence which tells listeners specifically what a speaker is going to talk about in a speech.

topical pattern: A method of organizing main ideas in a speech according to some classification of natural or conventional parts of the topic being discussed.

transition: Devices used to give unity and coherence to ideas, to give a sense of movement to the speech, and to emphasize important ideas.

trustworthiness: One of the five sources of ethos. Established by the appearance that the speaker is honest, just, and objective.

two-sided speech: A persuasive speech that presents arguments supporting the advocate's position, and presents refutation of main arguments opposing the advocate's position.

V

vitality: A forcefulness of style achieved essentially by word choice and the characteristics of sentences.

voice projection: The ability to cause the voice to carry to distant parts of the place in which a speech is given.

W

warrant: The link between the evidence and a claim. The basic premise on which the claim rests.

PHOTO CREDITS

Name Index

Carver, C. S., 58, 68
Catalan, J., 343
Cathcart, R. S., 268
Chaiken, S., 343
Chino, W., 188, 193
Church, J., 284, 295
Cialdini, R. B., 328, 343
Clark, K. B., 180, 193
Clement, F., 291, 292, 296
Clevenger, T., 31, 43, 44, 45, 96, 114
Coakley, C. G., 58, 68
Cohen, A. R., 149, 160, 173
Conant, J.B., 77, 86
Conger, H. M., 371
Converse, P. E., 113, 114
Cook, R. L., 143
Cooper, E., 153, 173
Cooper, J. B., 90, 113
Cooper, L., 85, 114
Copi, I. M., 250, 269
Corax, xvii
Costley, D. L., 252, 268, 269
Crocker, J., 343
Crowell, L., 136, 143
Culton, G. L., 345
Cuomo, M. M., 182, 193
Curry, H. L., xxi

D

Dabbs, J. M., Jr., 332, 344
Dance, F. E. X., 14, 18
Darby, B. L., 343
Darnell, D. K., 147, 172
de Haan, H., 147, 173
Delattre, E. J., xix, xxi
DeVito, J. A., 288, 292, 295, 296
Dickens, M., 43, 45
Dickson, H. W., 90, 113
Dinerman, H., 153, 173
Di Vesta, F. J., 173, 329, 343
Dresser, W. R., 268
Dubos, R., 239
Dunham, R. E., 244, 269
Dusenbury, D., 218
Dyer, C. S., 189, 193

E

Eaton, J. W., 114
Edwards, H., 186, 193
Edwards, R., 68
Ehninger, D., 161, 173
Ehrensberger, R., 314, 345
Eldridge, C., 201, 218
Ellsworth, P. C., 218
Epstein, S., 45
Ernest, C. H., 211, 218
Ernst, F. H., Jr., 59, 68
Exline, R. V., 201, 218

F

Fairbanks, G., 210, 218
Fast, J., 280, 295
Fazio, R. H., 113
Feieraband, R. L., 339, 345
Feinstein, D., 182, 193
Ferris, S. R., 195, 217
Feshbach, S., 331, 344
Festinger, L., 333, 344
Fiske, S. T., 343
Flanigan, W. H., 114
Fletcher, J., 50, 51, 54
Fosdick, H. E., 39
Fraser, S. C., 327, 343
Freedman, J. L., 323, 327, 342, 343
Frost, R., 140

G

Gallup, G., 105, 114, 248
Gardiner, J. C., 252, 268, 269
Gaudet, H., 342
Gergen, D., 249
Germond, J. W., 294
Gibson, F., 43, 45
Gibson, J. W., 295
Gibson, W. E., 181, 193
Gilkinson, H., 268, 269, 345
Ginsburg, G. P., 85
Gladney, K., 68
Goetsinger, C. S., Jr., 269
Golden, B., 81, 86
Goldsmith, J. A., 269
Goodman, E., 282, 295
Goolagong, E., 42
Gove, P. B., 214, 218
Greenfield, J., 269
Gulley, H. E., 339, 345

H

Haefner, D. P., 332, 344
Haiman, F. S., 76, 86
Hanford, G., 183, 189, 193
Harbert, J. M., xix, xxi
Harcleroad, F. F., 270
Harkins, S. G., 343
Harms, L. S., 206, 218
Harriman, P. L., 173
Hart, R. J., 195, 217
Harte, T. B., 269
Hay, J. M., 295
Hayakawa, S. I., 277, 284, 295
Hazen, M. D., 114
Henderlider, C. R., 87, 143
Henrikson, E. H., 40, 45, 195, 217
Hewgill, M. A., 74, 85, 332, 344
Hibbard, A., 296
Hildebrandt, H. W., 143

Niemi, R. G., 114
Niles, P., 332, 344
Nilsen, T.R., 47, 54, 269
Nixon, R. M., 79
Norman, G., 36, 45

O

Olson, K. B., 113, 172
Osgood, C. E., 85
Ostermeier, T. H., 263, 268, 270
Ostrom, T. M., 343

P

Pagano, F., 344
Parker, J. P., 147, 173
Parry, C. W., 183, 193
Paulson, S. F., 268, 269, 345
Peale, N. V., 132
Pearson, L. B., 263, 270
Perry, J. M., 270
Petty, R. E., 326, 342, 343
Phillips, W., xviii, xxi, 109
Pirie, M., 239
Plato, xvii, 140
Pond, J. B., 110
Powell, F. A., 333
Prall, C., 43, 45
Pritzker, H., 342
Pronovost, W., 210, 218

Q

Quintilian, 363

R

Rader, M. H., xxi
Rajecki, D. W., 113
Rankin, P. T., 57, 68
Rea, R. G., 339, 345
Reagan, R., 34, 51
Reed, J. S., 190, 193
Reinsch, N. L., Jr., 291, 296
Reston, J. B., 181, 193
Rhine, R., 343
Robinson, E. R., 39, 45
Ronstadt, L., 32, 45
Roosevelt, F. D., 136
Roper, B. W., 247, 248
Rosemier, R., 270
Rosenbaum, L., 320, 342
Rosenberg, M., 334, 344
Rosenthal, A., 179, 192
Roskens, R. W., 364, 367, 368, 369, 370

S

Saine, T. J., 86
Sanford, T., 181, 193
Satterthwaite, L., 270
Saunders, D. E., 296
Schambra, W., 269
Scheier, M. F., 58, 68
Schmidt, H., 173, 345
Schuller, C. F., 270
Schweitzer, D., 85
Secord, P. F., 85
Seligman, C., 327, 343
Severance, L., 343
Sharp, H., Jr., 148, 173
Sheets, B. V., 34, 40, 45
Sheffield, F. D., 336, 345
Sherif, C. W., 89, 113, 321, 323, 342
Sherif, M., 89, 113, 321, 323, 342, 343
Shriver, S., 178, 192
Siipola, E., 173
Sikkink, D. E., 268, 269, 345
Silber, J. R., 315
Simpson, R. H., 288, 295
Singer, R., 336, 344, 345
Sleemer, P., 270
Smith, M. C., 179, 192
Smith, R. G., 79, 86, 149, 173
Smith, W. F., 186, 193
Spicer, C., 147, 173
Sponberg, H., 345
Starr, P., 269
Steer, M. D., 214, 218
Stetler, C. J., 86
Stevens, W. W., 143
Stinson, G. A., 330, 344
Stockman, D., 254
Stokes, D. E., 113
Stotland, E., 149, 173
Sullivan, L. H., 178, 192
Svehla, G., 93, 113

T

Taft, H. W., 143
Tannenbaum, P., 85, 321, 342, 345
Taylor, A., 188, 193
Taylor, S. E., 343
Thistlethwaite, D. L., 147, 173, 345
Thomas, N., 131, 143
Thompson, E., 147, 172, 173
Thonssen, L., 49, 54
Thrall, W. F., 296
Tiffin, J., 211, 214, 218
Toulmin, S., 222, 223, 239
Trembley, G., 344
Truman, H. S., 131
Tubbs, S. L., 153, 173
Tucker, R. K., 269
Turner, J., 323, 342
Turner, R. H., 114
Twain, M., 280, 295

V

Vernon, M. D., 68
Vick, C. F., 295
Vincent, J. E., 343
Vohs, J. L., 196, 217
Volkhart, E. H., 321, 342

W

Wagner, G. A., 268
Waldhart, E. S., 59, 68
Walker, D., 315
Walker, M. H., xxi
Walpole, H. R., 296
Walster, E., 78, 86, 320
Watts, J. C., 332, 344
Weddle, P., 270
Weiss, W., 76, 80, 86
Wheeler, D., 343
White, E. E., 87, 143
Whitehead, A. E., 143
Whitehead, J. L., Jr., 85, 86
Whitehouse, A. W., Jr., 179, 192
Whittaker, J., 323, 342
Wiener, M., 218
Williams, M., 196, 217

Wilson, W., xviii, xxi
Winans, J. A., 27, 29
Witcover, J., 294
Wittich, W. A., 270
Woodruff, C., 329, 343
Wolfe, D. M., 149, 173
Wolvin, A. D., 58, 68
Wood, R. V., 295
Wrenchley, E. D. O., 34, 43, 45
Wunsch, A. P., xxi
Wyatt, L., 178, 192
Wylie, I. A. R., 36, 45

Y

Yeager, W. H., xxi

Z

Zanna, M. P., 113
Zimbardo, P. G., 285, 295
Zingle, N. H., 114

SUBJECT INDEX

A

Affective component, 90
Alliteration, 292
Ambiguity, 285–86
Amorality of speech communication
    principles, 47–48
Analogy, 228–30
    figurative, 229
    literal, 229
    tests of, 229–30
Analysis, 307
Anticlimax order, 339
Appeal, 188
Appropriateness, 286–88
Articulation problems, 207
Assimilation, 207–8
Asyndeton, 292
Attitude formation, 93–96
    cognitive consistency and, 95–96
    environment and, 93–94
    self-interest and, 94–95
Attitudes, 89–112
    affective component, 90
    behavioral component, 90–91
    belief and, 89–90
    centrality and, 92
    characteristics of, 92–93
    clarity of, 93
    cognitive component, 90
    components of, 90–92
    defined, 89–90
    degree of commitment and, 321
    direction of, 92–93
    discrepancy and, 322–24
    formation of, 93–96
    group pressure and, 324–25
    intensity of, 92
    methods of changing, 326–36
    motive and, 89
    neutral, 11–12
    opinion and, 90
    public commitment and, 321–22

    salience of, 92
    stability of, 93
Attraction, ethos and, 81–82
Audience adaptation, 106–12
    after the speech, 111–12
    before the speech, 107–8
    defined, 106
    during the speech, 109–11
Audience analysis, 96–106
    attitudes of potential listeners, 96
    defined, 96
    demographic analysis, 96–102
    obtaining data about listeners'
        attitudes, 103–6
    purpose-oriented analysis, 102–3
Audio-visual aids, 256–62

B

Backing for warrant, 224–26
Balanced development, 300–301
Balance theory, 95–96
Barriers to communication, 13
Behavioral component, 90–91
Belief, defined, 89–90
Bodily action, 196–205
Body of speech, 156
    informative speech and, 311–12
    persuasive speech and, 339–40
Boomerang effect, 153

C

Causal pattern of organization, 159–60
Causal reasoning, tests of, 230–33
Centrality of attitudes, 92
Challenge, 186–87
Changing attitudes, 326–36
    alternative value premise and, 330–31
    door-in-the-face technique, 328–29

406

Subject Index

N

Narration, 303–4
Noise. *See* Barriers to communication
Nonverbal communication, 195–216
    physical behavior, 196–206
    vocal behavior, 206–16
Note cards, sample, 127
Notes, use of, 133–34

O

Obstacles to changing attitudes, 317–25
    degree of commitment, 321
    discrepancy, 322–24
    group pressure, 324–25
    public commitment, 321–22
    selective exposure, 320–21
    selective perception, 318–19
    selective recall, 319–20
One-sidedness vs. two-sidedness, 336–38
One-sided speech, 336–37
Opinion, 247–51
Oral style, 278–88
Organization, 147–72
    attitude change and, 149
    ethos of speeches and, 148
    informative speech and, 300–303
    listener's comprehension of message
        and, 147–48
    listener's frustration and, 149
    one-sided speech and, 339
    two-sided speech and, 339–40
Outline, sample, 166–68

P

Parallel structure, 292
Patterns of organization, 156–62
    causal pattern, 159–60
    chronological pattern, 156–57
    motivated sequence, 161–62
    problem-solution, 160
    spatial pattern, 157–58
    topical pattern, 158–59
Pause, 213
Performance apprehension, 30–44
    bodily action and, 42
    concentration and, 42
    controlling, 39–44
    harmful, 38–39
    helpful reactions from, 35–37
    physiological reactions and, 43–44
    speaking experience and, 40
    students and, 33
Periodic sentences, 293
Personal experience, 262–63
Personal reference, 179–80
Persuasion, 316–41
    defined, 317

Persuasive speech, organization of, 338–40
Physical behavior, nonverbal and, 196–
    206
Pitch, 208–10
Polarization, 16
Posture, 197–98
Preparation outline, 164–65
Preview, 155
Primitive credulity, 242
Problem-solution, pattern of organization,
    160
Pronunciation, 214–16
Proof, 221
Public commitment, 321–22
Public opinion, 105–6
Purpose of speech, 123–25
Purpose-oriented analysis, 102–3
Pyramidal order, 339

Q

Qualifier, Toulmin model and, 224
Quality, 212
Quantitative data, 254–55
Quotation, 182–83, 185–86

R

Range, 210
Rate, 211
Reasoning, 221–39
    analogy, 228–30
    causal, 230–33
    generalization, 226–28
    special fallacies, 234–38
    Toulmin model, 222–25
    types of, 226–34
Reference to audience, 177
Reference to occasion, 178–79
Reference to subject, 178
Reluctant testimony, 251
Reporting, 304
Reservation, Toulmin model and, 224
Retention of material, informative
    speaking and, 311
Rhetorical question, 293

S

Salience of attitudes, 92
Selective exposure, 320–21
Selective perception, 318–19
Selective recall, 319–20
Semantic triangle, 276
Sentences, 292–93
Set, thesis sentence and, 152
Sign reasoning, tests of, 233–34
Similarity, ethos and, 79–81
Sincerity, ethos and, 82–84